# The Rosa Luxemburg Reader

# The Rosa Luxemburg Reader

*Edited by* PETER HUDIS *and* KEVIN B. ANDERSON

 MONTHLY REVIEW PRESS *New York*

*Copyright* © 2004 *by* MONTHLY REVIEW PRESS
*All Rights Reserved*

Library of Congress Cataloging-in-Publication Data
available from the publisher

ISBN 1-58367-103-x (paperback)
ISBN 1-58367-104-8 (cloth)

MONTHLY REVIEW PRESS
122 West 27th Street
New York, NY 10001

www.monthlyreview.org

*Printed in Canada* 10 9 8 7 6 5 4 3 2 1

# CONTENTS

# Introduction By Peter Hudis and Kevin B. Anderson

On January 12, 2003, over 100,000 people attended a rally in the Berlin sub-urb of Friedrichsfelde to commemorate the life and legacy of Rosa Luxem-burg and Karl Liebknecht. It may come as a surprise that so many turned out to commemorate these figures, who had been murdered by proto-fascist forces eighty-four years earlier. Yet the turnout was not completely unexpect-ed, since it occurred in the midst of growing opposition around the world to the new stage of military intervention signaled by the impending U.S. invasion of Iraq. Luxemburg and Liebknecht were among the most impor-tant antimilitarist figures in European history, and it is a testament to their enduring legacy that so many continue view them as a rallying point amid the challenges of imperialist war and terrorism.

The legacy of Rosa Luxemburg (1871–1919) extends far beyond her contri-bution as an antimilitarist, however. Her life and work also speak to the search for a liberating alternative to the globalization of capital. More than any other Marxist of her generation, Luxemburg theorized capitalism's incessant drive for self-expansion, focusing especially on its destructive impact upon the tech-nologically underdeveloped world. Her critique of capital's drive to destroy non-capitalist environments and her fervent opposition to imperialist expan-sion has taken on new importance in light of the emergence of a new genera-tion of activists and thinkers opposed to globalized capital. At the same time, her intense opposition to reformist compromise, bureaucratic intrigue, and elitist organizational methods speaks to the search for an anticapitalist alterna-tive that avoids the repressive and hierarchical formations that have defined radical movements and efforts to create socialist societies over the past hun-dred years. Her insistence on the need for revolutionary democracy *after* the seizure of power addresses some of the major unanswered questions of our time, such as: Is there an alternative to capitalism? Is it possible to stop global capital's drive for self-expansion without reproducing the horrors of bureau-cracy and totalitarianism? *Can humanity be free* in an era defined by global-ized capitalism and terrorism? Finally, her position as a woman leader and theoretician in a largely male-dominated socialist movement has prompted some new reflections on gender and revolution.

This *Reader* shows the full range of Luxemburg's contributions by including for the first time in one volume substantial extracts from both her economic and political writings. Several key texts, here translated into English for the first time, deal with 1) the impact of capitalist globalization on precapitalist communal forms of social organization, 2) women's emancipation as an integral dimension of socialist transformation, and 3) critiques of the hierarchical organizational methods that have defined so much of the history of Marxism. Finally, our selections from her correspondence attempt to convey her humanism and depth of vision. As a whole, this *Reader* aims to provide a resource for those trying to rethink the problems of radical social transformation today.

## I

Rosa Luxemburg was one of the most original characters ever to participate in the socialist movement. Born on March 5, 1871, to a Jewish family in Zamosc, in the Russian-occupied part of Poland, she joined the revolutionary movement as a teenager, becoming active with Proletariat, one of the first organizations of Polish Marxists. She was smuggled out of Poland in 1889 when the group was crushed by government forces. She attended the University of Zurich from 1889 to 1897, where she wrote a doctoral dissertation entitled *The Industrial Development of Poland*. Her activity in Polish revolutionary émigré circles in Switzerland and France in the early and mid-1890s already displayed the characteristics of political independence and theoretical assertiveness for which she later became renowned. In 1893 she attended the Third Congress of the Second International in Zurich, where she encountered such luminaries as Frederick Engels and Georgi Plekhanov, the founder of Russian Marxism. She argued against national self-determination for Poland, insisting instead on "strict" proletarian internationalism—a position that placed her in direct opposition to the most prominent socialist figures of the time, as well as to Marx's own writings on Poland.

It was also in Zurich, in 1890, that Luxemburg met the Polish revolutionary Leo Jogiches (1867–1919), who became her comrade and lover for the next seventeen years, and remained a close colleague until the end of her life. Jogiches, who joined the socialist movement in Vilna in 1885, was an outstanding strategist and organizer in the Polish, the Russian, and later the German, revolutionary movements. He worked closely with Luxemburg on many fronts, from offering constructive commentary on drafts of her articles and essays to propagating their ideas through tireless behind-the-scenes organizational work in the revolutionary underground. As the Luxemburg scholar Felix Tych has noted, the importance of Jogiches' contributions have tended to be underestimated, in part because he published little under his own name.[1] Yet he too was an original character. Luxemburg's close friend, the socialist feminist Clara Zetkin, once noted that Jogiches "was one of those very masculine personalities—an extremely rare phenomenon these days—who can tolerate a great female personality."[2] The passionate and stormy relationship between Luxemburg and Jogiches, both during and after their period of intimacy, reveals much about Luxemburg as woman, as thinker, and as revolutionary. As she once noted, "I cleave to the idea that a woman's character doesn't show itself when love begins, but when it ends."[3]

Luxemburg's independent character came fully to the fore upon her move to Germany in 1898, where she became active in the German Social Democratic Party (SPD), then the largest socialist organization in the world. As a Polish–Jewish woman, she encountered considerable resentment and opposition from many party leaders, who referred to her in terms of a "guest who comes to us and spits in our parlor."[4] Undeterred by such obstacles, she plunged directly into one of the most important disputes of the day, over Eduard Bernstein's effort to "revise" Marxism.

At the time Bernstein was one of the leading figures in Marxism; Engels had designated him as his literary executor. It therefore came as a shock to see Bernstein argue in a series of articles in 1896–98 that the central theses of Marx's work were now out of date. Bernstein wrote that Marx's predictions about the inevitable breakdown and collapse of capitalism were no longer borne out by experience, as seen in the decreasing frequency of economic crises. He argued that the formation of the credit system, trusts, and monopolies showed that the "anarchy" of the capitalist market was being overcome and that capitalism was moving on its own towards "socialized" production. Bernstein also contended that the ability of trade unions to obtain higher wages would eventually suppress the rate of profit to the point where capitalist exploitation would come to an end without the need for a social revolution. He based his views on political as much as economic considerations. Bernstein argued that the growing power of Social Democracy, with the SPD having become a mass party with millions of members and supporters, showed that the capitalist order was capable of reform through legal and parliamentary means. He concluded, "For me the movement is everything, the goal is nothing."

Luxemburg's response to Bernstein in her *Social Reform or Revolution* (1899) remains one of the most creative answers to the illusions engendered by the apparent stability of capitalism. She argued that the achievement of legal or political equality under capitalism does not and cannot resolve the underlying social antagonisms of a system based on value production, class exploitation, and wage labor. She did not *counterpose* reform to revolution. She *supported* the extension of democratic rights through legal means. However, she argued that the achievement of *genuine* democracy was impossible within the framework of capitalist relations of production. As she later put it, "Social Democracy has always contended that 'full democracy, not formal democracy, but real and effective democracy,' is conceivable only when economic and social equality, i.e., a socialist economic order, has become a reality. . . . On the other hand, the 'democracy' of a bourgeois national state is, in the last resort, always more or less humbug."5

Luxemburg also argued that Bernstein's economic arguments were groundless, because he viewed society from the standpoint of the individual capitalist or individual units of capital rather than grasping capitalism as a totality. For instance, the credit system may enable individual firms to overcome some of the "anarchic" features of market competition, but by helping to expand the productive apparatus, the credit system exacerbates the disproportion in power and privilege between those who own capital versus those who are employed by it. "Socialized production" within capitalism, Luxemburg argued, does not free capital of its inherent contradictions, but only pushes them to a higher level. Furthermore, she argued, the "socialized production" achieved under capitalism is not sustainable. She wrote, "Capital, already pretty much 'socialized' through [capitalist] organization, will tend to revert again to the form of private capital."6 By focusing on particular units or aspects of capital, instead of the nature of capitalism as a whole, Bernstein fell into the "vulgar empiricism" of mistaking temporary changes and variations in the system for the law of motion of capital itself. Far from stabilization, she wrote, one result of capitalist relations at the level of international politics is the ever-greater danger of war, for developed capitalist nations "are states pushed to war precisely as a result of their equally advanced capitalist development."7

*Reform or Revolution* provided Luxemburg with an instant reputation as a leading figure in the fight against reformist tendencies in the Second International. This, however, did not lead her to downplay the importance of defending democratic rights in existing society, as especially seen in her attitude to the

Dreyfus Affair. Luxemburg rarely commented on matters of concern to Jews, though she did contribute to the Jewish Bund's publication, *Der Yiddische Arbeter*, beginning in 1899. Nevertheless, she fully supported the campaign to defend Captain Eduard Dreyfus from the anti-Semitic attacks of the French Right. In contrast to a number of French Marxists, such as Jules Guesde—who refused to get involved in the controversy on the grounds that the Drefyus case had "nothing to do with the proletariat"—Luxemburg supported the French socialist Jean Jaurès in his passionate defense of Dreyfus. However, she did not agree with Jaurès that the ability of socialists and liberals to work together in the Dreyfus case defense showed that the political distance between them had narrowed. She fervently opposed any kind of "rotten compromise" with the liberal bourgeoisie, even when it brought socialists to power. In contrast to Jaurès, Luxemburg sharply condemned the decision of French socialist leader Alexandre Millerand to join the government of René Waldeck-Rousseau as Minister of Labor in July 1900; the Minister of Defense in the same government was the butcher of the Paris Commune, General Gaston de Gallifet.

In 1904, the Amsterdam Congress of the Second International condemned all forms of socialist participation in bourgeois governments. Luxemburg had a right to think that she had won the battle against revisionism. In fact, the reality was more complex. Bernstein was not off base in arguing that his revisionist views were in line with the SPD's actual practice. The SPD's reformist approach was seen in its reluctance to take a firm stand against imperialism and its increasing reliance on parliamentarianism. Yet the extent of its accommodation to existing society was papered over by the tendency of SPD leaders like August Bebel and Karl Kautsky to lambaste "revisionism" in theory, even as they accommodated it in practice. This duality was rooted in the structural position of the SPD as a mass party. What mattered above everything to the leaders of the SPD was organization. The continuous growth of the party was seen as *the* condition for creating a socialist society, and as a measure of the waning of the capitalist order. As J. P. Nettl, author of the most comprehensive biography of Luxemburg put it, "The party's sole purpose was growth."[8] Its overall outlook tended to merge together two things that were not necessarily the same, SPD membership growth and the proximity of systemic collapse. For as it turned out, SPD reformist policies helped in the long run to integrate parts of the working classes into the system. Luxemburg may have underestimated the dangers implied by the SPD's structural position, for she believed that mass pressure from below would eventually act as a corrective by forcing the party to the

Left. That is exactly what she felt was on the agenda when the 1905 Revolution erupted in Russia.

Luxemburg had continued her work in the Polish and Russian movement while in Germany, heading (with Jogiches) the Social Democracy of the Kingdom of Poland (SDKP) and its successor party, the Social Democracy of the Kingdom of Poland and Lithuania (SDKPiL). She tried to affiliate the Polish organization to the Russian Social Democratic Party (RSDRP) and took an active role in the Russian revolutionary affairs. The emergence of outright revolution in Russia in 1905 gave all of this new urgency. At the September 1905 SPD Congress in Jena, she stated, "Day by day we are reading news of revolution in the papers, we are reading the dispatches, but it seems that some of us don't have eyes to see or ears to hear."9 She viewed the novel feature of the 1905 Revolution—the spontaneous emergence of the political mass strike—not only as a tactic for Russia, but also as the universal form of struggle for a future German revolution as well. With that in mind she went to Warsaw in December 1905 to participate in the revolution.

Luxemburg's involvement in the revolution and her effort to draw out its lessons in *The Mass Strike, the Party, and the Trade Unions* (1906) completely shifted the terms of debate over the relation of "advanced" and "backward" countries. No longer was industrially-developed Germany, with the best-organized socialist party in the world, considered to be more advanced than Russia, where a unified Marxist party (the RSDRP) had been formed only a few years earlier, in 1898. With the political mass strike, she held, the Russian workers were *ahead* of their counterparts in Western Europe in initiating a new revolutionary perspective. Moreover, organization no longer took precedence over spontaneity: the spontaneous emergence of the mass strike as the engine of revolution, which was not anticipated by any organization, proved that "the masses do not exist to be schoolmastered."10 The unbridled radicalism of the Russian workers also convinced her that "revolution is everything, all else is bilge."11 She universalized the lessons of the revolutionary experience in the *Mass Strike* pamphlet, which she composed in Kuokkala, Finland, where she also had discussions with V. I. Lenin and other participants in the Revolution.

Luxemburg and Lenin had a number of political differences, especially over the national question, given Lenin's support for self-determination of oppressed nations. Luxemburg also disagreed with what she considered to be Lenin's overemphasis on organizational centralism. Their views largely coincided, however, on the 1905 Revolution and its international ramifications. In

May and June 1907, Luxemburg attended the Congress of the RSDRP in London, where she sharply criticized the Mensheviks for tailending the liberal bourgeoisie and affirmed her support for the overall approach of the Bolsheviks. Most importantly, she sought to relate the lessons of the 1905 Revolution directly to the legacy of Marx, stating, "The Russian Social Democracy is the first to whom has fallen the difficult but honorable task of applying the principles of Marx's teaching not in a period of quiet parliamentary course in the life of the state, but in a stormy revolutionary period." (The full text of her speech appears in chapter 7 of this volume.)

Upon her return to Germany, Luxemburg worked tirelessly to concretize the ferment the 1905 Russian Revolution had unleashed inside the German working class. As she often insisted, "Not through formal prohibitions or through discipline, but only by the maximum development of mass action whenever and wherever the situation permits, a mass action which brings into play the broadest masses of the proletariat. . . . Only in this way can the clinging mists of parliamentary cretinism, of alliances with the middle classes, and the rest of the petty-bourgeois localism be gotten rid of."[12] While this perspective made her one of the most popular speakers to German working-class audiences, it also brought her into increased conflict with the SPD leadership.

In a letter to Clara Zetkin in early 1907, Luxemburg wrote: "Since my return from Russia, I feel rather isolated. . . . I feel the irresolution and the pettiness of our whole party more glaringly and more painfully than ever before."[13] As early as February 1906, the SPD had secretly granted autonomy in all matters pertaining to trade unions to the largely reformist union leaders, who vigorously opposed the idea of a mass strike. Then, in the 1907 elections, the SPD's seats in the Reichstag fell from eighty-one to forty-three, and the party responded by muting its radical demands in order to focus everything on electoral politics. Luxemburg retorted, "German party life is nothing but a bad dream, or rather a dreamless leaden sleep."[14] Her criticism was directed not only at the revisionists or those who openly covered for them; it extended even to Karl Kautsky, often dubbed "the Pope of Marxism," who had taken her side in earlier party disputes. She wrote in a letter in 1908: "Soon I shall be quite unable to read anything written by Kautsky. . . . It is a disgusting series of spider's webs . . . which can be washed away only by the mental bath of reading Marx himself."[15]

The open break with Kautsky occurred in 1910. In March of that year, *Vorwärts,* the party's leading journal, refused to publish a Luxemburg article on the mass strike on the grounds that "for the time being" the editors would not allow this topic to be discussed. She then sent it to *Neue Zeit*, edited by Kautsky. He too refused to publish it, on the grounds that her call for a democratic republic to replace the monarchy was "inappropriate." Kautsky was as determined as anyone to mute the Party's radical demands in order to regain its parliamentary strength. Luxemburg now hit back publicly, accusing him of opportunism. Reformism, she argued, permeated not only the revisionist wing of the SPD, but also the thinking of its most "orthodox" spokesman. While Kautsky wrote "heaven-storming theory," she contended, he was allowing for the most banal descent into parliamentarianism.

In many respects Luxemburg's critique of Kautsky in the essay "Theory and Practice"[16] was even more important than her critique of Bernstein in *Reform or Revolution*. Bernstein *openly* tried to revise Marxism by bringing theory into line with reformist practice. Kautsky, on the other hand, continued to claim adherence to revolutionary Marxism, even as he led the party down a reformist path. In her 1910 critique of Kautsky, Luxemburg anticipated the SPD's eventual betrayal of socialism in 1914. In 1910, however, very few understood the ramifications of her break with Kautsky. Many chalked it up to "personal" differences. For her trouble, Luxemburg earned the enmity of the top SPD leaders, who used blatantly sexist invective in their private, i.e. all-male, discussions of her. In a letter of August 10, 1910, to Kautsky, Bebel let loose: "It is an odd thing about women. If their partialities or passions or vanities come anywhere into question and are not given consideration, then even the most intelligent of them flies off the handle and becomes hostile to the point of absurdity. Love and hate lie side by side; a regulating reason does not exist."[17] Bebel, the author of the widely circulated handbook, *Woman and Socialism*, which had earned him a public reputation as a feminist, was here referring to both Luxemburg and Zetkin, who had allied herself with Luxemburg.

Even Lenin stayed aloof during the Luxemburg–Kautsky dispute.[18] But for Luxemburg, a fundamental issue was involved in Kautsky's turn to the right: a growing refusal on the part of the SPD to take an *active* stand against imperialist expansion for the sake of short-term electoral gain. This became evident to her in the summer of 1911, when she sharply criticized Kautsky and the SPD leadership for failing to oppose German imperialist designs on Morocco. As she saw it, their pusillanimity was symptomatic of a failure on the part of established Marxism to grasp the inseparability of capitalism and imperialism and to take effective action against this new phenomenon.

## II

From the moment she entered the Marxist movement, Luxemburg was renowned as a principled internationalist. Even before the term "imperialism" was coined, she wrote in 1899:

> Around 1895, a basic change occurred [in world politics]: the Japanese war opened the Chinese doors and European politics, driven by capitalist and state interests, intruded into Asia. . . . From that, the European antagonisms in Africa have received new impulses; there, too, the struggle is breaking out with new force (Fashoda, Delegoa, Madagascar). It's clear that the dismemberment of Asia and Africa is the final limit beyond which European politics no longer has room to unfold. There follows then another such squeeze as has just occurred in the Eastern question, and the European powers will have no choice other than throwing themselves on one another, until the *period of the final crisis sets in within politics*.[19]

In addition to attacking imperialism in general, in the ensuing years Luxemburg actively opposed German imperialism's effort to exterminate the Nama and Herero peoples in modern-day Namibia, insisting that "the Negroes in Africa with whose bodies the Europeans play a game of catch, are just as near to me" as the "suffering of the Jews."[20]

Beginning in 1907, when she was invited to teach at the SPD's party school in Berlin, an opportunity arose for her to analyze *theoretically* the ramifications of imperialism. In connection with her lectures on economic theory and history, she began working on a book entitled *Introduction to Political Economy*, left unfinished at her death. Luxemburg biographer Paul Frölich writes that based on her correspondence,

> We know the general plan of the whole work, which was to have included the following chapters:
>
> 1. What Is Economics?
> 2. Social Labor.
> 3. Economic-Historical Perspectives: Primitive Communist Society.
> 4. Economic-Historical Perspectives: Feudal Economic System.
> 5. Economic-Historical Perspectives: The Medieval Town and the Craft Guild.
> 6. Commodity Production.
> 7. Wage-Labor.
> 8. The Profit of Capital.
> 9. The Crisis.

10. The Tendencies of Capitalist Development.

In the summer of 1916 the first two chapters were ready for printing and all the other chapters already in draft. However, only chapters 1, 3, 6, 7, and 10 could be found among her literary remains.[21]

The surviving text, only a small part of which has ever been published in English,[22] runs some 250 printed pages. Far from a standard introduction to political economy, about half of the surviving text, which has been published in German and French, concerns not early or modern capitalism, but "primitive communism" in a diverse group of precapitalist societies. These include not only early European societies like ancient Greece or the early Germanic tribes, but also a wide variety of non-Western societies, some of them still functioning, albeit in decline, in Luxemburg's own lifetime: the Russian *mir* (village community), the traditional villages of India, the Lunda Empire of South Central Africa, the Kabyles of North Africa, the Australian aborigines, the Bororo of the Amazon, and the Inca Empire. In one of the few treatments to date of this part of Luxemburg's work, Michael Löwy writes: "In relying on the work of the Russian historian Maxim Kovalevsky, something in which Marx also had a lively interest, Rosa Luxemburg insisted on the *universality* of agrarian communism as a general form of human society at a certain level of development, that one finds just as easily among the American Indians, the Incas, the Aztecs, as among the Kabyles, the African tribes, and the Hindus. The Peruvian case seemed particularly significant to her."[23]

Luxemburg was trying to grasp the external as well as internal factors that brought about the dissolution of precapitalist communal formations. Instead of emphasizing the "backwardness" of such formations, she singled out their "extraordinary tenacity and stability . . . [their] elasticity and adaptability." "Communist ownership of the means of production," she wrote, "afforded, as the basis of a rigorously organized economy, the most productive social labor process and the best assurance of its continuity and development for many epochs." European imperialism destroyed the world's remaining indigenous communal formations:

The intrusion of European civilization was a disaster in every sense for primitive social relations. The European conquerors are the first who are not merely after subjugation and economic exploitation, but the means of production itself, by ripping the land from underneath the feet of the native population. In this way, European capitalism deprives the primitive social order of its foundation. What emerges is something that is worse than all oppression and exploitation, total anarchy and a specifically European phenomenon, the uncertainty of social existence. The subjugated peoples, separated from their means of production, are regarded by European capitalism as mere laborers, and when they are useful for this end, they are made into slaves, and if they are not, they are exterminated. We have witnessed this method in the Spanish, English, and French colonies. Before the advance of capitalism, the primitive social order, which outlasted all previous historical phases, capitulates. Its last remnants are eradicated from the earth and its elements—labor power and means of production—are absorbed by capitalism.[24]

Few Marxists of her era matched her depth of concern over and knowledge of the Western destruction of noncapitalist social relations. We publish in this volume for the first time in English the second half of Luxemburg's discussion of these precapitalist communal forms, where she focuses on their dissolution, which she attributes both to internal factors, e.g. their growing social differentiation, and, in modern times, to the external impact of European imperialism.

No one at the time, including Luxemburg, was aware of the extent of Marx's own studies of precapitalist communal formations. The *Grundrisse*, with its now-famous section on "Pre-Capitalist Economic Formations," was not published until 1939. Marx's extensive writings during his last decade (1872–83) on communal formations in Russia, India, Java, North Africa, the Australian aborigines, and the Native Americans did not begin to be published until the 1970s, and many remain unpublished to this day.[25] Luxemburg studied some of Marx's unpublished writings in search of research material for her lectures at the party school, though many thousands of pages penned by Marx on the subject remained unknown to her. She did, however, make use of some of the same sources as had Marx, such as the work of the Russian sociologist Maxim Kovalevsky, the British ethnologist Henry Sumner Maine, and the American ethnologist Lewis Henry Morgan.

Luxemburg wrote other pieces dealing with precapitalist societies as part of her research for her lectures. These and many other texts have come to light only recently, since the collapse of the Soviet Union, where they were hidden away in the Communist Party archives. One of these is a text on Greek and Roman slavery written sometime after 1907, with the part on Greece published for the first time in English in this *Reader*. It was first published in 2002 by the Luxemburg scholar Narihiko Ito. As Ito notes, Luxemburg here "criticized Engels" for having held that slavery arose as a consequence of the rise of private property and in this essay develops a less unilinear view of the origins of slavery.[26]

Luxemburg's researches into history and theory from 1907 to 1914 led to her greatest theoretical work—*The Accumulation of Capital: A Contribution to the Economic Explanation of Imperialism* (1913).[27] No Marxist, including Marx, she held, had adequately explained the inner drive and *necessity* for imperialist expansion. In *Accumulation of Capital,* Luxemburg argued that the fundamental contradiction of capitalism lies in the "unlimited expansive capacity of the productive forces" and the "limited expansive capacity of social consumption." Since capitalist production rests upon the extraction of surplus value, it is impossible for the workers to obtain enough value in the form of wages to "buy back" the surplus product; the same is true for the capitalists, who must invest ever-larger amounts of surplus value in the productive process in order to obtain increased capital accumulation. It is simply impossible, she held, for workers and capitalists in a single capitalist society to *realize* the mass of surplus value. So how does capitalism realize surplus value and provide for continuous capital accumulation? The answer, she argued, is that a strata of buyers of the surplus product must be obtained from *outside* the capitalist societies, in the pre-capitalist world: "The decisive fact is that the surplus value cannot be realized by sale either to workers or to capitalists, but only if it is sold to such social organizations or strata whose own mode of production is not capitalistic."[28] Through this approach she sought to show that imperialism and the destruction of precapitalist communal formations were not *accidental* features but were *organic* to the very nature of capitalism:

> From the very beginning, the forms and laws of capitalist production aim to comprise the entire globe as a store of productive forces. Capital, impelled to appropriate productive forces for purposes of exploitation, ransacks the whole world, it procures its means of production from all corners of the earth, seizing them, if necessary by force, from all levels of civilization and from all forms of society.... It becomes necessary for capital progressively to dispose ever more fully of the whole globe, to acquire an unlimited choice of means of production, with regard to both quality and quantity, so as to find productive employment for the surplus value it has realized.[29]

Luxemburg's approach involved a challenge to Marx's theory of accumulation, as expressed in the diagrams on expanded reproduction in Volume II of *Capital.* Marx there assumed, for the sake of simplicity, a single capitalist society composed solely of workers and capitalists, from which foreign trade was excluded. This assumption flowed from Marx's view that the mass of surplus value is realized not by personal consumption but by the continuous expansion of constant capital, especially in the form of machinery. His point was that the entirety of surplus value earmarked for capital accumulation need not yield an equivalent in monetary form; it was possible, Marx held, for much of surplus value to be realized *directly*, without having to take the form of money and be consumed by live people.

Luxemburg sharply criticized this approach, arguing that Marx's diagrams on expanded reproduction implied that capital accumulation could occur without crises of disproportionality or objective limits. She found this to be deeply disturbing, since it indicated to her that the theory of expanded reproduction failed to account for the inevitable collapse of capitalism. She therefore argued that Marx had made a fundamental error in assuming a closed capitalist society composed solely of workers and capitalists.

Critics from within the Marxian tradition have raised a number of objections against Luxemburg's critique of Marx in *The Accumulation of Capital*.[30] First, the critics have argued, Marx's theory does not presume a smooth process of accumulation without internal barriers and limits, since expanded reproduction leads to a disproportionate growth of means of production at the expense of labor power, which tends to depress the rate of profit. While economic crises *manifest* themselves in an inability to consume the surplus product, they are *rooted* in a breakdown in capital accumulation due to the decline in the rate of profit. Second, the critics have held that Luxemburg failed to understand that Marx's diagrams of expanded reproduction in Volume II were not meant to refer to actually existing capitalist reality; they were abstractions meant to show that even if one assumes away the problem of the *realization* of surplus value the capitalist system still finds its objective limits in the *production* of surplus value. Third, Luxemburg's critics have maintained that her argument that capitalism would collapse once it has exhausted pre-capitalist strata (since no buyers would be left to realize the mass of surplus value) fails to specify the role of human, subjective forces in putting an end to capitalism and imperialism. This problem is especially critical because of her virulent objection to all forms of national self-determination and her rejection of the idea that national movements against imperialism could become a revolutionary force that would help bring the system down.[31]

Despite these criticisms, there is broad agreement that *The Accumulation of Capital* represents one of the most comprehensive efforts in the history of Marxism to account for what is now termed "the globalization of capital."

Few Marxists of Luxemburg's generation were as acutely aware as she of the devastating impact of imperialism upon the Third World and on its precapitalist communal formations in particular. Her devastating critique of the impact of French imperialism in Algeria, of British imperialism in India and China, of U.S. imperialism in the Pacific and Latin America, and of European colonialism upon Southern Africa remain a beacon of creative analysis. Moreover, her effort to tie imperialist expansion to the nature of capitalism has taken on new importance in light of the need to oppose the *structural* factors that are responsible for today's drive toward "permanent war." As she wrote in *The Accumulation of Capital—An Anti-Critique*:

> The belief in the possibility of accumulation in an "isolated capitalist society," the belief that "capitalism is conceivable even without expansion," is the theoretical formula for a certain definite tactical tendency. This conception tends to regard the phase of imperialism not as a historical necessity, not as the decisive contest between capitalism and socialism, but as the malicious invention of a certain number of interested parties. It is bent on persuading the bourgeoisie that imperialism and militarism are detrimental even from the standpoint of bourgeois interests, and on thus isolating the alleged handful of benefiting parties, so that it can form a block between the proletariat and the broad strata of the bourgeoisie with a view to "damping down" imperialism, starving it out by "partial disarmament," and "removing its sting."[32]

## III

Luxemburg remains the best-known woman theorist in the history of Marxism. For many years the predominant claim among scholars was that she paid little or no attention to the concerns of women, since she wrote relatively little on women's liberation. Moreover, her writings often attack "bourgeois feminism." Nor did she spend a great deal of time involved in activist work on behalf of women's rights. Soon after her arrival in Germany, she refused the suggestion of a number of SPD leaders that she devote herself to the women's section of the SPD, for she had no intention of becoming "marginalized," placed far away from the central issues being debated by the male leadership. More recent research—especially the Marxist-Humanist philosopher Raya Dunayevskaya's *Rosa Luxemburg, Women's Liberation, and Marx's Philosophy of Revolution* (1982)—has pointed to heretofore ignored feminist dimensions of Luxemburg's life and thought. As Paul Le Blanc noted recently, Luxemburg "had a vibrant sense of the interpenetration of women's liberation and working class liberation."33 Writing a decade ago, the feminist philosopher Andrea Nye suggested that Luxemburg's class perspective on feminism offers "a theoretical grounding which is lacking in both liberal tolerance of diversity and postmodern politics of difference."34 And in 1988 the German Marxist feminist Frigga Haug contested earlier notions whereby Luxemburg "was relegated to the category of masculine women, that is to say, one of those women who had to deny her femininity and conform to the masculine world in order to achieve success."35

Luxemburg was quite aware of the male chauvinist attitudes that permeated many SPD members and she fully supported, although often behind the scenes, the work of close friends like Clara Zetkin in projecting women's emancipation as an integral dimension of socialist transformation.36 This *Reader* brings together a number of Luxemburg's writings on women, including several never previously translated into English, that demonstrate her lively and ongoing involvement in women's struggles.

One of these newly translated writings is "A Tactical Question" (1902), a response to Belgian Socialist leader Emil Vandervelde's electoral pact with liberals, in which the new alliance supported universal male suffrage, but dropped the longstanding Social Democratic demand for women's suffrage. Luxemburg not only attacked this move as a shameful abandonment of basic socialist principles, but she also wrote of how women's emancipation would shake up Social Democracy, as well as the capitalist order: "In [Social Democracy's] political and social life as well, a strong, fresh wind would blow in with the political emancipation of women, which would clear out the suffocating air of the current, philistine family life that rubs itself off so unmistakably, even on our party members, workers and leaders alike."37 Her disputes with leaders of the Second International over "the woman question" were not restricted to this episode. In 1907 she addressed the International Socialist Women's Conference, arguing that it should maintain its independent existence from the central headquarters of the Second International in Brussels. In 1912 she also argued for a working-class women's movement independent of the middle-class German women's organizations, in "Women's Suffrage and Class Struggle." In 1914 she published an article called "Proletarian Women" (here translated into English for the first time), which provided a moving tribute to women's resistance in Europe as well as in Africa and Latin America:

> A world of female misery is waiting for relief. The wife of the peasant moans as she nearly collapses under the life's burdens. In German Africa, in the Kalahari

Desert, the bones of defenseless Herero women are bleaching in the sun, those who were hunted down by a band of German soldiers and subjected to a horrific death of hunger and thirst. On the other side of the ocean, in the high cliffs of Putumayo, the death cries of martyred Indian women, ignored by the world, fade away in the rubber plantations of the international capitalists. Proletarian women, the poorest of the poor, the most disempowered of the disempowered, hurry to join the struggle for the emancipation of women and of humankind from the horrors of capitalist domination! [38]

And in 1918, at the height of the German revolution, Luxemburg urged Zetkin to establish a women's section of the Spartacus League and its publication *Die Rote Fahne.* Zetkin was too ill at the time to do so.

Luxemburg's writings on women extended to her work in the Polish movement. She authored point 10 of the SDKPiL's program, which called for "the abolition of all state laws, both civil and criminal, which have been issued to the detriment of women, or which in any way restrict her personal freedom, her right to dispose of her wealth or the right to exercise parental care over children on equal terms with the father of those children." Luxemburg biographer Richard Abraham notes that "Luxemburg and Zetkin were making demands for women that were more radical than the mass organizations of bourgeois feminism at the time, tolerating no backsliding from their leaders."[39]

One of the most important facets in Luxemburg's development was her personal break from Leo Jogiches, which occurred shortly after her involvement in the 1905 Revolution. A few years later, she wrote to her lover Konstantin (Costia) Zetkin, "I am I once more since I am free of Leo."[40] Dunayevskaya has carefully explored the political implications of their separation, noting that Luxemburg's "further self-development was reaching new heights without leaning on Jogiches. . . . Her greatest intellectual accomplishments occurred after the break." Whereas prior to their breakup "Luxemburg, who had very little interest in organization, and Jogiches, who was 'all organization,' did not find this to be in any way divisive of their love relationship," by 1907 "her further self-development was reaching new heights without leaning on Jogiches for either theory or organization."[41] Indeed, one of the most important aspects of Luxemburg's legacy is her distinctive attitude regarding the relation between spontaneity and organization. As Dunayevskaya also noted, these new developments were missed in Nettl's authoritative biography, where the chapter on 1906–09 was entitled "The Lost Years." The feminist poet Adrienne Rich comments as follows on this critique of Nettl: "Most biographers of women still fail to recognize that a woman's central relationship can be to her work, even as lovers come and go."[42]


## IV

Luxemburg's disputes with Lenin reveal her overall attitude towards revolutionary organization. Luxemburg greatly admired Lenin, and it was only after her death that the myth was created that they inhabited completely opposite poles on issues of revolution and organization.[43] Nonetheless, her criticisms of Lenin's organizational conceptions have taken on new importance in light of the subsequent history of the radical movement.

In her 1904 "Organizational Questions of Russian Social Democracy," Luxemburg sharply opposed Lenin's ultracentralism, arguing that proletarian class consciousness calls for "a complete revision of the concept of organization." Lenin's effort to combat opportunism through strict organizational centralism, she held, threatened to stifle spontaneous initiative and democratic deliberation. Opportunism needs to be fought, she said, but not by replicating its organizational methods. Though Luxemburg, like Lenin, upheld a concept of a vanguard party, they approached the relation of revolutionary consciousness and organization from somewhat different directions. Lenin often posed the party as the essential vehicle of class consciousness, whereas Luxemburg located class consciousness in the everyday struggles of the masses that the party needed to capture and help realize. As she wrote in 1899 in *Reform or Revolution*, "As long as theoretical knowledge remains the privilege of a handful of 'intellectuals' in the party, it will face the danger of going astray. Only when the great mass of workers has taken into their own hands the keen and dependable weapon of scientific socialism will . . . all the opportunistic currents come to naught."[44]

While Luxemburg's 1904 critique of Lenin's *What is to be Done* is well known, other manuscripts that have recently been discovered cast new light on her critique of his organizational concepts. The most important of these is a lengthy unpublished article written in the fall of 1911 and published in 1991 by Feliks Tych, who discovered it in the archives of the SDKPiL in Moscow. Entitled "Credo," it is translated into English in this *Reader* for the first time. The "Credo" was written in the period when Lenin was trying to eliminate all non-Bolshevik tendencies from the RSDRP and when sharp tensions had broken out between him and Luxemburg and Jogiches's SDKPiL. In the

"Credo" Luxemburg makes clear her greater affinity for Lenin and the Bolsheviks than for the Mensheviks or Trotsky, but nonetheless strongly attacked what she called "the crude, revolutionary actions of the Leninist Left." The importance of this document has been singled out by Annelies Laschitza, author of the most recent biography of Luxemburg: "The 'Credo' belongs alongside the article 'Organizational Questions of Russian Social Democracy' (1904) and the manuscript on 'The Russian Revolution' (1918) as the most important works of Rosa Luxemburg about Lenin's politics and makes clear the principled differences between the two regarding the questions of party unity and internal party democracy."[45]

The most important instance of Luxemburg's projection of the need for revolutionary democracy is found in her lengthy 1918 essay, *The Russian Revolution*, published after her death in 1922.[46] While the essay makes many strong criticisms of the Bolshevik Revolution of October 1917, it should be remembered that this work is a *defense* of the October Revolution. Written while she was in prison for opposing World War I, it *praised* the Bolsheviks for their daring and initiative. At the same time, however—and it was these points that have drawn the most attention—Luxemburg sharply criticized a number of their policies upon coming to power, from granting land to the peasants and continuing to insist on national self-determination to the dispersal of the Constituent Assembly. Her strongest and most enduring criticism centered on the suppression of revolutionary democracy by Lenin and Trotsky.[47] Luxemburg was deeply concerned that the Bolsheviks' tendency to stifle freedom of speech, press, and association endangered the very movement toward a socialist society. Socialism and democracy, she held, were inextricably linked; one could not be achieved without the other. Moreover, by monopolizing power in a single party, Lenin and Trotsky risked destroying the basis of Russia's revolutionary development. In raising the need for freedom of thought and spontaneous expression after the overthrow of the old regime, she posed some of the most important and difficult questions facing the Marxist movement, such as: what happens *after* the revolution? What can be done to ensure that a new class or a bureaucracy does not take over afterwards? Is it possible for a revolutionary process to continue "in permanence" so that the *transcendence* of alienation can be achieved?

These questions have taken on much greater force ever since the rise of Stalinist totalitarianism from *within* the Marxist movement and the later collapse of the Stalinist regimes after decades of repression and terror—developments that Luxemburg herself did not live to witness. It is a testament to

Luxemburg's prescience that her critique of the Russian revolution, posed in such a radically different historical context, nevertheless speaks to a question that is on the minds of millions today—is there an alternative to *both* existing capitalism *and* its bureaucratic/totalitarian opponents?

Recently, a new myth has surfaced concerning Luxemburg's critique of the Russian Revolution—that as against the "daring" of Lenin, who recognized the need to leap over objective barriers and propagate "*the* revolutionary Event," Luxemburg's critique represented reluctance on her part to seize the historical initiative.[48] Nothing could be further from the truth. Luxemburg did not oppose the October Revolution. Nor did she ever shy away from the need to seize power, as seen in everything from her critique of Bernstein to her participation in the German Revolution of 1918–19. The key issue for her was the *character* of the seizure of power and what steps need to be taken immediately *afterwards* to ensure the broadest possible revolutionary democracy. As she wrote in *The Russian Revolution*:

> When the proletariat seizes power, it can never again follow Kautsky's good advice to dispense with a socialist transformation of a country on the grounds that "the country is unripe". . . It should and must in fact immediately embark on socialist measures in the most energetic, the most unyielding and the most ruthless way; in other words, it must exercise a dictatorship, but a dictatorship of the class, not of a party or of a clique—and dictatorship of the class means: in full view of the broadest public, with the most active, uninhibited participation of the popular masses in an unlimited democracy.

For Luxemburg, "It is the historic task of the proletariat, once it has attained power, to create socialist democracy in place of bourgeois democracy, not to do away with democracy altogether." She would settle for nothing less because, she insisted, "socialist practice means a total spiritual transformation in the masses degraded by centuries of bourgeois class rule."[49]

V

Luxemburg got an opportunity to test such ideas directly in an actual revolutionary process, in Germany in 1918–19. This opportunity arose after a trying period set into motion by the collapse of the Second International, when the SPD voted for war credits at the outbreak of World War I on August 4, 1914. Shocked and nearly suicidal over the great betrayal, Luxemburg soon composed herself and got to work developing a revolutionary opposition to the socialist movement's capitulation to imperialist war. On the very evening of August 4, she met with colleagues in her apartment to work out how to disassociate socialism from the betrayal of the SPD. She was soon joined by Karl Liebknecht, who was the sole Reichstag deputy openly to oppose the vote for war credits, this in late 1914. In early 1915, Luxemburg, Liebknecht and others formed *Die Gruppe Internationale* and published *Die Internationale* as its journal. Alhough its further publication was blocked by wartime censorship, it helped galvanize antiwar sentiment and led a year later to the formation of the Spartacus Group, headed by Luxemburg and Liebknecht.

By that time, Luxemburg was in prison. Her letters from prison reveal her multi-faceted personality and intellectual interests, as she delved into Russian literature by writing a study of Vladimir Korolenko, commented on German Romantic literature and French poetry, indulged herself in her life-long interest in art, and wrote one of her most important works—*The Accumulation of Capital: An Anti-Critique*—and, as we have seen, worked to ready the *Introduction to Political Economy* for publication. Luxemburg was never one to limit herself, even in the most difficult of circumstances. As she noted in a letter to her friend Luise Kautsky from prison, "Everyone who writes to me also moans and groans. I find nothing more ridiculous than that. . . . To abandon oneself completely to the woes of the day is altogether incomprehensible and intolerable. . . . A political fighter has even more the need to try to be on top of things; otherwise, he will sink right up to his ears in every piddling matter."[50]

It was also in prison, in 1915, that she wrote her great antiwar and antimilitarist manifesto—*The Crisis in German Social Democracy*, published under the pseudonym of "Junius," and known since then as the *Junius Pamphlet*. Smuggled out of prison and issued as a pamphlet in 1916, its scathing indictment of the SPD and the Second International acted as a powerful prod to revolutionary regrouping. Yet Luxemburg resisted calls to issue a complete organizational break from the SPD. Earlier, in 1908, she had opposed the decision of the Dutch revolutionary Henrietta Roland-Holst to leave the Dutch Social-Democratic Party, arguing that "the worst working class party is better than none."[51] The fetish of a unified organization, which so characterized the Marxists of the Second International, left its mark on Luxemburg. Despite her critique of the SPD in the Junius pamphlet and other writings, she advocated working from within the SPD as an opposition tendency for as long as possible in order not to lose touch with the masses.

By 1916 opposition to the war was growing within the working class, as seen in the formation of groups of radical workers in manufacturing centers such as Berlin, Bremen, Braunschweig, Stuttgart and Hamburg. Some were connected with the Spartacus Group, others not; a number of these groups sought an immediate break from the political legacy of the SPD and the Second International. With Luxemburg and Liebknecht in prison, the organizational work of maintaining the underground existence of the Spartacus League fell to Leo Jogiches. Due to his excellent conspiratorial skills, the Spartacus Group organized a widespread illegal campaign to distribute antiwar leaflets, many of them written by Luxemburg. This helped create the climate for the January 1918 mass strike for peace involving a million workers. This became known as the *Generalprobe* (dress rehearsal) for the German Revolution of November 1918. In 1917, after the SPD opposition, grouped around Hugo Haase and Georg Ledebour, had been expelled and formed its own Independent Social Democratic Party (USPD), the Spartacus Group affiliated itself with the USPD as an autonomous tendency, trying to push the moderate majority of the USPD in a revolutionary direction.

Finally, in October 1918 the German front collapsed, followed by the mutiny of German sailors in Kiel. The German Revolution had begun. Workers and soldiers' councils began forming and political prisoners like Liebknecht were freed. Luxemburg was released on November 8. Terrified by the mass upsurge, the last wartime chancellor, Max von Baden, announced the resignation of the Kaiser and appointed SPD leader Friedrich Ebert chancellor. SPD leaders Philipp Scheidemann and Ebert—a socialist who announced, "I hate revolution like a mortal sin"[52]—directed their energies to containing the workers and soldiers' revolt within bourgeois boundaries.

The toll that years of imprisonment had taken on Luxemburg's health was immediately recognizable to her comrades on her release from prison. Yet in the next two months she called forth a remarkable store of energy and creativity as she immersed herself in the effort to push for social revolution. There was the work of issuing the Spartacus League's publication, *Die Rote Fahne*, which appeared daily and sometimes twice a day; Luxemburg usually wrote over half the pieces for each issue. There were innumerable discussions with the Berlin USPD, with the Revolutionary Shop Stewards and speeches to workers and soldiers. And there was the intense work that led to the formation of the German Communist Party in December 1918, where Luxemburg made a firm break from the entire legacy of the German SPD. As Luxemburg wrote that December, "In the present revolution the defenders of the old order enter the lists not with shields and coats of arms of the ruling classes, but under the banner of a 'Social Democratic Party.'"[53]

This *Reader* offers a selection of some of Luxemburg's most important writings on the German Revolution of 1918–19. It contains "The Beginning," written on November 18, 1918, which evaluated the state of the revolution; "The Socialization of Society" (December 4, 1918), which includes one of her fullest discussions of the nature of postcapitalist society; "What Does the Spartacus League Want?"(December 14, 1918); and "Our Program and the Political Situation," her speech to the founding conference of the German Communist Party (KPD) on December 31, 1918. The latter marks not just an organizational but also a *conceptual* break from the politics of the Second International. In this speech, Luxemburg did not limit herself to a criticism of SPD leaders; she instead linked the betrayal of 1914 to the politics pursued by the Second International since its inception, when it adopted the Erfurt Program of 1891 with its sharp distinction between "minimum" and "maximum" demands. She did not shy away from criticizing Engels, who had consented to the establishment of the Second International, even though he had criticisms of the Erfurt Program. "The 4th of August [1914] did not come like thunder out of a clear sky," she declared. "What happened on the 4th of August was the logical outcome of all that we had been doing for many years." Although Luxemburg took aim at the founding programmatic document of the Second International;[54] she did not extend her criticism all the way to 1875, when Marx, in his *Critique of the Gotha Program,* had issued an attack on "the unprincipled unity" between his followers and those of the authoritarian socialist Ferdinand Lassalle. The way in which Marx's *Critique of the Gotha Program* projected a distinctive concept of organization that none of his followers built upon was not recognized by anyone at the time, including Luxemburg; it has taken our age to rediscover its importance.[55]

On January 4, 1919, within days of the formation of the KPD, Emil Eichhorn, the Berlin Chief of Police who was connected to the Left USPD, was dismissed by the SPD-controlled Prussian government. On Sunday, January 5, following a call drafted by the Berlin USPD, the Revolutionary Shop Stewards, and the KPD, over 100,000 workers came into the streets of Berlin to oppose Eichhorn's dismissal. That evening, groups of workers spontaneously occupied the offices of *Vorwärts* and the establishment press. Surprised by the unexpectedly large turnout and the revolutionary mood of the participants, a Revolutionary Committee was quickly formed by the Berlin USPD, the Revolutionary Shop Stewards, as well as Liebknecht and Wilhelm Pieck of the KPD. Without consulting Luxemburg, they voted on late Sunday night to overthrow the Ebert-Scheidemann government. The next day, on January 6, the movement against the government appeared even stronger when over half a million workers marched in Berlin. It was the largest working-class demonstration in the history of Germany. But the soldiers in the Berlin barracks did not join the uprising and many in the factories supported unity among the different socialist parties.

The complex and confusing turn of events over the next several days cannot be detailed here. There is little doubt that Luxemburg considered the call for an insurrection to be premature; the KPD was still a small and fledgling organization and it was not clear that the revolutionaries could count on the support of the workers and soldiers' councils, let alone the peasantry. Yet recent research by scholars such as Ottokar Luban has challenged the long-held contention that Luxemburg was fundamentally reluctant to participate in what came to be known as the Spartacus uprising. Neither Rosa Luxemburg nor other leaders of the KPD and USPD planned this uprising, as the SPD and others claimed at the time. But on January 7, after Luxemburg saw the huge crowds of workers in the streets demanding the dismissal of Ebert-Scheidemann government, she called for the "occupation of all positions of power" in *Die Rote Fahne*, and a day later she termed the overthrow of the Ebert–Scheidemann government "a necessary objective." Though Luxemburg was aware that the balance of forces did not favor the revolutionaries, she refused to oppose the uprising on the grounds that once in motion "a revolutionary development will not turn backward." The masses were clearly in the streets, and she felt it was incumbent upon revolutionaries to do all they could to make the best of the fight.[56]

The revolutionaries' failure to gain the support of the Berlin workers and soldiers councils and troops from the People's Naval Division helped doom the uprising; government forces went on the offensive and crushed it. Luxemburg and Liebknecht were forced into hiding, as the SPD issued not-so-veiled calls for their heads. Though some advised her to leave Berlin, Luxemburg refused to do so. She was arrested along with Liebknecht on January 15 by members of the Freikorps, forerunners of the Nazis who had been armed by the government, and both were brutally murdered the same day. Luxemburg's disfigured body was not discovered for months afterward.

VI

The era in which Rosa Luxemburg lived and worked is certainly one removed from our own, not only historically, but also conceptually. She died before seeing the transformation of the Russian Revolution into a full-fledged totalitarian society, let alone its collapse. She did not live to see anti-imperialist revolutions in Africa, Asia, and Latin America. She also died before the publication of an array of Marx's writings, which enabled later generations to gain a much deeper understanding of the breadth and depth of his thought. The discovery of his *Economic and Philosophic Manuscripts of 1844*, the *Grundrisse*, and the writings from his last decade on technologically developed societies, all lay in the future. Yet in spite of the historical and conceptual limitations of the time in which she lived, Rosa Luxemburg developed a concept of revolution and of freedom that speaks to us today, despite our radically different circumstances.

Her visionary commitment to socialist democracy and human liberation and her virulent opposition to bureaucracy, excessive entralism and elitism offer a permanent challenge to those who would narrow the struggle against capitalism to piecemeal reforms or unprincipled compromises with reactionary tendencies. Her work speaks to the need for a deeper form of democracy, a socialist democracy grounded in a humanist outlook, free of both authoritarianism and the claim that any attempt to go beyond the narrow horizons of capitalist democracy will necessarily end in chaos or totalitarianism.

Moreover, her critique of war and imperialism continues to resonate, as does her deep identification with those who suffer the most under the domination of global capitalism, from working-class women to those subjected to the barbarism of colonial rule.

Given our own situation today, we cannot afford to have a bad break between the generations—at least when it comes to absorbing and rethinking the contributions of so historic a figure as Rosa Luxemburg. In this sense, the final words that we have from her pen ring as loudly today as when she wrote them: "I was, I am, I shall be!"

# PART ONE

## Political Economy, Imperialism, and Non-Western Societies

# 1 — The Historical Conditions of Accumulation, from *The Accumulation of Capital*

EDITORS' NOTE: *The Accumulation of Capital*, first published in German in 1913 with the subtitle *A Contribution to an Explanation of Imperialism*, is regarded as Rosa Luxemburg's most important theoretical work. In this 450-page book, Luxemburg sought to uncover the economic roots of imperialism by focusing on the problem of expanded reproduction, which Marx discussed at the end of Volume II of *Capital*. Luxemburg held that Marx failed to provide an adequate account of expanded reproduction because Volume II of *Capital* assumed a closed capitalist society in which foreign trade is excluded. Luxemburg, in contrast, sought to show that expanded reproduction depends upon the ability of capitalism to realize surplus value through its exploitation of non-capitalist strata. *The Accumulation of Capital* therefore sought to demonstrate that capitalism is required by its very nature to dominate and exploit the non-capitalist world, without which it would collapse.

Section One of *The Accumulation of Capital* is entitled "The Problem of Reproduction"; Section Two "Historical Exposition of the Problem"; and Section Three "The Historical Conditions of Accumulation." We include here the first two chapters of Section Three—Chapter 25, "Contradictions Within the Diagram of Enlarged Reproduction," and Chapter 26, "The Reproduction of Capital and Its Social Setting"—as well as excerpts from Chapter 27, "The Struggle Against Natural Economy." The translation is by Agnes Schwarzschild. Footnotes supplied by the editors are to current English-language editions of Marx's works. The full text of *The Accumulation of Capital* has recently been reprinted by Routledge (London and New York, 2003).

## CONTRADICTIONS WITHIN THE DIAGRAM
## OF ENLARGED REPRODUCTION

In the first section, we ascertained that Marx's diagram of accumulation does not solve the question of who is to benefit in the end by enlarged reproduction. If we take the diagram literally as it is set out at the end of Volume II [of

*Capital*],[1] it appears that capitalist production would itself realize its entire surplus value, and that it would use the capitalized surplus value exclusively for its own needs. This impression is confirmed by Marx's analysis of the diagram where he attempts to reduce the circulation within the diagram altogether to terms of money, that is to say to the effective demand of capitalists and workers—an attempt which in the end leads him to introduce the "producer of money" as a *deus ex machina*. In addition, there is that most important passage in *Capital*, Volume I, which must be interpreted to mean the same.

> The annual production must in the first place furnish all those objects (use-values) from which the material components of capital, used up in the course of the year, have to be replaced. Deducting these there remains the net or surplus-product, in which the surplus-value lies. And of what does this surplus-value consist? Only of things destined to satisfy the wants and desires of the capitalist class, things which, consequently, enter into the consumption fund of the capitalists? Were that the case, the cup of surplus-value would be drained to the very dregs and nothing but simple reproduction would ever take place.
>
> To accumulate it is necessary to convert a portion of the surplus-product into capital. But we cannot, except by a miracle, convert into capital anything but such articles as can be employed in the labor-process (i.e. means of production), and such further articles as are suitable for the sustenance of the laborer (i.e. means of subsistence). Consequently, a part of the annual surplus-labor must have been applied to the production of additional means of production and subsistence, over and above the quantity of these things required to replace the capital advanced. In one word, surplus-value is convertible into capital solely because the surplus-product, whose value it is, already comprises the material elements of new capital.[2]

The following conditions of accumulation are here laid down: 1) The surplus value to be capitalised first comes into being in the natural form of capital (as additional means of production and additional means of subsistence for the workers). 2) The expansion of capitalist production is achieved exclusively by means of capitalist products, i.e. its own means of production and subsistence. 3) The limits of this expansion are each time determined in advance by the amount of surplus value which is to be capitalized in any given case; they cannot be extended, since they depend on the amount of the means of production and subsistence which make up the surplus product; neither can they be reduced, since a part of the surplus value could not then be employed in its natural form. Deviations in either direction (above and below) may give rise to periodical fluctuations and crises—in this context, however, these may be ignored, because in general the surplus product to be capitalized must be equal to actual accumulation. 4) Since capitalist production buys up its entire surplus product, there is no limit to the accumulation of capital.

Marx's diagram of enlarged reproduction adheres to these conditions. Accumulation here takes its course, but it is not in the least indicated who is to benefit by it, who are the new consumers for whose sake production is ever more enlarged. The diagram assumes, say, the following course of events: the coal industry is expanded in order to expand the iron industry in order to expand the machine industry in order to expand the production of consumer goods. This last, in turn, is expanded to maintain both its own workers and the growing army of coal, iron and machine operatives. And so on *ad infinitum*. We are running in circles, quite in accordance with the theory of Tugan-Baranovski.[3] Considered in isolation, Marx's diagram does indeed permit of such an interpretation since he himself explicitly states time and again that he aims at presenting the process of accumulation of the aggregate capital in a society consisting solely of capitalists and workers. Passages to this effect can be found in every volume of *Capital*.

In Volume I, in the very chapter on "The Conversion of Surplus-Value into Capital," he says: "In order to examine the object of our investigation in its integrity, free from all disturbing subsidiary circumstances, we must treat the whole world as one nation, and assume that capitalist production is everywhere established and has possessed itself of every branch of industry."[4]

In Volume II, the assumption repeatedly returns; thus in chapter 17 on "The Circulation of Surplus-Value": "Now, there are only two points of departure: The capitalist and the laborer. All third classes of persons must either receive money for their services from these two classes, or, to the extent that they receive it without any equivalent services, they are joint owners of the surplus-value in the form of rent, interest, etc. . . . The capitalist class, then, remains the sole point of departure of the circulation of money."[5]

Further, in the same chapter "On the Circulation of Money in Particular under Assumption of Accumulation": "But the difficulty arises when we assume, not a partial, but a general accumulation of money-capital on the part of the capitalist class. Apart from this class, there is, according to our assumption—the general and exclusive domination of capitalist production—no other class but the working class."[6]

And again in chapter 20: " . . . there are only two classes in this case, the working class disposing of their labor-power, and the capitalist class owning the social means of production and the money."[7]

In Volume III, Marx says quite explicitly, when demonstrating the process of capitalist production as a whole:

> Let us suppose that the whole society is composed only of industrial capitalists and wage workers. Let us furthermore make exceptions of fluctuations of prices which prevent large portions of the total capital from reproducing themselves under average conditions and which, owing to the general interrelations of the entire process of reproduction, such as are developed particularly by credit, must always call forth general stoppages of a transient nature. Let us also make abstraction of the bogus transactions, and speculations, which the credit system favors. In that case, a crisis could be explained only by a disproportion of production in various branches, and by a disproportion of the consumption of the capitalists and the accumulation of their capitals. But as matters stand, the reproduction of the capitals invested in production depends largely upon the consuming power of the non-producing classes; while the consuming power of the laborers is handicapped partly by the laws of wages, partly by the fact that it can be exerted only so long as the laborers can be employed at a profit for the capitalist class.[8]

This last quotation refers to the question of crises with which we are not here concerned. It can leave no doubt, however, that the movement of the total capital, "as matters stand," depends in Marx's view on three categories of consumers only: the capitalists, the workers and the "non-productive classes," i.e. the hangers-on of the capitalist class (king, parson, professor, prostitute, mercenary), of whom he quite rightly disposes in Volume II as the mere representatives of a derivative purchasing power, and thus the parasitic joint consumers of the surplus value or of the wage of labor.

Finally, in *Theories of Surplus Value*,[9] Marx formulates his general presuppositions with regard to accumulation as follows:

> Here we have only to consider the forms through which capital passes during the various stages of its development. Thus we do not set out the actual conditions of the real process of production, but always assume that the commodity is sold for what it is worth. We ignore the competition of capitalists and the credit system; we also leave out of account the actual constitution of society which never consists exclusively of the classes of workers and industrial capitalists, and where there is accordingly no strict division between producers and consumers. The first category (of consumers, whose revenues are partly of a secondary, not a prim-

itive nature, derived from profits and the wage of labor) is much wider than the second category (of producers).

Therefore the manner in which it spends its income, and the extent of such income, effects very large modifications in the economic household, and especially so in the process of circulation and reproduction of capital.

Speaking of the "actual constitution of society," Marx here also considers merely the parasitic joint consumers of surplus value and of the wage of labor, i.e. only the hangers-on of the principal categories of capitalist production.

There can be no doubt, therefore, that Marx wanted to demonstrate the process of accumulation in a society consisting exclusively of workers and capitalists, under the universal and exclusive domination of the capitalist mode of production. On this assumption, however, his diagram does not permit of any other interpretation than that of production for production's sake.

Let us recall the second example of Marx's diagram of enlarged reproduction:[10]

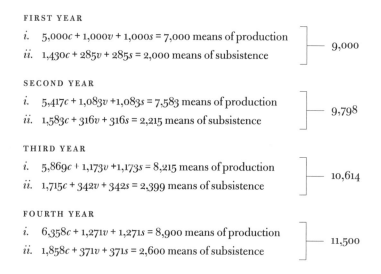

**FIRST YEAR**

*i.*   $5,000c + 1,000v + 1,000s = 7,000$ means of production

*ii.*   $1,430c + 285v + 285s = 2,000$ means of subsistence     9,000

**SECOND YEAR**

*i.*   $5,417c + 1,083v + 1,083s = 7,583$ means of production

*ii.*   $1,583c + 316v + 316s = 2,215$ means of subsistence     9,798

**THIRD YEAR**

*i.*   $5,869c + 1,173v + 1,173s = 8,215$ means of production

*ii.*   $1,715c + 342v + 342s = 2,399$ means of subsistence     10,614

**FOURTH YEAR**

*i.*   $6,358c + 1,271v + 1,271s = 8,900$ means of production

*ii.*   $1,858c + 371v + 371s = 2,600$ means of subsistence     11,500

Here accumulation continues year after year without interruption, the capitalists in each case consuming half of the surplus value they have gained and capitalizing the other half. In the process of capitalization, the same technical foundation, that is to say the same organic composition or division into constant and variable capital and also the same rate of exploitation (always amounting to 100 percent) is consecutively maintained for the additional capital as it was for the original capital. In accordance with Marx's assumption in

Volume I of *Capital*, the capitalized part of the surplus value first comes into being as additional means of production and as means of subsistence for the workers, both serving the purpose of an ever expanding production in the two departments. It cannot be discovered from the assumptions of Marx's diagram for whose sake production is progressively expanded. Admittedly, production and consumption increase simultaneously in a society. The consumption of the capitalists increases (in terms of value, in the first year it amounts to 500 + 142, in the second year to 542 + 158, in the third year to 586 + 171, and in the fourth year to 635 + 185); the consumption of the workers increases as well; the variable capital increasing year after year in both departments precisely indicates this growth in terms of value. And yet, the growing consumption of the capitalists can certainly not be regarded as the ultimate purpose of accumulation; on the contrary, there is no accumulation inasmuch as this consumption takes place and increases; personal consumption of the capitalists must be regarded as simple reproduction. Rather, the question is: if, and insofar as, the capitalists do not themselves consume their products but "practice abstinence," i.e. accumulate, for whose sake do they produce? Even less can the maintenance of an ever larger army of workers be the ultimate purpose of continuous accumulation of capital. From the capitalist's point of view, the consumption of the workers is a consequence of accumulation, it is never its object or its condition, unless the principles (foundations) of capitalist production are to be turned upside down. And in any case, the workers can only consume that part of the product which corresponds to the variable capital, not a jot more. Who, then, realizes the permanently increasing surplus value? The diagram answers: the capitalists themselves and they alone.—And what do they do with this increasing surplus value?—The diagram replies: They use it for an ever greater expansion of their production. These capitalists are thus fanatical supporters of an expansion of production for production's sake. They see to it that ever more machines are built for the sake of building—with their help—ever more new machines. Yet the upshot of all this is not accumulation of capital but an increasing production of producer goods to no purpose whatever. Indeed, one must be as reckless as Tugan-Baranovski, and rejoice as much in paradoxical statements, to assume that this untiring merry-go-round in thin air could be a faithful reflection in theory of capitalist reality, a true deduction from Marx's doctrine.[11]

Besides the analysis of enlarged reproduction roughed out in *Capital*, Volume II, the whole of Marx's work, Volume II in particular, contains a most elaborate and lucid exposition of his general views regarding the typical course of capitalist accumulation. If we once fully understand this interpretation, the deficiencies of the diagram at the end of Volume II are immediately evident.

If we examine critically the diagram of enlarged reproduction in the light of Marx's theory, we find various contradictions between the two.

To begin with, the diagram completely disregards the increasing productivity of labor. For it assumes that the composition of capital is the same in every year, that is to say, the technical basis of the productive process is not affected by accumulation. This procedure would be quite permissible in itself in order to simplify the analysis, but when we come to examine the concrete conditions for the realization of the aggregate product, and for reproduction, then at least we must take into account, and make allowance for, changes in technique which are bound up with the process of capital accumulation. Yet if we allow for improved productivity of labor, the material aggregate of the social product—both producer and consumer goods—will in consequence show a much more rapid increase in volume than is set forth in the diagram. This increase in the aggregate of use-values, moreover, indicates also a change in the value relationships. As Marx argues so convincingly, basing his whole theory on this axiom, the progressive development of labor productivity reacts on both the composition of accumulating capital and the rate of surplus value so that they cannot remain constant under conditions of increasing accumulation of capital, as was assumed by the diagram. Rather, if accumulation continues, $c$, the constant capital of both departments, must increase not only absolutely but also relatively to $v + c$ or the total new value (the social aspect of labor productivity); at the same time, constant capital and similarly the surplus value must increase relatively to the variable capital—in short, the rate of surplus value, i.e. the ratio between surplus value and variable capital, must similarly increase (the capitalist aspect of labor productivity). These changes need not, of course, occur annually, just as the terms of first, second and third year in Marx's diagram do not necessarily refer to calendar years but may stand for any given period. Finally, we may choose to assume that these alterations, both in the composition of capital and in the rate of surplus value, take place either in the first, third, fifth, seventh year, etc., or in the second, sixth and ninth year, etc. The important thing is only that they are allowed for somewhere and taken into account as periodical phenomena. If the diagram is amended accordingly, the result of this method of accumulation will be an increasing annual surplus in the consumer at the expense of producer goods. It is true that Tugan-Baranovski conquers all difficulties on paper: he simply constructs a diagram with different proportions where year by year the variable capital decreases by 25 percent.

And since this arithmetical exercise is successful enough on paper, Tugan triumphantly claims to have "proved" that accumulation runs smoothly like clockwork, even if the absolute volume of consumption decreases. Even he must admit in the end, however, that his assumption of such an absolute decrease of the variable capital is in striking contrast to reality. Variable capital is in point of fact a growing quantity in all capitalist countries; only in relation to the even more rapid growth of constant capital can it be said to decrease. On the basis of what is actually happening, namely a greater yearly increase of constant capital as against that of variable capital, as well as a growing rate of surplus value, discrepancies must arise between the material composition of the social product and the composition of capital in terms of value. If, instead of the unchanging proportion of five to one between constant and variable capital, proposed by Marx's diagram, we assume for instance that this increase of capital is accompanied by a progressive readjustment of its composition, the proportion between constant and variable in the second year being six to one, in the third year seven to one, and in the fourth year eight to one—if we further assume that the rate of surplus value also increases progressively in accordance with the higher productivity of labor so that, in each case, we have the same amounts as those of the diagram, although, because of the relatively decreasing variable capital, the rate of surplus value does not remain constant at the original 100 percent—and if finally we assume that one-half of the appropriated surplus value is capitalized in each case (excepting Department II[12] where capitalization exceeds 50 percent, 184 out of 285 being capitalized during the first year), the result will be as follows:

FIRST YEAR

i.   $5,000c + 1,000v + 1,000s = 7,000$ means of production

ii.   $1,430c + 285v + 285s = 2,000$ means of subsistence

SECOND YEAR

i.   $5,428 \, 4/7 \, c + 1,071 \, 3/7 \, v + 1,083s = 7,583$ means of production

ii.   $1,587 \, 5/7 \, c + 311 \, 2/7 \, v + 316s = 2,215$ means of subsistence

THIRD YEAR

i.   $5,903c + 1,139v + 1,173s = 8,215$ means of production

ii.   $1,726c + 331v + 342s = 2,399$ means of subsistence

FOURTH YEAR

i.   $6,424c + 1,205v + 1,271s = 8,900$ means of production

ii.   $1,879c + 350v + 371s = 2,600$ means of subsistence

If this were a true picture of the accumulative process, the means of production (constant capital) would show a deficit of sixteen in the second year, of forty-five in the third year and of eighty-eight in the fourth year; similarly, the means of subsistence would show a surplus of sixteen in the second year, of forty-five in the third year and of eighty-eight in the fourth year.

This negative balance for the means of production may be only imaginary in part. The increasing productivity of labor ensures that the means of production grow faster in bulk than in value, in other words: means of production become cheaper. As it is use value, i.e. the material elements of capital, which is relevant for technical improvements of production, we may assume that the quantity of means of production, in spite of their lower value, will suffice for progressive accumulation up to a certain point. This phenomenon amongst others also checks the actual decline of the rate of profit and modifies it to a mere tendency, though our example shows that the decline of the profit rate would not only be retarded but rather completely arrested. On the other hand, the same fact indicates a much larger surplus of unsaleable means of subsistence than is suggested by the amount of this surplus in terms of value. In that case, we should have to compel the capitalists of Department II to consume this surplus themselves, which Marx makes them do on other occasions; in which case, and insofar as those capitalists are concerned, there would again be no accumulation but rather simple reproduction. Alternatively, we should have to pronounce this whole surplus unsaleable.

Yet would it not be very easy to make good this loss in means of production which results from our example? We need only assume that the capitalists of Department I capitalize their surplus value to a greater extent. Indeed, there is no valid reason to suppose, as Marx did, that the capitalists in each case add only half their surplus value to their capital. Advances in labor productivity may well lead to progressively increasing capitalization of surplus value. This assumption is the more permissible in that the cheapening of consumer goods for the capitalist class, too, is one of the consequences of technological progress. The relative decrease in the value of consumable income (as compared with the capitalized part) may then permit of the same or even a higher standard of living for this class. We might for instance make good the deficit in producer goods by transferring a corresponding part of surplus value I to the constant capital of this department, a part which would otherwise be consumed, since this surplus value, like all other products of the department, originally takes the form of producer goods; eleven-and-four-sevenths would then be transferred in the second year, thirty-four in the third year and sixty-six in the fourth year.[13] The solution of one difficulty, however, only adds to another. It goes without saying that if the capitalists of Department I relatively restrict their consumption for purposes of accumulation, there will be a proportionately greater unsaleable residue of consumer goods in Department II; and thus it becomes more and more impossible to enlarge the constant capital even on its previous technological basis. If the capitalists in Department I relatively restrict their consumption, the capitalists of Department II must relatively expand their personal consumption in proportion. The assumption of accelerated accumulation in Department I would then have to be supplemented by that of retarded accumulation in Department II, technical progress in one department by regression in the other.

These results are not due to mere chance. The adjustments we have tried out on Marx's diagram are merely meant to illustrate that technical progress, as he himself admits, must be accompanied by a relative growth of constant as against variable capital. Hence the necessity for a continuous revision of the ratio in which capitalized surplus value should be allotted to $c$ and $v$ respectively. In Marx's diagram, however, the capitalists are in no position to make these allocations at will, since the material form of their surplus value predetermines the forms of capitalization. Since, according to Marx's assumption, all expansion of production proceeds exclusively by means of its own, capitalistically produced means of production and subsistence—since there are here no other places and forms of production and equally no other consumers than the two departments with their capitalists and workers—and since, on the other hand, the smooth working of the accumulative process depends on circulation wholly absorbing the aggregate product of both departments, the technological shape of enlarged reproduction is in consequence strictly prescribed by the material form of the surplus product. In other words: according to Marx's diagram, the technical organization of expanded production can and must be such as to make use of the aggregate surplus value produced in Departments I and II. In this connection we must bear in mind also that both departments can obtain their respective elements of production only by means of mutual exchange. Thus the allocation to constant or variable capital of the surplus value earmarked for capitalization, as well as the allotment of the additional means of production and subsistence (for the workers) to Departments I and II, is given in advance and determined by the relations between the two departments of the diagram—both in material and in terms of value. These relations themselves, however, reflect a quite determinate technical organization of production. This implies that, on the assumptions of Marx's diagram, the techniques of production given in each case predetermine the techniques of the subsequent periods of enlarged reproduction, if accumulation continues. Assuming, that is to say, in accordance with Marx's diagram, that the expansion of capitalist production is always performed by means of the surplus value originally produced in form of capital, and further—or rather, conversely—that accumulation in one department is strictly dependent on accumulation in the other, then no change in the technical organization of production can be possible insofar as the relation of $c$ to $v$ is concerned.

We may put our point in yet another way: it is clear that a quicker growth of constant as compared with variable capital, i.e. the progressive metamorphosis of the organic composition of capital, must take the material form of faster expansion of production in Department I as against production in Department II. Yet Marx's diagram, where strict conformity of the two departments is axiomatic, precludes any such fluctuations in the rate of accumulation in either department. It is quite legitimate to suppose that under the technical conditions of progressive accumulation, society would invest ever increasing portions of the surplus value earmarked for accumulation in Department I rather than in Department II. Both departments being only branches of the same social production—supplementary enterprises, if you like, of the "aggregate capitalist,"—such a progressive transfer, for technical reasons, from one department to the other of a part of the accumulated surplus value would be wholly feasible, especially as it corresponds to the actual practice of capital. Yet this assumption is possible only so long as we envisage the surplus value earmarked for capitalization purely in terms of value. The diagram, however, implies that this part of the surplus value appears in a definite material form which prescribes its capitalization. Thus the surplus value of Department II exists as means of subsistence, and since it is as such to be only realized by Department I, this intended transfer of part of the capitalized surplus value from Department II to Department I is ruled out, first because the material form of this surplus value is obviously useless to Department I, and secondly because of the relations of exchange between the two departments which would in turn necessitate an equivalent transfer of the products of Department I into Department II. It is therefore downright impossible to achieve a faster expansion of Department I as against Department II within the limits of Marx's diagram.

However we may regard the technological alterations of the mode of production in the course of accumulation, they cannot be accomplished without upsetting the fundamental relations of Marx's diagram.

And further: according to Marx's diagram, the capitalized surplus value is in each case immediately and completely absorbed by the productive process of the following period, for, apart from the portion earmarked for consumption, it has a natural form which allows of only one particular kind of employment. The diagram precludes the cashing and hoarding of surplus value in monetary form, as capital waiting to be invested. The free monetary forms of private capital, in Marx's view, are first the money deposited gradually against the wear and tear of the fixed capital, for its eventual renewal; and secondly those amounts of money which represent realized surplus value but are still too small for investment. From the point of view of the aggregate capital, both these sources of free money capital are negligible. For if we assume that even a portion of the social surplus value is realized in monetary form for purposes of future investment, then at once the question arises: who has bought the material items of this surplus value, and who has provided the money? If the answer is: other capitalists, of course—then, seeing that the capitalist class is represented in the diagram by the two departments, this portion of the surplus value must also be regarded as invested *de facto*, as employed in the productive process. And so we are back at immediate and complete investment of the surplus value.

Or does the freezing of one part of the surplus value in monetary form in the hands of certain capitalists mean that other capitalists will be left with a corresponding part of that surplus product in its material form? Does the hoarding of realized surplus value by some imply that others are no longer able to realize their surplus value, since the capitalists are the only buyers of surplus value? This would mean, however, that the smooth course of reproduction and similarly of accumulation as described in the diagram would be interrupted. The result would be a crisis, due not to overproduction but to a mere intention to accumulate, the kind of crisis envisaged by Sismondi.[14]

In one passage of his *Theories*,[15] Marx explains in so many words that he "is not at all concerned in this connection with an accumulation of capital greater than can be used in the productive process and might lie idle in the banks in monetary form, with the consequence of lending abroad." Marx refers these phenomena to the section on competition. Yet it is important to establish that his diagram veritably precludes the formation of such additional capital. Competition, however wide we may make the concept, obviously cannot create values, nor can it create capitals which are not themselves the result of the reproductive process.

The diagram thus precludes the expansion of production by leaps and bounds. It only allows of a gradual expansion which keeps strictly in step with the formation of the surplus value and is based upon the identity between realization and capitalization of the surplus value.

For the same reason, the diagram presumes an accumulation which affects both departments equally and therefore all branches of capitalist production. It precludes expansion of the demand by leaps and bounds just as much as it prevents a one-sided or precocious development of individual branches of capitalist production.

Thus the diagram assumes a movement of the aggregate capital which flies in the face of the actual course of capitalist development. At first sight, two facts are typical for the history of the capitalist mode of production: on the one hand the periodical expansion of the whole field of production by leaps and bounds, and on the other an extremely unequal development of the different branches of production. The history of the English cotton industry from the first quarter of the eighteenth to the seventies of the nineteenth century, the most characteristic chapter in the history of the capitalist mode of production, appears quite inexplicable from the point of view of Marx's diagram.

Finally, the diagram contradicts the conception of the capitalist total process and its course as laid down by Marx in *Capital*, Volume III. This conception is based on the inherent contradiction between the unlimited expansive capacity of the productive forces and the limited expansive capacity of social consumption under conditions of capitalist distribution. Let us see how Marx describes this contradiction in detail in chapter 15 on "Unravelling the Internal Contradictions of the Law" (of the declining profit rate):

> The creation of surplus-value, assuming the necessary means of production, or sufficient accumulation of capital, to be existing, finds no other limit but the laboring population, when the rate of surplus-value, that is, the intensity of exploitation, is given; and no other limit but the intensity of exploitation, when the laboring population is given. And the capitalist process of production consists essentially of the production of surplus-value, materialized in the surplus-product, which is that aliquot portion of the produced commodities, in which unpaid labor is materialized. It must never be forgotten, that the production of this surplus-value—and the reconversion of a portion of it into capital, or accumulation, forms an indispensable part of this production of surplus-value—is the immediate purpose and the compelling motive of capitalist production. It will not do to represent capitalist production as something which it is not, that is to say, as a production having for its immediate purpose the consumption of goods, or the production of means of enjoyment for the capitalists. (And, of course, even less for the worker.—R.L.) This would be overlooking the

specific character of capitalist production, which reveals itself in its innermost essence. The creation of this surplus-value is the object of the direct process of production, and this process has no other limits than those mentioned above. As soon as the available quantity of surplus-value has been materialized in commodities, surplus-value has been produced. But this production of surplus-value is but the first act of the capitalist process of production, it merely terminates the act of direct production. Capital has absorbed so much unpaid labor. With the development of the process, which expresses itself through a falling tendency of the rate of profit, the mass of surplus-value thus produced is swelled to immense dimensions. Now comes the second act of the process. The entire mass of commodities, the total product which contains a portion which is to reproduce the constant and variable capital as well as a portion representing surplus-value must be sold. If this is not done, or only partly accomplished, or only at prices which are below the prices of production, the laborer has been none the less exploited, but his exploitation does not realize as much for the capitalist. It may yield no surplus-value at all for him, or only realize a portion of the produced surplus-value, or it may even mean a partial or complete loss of his capital. The conditions of direct exploitation and those of the realization of surplus-value are not identical. They are separated logically as well as by time and space. The first are only limited by the productive power of society, the last by the proportional relations of the various lines of production and by the consuming power of society. This last-named power is not determined either by the absolute productive power or by the absolute consuming power, but by the consuming power based on antagonistic conditions of distribution, which reduces the consumption of the great mass of the population to a variable minimum within more or less narrow limits. The consuming power is furthermore restricted by the tendency to accumulate, the greed for an expansion of capital and a production of surplus-value on an enlarged scale. This is a law of capitalist production imposed by incessant revolutions in the methods of production themselves, the resulting depreciation of existing capital, the general competitive struggle and the necessity of improving the product and expanding the scale of production, for the sake of self-preservation and on penalty of failure. The market must, therefore, be continually extended, so that its interrelations and the conditions regulating them assume more and more the form of a natural law independent of the producers and become ever more uncontrollable. This eternal contradiction seeks to balance itself by an expansion of the outlying fields of production. But to the extent that the productive power develops, it finds itself at variance with the narrow basis on which the conditions of consumption rest. On this self-contradictory basis it is no contradiction at all that there should be an excess of capital simultaneously with an excess of population. For while a combination of these two would indeed increase the mass of the produced surplus-value, it would at the same time intensify the contradiction between the conditions under which this surplus-value is produced and those under which it is realized.[16]

If we compare this description with the diagram of enlarged reproduction, the two are by no means in conformity. According to the diagram, there is no inherent contradiction between the production of the surplus value and its realization, rather, the two are identical. The surplus value here from the very beginning comes into being in a natural form exclusively designed for the requirements of accumulation. In fact it leaves the place of production in the very form of additional capital, that is to say it is capable of realization in the capitalist process of accumulation. The capitalists, as a class, see to it in advance that the surplus value they appropriate is produced entirely in that material form which will permit and ensure its employment for purposes of further accumulation. Realization and accumulation of the surplus value here are both aspects of the same process, they are logically identical. Therefore according to the presentation of the reproductive process in the diagram, society's capacity to consume does not put a limit to production. Here production automatically expands year by year, although the capacity of society for consumption has not gone beyond its "antagonistic conditions of distribution." This automatic continuation of expansion, of accumulation, truly is the "law of capitalist production . . . on penalty of failure." Yet according to the analysis in Volume III, "the market must, therefore, be continually extended," "the market" obviously transcending the consumption of capitalists and workers. And if Tugan-Baranovski interprets the following passage "this eternal contradiction seeks to balance itself by an expansion of the outlying fields of production" as if Marx had meant production itself by "outlying fields of production," he violates not only the spirit of the language but also Marx's clear train of thought. The "outlying fields of production" are clearly and unequivocally not production itself but consumption which "must be continually extended." The following passage in *Theories of Surplus Value*, amongst others, sufficiently shows that Marx had this in mind and nothing else: "Ricardo[17] therefore consistently denies the necessity for an expansion of the market to accompany the expansion of production and the growth of capital. The entire capital existing within a country can also be profitably used in that country. He therefore argues against Adam Smith[18] who had set up his (Ricardo's) opinion on the one hand but also contradicted it with his usual sure instinct."[19]

In yet another passage, Marx clearly shows that Tugan-Baranovski's notion of production for production's sake is wholly alien to him:

> Besides, we have seen in Volume II part III that a continuous circulation takes place between constant capital and constant capital (even without considering any accelerated accumulation), which is in so far independent of individual consumption, as it never enters into such consumption, but which is nevertheless definitely limited by it, because the production of constant capital never takes place for its own sake, but solely because more of this capital is needed in those spheres of production whose products pass into individual consumption.[20]

Admittedly, in the diagram in Volume II, Tugan-Baranovski's sole support, market and production coincide—they are one and the same. Expansion of the market here means extended production, since production is said to be its own exclusive market—the consumption of the workers being an element of production, i.e. the reproduction of variable capital. Therefore the limit for both the expansion of production and the extension of the market is one and the same: it is given by the volume of the social capital, or the stage of accumulation already attained. The greater the quantity of surplus value that has been extracted in the natural form of capital, the more can be accumulated; and the greater the volume of accumulation, the more surplus value can be invested in its material form of capital, i.e. the more can be realized. Thus the diagram does not admit the contradiction outlined in the analysis of Volume III. In the process described by the diagram there is no need for a continual extension of the market beyond the consumption of capitalists and workers, nor is the limited social capacity for consumption an obstacle to the smooth course of production and its unlimited capacity for expansion. The diagram does indeed permit of crises but only because of a lack of proportion within production, because of a defective social control over the productive process. It precludes, however, the deep and fundamental antagonism between the capacity to consume and the capacity to produce in a capitalist society, a conflict resulting from the very accumulation of capital which periodically bursts out in crises and spurs capital on to a continual extension of the market.

## THE REPRODUCTION OF CAPITAL AND ITS SOCIAL SETTING

Marx's diagram of enlarged reproduction cannot explain the actual and historical process of accumulation. And why? Because of the very premises of the diagram. The diagram sets out to describe the accumulative process on the assumption that the capitalists and workers are the sole agents of capitalist consumption. We have seen that Marx consistently and deliberately assumes the universal and exclusive domination of the capitalist mode of production as a theoretical premise of his analysis in all three volumes of *Capital*. Under these conditions, there can admittedly be no other classes of society than capitalists and workers; as the diagram has it, all "third persons" of capitalist society—civil servants, the liberal professions, the clergy, etc.—must, as consumers, be counted in with these two classes, and preferably with the capitalist class. This axiom, however, is a theoretical contrivance—real life has never known a self-sufficient capitalist society under the exclusive domination of the capitalist mode of production. This theoretical device is perfectly admissible so long as it merely helps to demonstrate the problem in its integrity and does not interfere with its very conditions. A case in point is the analysis of simple reproduction of the aggregate social capital, where the problem itself rests upon a fiction: in a society producing by capitalist methods, i.e. a society which creates surplus value, the whole of the latter is taken to be consumed by the capitalists who appropriate it. The object is to present the forms of social production and reproduction under these given conditions. Here the very formulation of the problem implies that production knows no other consumers than capitalists and workers and thus strictly conforms to Marx's premise: universal and exclusive domination of the capitalist mode of production. The implications of both fictions are the same. Similarly, it is quite legitimate to postulate absolute dominance of capital in an analysis of the accumulation of individual capitals, such as is given in *Capital*, Volume I. The reproduction of individual capitals is an element in total social reproduction but one which follows an independent course, contrary to the movements of the other elements. In consequence it will not do simply to take together the individual movements of the respective capitals in order to arrive at the total movement of social capital, since the latter is essentially different. The natural conditions of reproducing individual capitals therefore neither conform with one another, nor do they conform to the relations of the total capital. Under normal conditions of circulation, every individual capital engages in the process of circulation and of accumulation entirely on its own account, depending upon others only insofar, of course, as it is compelled to find a market for its product and must find available the means of production it requires for its specific activities. Whether the strata who afford this market and provide the necessary means of production are themselves capitalist producers or not is completely immaterial for the individual capital, although, in theory, the most favorable premise for analyzing the accumulation of individual capital is the assumption that capitalist production has attained universal and exclusive domination and is the sole setting of this process.[21]

Now, however, the question arises whether the assumptions which were decisive in the case of individual capital, are also legitimate for the consideration of aggregate capital.

"We must now put the problem in this form: *given universal accumulation*, that is to say provided that in all branches of production there is greater or less accumulation of capital—which in fact is a condition of capitalist production, and which is just as natural to the capitalist *qua* capitalist as it is natural to the miser to amass money (but which is also necessary for the perpetuation of capitalist production)—what are the conditions of this universal accumulation, to what elements can it be reduced?"

And the answer: "*The conditions for the accumulation of capital are precisely those which rule its original production and reproduction in general*: these conditions being that one part of the money buys labor and the other commodities (raw materials, machinery, etc.) . . . Accumulation of new capital can only proceed therefore under the same conditions under which already existing capital is reproduced."[22]

In real life the actual conditions for the accumulation of the aggregate capital are quite different from those prevailing for individual capitals and for simple reproduction. The problem amounts to this: If an increasing part of the surplus value is not consumed by the capitalists but employed in the expansion of production, what, then, are the forms of social reproduction? What is left of the social product after deductions for the replacement of the constant capital cannot, *ex hypothesi*, be absorbed by the consumption of the workers and capitalists—this being the main aspect of the problem—nor can the workers and capitalists themselves realize the aggregate product. They can always only realize the variable capital, that part of the constant capital which will be used up, and the part of the surplus value which will be consumed, but in this way they merely ensure that production can be renewed on its previous scale. The workers and capitalists themselves cannot possibly realize that part of the surplus value which is to be capitalized. Therefore, the realization of the surplus value for the purposes of accumulation is an impossible task for a society which consists solely of workers and capitalists. Strangely enough, all theorists who analyzed the problem of accumulation, from Ricardo and Sismondi to Marx, started with the very assumption which makes their problem insoluble. A sure instinct that realization of the surplus

value requires "third persons," that is to say consumers other than the immediate agents of capitalist production (i.e. workers and capitalists) led to all
kinds of subterfuges: "unproductive consumption" as presented by Malthus
in the person of the feudal landowner, by Vorontsov in militarism, by Struve
in the "liberal professions" and other hangers-on of the capitalist class;[23] or
else foreign trade is brought into play which proved a useful safety valve to all
those who regarded accumulation with skepticism, from Sismondi to Nicolayon.[24] Because of these insoluble difficulties, others like v. Kirchmann and
Rodbertus[25] tried to do without accumulation altogether, or, like Sismondi
and his Russian "populist" followers, stressed the need for at least putting
the dampers on accumulation as much as possible.

The salient feature of the problem of accumulation, and the vulnerable
point of earlier attempts to solve it, has only been shown up by Marx's more
profound analysis, his precise diagrammatic demonstration of the total
reproductive process, and especially his inspired exposition of the problem
of simple reproduction. Yet he could not supply immediately a finished solution either, partly because he broke off his analysis almost as soon as he had
begun it, and partly because he was then preoccupied, as we have shown,
with denouncing the analysis of Adam Smith and thus rather lost sight of the
main problem.[26] In fact, he made the solution even more difficult by assuming the capitalist mode of production to prevail universally. Nevertheless, a
solution of the problem of accumulation, in harmony both with other parts of
Marx's doctrine and with the historical experience and daily practice of capitalism, is implied in Marx's complete analysis of simple reproduction and his
characterization of the capitalist process as a whole which shows up its
immanent contradictions and their development (in *Capital*, vol. III). In the
light of this, the deficiencies of the diagram can be corrected. All the relations
being, as it were, incomplete, a closer study of the diagram of enlarged reproduction will reveal that it points to some sort of organization more advanced
than purely capitalist production and accumulation.

Up to now we have only considered one aspect of enlarged reproduction,
the problem of realizing the surplus value, whose difficulties hitherto had
claimed the skeptics' whole attention. Realization of the surplus value is
doubtless a vital question of capitalist accumulation. It requires as its prime
condition—ignoring, for simplicity's sake, the capitalists' fund of consumption altogether—that there should be strata of buyers outside capitalist society. Buyers, it should be noted, not consumers, since the material form of the
surplus value is quite irrelevant to its realization. The decisive fact is that the

surplus value cannot be realized by sale either to workers or to capitalists, but only if it is sold to such social organizations or strata whose own mode of production is not capitalistic. Here we can conceive of two different cases:

1) Capitalist production supplies consumer goods over and above its own requirements, the demand of its workers and capitalists, which are bought by non-capitalist strata and countries. The English cotton industry, for instance, during the first two-thirds of the nineteenth century, and to some extent even now, has been supplying cotton textiles to the peasants and petty-bourgeois townspeople of the European continent, and to the peasants of India, America, Africa and so on. The enormous expansion of the English cotton industry was thus founded on consumption by non-capitalist strata and countries.[27] In England herself, this flourishing cotton industry called forth large-scale development in the production of industrial machinery (bobbins and weaving-looms), and further in the metal and coal industries and so on. In this instance, Department II realized its products to an increasing extent by sale to non-capitalist social strata, and by its own accumulation it created on its part an increasing demand for the home produce of Department I, thus helping the latter to realize its surplus value and to increase its own accumulation.

2) Conversely, capitalist production supplies means of production in excess of its own demand and finds buyers in non-capitalist countries. English industry, for instance, in the first half of the nineteenth century supplied materials for the construction of railroads in the American and Australian states. (The building of railways cannot in itself be taken as evidence for the domination of capitalist production in a country. As a matter of fact, the railways in this case provided only one of the first conditions for the inauguration of capitalist production.) Another example would be the German chemical industry which supplies means of production such as dyes in great quantities to Asiatic, African and other countries whose own production is not capitalistic.[28] Here Department I realizes its products in extra-capitalist circles. The resulting progressive expansion of Department I gives rise to a corresponding expansion of Department II in the same (capitalistically producing) country in order to supply the means of subsistence for the growing army of workers in Department I.

Each of these cases differs from Marx's diagram. In one case, the product of Department II exceeds the needs of both departments, measured by the variable capital and the consumed part of the surplus value. In the second case, the product of Department I exceeds the volume of constant capital in both departments, enlarged though it is for the purpose of expanding production. In both cases, the surplus value does not come into being in that natural form which would make its capitalization in either department possible and necessary. These two prototypes continually overlap in real life, supplement each other and merge.

In this contest, one point seems still obscure. The surplus of consumer goods, say cotton fabrics, which is sold to non-capitalist countries, does not exclusively represent surplus value, but, as a capitalist commodity, it embodies also constant and variable capital. It seems quite arbitrary to assume that just those commodities which are sold outside the capitalist strata of society should represent nothing but surplus value. On the other hand, Department I clearly can in this case not only realize its surplus value but also accumulate, and that without requiring another market for its product than the two departments of capitalist production. Yet both these objections are only apparent. All we need remember is that each component of the aggregate product represents a proportion of the total value, that under conditions of capitalist production not only the aggregate product but every single commodity contains surplus value; which consideration does not prevent the individual capitalist, however, from computing that the sale of his specific commodities must first reimburse him for his outlay on constant capital and secondly replace his variable capital (or, rather loosely, but in accordance with actual practice: it must first replace his fixed, and then his circulating capital); what then remains will go down as profit. Similarly, we can divide the aggregate social product into three proportionate parts which, in terms of value, correspond to 1) the constant capital that has been used up in society, 2) the variable capital, and 3) the extracted surplus value. In the case of simple reproduction these proportions are also reflected in the material shape of the aggregate product: the constant capital materializes as means of production, the variable capital as means of subsistence for the workers, and the surplus value as means of subsistence for the capitalist. Yet as we know, the concept of simple reproduction with consumption of the entire surplus value by the capitalists is a mere fiction. As for enlarged reproduction or accumulation, in Marx's diagram the composition of the social product in terms of value is also strictly in proportion to its material form: the surplus value, or rather that part of it which is earmarked for capitalization, has from the very beginning the form of material means of production and means of subsistence for the workers in a ratio appropriate to the expansion of production on a given technical basis. As we have seen, this conception, which is based upon the self-sufficiency and isolation of capitalist production, falls down as soon as we consider the realization of the surplus value. If we assume, however, that the surplus value is realized outside the sphere of capitalist production, then its material form is independent of the requirements of capitalist production itself. Its material form conforms to the requirements of those non-capitalist circles who help to realize it, that is to say, capitalist surplus value can take the form of consumer goods, e.g. cotton fabrics, or of means of production, e.g. materials for railway construction, as the case may be. If one department realizes its surplus value by exporting its products, and with the ensuing expansion of production helps the other department to realize its surplus value on the home market, then the fact still remains that the social surplus value must yet be taken as realized outside the two departments, either mediately or immediately. Similar considerations enable the individual capitalist to realize his surplus value, even if the whole of his commodities can only replace either the variable or the constant capital of another capitalist.

Nor is the realization of the surplus value the only vital aspect of reproduction. Given that Department I has disposed of its surplus value outside, thereby starting the process of accumulation, and further, that it can expect a new increase in the demand in non-capitalist circles, these two conditions add up to only half of what is required for accumulation. There is many a slip 'twixt the cup and the lip'. The second requirement of accumulation is access to material elements necessary for expanding reproduction. Seeing that we have just turned the surplus product of Department I into money by getting rid of the surplus means of production to non-capitalist circles, from where are these material elements then to come? The transaction which is the portal for realizing the surplus value is also, as it were, a backdoor out of which flies all possibility of converting this realized surplus value into productive capital—one leads to the nether regions and the other to the deep sea. Let us take a closer look.

Here we use $c$ in both Departments I and II as if it were the entire constant capital in production. Yet this we know is wrong. Only for the sake of simplifying the diagram have we disregarded that the $c$ which figures in Departments I and II of the diagram is only part of the aggregate constant capital of society, that is to say that part which, circulating during one year, is used up and embodied in the products of one period of production. Yet it would be perfectly absurd if capitalist production—or any other—would use up its entire constant capital and create it anew in every period of production. On the contrary, we assume that the whole mass of means of production, for the periodical total renewal of which the diagram provides in annual instalments—renewal of the used-up part—lies at the back of production as presented in the diagram.

With progressing labor productivity and an expanding volume of production, this mass increases not only absolutely but also relatively to the part which is consumed in production in every case, together with a corresponding increase in the efficiency of the constant capital. It is the more intensive exploitation of this part of the constant capital, irrespective of its increase in value, which is of paramount importance for the expansion of production.

> In the extractive industries, mines, etc., the raw materials form no part of the capital advanced. The subject of labor is in this case not a product of previous labor, but is furnished by Nature gratis, as in the case of metals, minerals, coal, stone, etc. In these cases the constant capital consists almost exclusively of instruments of labor, which can very well absorb an increased quantity of labor (day and night shifts of laborers, e.g.). All other things being equal, the mass and value of the product will rise in direct proportion to the labor expended. As on the first day of production, the original produce-formers, now turned into the creators of the material elements of capital—man and Nature—still work together. Thanks to the elasticity of labor-power, the domain of accumulation has extended without any previous enlargement of constant capital.—In agriculture the land under cultivation cannot be increased without the advance of more seed and manure. But this advance once made, the purely mechanical working of the soil itself produces a marvellous effect on the amount of the product. A greater quantity of labor, done by the same number of laborers as before, thus increases the fertility, without requiring any new advance in the instruments of labor. It is once again the direct action of man on Nature which becomes an immediate source of greater accumulation, without the intervention of any new capital. Finally, in what is called manufacturing industry, every additional expenditure of labor presupposes a corresponding additional expenditure of raw materials, but not necessarily of instruments of labor. And as extractive industry and agriculture supply manufacturing industry with its raw materials and those of its instruments of labor, the additional product the former have created without additional advance of capital, tells also in favor of the latter.—General result: by incorporating with itself the two primary creators of wealth, labor-power and the land, capital acquires a power of expansion that permits it to augment the elements of its accumulation beyond the limits apparently fixed by its own magnitude, or by the value and the mass of the means of production, already produced, in which it has its being.[29]

In addition, there is no obvious reason why means of production and consumer goods should be produced by capitalist methods alone. This assumption, for all Marx used it as the cornerstone of his thesis, is in conformity neither with the daily practice, and the history, of capital, nor with the specific character of this mode of production. In the first half of the nineteenth century, a great part of the surplus value in England was produced in form of cotton fabrics. Yet the material elements for the capitalization of this surplus value, although they certainly represented a surplus product, still were by no means all capitalist surplus value, to mention only raw cotton from the slave states of the American Union, or grain (a means of subsistence for the English workers) from the fields of serf-owning Russia. How much capitalist accumulation depends upon means of production which are not produced by capitalist methods is shown for example by the cotton crisis in England during the American War of Secession, when the cultivation of the plantations came to a standstill, or by the crisis of European linen-weaving during the war in the East, when flax could not be imported from serf-owning Russia. We need only recall that imports of corn raised by peasants—i.e. not produced by capitalist methods—played a vital part in the feeding of industrial labor, as an element, that is to say, of variable capital, for a further illustration of the close ties between non-capitalist strata and the material elements necessary to the accumulation of capital.

Moreover, capitalist production, by its very nature, cannot be restricted to such means of production as are produced by capitalist methods. Cheap elements of constant capital are essential to the individual capitalist who strives to increase his rate of profit. In addition, the very condition of continuous improvements in labor productivity as the most important method of increasing the rate of surplus value, is unrestricted utilization of all substances and facilities afforded by nature and soil. To tolerate any restriction in this respect would be contrary to the very essence of capital, its whole mode of existence. After many centuries of development, the capitalist mode of production still constitutes only a fragment of total world production. Even in the small Continent of Europe, where it now chiefly prevails, it has not yet succeeded in dominating entire branches of production, such as peasant agriculture and the independent handicrafts; the same holds true, further, for large parts of North America and for a number of regions in the other continents. In general, capitalist production has hitherto been confined mainly to the countries in the temperate zone, whilst it made comparatively little progress in the East, for instance, and the South. Thus, if it were dependent exclusively on elements of production obtainable within such narrow limits, its present level and indeed its development in general would have been impossible. From the very beginning, the forms and laws of capitalist production aim to comprise the entire

globe as a store of productive forces. Capital, impelled to appropriate productive forces for purposes of exploitation, ransacks the whole world, it procures
its means of production from all corners of the earth, seizing them, if necessary
by force, from all levels of civilization and from all forms of society. The problem of the material elements of capitalist accumulation, far from being solved
by the material form of the surplus value that has been produced, takes on
quite a different aspect. It becomes necessary for capital progressively to dispose ever more fully of the whole globe, to acquire an unlimited choice of
means of production, with regard to both quality and quantity, so as to find
productive employment for the surplus value it has realized.

The process of accumulation, elastic and spasmodic as it is, requires
inevitably free access to ever new areas of raw materials in case of need, both
when imports from old sources fail or when social demand suddenly increases. When the War of Secession interfered with the import of American cotton, causing the notorious "cotton famine" in the Lancashire district, new
and immense cotton plantations sprang up in Egypt almost at once, as if by
magic. Here it was Oriental despotism, combined with an ancient system of
bondage, which had created a sphere of activity for European capital. Only
capital with its technical resources can effect such a miraculous change in so
short a time—but only on the pre-capitalist soil of more primitive social conditions can it develop the ascendancy necessary to achieve such miracles.
Another example of the same kind is the enormous increase in the world
consumption of rubber which at present (1912) necessitates a supply of latex
to the value of £50,000,000 *per annum*. The economic basis for the production of raw materials is a primitive system of exploitation practiced by European capital in the African colonies and in America, where the institutions of
slavery and bondage are combined in various forms.[30]

Between the production of surplus value, then, and the subsequent period
of accumulation, two separate transactions take place—that of realizing the surplus value, i.e. of converting it into pure value, and that of transforming this
pure value into productive capital. They are both dealings between capitalist
production and the surrounding non-capitalist world. From the aspect both of
realising the surplus value and of procuring the material elements of constant
capital, international trade is a prime necessity for the historical existence of
capitalism—an international trade which under actual conditions is essentially
an exchange between capitalistic and non-capitalistic modes of production.

Hitherto we have considered accumulation solely with regard to surplus
value and constant capital. The third element of accumulation is variable capi-

tal which increases with progressive accumulation. In Marx's diagram, the social product contains ever more means of subsistence for the workers as the material form proper to this variable capital. The variable capital, however, is not really the means of subsistence for the workers but is in fact living labor for whose reproduction these means of subsistence are necessary. One of the fundamental conditions of accumulation is therefore a supply of living labor which can be mobilized by capital to meet its demands. This supply can be increased under favorable conditions—but only up to a certain point—by longer hours and more intensive work. Both these methods of increasing the supply, however, do not enlarge the variable capital, or do so only to a small extent (e.g. payment for overtime). Moreover, they are confined to definite and rather narrow limits which they cannot exceed owing to both natural and social causes. The increasing growth of variable capital which accompanies accumulation must therefore become manifest in ever greater numbers of employed labor. Where can this additional labor be found?

In his analysis of the accumulation of individual capital, Marx gives the following answer:

> Now in order to allow of these elements actually functioning as capital, the capitalist class requires additional labor. If the exploitation of the laborers already employed does not increase, either extensively or intensively, then additional labor-power must be found. For this the mechanism of capitalist production provides beforehand, by converting the working class into a class dependent on wages, a class whose ordinary wages suffice, not only for its maintenance, but for its increase. It is only necessary for capital to incorporate this additional labor-power, annually supplied by the working class in the shape of laborers of all ages, with the surplus means of production comprised in the annual produce, and the conversion of surplus-value into capital is complete.[31]

Thus the increase in the variable capital is directly and exclusively attributed to the natural physical increase of a working class already dominated by capital. This is in strict conformity with the diagram of enlarged reproduction which recognizes only the social classes of capitalists and workers, and regards the capitalist mode of production as exclusive and absolute. On these assumptions, the natural increase of the working class is the only source of extending the labor supply commanded by capital. This view, however, is contrary to the laws governing the process of accumulation. The natural propagation of the workers and the requirements of accumulating capital are not correlative in respect of time or quantity. Marx himself has most brilliantly shown that natural propagation cannot keep up with the sudden expansive needs of capital. If natural propagation were the only foundation for the development of capital, accumulation, in its periodical swings from over-strain to exhaustion, could not continue, nor could the productive sphere expand by leaps and bounds, and accumulation itself would become impos-sible. The latter requires an unlimited freedom of movement in respect of the growth of variable capital equal to that which it enjoys with regard to the ele-ments of constant capital—that is to say it must needs dispose over the sup-ply of labor power without restriction. Marx considers that this can be achieved by an "industrial reserve army of workers." His diagram of simple reproduction admittedly does not recognize such an army, nor could it have room for it, since the natural propagation of the capitalist wage proletariat cannot provide an industrial reserve army. Labor for this army is recruited from social reservoirs outside the dominion of capital—it is drawn into the wage proletariat only if need arises. Only the existence of non-capitalist groups and countries can guarantee such a supply of additional labor power for capitalist production. Yet in his analysis of the industrial reserve army[32] Marx only allows for a) the displacement of older workers by machinery, b) an influx of rural workers into the towns in consequence of the ascendancy of capitalist production in agriculture, c) occasional labor that has dropped out of industry, and d) finally the lowest residue of relative over-population, the paupers. All these categories are cast off by the capitalist system of produc-tion in some form or other, they constitute a wage proletariat that is worn out and made redundant one way or another. Marx, obviously influenced by English conditions involving a high level of capitalist development, held that the rural workers who continually migrate to the towns belong to the wage proletariat, since they were formerly dominated by agricultural capital and now become subject to industrial capital. He ignores, however, the problem which is of paramount importance for conditions on the continent of Europe, namely the sources from which this urban and rural proletariat is recruited: the continual process by which the rural and urban middle strata become proletarian with the decay of peasant economy and of small artisan enterprises, the very process, that is to say, of incessant transition from non-capitalist to capitalist conditions of a labor power that is cast off by pre-capi-talist, not capitalist, modes of production in their progressive break-down and disintegration. Besides the decay of European peasants and artisans we must here also mention the disintegration of the most varied primitive forms of production and of social organization in non-European countries.

Since capitalist production can develop fully only with complete access to all territories and climes, it can no more confine itself to the natural resources and productive forces of the temperate zone than it can manage with white labor alone. Capital needs other races to exploit territories where the white man cannot work. It must be able to mobilize world labor power without restriction in order to utilize all productive forces of the globe—up to the limits imposed by a system of producing surplus value. This labor power, however, is in most cases rigidly bound by the traditional pre-capitalist organization of production. It must first be "set free" in order to be enrolled in the active army of capital. The emancipation of labor power from primitive social conditions and its absorption by the capitalist wage system is one of the indispensable historical bases of capitalism. For the first genuinely capitalist branch of production, the English cotton industry, not only the cotton of the Southern states of the American Union was essential, but also the millions of African Negroes who were shipped to America to provide the labor power for the plantations, and who later, as a free proletariat, were incorporated in the class of wage laborers in a capitalist system.[33] Obtaining the necessary labor power from non-capitalist societies, the so-called "labor-problem," is ever more important for capital in the colonies. All possible methods of "gentle compulsion" are applied to solving this problem, to transfer labor from former social systems to the command of capital. This endeavor leads to the most peculiar combinations between the modern wage system and primitive authority in the colonial countries.[34] This is a concrete example of the fact that capitalist production cannot manage without labor power from other social organizations.

Admittedly, Marx dealt in detail with the process of appropriating non-capitalist means of production as well as with the transformation of the peasants into a capitalist proletariat. Chapter XXIV of *Capital*, vol. I, is devoted to describing the origin of the English proletariat, of the capitalistic agricultural tenant class and of industrial capital, with particular emphasis on the looting of colonial countries by European capital. Yet we must bear in mind that all this is treated solely with a view to so-called primitive accumulation. For Marx, these processes are incidental, illustrating merely the genesis of capital, its first appearance in the world; they are, as it were, travails by which the capitalist mode of production emerges from a feudal society. As soon as he comes to analyze the capitalist process of production and circulation, he reaffirms the universal and exclusive domination of capitalist production.

Yet, as we have seen, capitalism in its full maturity also depends in all respects on non-capitalist strata and social organizations existing side by side with it. It is not merely a question of a market for the additional product, as Sismondi and the later critics and doubters of capitalist accumulation would have it. The interrelations of accumulating capital and non-capitalist forms of production extend over values as well as over material conditions, for constant capital, variable capital and surplus value alike. The non-capitalist mode of production is the given historical setting for this process. Since the accumulation of capital becomes impossible in all points without non-capitalist surroundings, we cannot gain a true picture of it by assuming the exclusive and absolute domination of the capitalist mode of production. Sismondi and his school, when they attributed their difficulties entirely to the problem of realizing the surplus value, indeed revealed a proper sense for the conditions vital to accumulation. Yet the conditions for augmenting the material elements of constant and variable capital are quite a different matter from those which govern the realization of surplus value. Capital needs the means of production and the labor power of the whole globe for untrammelled accumulation; it cannot manage without the natural resources and the labor power of all territories. Seeing that the overwhelming majority of resources and labor power is in fact still in the orbit of pre-capitalist production—this being the historical *milieu* of accumulation—capital must go all out to obtain ascendancy over these territories and social organizations. There is no *a priori* reason why rubber plantations, say, run on capitalist lines, such as have been laid out in India, might not serve the ends of capitalist production just as well. Yet if the countries of those branches of production are predominantly non-capitalist, capital will endeavor to establish domination over these countries and societies. And in fact, primitive conditions allow of a greater drive and of far more ruthless measures than could be tolerated under purely capitalist social conditions.

It is quite different with the realization of the surplus value. Here outside consumers *qua* other-than-capitalist are really essential. Thus the immediate and vital conditions for capital and its accumulation is the existence of non-capitalist buyers of the surplus value, which is decisive to this extent for the problem of capitalist accumulation.

Whatever the theoretical aspects, the accumulation of capital, as an historical process, depends in every respect upon non-capitalist social strata and forms of social organization.

The solution to this problem which for almost a century has been the bone of contention in economic theory thus lies between the two extremes of the petty-bourgeois skepticism preached by Sismondi, v. Kirchmann,

Vorontsov and Nicolayon, who flatly denied accumulation, and the crude optimism advocated by Ricardo, Say[35] and Tugan-Baranovski who believed in capital's unlimited capacity for parthenogenesis, with the logical corollary of capitalism-in-perpetuity: The solution envisaged by Marx lies in the dialectical conflict that capitalism needs non-capitalist social organizations as the setting for its development, that it proceeds by assimilating the very conditions which alone can ensure its own existence.

At this point we should revise the conceptions of internal and external markets which were so important in the controversy about accumulation. They are both vital to capitalist development and yet fundamentally different, though they must be conceived in terms of social economy rather than of political geography. In this light, the internal market is the capitalist market, production itself buying its own products and supplying its own elements of production. The external market is the non-capitalist social environment which absorbs the products of capitalism and supplies producer goods and labor power for capitalist production. Thus, from the point of view of economics, Germany and England traffic in commodities chiefly on an internal, capitalist market, whilst the give and take between German industry and German peasants is transacted on an external market as far as German capital is concerned. These concepts are strict and precise, as can be seen from the diagram of reproduction. Internal capitalist trade can at best realize only certain quantities of value contained in the social product: the constant capital that has been used up, the variable capital, and the consumed part of the surplus value. That part of the surplus value, however, which is earmarked for capitalisation, must be realized elsewhere. If capitalization of surplus value is the real motive force and aim of production, it must yet proceed within the limits given by the renewal of constant and variable capital (and also of the consumed part of the surplus value). Further, with the international development of capitalism the capitalization of surplus value becomes ever more urgent and precarious, and the substratum of constant and variable capital becomes an ever-growing mass—both absolutely and in relation to the surplus value. Hence the contradictory phenomena that the old capitalist countries provide ever larger markets for, and become increasingly dependent upon, one another, yet on the other hand compete ever more ruthlessly for trade relations with non-capitalist countries.[36] The conditions for the capitalization of surplus value clash increasingly with the conditions for the renewal of the aggregate capital—a conflict which, incidentally, is merely a counterpart of the contradictions implied in the law of a declining profit rate.

## THE STRUGGLE AGAINST NATURAL ECONOMY

Capitalism arises and develops historically amidst a non-capitalist society. In Western Europe it is found at first in a feudal environment from which it in fact sprang—the system of bondage in rural areas and the guild system in the towns—and later, after having swallowed up the feudal system, it exists mainly in an environment of peasants and artisans, that is to say in a system of simple commodity production both in agriculture and trade. European capitalism is further surrounded by vast territories of non-European civilization ranging over all levels of development, from the primitive communist hordes of nomad herdsmen, hunters and gatherers to commodity production by peasants and artisans. This is the setting for the accumulation of capital.

We must distinguish three phases: the struggle of capital against natural economy, the struggle against commodity economy, and the competitive struggle of capital on the international stage for the remaining conditions of accumulation.

The existence and development of capitalism requires an environment of non-capitalist forms of production, but not every one of these forms will serve its ends. Capitalism needs non-capitalist social strata as a market for its surplus value, as a source of supply for its means of production and as a reservoir of labor power for its wage system. For all these purposes, forms of production based upon a natural economy are of no use to capital. In all social organizations where natural economy prevails, where there are primitive peasant communities with common ownership of the land, a feudal system of bondage or anything of this nature, economic organization is essentially in response to the internal demand; and therefore there is no demand, or very little, for foreign goods, and also, as a rule, no surplus production, or at least no urgent need to dispose of surplus products. What is most important, however, is that, in any natural economy, production only goes on because both means of production and labor power are bound in one form or another. The communist peasant community no less than the feudal corvée farm and similar institutions maintain their economic organization by subjecting the labor power, and the most important means of production, the land, to the rule of law and custom. A natural economy thus confronts the requirements of capitalism at every turn with rigid barriers. Capitalism must therefore always and everywhere fight a battle of annihilation against every historical form of natural economy that it encounters, whether this is slave economy, feudalism, primitive communism, or patriarchal peasant economy. The principal methods in this struggle are political force (revolution, war), oppressive taxation by the state, and cheap goods; they are partly applied simultaneously, and partly they succeed and complement one another. In Europe, force assumed revolutionary forms in the fight against feudalism (this is the ultimate explanation of the bourgeois revolutions in the seventeenth, eighteenth and nineteenth centuries); in the non-European countries, where it fights more primitive social organizations, it assumes the forms of colonial policy. These methods, together with the systems of taxation applied in such cases, and commercial relations also, particularly with primitive communities, form an alliance in which political power and economic factors go hand in hand.

In detail, capital in its struggle against societies with a natural economy pursues the following ends:

1. To gain immediate possession of important sources of productive forces such as land, game in primeval forests, minerals, precious stones and ores, products of exotic flora such as rubber, etc.
2. To "liberate" labor power and to coerce it into service.
3. To introduce a commodity economy.
4. To separate trade and agriculture.

At the time of primitive accumulation, i.e. at the end of the Middle Ages, when the history of capitalism in Europe began, and right into the nineteenth century, dispossessing the peasants in England and on the Continent was the most striking weapon in the large-scale transformation of means of production and labor power into capital. Yet capital in power performs the same task even today, and on an even more important scale—by modern colonial policy. It is an illusion to hope that capitalism will ever be content with the means of production which it can acquire by way of commodity exchange. In this respect already, capital is faced with difficulties because vast tracts of the globe's surface are in the possession of social organizations that have no desire for commodity exchange or cannot, because of the entire social structure and the forms of ownership, offer for sale the productive forces in which capital is primarily interested. The most important of these productive forces is of course the land, its hidden mineral treasure, and its meadows, woods and water, and further the flocks of the primitive shepherd tribes. If capital were here to rely on the process of slow internal disintegration, it might take centuries. To wait patiently until the most important means of production could be alienated by trading in consequence of this process were tantamount to renouncing the productive forces of those territories altogether. Hence derives the vital necessity for capitalism in its relations with colonial countries to appropriate the most important means of production. Since the primitive associations of the natives are the strongest protection for their social organizations and for their material bases of existence, capital must begin by planning for the systematic destruction and annihilation of all the non-capitalist social units which obstruct its development. With that we have passed beyond the stage of primitive accumulation; this process is still going on. Each new colonial expansion is accompanied, as a matter of course, by a relentless battle of capital against the social and economic ties of the natives, who are also forcibly robbed of their means of production and labor power. Any hope to restrict the accumulation of capital exclusively to "peaceful competition," i.e. to regular commodity exchange such as takes place between capitalist producer-countries, rests on the pious belief that capital can accumulate without mediation of the productive forces and without the demand of more primitive organizations, and that it can rely upon the slow internal process of a disintegrating natural economy. Accumulation, with its spasmodic expansion, can no more wait for, and be content with, a natural internal disintegration of non-capitalist formations and their transition to commodity economy, than it can wait for, and be content with, the natural increase of the working population. Force is the only solution open to capital; the accumulation of capital, seen as an historical process, employs force as a permanent weapon, not only at its genesis, but further on down to the present day. From the point of view of the primitive societies involved, it is a matter of life or death; for them there can be no other attitude than opposition and fight to the finish—complete exhaustion and extinction. Hence permanent occupation of the colonies by the military, native risings and punitive expeditions are the order of the day for any colonial regime. The method of violence, then, is the immediate consequence of the clash between capitalism and the organizations of a natural economy which would restrict accumulation. Their means of production and their labor power no less than their demand for surplus products is necessary to capitalism. Yet the latter is fully determined to undermine their independence as social units, in order to gain possession of their means of production and labor power and to convert them into commodity buyers. This method is the most profitable and gets the quickest results, and so it is also the most expedient for capital. In fact, it is invariably accompanied by a growing militarism whose importance for accumulation will be demonstrated below in another connection. British policy in India and French policy in Algeria are the classical examples of the application of these methods by capitalism.

The ancient economic organizations of the Indians—the communist village community—had been preserved in their various forms throughout thousands of years, in spite of all the political disturbances during their long history. In the sixth century B.C. the Persians invaded the Indus basin and subjected part of the country. Two centuries later the Greeks entered and left behind them colonies, founded by Alexander on the pattern of a completely alien civilisation. Then the savage Scythians invaded the country, and for centuries India remained under Arab rule. Later, the Afghans swooped down from the Iran mountains, until they, too, were expelled by the ruthless onslaught of Tartar hordes. The Mongols' path was marked by terror and destruction, by the massacre of entire villages—the peaceful countryside with the tender shoots of rice made crimson with blood. And still the Indian village community survived. For none of the successive Mahometan conquerors had ultimately violated the internal social life of the peasant masses and its traditional structure. They only set up their own governors in the provinces to supervise military organization and to collect taxes from the population. All conquerors pursued the aim of dominating and exploiting the country, but none was interested in robbing the people of their productive forces and in destroying their social organization. In the Moghul Empire, the peasant had to pay his annual tribute in kind to the foreign ruler, but he could live undisturbed in his village and could cultivate his rice on his *sholgura* as his father had done before him. Then came the British—and the blight of capitalist civilization succeeded in disrupting the entire social organization of the people; it achieved in a short time what thousands of years, what the sword of the Nogaians,[37] had failed to accomplish. The ultimate purpose of British capital was to possess itself of the very basis of existence of the Indian community: the land.

This end was served above all by the fiction, always popular with European colonizers, that all the land of a colony belongs to the political ruler. In retrospect, the British endowed the Moghul and his governors with private ownership of the whole of India, in order to "legalize" their succession. Economic experts of the highest repute, such as James Mill,[38] duly supported this fiction with "scientific" arguments, so in particular with the famous conclusion given below.[39]

As early as 1793, the British in Bengal gave landed property to all the *zemindars* (Mahometan tax collectors) or hereditary market superintendents they had found in their district so as to win native support for the campaign against the peasant masses. Later they adopted the same policy for their new conquests in the Agram province, in Oudh, and in the Central Provinces.

Turbulent peasant risings followed in their wake, in the course of which tax collectors were frequently driven out. In the resulting confusion and anarchy British capitalists successfully appropriated a considerable portion of the land.

The burden of taxation, moreover, was so ruthlessly increased that it swallowed up nearly all the fruits of the people's labor. This went to such an extreme in the Delhi and Allahabad districts that, according to the official evidence of the British tax authorities in 1854, the peasants found it convenient to lease or pledge their shares in land for the bare amount of the tax levied. Under the auspices of this taxation, usury came to the Indian village, to stay and eat up the social organization from within like a canker.[40] In order to accelerate this process, the British passed a law that flew in the face of every tradition and justice known to the village community: compulsory alienation of village land for tax arrears. In vain did the old family associations try to protect themselves by options on their hereditary land and that of their kindred. There was no stopping the rot. Every day another plot of land fell under the hammer; individual members withdrew from the family unit, and the peasants got into debt and lost their land.

The British, with their wonted colonial stratagems, tried to make it appear as if their power policy, which had in fact undermined the traditional forms of land ownership and brought about the collapse of the Hindu peasant economy, had been dictated by the need to protect the peasants against native oppression and exploitation and served to safeguard their own interests.[41] Britain artificially created a landed aristocracy at the expense of the ancient property-rights of the peasant communities, and then proceeded to "protect" the peasants against these alleged oppressors, and to bring this illegally usurped land into the possession of British capitalists.

Thus large estates developed in India in a short time, while over large areas the peasants in their masses were turned into impoverished small tenants with a short-term lease.

Lastly, one more striking fact shows the typically capitalist method of colonization. The British were the first conquerors of India who showed gross indifference to public utilities. Arabs, Afghans and Mongols had organized and maintained magnificent works of canalization in India, they had given the country a network of roads, spanned the rivers with bridges and seen to the sinking of wells. Timur or Tamerlane,[42] the founder of the Mongol dynasty in India, had a care for the cultivation of the soil, for irrigation, for the safety of the roads and the provision of food for travellers.[43] The primitive Indian Rajahs, the Afghan or Mongol conquerors, at any rate, in spite of occasional cruelty against individuals, made their mark with the marvellous constructions we can find today at every step and which seem to be the work of a giant race. "The (East India) Company which ruled India until 1858 did not make one spring accessible, did not sink a single well, nor build a bridge for the benefit of the Indians."[44]

Another witness, the Englishman James Wilson, says:

> In the Madras Province, no-one can help being impressed by the magnificent ancient irrigation systems, traces of which have been preserved until our time. Locks and weirs dam the rivers into great lakes, from which canals distribute the water for an area of sixty or seventy miles around. On the large rivers, there are thirty to forty of such weirs. . . . The rain water from the mountains was collected in artificial ponds, many of which still remain and boast circumferences of between fifteen and twenty-five miles. Nearly all these gigantic constructions were completed before the year 1750. During the war between the Company and the Mongol rulers—and, be it said, during the entire period of our rule in India—they have sadly decayed.[45]

No wonder! British capital had no object in giving the Indian communities economic support or helping them to survive. Quite the reverse, it aimed to destroy them and to deprive them of their productive forces. The unbridled greed, the acquisitive instinct of accumulation must by its very nature take every advantage of the "conditions of the market" and can have no thought for the morrow. It is incapable of seeing far enough to recognize the value of the economic monuments of an older civilization. (Recently British engineers in Egypt feverishly tried to discover traces of an ancient irrigation system rather like the one a stupid lack of vision had allowed to decay in India, when they were charged with damming the Nile on a grand scale in furtherance of capitalist enterprise.) Not until 1867 was England able to appreciate the results of her noble efforts in this respect. In the terrible famine of that year a million people were killed in the Orissa district alone; and Parliament was shocked into investigating the causes of the emergency. The British government has now introduced administrative measures in an attempt to save the peasant from usury. The Punjab Alienation Act of 1900 made it illegal to sell or mortgage peasant lands to persons other than of the peasant caste, though exceptions can be made in individual cases, subject to the tax collector's approval.[46] Having deliberately disrupted the protecting ties of the ancient Hindu social associations, after having nurtured a system of usury where nothing is thought of a 15 percent charge of interest, the British now entrust the ruined Indian peasant to the tender care of the Exchequer and its officials, under the "pro-tection," that is to say, of those draining him of his livelihood.

Next to tormented British India, Algeria under French rule claims pride of place in the annals of capitalist colonization. When the French conquered Algeria, ancient social and economic institutions prevailed among the Arab-Kabyle population. These had been preserved until the nineteenth century, and in spite of the long and turbulent history of the country they survive in part even to the present day.

Private property may have existed no doubt in the towns, among the Moors and Jews, among merchants, artisans and usurers. Large rural areas may have been seized by the state under Turkish suzerainty—yet nearly half of the productive land is jointly held by Arab and Kabyle tribes who still keep up the ancient patriarchal customs. Many Arab families led the same kind of nomad life in the nineteenth century as they had done since time immemorial, an existence that appears restless and irregular only to the superficial observer, but one that is in fact strictly regulated and extremely monotonous. In summer they were wont, man, woman and child, to take their herds and tents and migrate to the sea-swept shores of the Tell district; and in the winter they would move back again to the protective warmth of the desert. They travelled along definite routes, and the summer and winter stations were fixed for every tribe and family. The fields of those Arabs who had settled on the land were in most cases the joint property of the clans, and the great Kabyle family associations also lived according to old traditional rules under the patriarchal guidance of their elected heads.

The women would take turns for household duties; a matriarch, again elected by the family, being in complete charge of the clan's domestic affairs, or else the women taking turns of duty. This organization of the Kabyle clans on the fringe of the African desert bears a startling resemblance to that of the famous Southern Slavonic *Zadruga*[47]—not only the fields but all the tools, weapons and monies, all that the members acquire or need for their work, are communal property of the clan. Personal property is confined to one suit of clothing, and in the case of a woman to the dresses and ornaments of her dowry. More valuable attire and jewels, however, are considered common property, and individuals were allowed to use them only if the whole family approved. If the clan was not too numerous, meals were taken at a common table; the women took it in turns to cook, but the eldest were entrusted with the dishing out. If a family circle was too large, the head of the family would each month ration out strictly proportionate quantities of uncooked food to the individual families who then prepared them. These communities were bound together by close ties of kin-ship, mutual assistance and equality, and a patriarch would implore his sons on his deathbed to remain faithful to the family.[48]

These social relations were already seriously impaired by the rule of the Turks, established in Algeria in the sixteenth century. Yet the Turkish excheq-uer had by no means confiscated all the land. That is a legend invented by the French at a much later date. Indeed, only a European mind is capable of such a flight of fancy which is contrary to the entire economic foundation of Islam both in theory and practice. In truth, the facts were quite different. The Turks did not touch the communal fields of the village communities. They merely confiscated a great part of uncultivated land from the clans and converted it into crown land under Turkish local administrators (*Beyliks*). The state worked these lands in part with native labor, and in part they were leased out on rent or against payment in kind. Further the Turks took advantage of every revolt of the subjected families and of every disturbance in the country to add to their possessions by large-scale confiscation of land, either for military establishments or for public auction, when most of it went to Turkish or other usurers. To escape from the burden of taxation and confiscation, many peas-ants placed themselves under the protection of the Church, just as they had done in medieval Germany. Hence considerable areas became Church prop-erty. All these changes finally resulted in the following distribution of Algerian land at the time of the French conquest: crownlands occupied nearly 3,750,000 acres, and a further 7,500,000 acres of uncultivated land as com-mon property of All the Faithful (*Bled-el-Islam*). 7,500,000 acres had been privately owned by the Berbers since Roman times, and under Turkish rule a further 3,750,000 acres had come into private ownership, a mere 12,500,000 acres remaining communal property of individual Arab clans. In the Sahara, some of the 7,500,000 acres of fertile land near the Sahara Oases was commu-nally owned by the clans and some belonged to private owners. The remain-ing 57,500,000,000 acres were mainly waste land.

With their conquest of Algeria, the French made a great ado about their work of civilization, since the country, having shaken off the Turkish yoke at the beginning of the eighteenth century, was harboring the pirates who infest-ed the Mediterranean and trafficked in Christian slaves. Spain and the North American Union in particular, themselves at that time slave traders on no mean scale, declared relentless war on this Moslem iniquity. France, in the very throes of the Great Revolution, proclaimed a crusade against Algerian anarchy. Her subjection of that country was carried through under the slogans of "combating slavery" and "instituting orderly and civilized conditions." Yet practice was soon to show what was at the bottom of it all. It is common knowledge that in the forty years following the subjection of Algeria, no European state suffered so many changes in its political system as France: the restoration of the monarchy was followed by the July Revolution[49] and the reign of the "Citizen King," and this was succeeded by the February Revolution, the Second Republic, the Second Empire, and finally, after the disaster of 1870, by the Third Republic. In turn, the aristocracy, high finance, petty bourgeoisie and the large middle classes in general gained political ascendancy.

Yet French policy in Algeria remained undeflected by this succession of events; it pursued a single aim from beginning to end; at the fringe of the African desert, it demonstrated plainly that all the political revolutions in nineteenth-century France centered in a single basic interest: the rule of a capitalist bourgeoisie and its institutions of ownership.

"The bill submitted for your consideration," said Deputy Humbert on June 30, 1873, in the Session of the French National Assembly as spokesman for the Commission for Regulating Agrarian Conditions in Algeria, "is but the crowning touch to an edifice well founded on a whole series of ordinances, edicts, laws and decrees of the Senate which together and severally have as the same object: the establishment of private property among the Arabs."

In spite of the ups and downs of internal French politics, French colonial policy persevered for fifty years in its systematic and deliberate efforts to destroy and disrupt communal property. It served two distinct purposes: The breakup of communal property was primarily intended to smash the social power of the Arab family associations and to quell their stubborn resistance against the French yoke, in the course of which there were innumerable risings so that, in spite of France's military superiority, the country was in a continual state of war. Secondly, communal property had to be disrupted in order to gain the economic assets of the conquered country; the Arabs, that is to say, had to be deprived of the land they had owned for a thousand years, so that French capitalists could get it. Once again the fiction we know so well, that under Moslem law all land belongs to the ruler, was brought into play. Just as the English had done in British India, so Louis Philippe's[50] governors in Algeria declared the existence of communal property owned by the clan to be "impossible." This fiction served as an excuse to claim for the state most of the uncultivated areas, and especially the commons, woods and meadows, and to use them for purposes of colonization....

## 2 — The Dissolution of Primitive Communism: From the Ancient Germans and the Incas to India, Russia, and Southern Africa, from *Introduction to Political Economy*

EDITORS' NOTE: This selection is drawn from Luxemburg's *Introduction to Political Economy*, an unfinished book begun around 1908 and based on her lectures at the Social Democratic Party School in Berlin. As late as 1916, she wrote from prison to her publisher, I. H. W. Dietz, of plans to revise the manuscript for book publication, with the following chapters: 1) What Is Political Economy? 2) Social Labor, 3) Elements of Economic History: Primitive Communism, 4) Elements of Economic History: The Feudal Economic System, 5) Elements of Economic History: The Medieval City and the Craft Guilds, 6) Commodity Production, 7) Wage Labor, 8) Capitalist Profit, 9) Crisis, 10) Tendencies of Capitalist Development. After Luxemburg's murder, only the manuscripts for chapters 1, 3, 6, 7, and 10 were found and they were first published by Paul Levi in 1925. What follows is the second half of chapter 3, translated from the version of the *Introduction* that appears in Vol. 5 of Luxemburg's *Gesammelte Werke* (Berlin: Dietz Verlag, 1975). We have also consulted the excellent French translation of the *Introduction* by Irène Petit (Paris: Éditions Anthropos, 1970). Unless otherwise indicated, footnotes below are by the editors, often based on those in the *Gesammelte Werke*. The present translation is by Ashley Passmore and Kevin B. Anderson. We would like to thank Olga Avedeyeva, A. Z. Hilali, Waheed Khan, and Albert Resis for background information. The title and the subheadings have been supplied by the editors.

### THE MARK COMMUNITY OF THE ANCIENT GERMANS

Let us take a look at the mark community[1] that has been researched most thoroughly in terms of its internal structures, the German one. As we know, the Germans settled into tribes and clans. In each clan, the male head of the household obtained a designated building site next to a plot of land in order to set up house and farm there. Then, a portion of the area would be used for agriculture, and in fact each family would get a lot on it. According to Caesar, around the beginning of the Christian era, a tribe of Germans (the Suebi or Swabians) cultivated their farms collectively without first partitioning it among the families. Indeed, yearly repartitioning of the lots was already a common practice in the time of Tacitus, the Roman historian, in the second century. In scattered regions, such as the township of Frickhofen in Nassau, yearly repartitionings were still common in the seventeenth and eighteenth centuries. In the nineteenth century, it was still common in a few regions of the Bavarian Palatinate and on the Rhine to draw lots for farmland, although they took place at larger intervals: every three, four, nine, twelve, fourteen, and eighteen years. These farms were therefore definitively turned into private property only around the middle of the last century. In a few regions of Scotland as well, there were repartitionings of farmland up until recently. All of the lots were originally the same and their size was fitted to the average needs of a family and to the potential yield of the soil. Depending on the quality of soil in the various regions, they amounted to fifteen, thirty, forty or more acres of land. In most parts of Europe, the lots were passed down through inheritance by individual families, as the repartitioning of land became rare and eventually fell out of practice in the fifth and sixth centuries. Still, this only applied to the farms. All of the land that was left over—forests, meadows, bodies of water and unused portions—remained the unpartitioned, collective property of the mark. From the yields of the forest, for example, the needs of the community were negotiated and what remained was dispersed among individuals.

The pastures were used in common. This unpartitioned mark or common land existed for a significant period of time; it still exists today in the Bavarian Alps, Switzerland, the Tyrol, and France (in the Vendée), and in Norway and Sweden.

In order to ensure complete equality in the partitioning of the farmlands, the land was first divided by quality and condition into a few fields, and each field was then cut into a number of smaller strips that corresponded to the number of mark members there were. If a member of the mark had doubts about whether he had received an equal share, he was allowed to call for the total re-measurement of the land. Whoever resisted him was punished.

But after the periodic re-partitioning and drawings by lot fell into disuse, the *work* of the members of the mark community, including farm work, remained totally communal and was mandated for the community by strict regulation. At first, this resulted in the general obligation of every owner of a portion of the mark to work, since residency alone was not enough to be an actual member of the mark. For this, each person not only had to live in the mark, but also had to cultivate his farm himself. Whoever neglected to cultivate his portion of land over a number of years lost it for good and the mark could hand it over to someone else to cultivate. Work itself, then, was under the direction of the mark. Early on, after the Germans established settlements, the centerpiece of German economic life was tending livestock, conducted on communal fields and meadows under the watch of communal, village herdsmen. They used fallow land, such as farmland after the harvest, as pastures for livestock. This was due to the fact that the times for seeding and harvesting, the variation in fallow and harvest years for each field, and the sequence of sowings were collectively decided and everyone had to comply with the communal directives. Each field was surrounded by a fence with gates that were closed until the harvest; the opening and closing dates of the field were decided by the entire village. Each field had an overseer, or field guardian, who was to uphold the prescribed order as an official functionary of the mark. The so-called field processions of all the villages turned into festivals, to which one also brought children and boxed their ears to make them remember the borders in order that they might later be able to give testimony.

Livestock breeding was conducted in common; keeping individual herds was forbidden by the mark community. All the animals of the village were split into common herds according to the type of animal, each with a village herdsman and an animal to lead the herd. It was also decreed that the herds have bells. The right to hunt and fish on the mark was also determined communally. One could not lay any snares or dig any pits without first notifying the rest of the community. Brass and similar items that were dug out of the soil of the mark and were deeper than a ploughshare belonged to the community and not to the individual finder. The necessary craftsmen had to reside in each mark. Yet each farming family made most of the items they needed for everyday life themselves. They baked, brewed, spun and wove at home. Yet many crafts became specialized early on, especially those having to do with the manufacture of farm implements. Thus, in the communal forests of Wölpe in Lower Saxony, the members of the mark were supposed to "have a man of each craft in the forest to make something useful out of the wood."[2] For the craftsmen, the amount and kind of wood one used was regulated in order to protect the forest and for the members of the mark to make necessary preparations. The craftsmen received their necessities from the mark and generally lived the same way as the mass of other peasants. Yet, they did not have full rights, partly because they were transient people, and not an indigenous element. For this reason, the craftsmen were not necessary for farming, which was at the center of economic life at that time and served as the axis around which the rights of the members of the mark, their public life, and their obligations revolved. 3 Thus, not everyone could push their way into the society of the mark community. The acceptance of a foreigner had to be unanimously approved by all of the members of the mark. One could only divest himself of his lot to another mark member, never a foreigner, and only before the mark tribunal.

At the head of the mark community was the village count, or the village mayor, in other places called the mark master or *centener*. His fellow mark members voted him into his position of authority. This election was not only an honor but also a duty for the chosen individual; those who refused to serve incurred legal sanctions. It is likely that with the passage of time, the office of mark leader became hereditary in certain families. Because of its power and income, it was only a small step before this office could be bought, or for the land to be given out as a fiefdom. It was only a short period of time before the position developed from that of a purely democratically elected leader of a community into a tool for the domination of the community. In the heyday of the mark community, however, the mark leader was nothing more than the executor of the wishes of the collectivity. The assembly of the mark community regulated all of the communal affairs, reconciled disputes, and imposed punishments. The entire system of agricultural work, the paths and buildings, as well as the field and village police, were all decided upon by the assembly majority. The assembly was also responsible for the computation of the "communal books," which accounted for the business affairs of the mark. Maintaining the peace and administering justice within the mark were carried out by the mark leader and the surrounding members (the "court of jurisdiction"), who rendered judgments orally and publicly. Only members of the mark were allowed to attend the tribunal; foreigners were denied entry. The members of the mark were obligated to take oaths and act as witnesses for one another, since they were generally required to assist one another in a brotherly and loyal manner in case of emergency, fire, or enemy attack. In their army, the mark members created their own battalions and defended themselves side by side. No one was allowed to abandon his comrade to an enemy spear. When there were burglaries or crimes that either occurred in the mark or were perpetrated by a member of the mark on an outsider, the whole mark banded together in solidarity. Members of the mark were also obliged to harbor travelers and to support the needy. Each mark originally

consisted of a religious community, and after the introduction of Christianity—which, as with the Saxons, occurred quite late among the Germans, only
in the 9th century—the community was a religious congregation. Finally, the
mark typically kept a schoolteacher for the youth of the village.

One cannot imagine anything any simpler and more harmonious than the
economic system of the old Germanic mark. Evidently, we have the entire
mechanism of social life. A strict plan and a tight organization incorporate
everything each individual does and places him as a part into the whole. The
immediate needs of everyday life and the equal fulfillment of everyone; this is
the starting point and endpoint of the organization. Everyone works for
everyone else and collectively decides on everything. Whence does this
spring, on what does it base itself, this organization, this power of the collective over the individual? It is nothing other than the communism of land and
soil, that is to say, the common possession of the most important means of
production on the part of those who work. The typical characteristics of the
communistic, agrarian economic organization can be brought out more easily if one studies them comparatively on an international scale in order to
grasp it as a global form of production in all its diversity and flexibility.

## THE INCA EMPIRE

Let us turn to the old Inca Empire in South America. The area of this empire,
which today consists of the republics of Peru, Bolivia, and Chile in an area of
2.1 million square miles, with a population today of twelve million inhabitants,
was organized at the time of the Spanish conquest under Pizarro the same way
it had been for many centuries before then. At first, we find the same organization as among the ancient Germans. Each tribal community, together a hundred men, was capable of defending itself militarily. They took over a specific
area that henceforth belonged to them, curiously resembling the German one
in its name, *marca*. The farmland was separated from the mark region, divided
into lots and annually raffled off to families before the sowing of crops. The size
of the lots was determined according to the size of the family, or according to its
needs. The leader of the village, whose position had already developed from an
elected one into a hereditary one around the time of the formation of the Inca
Empire in the tenth and eleventh centuries,[4] received the largest share of the
lots. In northern Peru, the male head of household did not cultivate his plot of
land by himself; rather, they worked in groups of ten under the direction of a
leader. This is an arrangement that resembles certain aspects of the Germanic

structure. The ten-man group cultivated on rotation the lots of all of their members, even those who were absent, serving in war, or doing compulsory labor for the Incas. Each family received the fruits that grew on their lot. Only those who lived in the mark and belonged to the clan had the right to a plot of land. Yet everyone was obliged to cultivate his plot himself as well. Whoever let his field lie fallow for a certain number of years (in Mexico, it was three) lost his claim to his land. The plots could not be sold or given away. It was strictly forbidden to leave one's own mark and settle into an external one, which was probably connected to the strict bloodlines of the village tribes.

Agriculture in the coastal areas, where there was only periodic rainfall, always required artificial irrigation through canals, which were constructed through the collective labor of the entire mark. There were strict rules governing the use of water and its distribution among separate villages, and within the same ones. Each village also had "paupers' fields," which were cultivated by all the members of the mark and whose yields the village leaders distributed among the elderly, widows, and other needy individuals. The rest of the area apart from agricultural lands was *marcapacha* (common lands). In the mountainous region of the country, where field agriculture could not thrive, there was modest livestock farming, which consisted almost exclusively of llamas, which was the basis of the existence of the inhabitants, and periodically brought their main product, wool, into the valley in order to trade it with the peasants for corn, pepper, and beans. At the time of the conquest there were already private herds and significant differences in wealth in the mountain regions. An average member of the mark probably owned between three and ten llamas, while a leader might have between fifty and a hundred of them. Only the forest, soil and pasture were common property there, and outside of private herds, there were village herds that could not be divided up. At certain times, portions of the communal herd were slaughtered and the meat and wool divided among the families. There were no specialized craftsmen; each family made the necessary items for the household itself. There were, however, villages that demonstrated special skill in a certain craft, whether as weavers, potters, or metal workers. At the head of the village was the village leader, originally an elected office, but later a hereditary one, who oversaw the cultivation, but in every important matter he consulted with the assembly of the council of elders, which was called together with the sounding of a conch shell trumpet.

Thus far, the old Peruvian mark community offers a faithful copy of the German one in all the essential characteristics. Yet it is even better suited to offer us more in our investigation of the essence of this social system, insofar as

## SPANISH COLONIALISM IN THE AMERICAS

The internal organization of the Peruvian Inca state uncovered for us an important side of this primitive social form and, at the same time, pinpointed the specific historical process of its downfall. Another turn in the destiny of this social form will appear when we pursue the next chapter in the history of the Peruvian Indians as well as the other Spanish colonies in America. Here we encounter primarily a completely new method of domination of which the Inca rulers, for example, had no idea. The Spanish, the first Europeans in the New World, began their rule with the relentless extermination of the sub-jugated population. According to the reports of the Spanish themselves, the number of Indians exterminated in the space of only a few years after the dis-covery of America reached as high as between twelve and fifteen million. "We believe it is justified to maintain," Las Casas says, "that the Spanish, through their monstrous and inhuman treatment, have exterminated twelve million people, among them women and children." He further states, "In my person-al opinion, the number of those natives murdered in this period exceeded even fifteen million."9 "On the island of Haiti," says Handelmann, "the num-ber of natives before the Spanish encountered them in 1492 was around one million; in 1508 there were only sixty thousand remaining of these million people and nine years later there were only fourteen thousand, so that the Spanish had to seize upon the introduction of Indians from the neighboring islands in order to have enough working hands. In 1508 alone, forty thousand natives from the Bahamas were transported to the island of Haiti and made into slaves."10 The Spanish regularly hunted down the redskins, as described for us by an eyewitness and participant, the Italian Girolamo Benzoni. "In part because of a lack of food, and in part out of fear after the separation from their fathers, mothers, and children," says Benzoni after one such manhunt on the island of Kumagna, in which four thousand Indians were captured,

the majority of the enslaved natives died on the way to the port of Cumana.[11] Each time someone among the slaves was too tired to march as quickly as his comrades, the Spanish stabbed him in the back with their daggers, inhumanly murdering him out of fear that he wanted to remain in order to lead a counterattack. It was a heart-breaking scene, seeing these poor souls, totally naked, tired, wounded and so exhausted from hunger that they could hardly stand on their feet. Iron chains bound their necks, hands and feet. There was not a virgin among them who would not have been raped by these robbers (the Spanish), who were so addicted to this repulsive debauchery that many of them remained marred by syphilis forever. . . . All of the natives put into slavery were branded with hot irons. Then the captains took a number of them for themselves, and divided the rest among the soldiers. They either gambled them away to each other or sold them to Spanish colonists. Traders, who traded these wares for wine, flour, sugar and other daily necessities, transported the slaves into the parts of the Spanish colonies where there was the greatest demand for them. During their transport, a number of these unfortunates died because of lack of water and the bad air in the cabins, which was due to the fact that the traders herded the slaves into the lowest level of the ship without giving them enough water to drink or enough air to breathe.[12]

However, in order to relieve themselves of the trouble of hunting the Indians down and the cost of their acquisition, the Spanish created a system known as *Repartimientos* in their West Indian possessions and on the American mainland. The entire conquered area was divided by the governors into districts, whose village leaders, "Caciques," were obligated simply to supply on demand the number of natives for slavery requested by the Spanish. Spanish colonists periodically received the requested number of slaves that were delivered to them by the governor under the condition that they "take the trouble to convert them to Christianity."[13] The abuse of the slaves by the colonists defied all understanding. Suicide became a salvation for the Indians. "All of the natives captured by the Spanish," according to a witness,

were forced by them to do hard and strenuous labor in the mines, away from their homes and families and under constant threat of beatings. No wonder that thousands of slaves saw no other possibility than to escape from their gruesome fate by not only violently taking their own lives, by hanging or drowning themselves or in other ways, but before then also murdering their wives and children, in order to end an unfortunate and inescapable situation for everyone all at once. In other cases, women resorted to aborting their children in the womb or avoiding sexual contact with men so that they did not have to bear slaves.[14]

Through the intervention of the imperial confessor, the pious Father Garcia de Loyosa, the colonists were finally able to have a decree issued by the Hapsburg Emperor, Charles V, summarily declaring the Indians to be hereditary slaves of the Spanish colonists. Benzoni in fact says the decree only applied to Caribbean cannibals, but was extended to and applied to all Indians in general. In order to justify the horrors they caused, the Spanish systematically spread dramatic horror stories about cannibalism and other vices of the Indians so that a contemporary French historian, Marly de Châtel, in his "General History of the West Indies" (Paris, 1569) could write of them: "God punished them with slavery for their evil and vice, since not even Ham[15] sinned against his father Noah to the degree of the Indians against the Holy Father." And around the same time the Spaniard Acosta wrote in his *Historia natural y moral de las Indias* (Barcelona, 1591) about these same Indians, that they were a "good-natured people that is always ready to prove itself of service to the Europeans; a people that, in its behavior, shows such a touching harmlessness and sincerity, that those not completely stripped of all humanity could not treat them any other way than with tenderness and love."

Naturally, there were also attempts to stop the horror. In 1531, Pope Paul III published a bull decreeing that the Indians were members of the human race and therefore free from slavery. The Spanish Imperial Council for the West Indies also made a declaration against slavery, but the need for these repeated decrees testified more to the fruitlessness than to the sincerity of these attempts.

What freed the Indians from slavery was not the pious action of the Catholic clergy, nor the protests of the Spanish kings, but rather the simple fact that the Indians' mental and physical constitution rendered them worthless for hard slave labor. Against this bare impossibility, the intense cruelty of the Spanish did not help in the long run; the redskins died under slavery like flies, fled, took their own lives, in short: the entire affair was thoroughly unprofitable. And only when the warm and untiring defender of the Indians, Bishop Las Casas, came upon the idea of importing the more robust Africans as slaves rather than the unfit Indians, were the useless experiments with the Indians immediately abandoned. This practical discovery took effect more quickly and more thoroughly than all of Las Casas's pamphlets on the cruelties of the Spanish. The Indians were freed from slavery after a few decades and the enslavement of the Negroes began, which would last for four more centuries. At the end of the eighteenth century a respectable German, the "good old Nettelbeck" from Kolberg, was the captain of a ship taking hundreds of Africans from Guinea to Guyana in South America, where other "good East Prussians" exploited plantations and sold slaves along with other goods from Africa, herding them into the lowest parts of the ship, as the Spanish captains had done in the sixteenth century. The progress of the humanistic era of the Enlightenment showed itself in how Nettelbeck, to alleviate their melancholy and to keep them from dying off, allowed them to dance on the ship's deck with music and whip cracks every evening, something to which the more brutal Spanish traders had not yet resorted. And in 1871, at the end of the nineteenth century, the noble David Livingstone, who had spent thirty years in Africa searching for the sources of the Nile, wrote in his famous letters to the American Gordon Bennett: "And if my disclosures regarding the terrible Ujijian[16] slavery should lead to the suppression of the east coast slave trade, I shall regard that as a greater matter by far than the discovery of all the Nile sources together. Now that you have done with domestic slavery forever, lend us your powerful aid toward this great object. This fine country is blighted, as with a curse from above...."[17]

Yet the lot of the Indians in the Spanish colonies was not made significantly better by this transformation. A new system of colonization had taken the place of the old one. Instead of *Repartimientos*, which were created for the direct enslavement of the population, the so-called *"encomiendas"* were introduced.[18] Formally, the inhabitants were awarded personal freedom and full property rights to their land. But the areas were under the administrative direction of the Spanish colonists, primarily placed into the hands of the descendants of the first *Conquistadores*, the conquerors, who, as *encomenderos*, were the guardians of the Indians, who were in turn declared to be minors. The *encomenderos* were supposed to spread Christianity among the Indians. To cover the cost of constructing churches for the natives and as compensation for their labor as guardians, the *encomenderos* legally acquired the right to demand "moderate payments in money and in kind" from the population. These provisions soon were enough to make the *encomiendas* hell for the Indians. The land was of course left to them as the undivided property of the tribes. The Spanish only understood, or only wanted to understand, this to be farmland, which was to be ploughed. The undivided mark and the unused estates, and often even the areas left to lay fallow were taken over by the Spanish as "deserted land." And they did so with such thoroughness and shamelessness that Zurita wrote on this subject:

> There is not a parcel of land, not a farm, that was not determined to be the property of the Europeans, without regard for the encroachments onto the interests and the property rights of the natives, who were thus forced to leave this land, which had been inhabited by them since ancient times. They often seized cultivated lands from them, under the pretext that they were being utilized only to prevent their acquisition by the Europeans. Thanks to this system, in a few provinces, the Spanish expanded their property so widely that the natives had no land left to cultivate themselves.[19]

At the same time, the "moderate" payments were increased by the *encomenderos* so shamelessly that the Indians were crushed under them. "All of the belongings of the Indian," Zurita says,

> are not enough to pay the taxes that are levied against him. One meets many people among the redskins whose assets do not even come out to one peso and who live by daily wage labor; in this way, there were no means remaining for these unfortunates to support their families. This is the reason why so often young people prefer sexual relations out of wedlock rather than sexual relations within wedlock, especially when their parents do not even have four or five *real* at their disposal. The Indians can only barely afford the luxury of clothing themselves; many who have no resources to buy themselves a dress are not able to take communion. It is no wonder, then, that the majority of them become desperate, since they cannot find any means to acquire the necessary food for their families. . . . During my early travels, I discovered that many Indians hung themselves out of despondency, after they explained to their wives and children that they did this in the face of the impossibility of being able to afford the taxes demanded of them.[20]

Finally, in addition to land theft and the pressure of taxation, came forced labor. At the beginning of the seventeenth century, the Spanish openly returned to the system that had been formally abandoned in the sixteenth century. Though slavery was abolished for the Indians, in its place came a unique system of forced wage labor, which did not significantly differ from the system that preceded it. Already in the mid-sixteenth century, Zurita portrays for us the situation of the Indian wage laborers under the Spanish in the following way:

> The whole time, the Indians received no other nourishment than cornbread. . . . The *encomendor* has them work from morning to night, letting them work naked, whether in morning or evening frosts, in storms and thunder, without ever giving them any food other than half-spoiled bread. The Indians spend the night under the open sky. Because the wage is only paid out at the end of the term of their forced labor, the Indians have no means to buy the necessary warm clothing for themselves. It is no surprise that under such circumstances in the *encomenderos*, the work is utterly exhausting for them and can be identified as one of the causes of the Indians dying off so rapidly.[21]

This system of forced wage labor was introduced at the beginning of the seventeenth century by the Spanish crown, making it officially and universally legal.

The stated reason for the law was that the Indians would not work voluntarily and that without them, the mines could only be run with great difficulty, despite the presence of the African slaves. The Indian villagers were thus required to place the demanded number of workers (in Peru, one-seventh, and in New Spain, four percent of the population), who were at the mercy of the *encomenderos*. The deadly consequences of this system were immediately apparent. In an anonymous memorandum sent to Philip IV, carrying the title "Report on the Dangerous Situation of the Kingdom of Chile from the Temporal and Spiritual Point of View," it states: "The known cause of the rapid decrease in the number of natives is the system of forced labor in the mines and on the fields of the *encomenderos*. Although the Spanish have an enormous number of Negroes at their disposal, although they have taxed the Indians at a higher rate than they paid their leaders before the conquest, they nevertheless regard it as impossible to give up this system of forced labor."[22] In addition, forced labor resulted in the Indians in many cases not being able to cultivate their fields, which the Spanish then used as a pretext to seize the land for themselves as "waste land." The ruin of Indian farming offered a fertile ground for extortion. "Among their native rulers," according to Zurita, "the Indians did not know any usurers." The Spanish taught them well the fruits of the money economy and taxation. Eaten up by debt, huge estates owned by the Indians—those that had not already been simply stolen by the Spanish—fell into the hands of Spanish capitalists, whereby the estimation of the fundamental value of these estates formed a special chapter in European perfidy. Taken together, the theft of land, taxation, forced labor and usury close a circle in which the existence of the Indian mark community collapsed. The traditional public order and the traditional social bonds of the Indians were dissolved by the collapse of their economic base—mark community farming. For their part, the Spanish methodically destroyed it through the disruption of all traditional forms of authority. The village leaders and the tribal leaders had to be confirmed by the *encomenderos*, something the latter used for the purpose of filling these positions only with their protégés, the most depraved subjects of the Indian society. A preferred method of the Spanish was also the systematic instigation of the Indians against their leaders. Under the auspices of their Christian aims, to protect the natives from being exploited by their leaders, they declared them free from payment of the dues that had been paid to their leaders since time immemorial. "The Spanish," writes Zurita, "supported by what is going on in Mexico today, maintain that the leaders were plundering their own tribes, but they carry the blame for this extortion, since they themselves and nobody else robbed the early leaders of their position and their means of income and replaced them with ones from among their protégés."[23] Likewise, they looked to instigate mutinies whenever the village or tribal leaders protested against the illicit sale of land by individual members of the mark to the Spanish. Chronic revolutions and an endless succession of legal proceedings among the natives over unlawful land sales were the result. Along with ruin, hunger, and slavery, anarchy was added into the mix in order to make the existence of the Indians hell. The stark result of this Spanish-Christian guardianship can be summed up in two phrases: the land going into the hands of the Spanish, and the extinction of the Indians. "In all the Spanish areas of the Indies," Zurita writes,

> either the native tribes disappear completely or they become much smaller, although others have claimed the opposite. The natives leave their dwellings and farms, since these have lost all value for them in the face of the exorbitant dues in money and kind; they emigrate to other regions, continuously wandering from one region to another, or they hide themselves in the forest and run the danger of becoming, sooner or later, the prey of wild animals. Many Indians end their lives by suicide, as I personally witnessed several times and understood from interviews with the local population.[24]

And half a year later, another high official of the Spanish government in Peru, Juan Ortiz de Cervantes, reported: "The native population in the Spanish colonies gets thinner and thinner; they leave the areas they formerly inhabited, leaving the soil uncultivated, and the Spanish have to struggle to find the necessary number of peasants and herdsmen. The so-called Mitayos, a tribe without whom the labor in the gold and silver mines would be impossible, either completely abandoned the cities occupied by the Spanish, or if they stayed, died out at an astonishing rate."[25]

One must truly wonder at the incredible tenacity of the Indian people and their organization of the mark community, since both of these have been preserved well into the nineteenth century, despite these conditions.

### THE VILLAGES OF INDIA

The great English colony of India shows us another aspect of the fate of the mark community. Here, as in no other corner of the earth, one can study the most varying forms of property that represent the history of several millennia, like Herschel's[26] star gage model of the sky, projected onto a flat surface.

Village communities next to tribal communities; periodic repartitionings of equal portions of land next to the lifelong ownership of unequal portions of land; communal labor next to private, individual enterprise; the equal rights of all villagers to community lands next to the privileges of certain groups; and finally, next to all of these forms of communal property, private property in the land in the form of smaller subplots of rural land, short-term leaseholds, and enormous *latifundia*. All of this one could study, as large as life, in India until a few decades ago. Indian legal sources attest that the mark community in India is an ancient system. The oldest common law, the Code of Manu from the ninth century B.C., contains countless ordinances concerning border disputes between marks, unpartitioned marks, and the establishment of daughter villages on unpartitioned estates of older marks. The code knows only ownership based on one's own labor; it mentions handcrafts as well as a side-occupation of agriculture; it attempts to rein in the power of the Brahmins, the priests, by only allowing them to be granted moveable property. The future indigenous sovereigns, the rajas, appear in these codes still as elected tribal leaders. The two later codes, *Yajnavalkya* and *Narada*, which are from the fifth century, accept the clan as the social organization, while public and judicial authority lie in the hands of the assembly of the mark members. They are, collectively and in solidarity, responsible for the misdeeds and offenses of individuals. Standing at the head of the village is the elected mark leader. Both legal codes offer advice on how to elect the best, most peace-loving, and most evenhanded community member to this office and to offer him obedience. The Code of Narada distinguishes between two kinds of mark communities: "relatives," or clan-based communities, and "cohabitants," or neighboring communities as local associations of non-blood relatives. Yet, at the same time, both legal codes recognize ownership based on only individual labor. Abandoned land belongs to the person who takes it over for cultivation. An unlawful ownership is not recognized for three generations if the individuals in question do not cultivate the land. Up to this point, we therefore see the Indian people still enclosed within the same primitive social groups and economic relations, as it existed for centuries in the area of the Indus and afterwards in the heroic period of the Ganges conquest, from which the great folk epics the *Ramayana* and the *Mahabharata* were born. It is only with the commentaries on the old legal codes, which are always the characteristic symptom of deep social changes and aspirations, that one sees old legal views reinterpreted in light of new interests. This is clear proof that up to the fourteenth century— the epoch of the commentators—Indian society went through a significant adjustment in its social structure. In the meantime, an influential priestly class developed, rising above the mass of peasants both materially and legally. The commentators seek the precise language of the old legal codes—just like their Christian colleagues in the feudal West—to "lay out" there the justification for priestly ownership of property and to encourage the donation of land to the Brahmins and thereby the division of the mark estates and the formation of a clerical estate at the expense of the mass of peasant farmers. This development typified the fate of all Oriental societies.

The life-and-death question for every form of developed agriculture in most parts of the Orient is irrigation.[27] Early on, we see in India and Egypt large irrigation systems forming the foundation of their agriculture, along with channels, streams and systematic precautionary measures to protect the land from periodic flooding. From the outset, all of these well-financed undertakings not only surpassed the individual mark communities in terms of their abilities, but also in terms of their budget and initiative. Their direction and execution are products of an authority that stands over the individual village marks, one that can bring the labor force together in a higher degree of unity. Relating to this as well was a form of domination of nature greater than that available to the observational and experiential realm of the masses enclosed within the limits of their villages. Out of these needs arose the important function of the priests in the Orient, who were able to direct large public works such as irrigation systems, due to their observation of nature, which is an integral part of every nature-based religion. Because of the priests' exemption from direct participation in agricultural labor, they attained a freedom that was the product of a certain stage of development. Naturally, over time, this purely economic function grew into a particular type of social power held by the priests. The specialization of these members of society, which emerged from the division of labor, turned into a hereditary, exclusive caste with privileges over and interest in the exploitation of the peasant masses. The speed and extent to which this process occurred for a specific people, whether it remained an embryonic form as in the case of the Peruvian Indians, or whether it developed into official state rule by the priestly caste, or a theocracy, as in Egypt or among the ancient Hebrews, was always dependent on the specific geographical and historical circumstances. But it also depended on whether frequent contact with surrounding peoples allowed a strong warrior caste to emerge outside of the priestly caste, rising up as a military aristocracy in competition with or indeed above the priests. In either case, it was the specific, particularistic narrowness of the ancient communistic mark, whose organization was scarcely suited for larger economic or political tasks, and thus must have abandoned the idea of controlling the regions beyond its own territories, ceding them to the domination of powers that took over these functions. This was the key to the political domination and the economic exploitation of the peasant masses. Many barbarian conquerors in the Orient, whether Mongols, Persians, or Arabs, were forced, alongside of their military power, to take control of the management and execution of these large public undertakings, which were required for the agricultural economy. Just as the Incas in Peru regarded the supervision of artificial irrigation projects and of road and bridge construction as a privilege and a duty, so too did the various Asiatic despotic dynasties that succeeded one another in India set the same task. Despite the formation of castes, despite the despotic, foreign rule that set up camp on the land, despite the political upheavals, the quiet village eked out an existence for itself in the nether regions of Indian society. Inside each village reigned the ancient traditional statutes of the mark's basic law, which survived behind the scenes of a stormy political history, with its own quiet and unnoticeable internal history, stripping away old forms, adopting new ones, experiencing prosperity and decline, dissolution and regeneration. No chronicler ever portrayed these events, and while world history describes the bold campaign of Alexander of Macedon all the way to the sources in the Indus and satisfies itself with the sound of swords emanating from bloody Timur and his Mongols,[28] they remain completely silent about the internal economic history of the Indian people. We can only reconstruct a hypothetical pattern of development of Indian society from the remnants of all of the old layers from this history. It is the achievement of Kovalevsky to have unraveled this. According to Kovalevsky, the various types of agrarian communities that were still observed in the mid-nineteenth century in India can be organized in the following historical sequence:

1) The oldest form can be characterized as a purely tribal community encompassing the entirety of the blood relatives of a tribe (clan), which owns the land and cultivates it communally. The communal lands are therefore unpartitioned, and the fruits of the harvest, as well as those kept in communal storage, were shared. This most primitive type of village community continued only in a few districts of northern India, yet their inhabitants were largely confined to a few sectors (*putti*) of the old gens. Kovalevsky sees in this analogy to the *zadruga* of Bosnia-Herzegovina,[29] where the original blood relations were dissolved with the growth of the population, breaking into a few large families that withdrew from the community with their lands. Even in the middle of the previous century, there were considerable village communi-

ties of this type, some of them with more than 150 members, while others boasted four hundred. More predominant, however, was the type of small village that assembled with their larger familial groups in the area of the old gens only in exceptional cases, i.e., the sale of land. In ordinary life, they led an isolated and strongly regulated existence that Marx, using English sources, portrays in a few short passages:[30]

These small and extremely ancient Indian communities, for example, some of which continue to exist to this day, are based on the possession of the land in common, on the blending of agriculture and handicrafts and on an unalterable division of labor, which serves as a fixed plan and basis for action whenever a new community is started. The communities occupy areas of from a hundred up to several thousand acres, and each forms a compact whole producing all it requires. Most of the products are destined for direct use by the community itself, and are not commodities. Hence production here is independent of that division of labor brought about in Indian society as a whole by the exchange of commodities. It is the surplus alone that becomes a commodity, and a part of that surplus cannot become a commodity until it has reached the hands of the state, because from time immemorial a certain quantity of the community's production has found its way to the state as rent in kind. The form of the community varies in different parts of India. In the simplest communities, the land is tilled in common, and the produce is divided among the members. At the same time, spinning and weaving are carried on in each family as subsidiary industries. Alongside the mass of people thus occupied in the same way, we find the *"chief inhabitant,"* who is judge, police authority and tax-gatherer in one; the *book-keeper*, who keeps the accounts of the tillage and registers everything relating to this; another official, who prosecutes criminals, protects strangers traveling through and escorts them to the next village; the *boundary man*, who guards the boundaries against neighboring communities; the *water-overseer*, who distributes the water from the common tanks for irrigation; the *Brahmin*, who conducts the religious services; the *schoolmaster*, who on the sand teaches the children reading and writing; the *calendar Brahmin*, or astrologer, who makes known the lucky or unlucky days for seed-time and harvest, and for every other kind of agricultural work; a *smith* and a *carpenter*, who make and repair all the agricultural implements; the *potter*, who makes all the pottery of the village; the *barber*, the *washerman*, who washes clothes, the *silversmith*, here and there the *poet*, who in some communities replaces the silversmith, in others the schoolmaster. This dozen or so of individuals is maintained at the expense of the whole community. If the population increases, a new community is founded, on the pattern of the old one, on unoccupied land. . . . The law that regulates the division of labor in the community acts with the irresistible authority of a law of nature. . . . The simplicity of the productive organism in these self-sufficing communities which constantly reproduce themselves in the same form and, when accidentally destroyed, spring up again on the same spot and with the same name—this simplicity supplies the key to he riddle of the *unchangeability* of Asiatic *societies*, which is in such striking contrast with the constant dissolution and refounding of Asiatic *states*, and their never-ceasing changes of dynasty. The structure of the fundamental economic elements of society remains untouched by the storms which blow up in the cloudy regions of politics."[31] [Emphasis added—RL]

2) At the time of the English conquest, the original tribal community had for the most part already been dissolved. From its dissolution, however, emerged a new form, a kinship community with partitioned agricultural land, though not equally divided. The unequal lots of land were given to individual families and their size was based on the family's relationship to the tribal forefathers. This form was prevalent in northwestern India as well as in Punjab. The lots were neither held for life nor were they hereditary; they remained in the family's possession until such time as the growth of the population or the need to allocate a lot to a relative who had been temporarily absent made a repartitioning necessary. Yet frequently, new claims were satisfied not by a general repartitioning, but through allocation of new parcels of uncultivated communal land. In this way, the familial lots of land were often, however illegally, virtually theirs for the duration of their lives, and were even inheritable. Next to this unevenly partitioned communal land, there were still forests, marshes, fields, and uncultivated estates belonging to all the families that were utilized collectively. The unusual communistic organization based on inequality came into contradiction with new interests. With each new generation, determining the degree of relationship between each person became more difficult, the tradition of the blood lineages faded, and the inequality of the familial lots of land was increasingly felt to be an injustice by those disadvantaged by them. On the other hand, in many regions, a mixing of the population unavoidably began, whether because of the departure of a section of the family, because of war or extermination of another part of the population, or because of new settlements and the acceptance of new members. Thus, the population of the community, despite all the apparent immobility and immutability of their relations, was indeed subdivided according to the quality of the soil into fields (*wund*), and each family received a few strips of land

both in the better, irrigated fields (which were called *sholgura* from *shola*, or rice) and in the inferior fields (*lulmee*).[32] Reallotments were not periodic at first, at least before the English conquest; rather, they took place each time population growth caused a real inequality in the economic situation of the families. This was especially true in communities rich in land that had a supply of utilizable fields. In smaller communities, repartitioning occurred every ten, eight, or five years, often every year. The latter took place especially where there was a lack of good fields, making equal distribution each year to all members of the mark impossible. Therefore, only by rotating the use of the various fields could an equitable balance be achieved. Thus, the Indian tribal community ends, as it is disintegrating, by assuming the form that is historically established as the original German mark community.

With British India and Algeria,[33] we have become acquainted with two classic examples of the desperate struggle and the tragic end of the ancient communist economic organization through contact with European capitalism. The picture of the changeable fate of the mark community would not be complete if we neglected to take into consideration the remarkable example of the country where history apparently took an entirely different course. In this case, the state did not seek to destroy the communal property of the peasants through force, but on the contrary, attempted to rescue and preserve it with all the means at its disposal. This country is tsarist *Russia*.

## THE RUSSIAN VILLAGE

We do not need to concern ourselves with the enormous theoretical debate concerning the origins of the Russian peasant commune that has gone on for decades. It was in complete accord with the hostile attitude toward primitive communism among contemporary bourgeois scholarship, that the "discovery" by the Russian Professor Chicherin[34] in 1858, according to whom the agricultural commune in Russia was not an original historical product at all, but supposedly an artificial product of the fiscal politics of Tsarism, should have achieved such a favorable reception and acceptance among German scholars.[35] Chicherin, who yet again provides the proof that the liberal scholars are, as historians, for the most part much more ineffectual than their reactionary colleagues, still accepts the theory, which has already been definitively abandoned for Western Europe since Maurer, that the Russians settled in individual colonies from which the communities developed, supposedly only in the sixteenth and seventeenth centuries. Chicherin thereby derives the collective crop rotation and the imposition of plots of land from the overlapping uses of crops in the strips of land, while he views collective ownership of the land as a result of border disputes, and the public power of the mark community from the collective burden of the poll tax introduced in the sixteenth century. Thus, in a typically liberal fashion, he seems to turn all historical contexts, causes, and consequences upside down.

Whatever one thinks about the antiquity of the peasant agricultural commune or about its origins, it has, in any case, outlived the rather long history of serfdom and its dissolution, up to recent times. We will be concerned here only with its fate in the nineteenth century.

When Tsar Alexander II enacted his so-called emancipation of the peasant, the peasants' land was sold to them by the lords—following the Prussian example—whereby the lands were well indemnified by the treasury with bonds for the worst areas of the land ostensibly owned by the lords, imposing a debt in the amount of nine hundred million rubles, that was to be paid off to the treasury at a repayment rate of 6 percent within forty-nine years. This land was not, as in Prussia, assigned to individual peasant families as private property, but to whole communities as inalienable and unmortgageable communal property. The entire community took responsibility for the debt repayment together, just as they had with various taxes and dues, while individual members were exempt from the assessment of the debt. In this way, the entire massive area of the Great Russian peasant masses was organized. At the beginning of the nineties, the arrangement of the complete ownership of land in European Russia (without Poland, Finland, and the region of the Don Cossacks) was as follows: The public domains, which mostly consist of enormous forest regions in the north and desert lands, encompassed 150 million dessatines [1 dessatine = 2.69 acres]; imperial appanages, seven million; church and municipal property, less than nine million; in private ownership, ninety-three million, of which only 5 percent belong to the peasants, while the rest belongs to the aristocracy, although 131 million dessatines were the communal property of the peasantry. In Russia as late as 1900, there were 122 million hectares [1 hectare = 2.47 acres] belonging to the communal property of the peasantry and only twenty-two million that were the property of individual peasants.

Looking at the economy of the Russian peasantry in this enormous area, as it existed until recently and in part still exists today, one easily recognizes again the typical structures of the mark community, as it was commonly observed, whether in Germany or Africa, on the Ganges or in Peru. The fields were partitioned, while forests, grasslands and bodies of water formed the undivided communal lands. With the general prevalence of the primitive three-field crop rotation, summer and winter fields were divided according to soil quality into strips ("charts"), and each strip into smaller segments. The summer strips were distributed in April and the winter ones in June. With the scrupulous surveillance of equal land distribution, the diversity of land uses had become so developed that, for example, the government of Moscow found, on average, that in the summer and winter fields there were eleven strips a piece, so that each peasant had at least twenty-two scattered parcels of land to cultivate. The community usually parceled out pieces of land to be cultivated for the use of the community or laid inventory stocks aside for the same purpose, to which each individual member had to supply grain. The arrangements for the technical advancement of this economic unit were made so that each peasant family could keep their land for ten years on condition that they fertilize it, or on each field they divided parcels of land that were fertilized from the outset and only available for repartitioning every ten years. Most of the flax fields and the fruit and vegetable gardens were subject to the same rule.

The allocation of various grasslands and pastures for the community herds, the fencing of the pastures, the conservation of the fields, as well as the designation of the field system, the times for individual field work, and the date and means of repartitionings—all of this was the domain of the community, or more specifically, the village assembly. Concerning the frequency of repartitionings, there was great diversity. In a single province, for example, Saratov, nearly half of the 278 researched village communities in 1877 undertook a reallotment each year, while the other half did so every two, three, five, six, eight, and eleven years. At the same time, thirty-eight communities that universally practiced fertilization had given up repartitionings altogether.[36]

What is unique about the Russian mark community is the method of land apportionment. The principle of equal lots common among the Germans was not prevalent in the Russian case, nor was a determination based on the needs of a particular family, as in Peru. Instead, the principle of taxability was the single determining factor. The fiscal concern with taxation dominated the life of the commune after the "emancipation of the peasant," and all of the village institutions revolved around taxation. For the tsarist government, taxation was based on the so-called legally auditable souls, that is, all of the male inhabitants of the community without distinction of age, which had been determined every twenty years, ever since the first peasant census under Peter the Great, by the famous "audits" that were the terror of the Russian people and tore whole communities apart.[37]

The government taxed the villages based on the number of audited "souls." Yet the commune assessed the lump sum of taxes they were liable for onto the farms according to the number of laborers. The taxability of the farms determined how each portion of land was measured. The land allotment thus appeared in Russia not as the source of nourishment for the peasants, but as the source of taxation. It was not a benefit to which each farm was entitled, but an obligation imposed on every member of the community as a service to society. For this reason, there was nothing more original than a Russian village assembly, in which the land partitioning took place. Everywhere one could hear protests against parcels of land that had been too generously allotted. Poor families without any real laborers and with predominantly women or minors as their members were completely spared with a pardon from taking on an allotment, while wealthy peasants were forced by the masses of poorer peasants to take on the larger allotments. The tax burden at the center of Russian village life is also enormous. On top of the debt repayments, there were also poll taxes, a village tax, the church tax, the salt tax, etc. In the eighties, the poll tax and the salt tax were abolished, yet the tax burden remained so enormous that it devoured all of the peasantry's economic resources. According to a statistic from the nineties, 70 percent of the peasantry eked out less than a minimum existence from their land allotments, 20 percent were able to feed themselves, but not to keep livestock, and only 9 percent had a surplus above their own needs that could be taken to market. Thus, a frequent occurrence of the Russian village immediately after the "emancipation of the peasant" was tax arrearage. Already in the seventies, an average yearly output of fifty million rubles for the poll tax was accompanied by an annual deficit of eleven million rubles in taxes. Once the poll tax was lifted, the poverty of the Russian village continued to grow, due to the simultaneous escalation of indirect taxation from the eighties onward. In 1904, the tax arrears amounted to 127 million rubles, a debt that was almost completely cancelled because collecting it had become totally impossible and because of the general revolutionary ferment. The taxes not only ate up all of the peasants' income, they also forced them to seek side occupations. One of these was seasonal farm labor, which brought about whole migrations of peoples into the interior of Russia. As a result, the strongest male villagers migrated to the large manorial estates in order to be hired on as a day laborers, while their own fields back home were left in the weaker hands of older, female, and half-grown workers. The beckoning of the city offered another possibility, namely, the manufacturing industries. In the central industrial region, therefore, this class of temporary workers migrated to the city only for the winter, mostly to textile factories, in order to return to their village in the spring with their earnings to work in the fields. Finally, in many regions, there was industrial homework or occasional agricultural work on the side, such as transport or chopping wood. And with all of this, the large majority of the peasant masses could hardly support themselves. Not only were all of the fruits of the farm eaten up by taxation, but their extra earnings as well. The mark community, which was collectively liable for the taxes, was equipped with strong means of enforcement vis-à-vis its members. They could rent out those whose taxes were in arrears to the outside for wage labor and requisition their earned income. They issued and denied internal passports to their members, without which a peasant was unable to leave the village. Finally, they had the legal right to enact corporal punishment upon those whose taxes were intractably in arrears. Periodically, this made the Russian village in the enormous stretches of the Russian interior a horrific sight. Upon the arrival of the tax collectors, a procedure began for which tsarist Russia coined the term "flogging out those in arrears." As the entire village assembly came together, the "evaders" had to take off their trousers and lay themselves down on a bench, whereupon they were brutally whipped by their fellow mark members, one after the other, with a stroke of the birch. The moaning and weeping of those being thrashed—most often male heads of household or even white-haired old men—accompanied the higher authorities, who, after they had completed their task with the ringing of bells, went off in their troikas to hunt down another community and proceed to carry out the same punishments. It was not uncommon for a peasant to spare himself this public punishment by committing suicide. Another unique product of those circumstances was the "tax beggar," an impoverished old peasant who took to begging as a tramp in order to cobble together the taxes due and bring them back to the village. The state watched over the mark community, which had been turned into a tax machine, with severity and persistence. The law of 1881 decreed, for example, that the community could only sell agricultural land if two-thirds of the peasants made that decision, after which it was still necessary to get the consent of the Ministry of the Interior, the Ministry of Finance, and the Ministry of Crown Lands. Individual peasants were allowed to sell their inherited lands only to other members of the mark community. Taking on a mortgage was forbidden. Under Alexander III, the village community was robbed of all autonomy and was placed under the thumb of the "Land Captains," an institution similar to that of the Prussian district administrators. Decisions made by the village assem-

bly required the consent of these officials; repartitionings of land were undertaken under their supervision, as well as tax assessment and debt collection.
The law of 1893 made a partial concession to time pressures by declaring
repartitionings permissible every twelve years. Yet, at the same time, with-
drawing from the mark community required the consent of the community
and took place only under the condition that the person involved contributed the entire sum of his individual portion of the repayment debt.

Despite all of these artificial legal binds that squeezed the village community, despite the guardianship of three ministries and a swarm of *chinovniks*
[petty officials], the dissolution of the mark community could no longer be
prevented. There was the crushing tax burden; the deterioration of the farming economy in the wake of peasants earning extra wages in agricultural and
industrial work on the side; a shortage of land, especially pasture and forest
land, which had already been grabbed by the aristocracy during the displacement of the peasantry, and a shortage of arable fields due to increasing population. All of this resulted in two critical events: the escape to the city and the
rise of usury within the village. To the extent that a tract of land, along with
work on the side in industry or elsewhere, increasingly served only to alleviate a tax burden, without ever providing a subsistence, membership in the
mark community became like an iron chain of hunger on the necks of the
peasants. The natural desire of the poorer members of the community
became escape from this chain. Hundreds of fugitives were sent back by the
police as undocumented vagabonds to their communities and were then
made an example of by their mark comrades by being beaten on a bench with
rods. But the rods and the enforcement of passport controls proved themselves to be powerless against the mass flight of the peasants, who wanted to
flee the hell of their "village communism" by night and fog into the city, to
plunge themselves into the sea of the industrial proletariat. Others, for whom
family bonds or other circumstances made escape inadvisable, sought by a
legal path to accomplish their exit from the agricultural commune. For this to
occur, they had to contribute their share of the debt repayment and here,
they were assisted—by usurers. Early on, both the tax burden alone and the
forced sale of grain on the most unacceptable terms in order to repay these
debts exposed the Russian peasant to the usurers. Every emergency, every
bad crop made turning to the usurers unavoidable. And ultimately, emancipation from under the yoke of the community was unattainable for most
unless they put themselves again under the yoke of the usurer, to whom they
made themselves indebted, and whom they would have to serve and pay dues

to for an incalculable length of time. While the impoverished peasants sought to flee the mark community in order to free themselves from misery, many wealthy peasants turned their backs on it and in many cases they stepped out of the commune in order to escape the communal tax burden of the poorer ones. Although the official departure of the wealthy peasants abated, these individuals, who were in large part also the village usurers, formed into a ruling power over the peasant masses, and knew how to extract convenient resolutions for themselves from the indebted, dependent majority. Thus, in the heart of a village community officially based on equality and communal property, grew a clear division of classes into a small but influential village bourgeoisie and a mass of dependent and effectively proletarianized peasants. The internal breakup of the village commune—crushed by taxes, eaten by usurers, and internally divided—eventually made waves on the outside: famine and peasant revolts were frequent occurrences in Russia in the eighties. The internal government went after them with the same implacability as the tax executors and the military showed when coming after them to "pacify" the village. In many regions, Russian fields became the scene of horrific death by starvation and bloody turmoil. The Russian *muzhik* [peasant] experiences the fate of the Indian peasant and Orissa[38] is in this case Saratov, Samara, and so on down the Volga.[39] When the revolution of the urban proletariat finally broke out in Russia in 1904 and 1905, the peasant insurrections, which had been chaotic up to that point, became a political factor by their sheer weight, tipping the scales of revolution and making the agricultural question a central issue. Now, as the peasants, like an irresistible flood, flowed over the aristocratic estates and set the "aristocratic nests" on fire with their cry for land, and as the workers' party formulated the distress of the peasantry into a revolutionary demand to expropriate state property and the landed estates without compensation and to place them into the hands of the peasants, Tsarism finally retreated from the centuries-old agrarian policies that it had pursued with an iron persistence. The mark community could no longer be resuscitated; it had to be abandoned. Already in 1902, the very roots of the village community in its specific Russian incarnation got the axe: The collective liability for taxes was abolished. Of course, this measure was actively prepared by the financial policies of Tsarism itself. The treasury could easily forgo the collective liability when it came to direct taxation, with the indirect taxation having reached such a level that, for example, in the budget of 1906, with a total revenue of 2,030 million rubles, only 148 million came from direct taxes and 1,100 million from indirect taxes, among which

558 million came from the spirits monopoly alone, a tax that was implemented by the "liberal" minister, Count Witte,[40] to combat drunkenness. The
poverty, hopelessness, and ignorance of the peasants contributed to the time-
ly establishment of *this* tax, the most reliable form of collective liability. In
1905 and 1906, the remaining amount of the debt for the repayment for emancipation was halved, and was canceled in 1907. And then the "Agrarian
Reform" implemented in 1907 publicly set itself the task of creating peasant
private property. The means for this would come from the parceling of
domains, appanages, and, in part, landed estates. Thus, the proletarian revolution of the twentieth century, even in its first, incomplete phase, had already
destroyed, at the same time, the last remainders of bondage and the mark
community, which had been artificially preserved by Tsarism.

### THE DISSOLUTION OF PRIMITIVE COMMUNISM
### AS A GENERAL PHENOMENON

With the Russian village commune, the varied fate of primitive agrarian communism comes to an end; the circle is closed. Beginning as a natural product
of social development, as the best guarantee of economic progress, and of the
material and intellectual flourishing of society, the mark community ends
here as an abused tool of political and economic backwardness. The Russian
peasant, who is beaten with rods by his fellow community members in the
service of tsarist absolutism, offers the most horrific historical critique of the
limits of primitive communism and the most evident expression of the fact
that even this social form is subject to the dialectical law: reason becomes
irrationality; benefit becomes scourge.

Two facts spring to mind when one contemplates closely the fate of the
mark community in various lands and parts of the earth. Far from being a rigid,
unchangeable pattern, this highest and last form of the primitive communist
economic system displays above all endless diversity, flexibility and adaptability, as seen in its various forms. In so doing, it undergoes a quiet transformation
process in each context and under all circumstances, which, because of its slow
pace, may hardly be apparent at first from the outside. Inside the society, however, new forms are replacing old ones and thus it survives under each political
superstructure of native or foreign institutions, and within economic and social
life, it is constantly developing and decaying, advancing and declining.

At the same time, this social form shows an extraordinary tenacity and
stability, precisely because of its elasticity and adaptability. It defies all the

storms of political history; or rather it tolerates them passively, lets them pass and patiently endures for centuries the strains of every form of conquest, foreign rule, despotism, and exploitation. There is only one contact that it cannot tolerate or overcome; this is the contact with European civilization, i.e. with capitalism. For the old society, this encounter is deadly, universally and without exception, and it accomplishes what centuries and the most savage Oriental conquerors could not: the dissolution of the whole social structure from the inside, tearing apart all traditional bonds and transforming the society in a short period of time into a shapeless pile of rubble.

But this whiff of death from European capitalism is simply the last and not the sole factor that brings about the inevitable decline of primitive society. The seeds of this lay inside the society itself. If we take the various means of its decline together, those that we know from various examples, this establishes a certain historical order of succession. Communist ownership of the means of production afforded, as the basis of a rigorously organized economy, the most productive social labor process and the best material assurance of its continuity and development for many epochs. But even the progress in labor productivity secured by it, albeit slowly, necessarily falls into conflict with the communistic organization over time. After the decisive progress—to a higher form of agriculture, or to the use of the ploughshare—had been accomplished and the mark community had retained its solid form on this basis, the next step in the development of the technology of production after a certain amount of time necessitates a *more intensive* land cultivation that for its part could only be achieved at that stage of agricultural technology by more intensive smallholding and by a stronger, closer relationship of the individual laborer to the soil. Longer use of the same parcel of land by a single peasant family became the precondition of the more careful treatment of this land. Fertilization of the soil became, in Germany, and concurrently in Russia, the reason behind the gradual abandonment of land repartitionings. In general, we can identify a trait that is constant everywhere in the life of the mark community: the movement toward increasingly larger intervals of time between land reallotments, which sooner or later leads universally to a transition from allotted land to inherited land. In the same way that the transformation of communal property into private property keeps pace with the intensification of labor, one can trace the fact that forest and pasture lands remained communal the longest, while the intensively worked farmland led first to the partitioned mark and then to hereditary property. By attaching private property to parcels of arable land, one does not unmake the entire communal economic organization, since it continues to be upheld by the diverse composition of the fields and enforced by the communal forest and grazing lands. The economic and social equality at the heart of ancient society are still not destroyed by it either. It initially forms only a single mass of peasants, equal in their living conditions, who generally can work and live according to these old traditions for centuries. Yet the gates have indeed already been opened to future inequality by the inheritability of property, and then especially by the purchasability and the universal salability of the peasant properties.

The very burying of the traditional social organization by the process referred to above proceeds extremely slowly. There are other historical factors at work, which take care of this job more quickly and thoroughly, and these are the comprehensive public works projects, which the mark community is not able to cope with by its very nature due to its narrow limits. We have already seen the critical importance that artificial irrigation had for the agriculture of the Orient. This greater intensification of labor and powerful rise in productivity led to quite different, wide-ranging results such as the changeover to fertilization in the West. From the outset, the carrying out of artificial irrigation is, in large measure, intended for a large-scale enterprise. Because of this, there is no suitable institution within the organization of the mark community and thus special institutions had to be created above the mark community. We know that the direction of the public water works was at the root of the domination by the priests and every Oriental ruler. But also in the West, and more generally, there are various public affairs that, although simple in comparison to contemporary state organization, nevertheless had to be dealt with in every primitive society. These affairs of state grew with the development and progress of the society, therefore eventually requiring special organizations. Everywhere in Germany and Peru, in India and Algeria—we can define the path of development as the tendency in primitive societies to transform elected public offices to inherited ones. Yet, initially, this turnaround, proceeding slowly and intangibly, is still not a break with the foundations of communistic society. Rather, the inheritability of these public offices is a natural result of the fact that here too, as is in the nature of primitive societies, tradition and personal, collective experience ensure the successful handling of this office. With time, the inheritability of the offices has to lead unavoidably to the creation of a small, indigenous aristocracy, whose rulers are composed of servants to the community. The undivided mark estates, the *ager publicus* of the Romans, served as the economic basis of advancing the status of this aristocracy, to which power swung. Theft of the undemarcated or unused lands of the mark is the common method of all indigenous and foreign rulers, who vault themselves above the peasant masses and subjugate them politically. If it concerns a people that is cut off from the major centers of civilization, the aristocracy may not distinguish itself greatly in their lifestyle from that of the masses, and it may take part directly in the production process while a certain democratic and customary simplicity may cover up differences in wealth. This is true with the tribal aristocracy of the Yakut people, which is merely endowed with more livestock than the masses and more influence in public affairs. If an encounter with more civilized peoples and active trade is added, then the need for refined goods and the relief from labor are added to the privileges of the aristocracy, and a true status differentiation takes place in society. The most typical example is Greece in the post-Homeric period.

Thus, the division of labor in the heart of the primitive society unavoidably leads, sooner or later, to the breakup of political and economic equality from inside. One public enterprise, however, plays an important role in this process and accomplishes the work more aggressively than the public offices of a peaceful nature. This is warfare. It is first a matter of the masses of society, and then, in the wake of the advances in production, it is turned into the specialty of certain circles within primitive society. The more advanced, continuous and systematic the labor process of the society, the less it tolerates the irregularities and the drain of time and energy resulting from war. If occasional military campaigns are the direct result of the economic system of hunting and nomadic herding, then agriculture is connected to a great peacefulness and passivity among the masses of society. Because of this, a special caste of warriors is often needed for protection. In one way or another, the existence of war, itself just an expression of the limits of labor productivity, plays an important role for all primitive peoples and universally leads over time to a new form of the division of labor. The segregation of a military aristocracy or a military leadership is the most difficult blow that the social equality of the primitive society must endure. Thus, it happens that wherever we learn of primitive societies, whether still existing today or transmitted to us through history, we almost never come across those free and equal relations any longer, such as Morgan was able to convey to us with the serendipitous example of the Iroquois. To the contrary, universal inequality and exploitation are the characteristics of all primitive societies, as they cross our paths as the product of a long history of disintegration, whether it pertains to the ruling castes of the Orient, or to the tribal aristocracy of the Yakuts, to the "Great Clansmen" of the Scottish Celts or to the military aristocracy of the Greeks, Romans, and the migrating Germans, or lastly, to the small despots of the African empires.

## SOUTHERN AFRICA

If we look, for example, at the famous Empire of Mwata Kazembe in South Central Africa, to the east of the Lunda Empire,[41] and into which the Portuguese penetrated at the beginning of the nineteenth century, we can see, right in the heart of Africa, in a region hardly touched by Europeans, primitive Negro social relations in which there is not much equality or freedom to be found. The 1831 expedition of Major Monteiro and Captain Gamitto, undertaken from the Zambezi into the interior for scientific and trading purposes, gives us the following portrait: Initially, the expedition came into the land of the Malawi, who were primitive hoe farmers and lived in small, conical palisade houses and wore only a loincloth on their bodies. At the time that Monteiro and Gamitto traveled through Malawiland, it was under the rule of a despotic leader who went by the title *Nede*. He adjudicated all disputes in his capital city, Muzenda, and disputing his decision was not allowed. True to form, he convened a council of elders who were required, however, to agree with his opinion. The land fell into provinces, which were governed by *Mambos*, and these were then further divided into districts that were led by *Funos*. All of these titles were hereditary.

> On the eighth of August we reached the residence of Mukanda, the powerful leader of the Chewa.[42] Mukanda, who had been sent a gift of various cotton goods, a red cloth, various pearls, salt, and cowries, came on the following day, riding on a black person into the encampment. Mukanda was a man sixty or seventy years old, with a pleasant, majestic appearance. His only garment consisted of a dirty cloth that he had wrapped around his hips. He stayed for about two hours and when he was leaving, asked everyone in a friendly and irresistible manner for a gift. . . . The burial of the Chewa leaders is accompanied by extremely barbaric ceremonies. All of the wives of the recently departed are locked up with the corpse in the same hut until everything is ready for the burial. Then the funeral cortege moves. . . . toward the crypt, and once it arrives, the favorite wife of the deceased, along with some others, climb into the crypt and sit down with their legs outstretched. This living foundation is then covered with draping and the cadaver is then laid on top of them, along with six other women who are thrown into the crypt after having their necks broken. Once the grave is covered, the shuddering ceremony ends with the impaling of two male youths, who are arranged atop the grave, one at the head with a drum, the other at the feet with a bow and arrow. Major Monteiro, during his stay in Chewaland, was a witness to one such burial." From here they went uphill into the middle of the empire. The Portuguese came "to a barren region, situated up high and almost

entirely lacking in foodstuffs. Everywhere one sees the signs of destruction by previous military campaigns, and famine plagued the expedition to a disturbing degree.
Messengers were sent with a few gifts to the next *Mambo*, in order to get leaders, but
those who were sent returned with the dispiriting news that they had encountered
the *Mambo* next to his family, close to starvation and death, completely alone in the
village. . . . Even before one reached the heart of the empire, one got samples of the
barbarian justice that was part of everyday life there. One frequently encountered
young people whose noses, hands, ears and other appendages had been cut off as
punishment for some minor offense. On the nineteenth of November we entered the
capital city, where the ass that Captain Gamitto was riding caused a stir. Soon we
arrived at a road about forty-five miles long that was fenced in on both sides by two
to three meter-high fences made of interwoven poles so elaborately constructed that
they looked like walls. In these straw walls there were small open doors spaced apart
from each other. At the end of the road, there is a small square barracks that is only
open to the west, and in the middle of which stands a human figure, crudely carved
out of wood, seventy centimeters tall, on a wooden pedestal. In front of the open
side lay a heap of more than three hundred skulls. Here, the road turns into a large
square area, at the end of which is a large forest that is only separated from the
square by a fence. On the outside of it, on both sides of the gate, is a line tied on
either side of the gate with thirty skulls strung onto it for ornamentation. . . . Following this was the reception at Mwata's with all of the barbarian pageantry and surrounded by his army of between five thousand and six thousand men. He sat on a
chair covered by a green cloth spread over a pile of leopard and lion skins. His head
covering consisted of a scarlet conical cap, which was composed of half-meter long
feathers. Wrapped around his forehead was a diadem made of glimmering stone; his
neck and shoulders were covered by a kind of necklace made of shells, square pieces
of mirror, and *faux* gems. Each arm had a piece of blue cloth wrapped around it,
decorated with fur, and the forearms also had ornamental strings made of blue
stones. A yellow, red, and blue-fringed cloth that was held together by a belt covered
the lower body. The legs, like the arms, were decorated with blue jewels.

Mwata proudly sat there with seven parasols protecting him from the sun and
swung around the tail of a wildebeest for a scepter, while twelve Negroes armed
with brooms were busy removing every piece of dust on the ground, every impurity
from his holy vicinity. A rather complicated court life developed around the rulers.
First, guarding his throne were two rows of figures, forty centimeters high, in the
shape of the upper body of a Negro adorned with animal horns and between these
figures sat two Negroes who burned aromatic leaves in coal pans. The place of
honor was occupied by the two main wives, with the first one dressed more or less

like Mwata. In the background, the harem of four hundred women was deployed, and indeed these women, apart from the aprons on their lower bodies, were completely naked. In addition, there were two hundred black women who stood waiting for the slightest command. Inside the quadrangle built by women sat the highest dignitaries of the kingdom, the *Kilolo*, sitting on lion and leopard skins, each with an umbrella and dressed similarly to Mwata. There were also several corps of musicians, who made a deafening noise with their strangely shaped instruments, while a few court jesters, dressed in animal pelts and horns, ran around completing the entourage of the Kazembe who, armed in this dignified manner, awaited the Portuguese advance. Mwata is the absolute ruler of this people, his title meaning simply "Lord". Underneath him are the Kilolo, or the aristocrats, who are in turn divided into two classes. Among the more noble aristocrats are the crown prince, Mwata's closest relatives, and the high commanders of his army. But the very lives and property of these nobles are only possible because of Mwata's absolute power.

If this tyrant is in a bad mood, he will have a person's ears cut off if he does not understand a command and asks for it to be repeated, "in order to teach him to listen more carefully." Every theft in his kingdom is punished by the amputation of the ears and hands; whoever gets together with one of his women or attempts to talk to her is killed or has all his limbs hobbled. The reputation he has among his superstitious people is that one cannot touch him without falling prey to his magical powers. Since it is impossible to avoid all contact with him, the people have discovered a means to avoid death. Whoever touches the lord, kneels down before him, and the lord lays the palm of his hand in a mysterious manner onto the one kneeling and thereby absolves him from the death curse.[43]

This is a picture of a society that has moved a long way away from the original foundations of every primitive community, from equality and democracy. It should not, however, be a foregone conclusion that under this kind of political despotism, the relations of the mark community, the communal ownership of the land and soil, and communally organized labor, ceased to exist. As for the Portuguese, who are able to record exactly the superficial rubbish such as costume and courtesans, when it comes to things that run counter to the European system of private ownership, they have, just as all Europeans, no eyes, no interest, no frame of reference. In any case, the social inequality and the despotism of primitive societies are completely distinct from the inequality common in civilized societies, which transplanted itself onto the primitive. The increase in status of the primitive aristocracy and the despotic power of the primitive leader are all natural products of the society, like all of its other necessities of life. They are only another expression for the helplessness of the society with respect to its natural surroundings and to its own social relations, a helplessness that appears both in the magical practices of the cult and in the periodic famines that either partly or completely starve the despotic leader along with the masses of his subjects. This rule by an aristocracy and a leader is therefore in complete harmony with the other material and intellectual aspects of the society, and it becomes visible in the significant fact that the political power of the primitive ruler is always closely bound up with the primitive nature religion, with the cult of the dead, and is sustained by it.

From this standpoint, Mwata Kazembe is the Lunda whom fourteen wives would follow into the grave alive and who rules over the death and life of his subjects according to his erratic moods, because he believes himself to be, and his people hold the rock solid conviction that he is, a magician. The despotic "Prince Kasongo" on the Lomami River who, forty years later, with great dignity among his noblemen and his people, presented a dance with his two naked daughters to the Englishman Cameron in a woman's skirt braided by monkey skins and a filthy handkerchief on his head, which consisted of him hopping up and down as a form of greeting, is in fact a much less absurd and insanely comical phenomenon than the rule of a person "by the grace of God" over sixty-seven million members of a people who produced the likes of Kant, Helmholtz, and Goethe. And yet even the worst enemy of this ruler could not call him a magician.

Primitive communist society, through its own internal development, leads to the formation of inequality and despotism. It has not yet disappeared; on the contrary, it can persist for many thousands of years under these tribal conditions. Such societies, however, sooner or later succumb to a foreign occupation and then undergo a more or less wide-ranging social reorganization. Foreign rule by Muslims is a foreign rule of special historical significance, because it predated European rule in vast stretches of Asia and Africa. Everywhere that nomadic Mohammedan peoples—whether Mongol or Arab—instituted and secured their foreign rule, a social process began that Henry Maine[44] and Maxim Kovalevsky called the *feudalization of the land*. They did not make the land their own property, but instead turned their attention to two objectives, the institution of taxes and the military consolidation of their domination of the country. Both goals served a specific administrative-military organization, under which the land was divided into several ethnic groups and given as a kind of fiefdom to Muslim officials, who were also tax collectors and military administrators. Large portions of uncultivated mark lands were utilized for the founding of military colonies. These institutions, together with the spread of Islam, implemented a profound change in the general conditions of existence of primitive societies. Their economic conditions alone were little changed. The foundations and the organization of production remained the same and persisted for many centuries, despite exploitation and military pressure. Of course, Muslim rule was not universally so considerate of the living conditions of the natives. For example, the Arabs on the eastern coast of Africa operated for centuries from the Zanzibar Sultanate an extensive slave trade in Negroes, which led to frequent slave hunts in the interior of Africa, to the depopulation and destruction of whole African villages, and to the escalation of despotic violence by the native leaders, who found an enticing business venture in the sale of their own subjects or the subjugated members of their neighboring tribes. This transformation in conditions was the most profound for the fate of African society, until the still greater consequences of European influence took place: This slave trade in Negroes came to pass only after the discoveries and conquests of the Europeans in the sixteenth century, in order to service the plantations and all the mines exploited by the Europeans that were in full bloom in Asia and America.

The intrusion of European civilization was a disaster in every sense for primitive social relations. The European conquerors are the first who are not merely after subjugation and economic exploitation, but the means of production itself, by ripping the land from underneath the feet of the native population. In this way, European capitalism deprives the primitive social order of its foundation. What emerges is something that is worse than all oppression and exploitation, total anarchy and a specifically European phenomenon, the uncertainty of social existence. The subjugated peoples, separated from their means of production, are regarded by European capitalism as mere laborers, and when they are useful for this end, they are made into slaves, and if they are not, they are exterminated. We have witnessed this method in the Spanish, English, and French colonies. Before the advance of capitalism, the primitive social order, which outlasted all previous historical phases, capitulates. Its last remnants are eradicated from the earth and its elements—labor power and means of production—are absorbed by capitalism. The early communist society thus fell everywhere—primarily because it was made obsolete by economic progress—in order to make room for prospects for development. This development and this progress shall, in the long run, be represented by the base methods of a class society, until this too will be made obsolete and be pushed aside by further progress. Here too, violence will be the mere servant of economic development.

# 3 — Slavery

EDITORS' NOTE: This text, written sometime after 1907 for Luxemburg's cours-
es at the Social Democratic Party School in Berlin, was locked away in the Russian
regime's archives until the 1990s. It is part of a large group of hitherto unknown
texts by Luxemburg that have recently come to light. It was published for the first
time in the 2002 issue of the *Jahrbuch für Historische Kommunismusforschung* by
the noted Luxemburg scholar Narihiko Ito, who also provided a lengthy introduction. In Ito's edition, which we have followed, long ellipses, e.g. "....." indicate
illegible passages in the surviving copy of the typescript; editors' clarifications are in
square brackets. The translators, Ashley Passmore and Kevin B. Anderson, have
attempted to preserve the sometimes unpolished language of the original. The
second half of the text, on Roman slavery, has not been included here.

The tendency of the mark community is to disintegrate and to make room for
new relations, though always according to milieu or to other conditions and
consequences.

The oldest form to establish itself after the mark, to a greater or lesser
extent in the ancient world, is slavery, the oldest form of class domination and
economic exploitation.

*Engels* says in his *Anti-Dühring* (pp. 162–195 [MECW 25, pp. 146–71])
that after the emergence of private property, the opportunity to employ foreign labor arose. But war supplied them; prisoners of war who were, until
this period, slain, and even earlier, eaten, were now used as laborers. (See
*Anti-Dühring*, pp. 188–89 [MECW 25, pp. 168–69]).

This explanation cannot, strictly speaking, satisfy us.

We are far too inadequately informed about the facts of the slave economy
and its origins. Even until recently there have been disagreements among the
bourgeois researchers about the meaning and the extent of slavery and the
ways it emerged. We are more or less dependent on hypotheses.

It is necessary that one trace out the manner in which slavery emerged out
of the mark and the gentile constitution. If we search for the point after which

we see the mark and the gens exhibiting the oldest forms of exploitation and servitude, we will not immediately encounter slavery, but other forms, which might lead to slavery.

Unlike Engels, we do not need to place exploitation after the emergence of private property. The mark itself allows for exploitation and servitude. The grafting of a foreign mark onto another allows for and creates a relationship of exploitation and servitude *toward the outside*. (In fact, the mark ensured communism internally, but not externally.) An example of this is the *Inca Empire*. Moreover, the Inca Empire teaches us something else: although the conquerors, the Incas, themselves lived together in municipalities, we find in their case four ruling lineages, whose representatives governed the four provinces into which the country was divided. The Incas also had a standing army, necessary for maintaining domination. Thus, there was already a certain aristocracy within the mark. How did this develop?

The four lineages would have taken control of the conquest. These four houses would have probably held an even greater position had the Spanish conquest not put an end to this process.

Similar examples that correspond . . . . . . the mark, there are many. E.g., the oldest historical reference from the island of Crete is that it was conquered by the Dorians. The Dorians were one of the main tribes of Greece. The conquest took place in prehistoric times. We do not know who lived on Crete. The conquered people on Crete must have handed over the yields from their crops, excluding the necessary sustenance for themselves and their families, to the conquerors. From these contributions from the subjugated people of Crete, the costs of the common meals of the free people were determined. This is due to the fact that the Dorians lived under communism. An example that the mark was compatible with the exploitation of other marks. The land continued to belong to the Cretan population; they only had to be able to afford the dues. (The Greek legend of the Minotaur that ate young boys and virgins can be explained by the fact that the subjugated had to hand over their young boys and virgins to the conquerors, similar to the Quechua tribes in the Inca Empire.)

Similar relationships existed elsewhere in Greece.

In Thessaly, the early inhabitants, who lived there before the Greeks, were conquered by the Aeolians and forced to become tenant farmers. They had a name that meant "poor people." Originally, this was one of their folk names.

The . . . . . . are from . . . . . . wandered to Asia Minor, conquered Bithynia and similarly subjugated the people living there and subjected them to taxes.

The most interesting and fruitful example is *Sparta* itself. In Sparta, we still find a strong tradition of gentile law. The Spartans used the peasant population of the helots as state slaves. They were handed over by the state, that is, by the mark community, to individuals. The individuals were not allowed, however, to kill or sell them to the outside, because the slaves remained communal property. The helots supplied the landless among the Spartans and had to relinquish a certain portion of their yields. Whatever they obtained beyond this amount belonged to them. The land still belonged to the Spartans. It was taken from them by the Spartans, so that they now worked on a foreign land that had previously belonged to them. They also had military obligations.

The Spartans also married the helots. The children of these marriages were, if they were raised as Spartans, not only free, but also citizens. For that reason, their education determined their fate. They were called *mothaken*: half-breeds.

Aside from the Spartans and the helots, there was another population, that of the *Periokoi*, e.g.: those that lived around the city (thus the word periphery). The *Periokoi* had no political rights, but were personally free.

The Spartans continued to live in the gens. Marriage was forbidden within the gens; the gentile law of inheritance was in effect, and thus the wealth remained in the gens. Marriage within the gens was only allowed to heiresses, in order that the wealth remain in the gens. From the dues of the helots, the Spartans ran a communist economic organization. Bourgeois historians construe the communist meals in Sparta as militaristic club feasts.

## WHAT IS THE DIFFERENCE BETWEEN CRETE AND SPARTA?

In Crete, the land remained the property of the inhabitants, even after the conquest by the Dorians, who only demanded dues from the subjugated.

In Sparta, the Spartans took the land from the helots and the helots were forced to work this land for the Spartans. The helots could therefore subsist only if they fed both themselves and their masters. They were dominated completely by the mark community of the Spartans and were assigned to individuals, that is, treated like objects. They therefore worked as labor power on foreign soil. They have no social cohesion of their own anymore; they are integrated into the mark of the Spartans. But they are not an active part of the mark of the Spartans, only the labor power for their subjugators. They have no more land, which was the basis of their social cohesion. They can only become Spartans if they are children of Spartans and helots, and if they are in such a way raised as Spartans; apart from this, they can only become fully entitled members of the Spartan mark through distinction in military service. Thus they are already slaves; they live in a *class state*.

If we compare the Peruvians, Crete, and Sparta, we would have to locate the Peruvian and the Cretan forms as the older forms and the Spartan as the newer one. In Peru and Crete, the subjugated are not yet slaves. They are members of the mark as before. There is no class domination, no class society in effect here. A class society is the grouping of classes *within* a given society. In Peru and Crete, it is a matter of the exploitation of *one society* by *another society*.

However, the helots form *a social bond* with the Spartans. Therefore, they live in a class society.

Slavery accelerates the dissolution of the communist association and goes hand in hand with the rise of private property. This stands in contrast to Engels, who saw slavery as arising only *after* the introduction of private property.

Slavery appeared naturally in several phases, depending on the level of development of the specific society.

The first beginning of slavery is a kind of tenant relationship. Communism is carried over, except that certain dues have to be paid. This has a corrosive effect on the conquered, as well as the conquerors. In a later stage, the land is taken from the conquered and already slavery has arrived. But the conquered are still being exploited communistically. Then the disintegration of communism. The rise of private property. Thereby the slaves also become private property. While before the slaves were not to be killed or sold, because they were communal property, once private property arose, the individual could do with the slave what he wanted.

The exploitation of a mark by another has a corrosive effect on the exploited mark, something we see already with the Incas. The disintegrative process is accelerated. First the conquest occurs and then a reconfiguration of the organization takes place. In order to fortify this, a specific class develops, the military, and thus inequality in the mark. Domination from above evolves faster when conquests and wars occur.

### THE DEVELOPMENT OF SLAVERY AMONG THE GREEKS

At the moment the Greeks enter history, their situation is that of a disintegrated gens. Though there are strong vestiges of the gentile law remaining, nevertheless there already exists a *rural system of private property* and the free right to dispose of that land. The peasantry is already in a state of deep indebtedness. Along with them, there is an *aristocracy*. Its representatives can already be found in the gentile constitution. The aristocrats are the descendants of the public officeholders in the gentile constitution: chiefs of the mark, herdsmen, etc. In the mark, they generally come from the undivided mark and over time, they confiscate more and more from it. In this way, they obtain greater assets and with the advent of hereditary power, they develop more and more into a mass that is supported by the peasantry. In this way, a minor aristocracy develops, one that already possesses privileges and goods. The earliest members of the mark are already the indebted peasants, who have to pay dues to the aristocracy.

*These relationships were strongly influenced by the culture of the Orient*, which was older and more prosperous. In order to be able to understand all the events of the ancient world in Greece and Rome, the influence of the Orient must, generally speaking, be taken into account, such as in the Near East, Assyria, Babylonia, Egypt, and Phoenicia. Historians and scholars of prehistory place great emphasis on the influence of the Near East. In particular, the Oriental technologies of war were especially influential. The Greek war chariot originated in the Near East.

*Exchange of goods with the Orient was critical.* Luxury items were exchanged for the refinement of their way of life. The reason for the exchange was in order to get their hands on these items. Since in the old empires, there was as yet no strong differentiation among the classes; the upper strata lived quite luxuriously. Already in the ninth, tenth centuries before Christ, there existed a strong disintegration within the society.

Exchange with the Orient led to two things:

1. provided an incentive to the aristocracy to have *various products manufactured*, which could be exchanged for luxury items from the Orient. Among these items were oil, wine, and metals.

2. spread, in association with exchange, a *monetary economy* in place of the earlier natural economy, since metal as a means of exchange comes from the Orient. In a natural economy, all products are produced only for subsistence and in fact mainly by the people who themselves consume, sell, or exchange them. The leader of the mark receives foodstuffs as income. Yet, once the leaders become an aristocracy and the monetary economy is in place, the public dues had to be paid in money and in kind. This creates a situation wherein the peasantry falls increasingly into debt [to] the large landowners.

In Homer's time, around the same time as the great migration of the Germanic peoples, raising livestock prevailed over agriculture, which was [already] important in this period. At this time, *the aristocracy* themselves took part in production, which ended after Homer. The aristocracy positioned the fighters; *it had trade with the Orient in its hands.* This can also be deduced from the mark itself. The mark itself engaged in trade, but with the outside, not within its own borders. The mark as a *whole* was engaged in trade. Since the mark as such could not carry on trade, it came about that the natural or customary public officials became, at the same time, the natural public organs of trade. And it is from these public officials that the aristocracy was later derived.

As seats for the reigning military aristocracy, there were castles that served as permanent constructions of militarism. *Building the castles was a form of compulsory labor for the surrounding peasantry.* The more hereditary the mark's earlier leadership positions became, the greater the dues paid by the peasants. Instead of money, the only thing they could afford was compulsory labor. It was *compulsory labor* for them, because the peasants no longer paid their dues to an *elected* organization. An historically handed down inverted relationship from the past.

The refinement of the lives of the aristocracy led to an increasing division between them and the peasantry. It developed into, on the one hand, the mass of peasants, who bore the brunt of the work, and on the other hand, the small body of aristocratic families, who saw as their only occupations the conduct of war and trade, with the latter helping to enhance their way of life. *Eventually, the aristocracy ceased to participate in the production process.* This increased their standard of living even more. This increase resulted in an even greater trade, and in order to support it, production had to be adapted for trade.

*Passive trade gave way to active trade.* That is, while the aristocracy originally needed surplus for trade, it later had goods manufactured for the sole purpose of exchange: oil, wine, and metals. These items were exchanged for fine linen, perfumes, purple robes, etc. With increasing trade came a growing use of precious metals. Increasingly, the peasants had to pay their dues in money; they fell more and more into debt.

*This leads to the establishment of debt slavery.* Peasants who cannot afford their dues are turned into slaves, who thus give over their life and death to the aristocracy. Everything for which they labor, they do for the aristocracy.

In conjunction with this, a new social form emerged, *the ancient city.* This was the area in which the aristocrats lived. Within the city they had their houses and outside of the city they kept their goods. Living in the city meant that one was not a participant in the production process, since the fields, the key source of production, lay further out.

In order to be able to live in the city, it was necessary for the aristocracy to have artisans living around them as well as city merchants, who acted as brokers for them, and in addition there were a whole series of personal servants. Here for the first time the foundations of a true slavery begin to take shape, one that we also see later in Greece.

Already during the time of Homer there were traces of slavery, though only in aristocratic families and in small numbers. *In this first phase of slavery, there was a preponderance of the female element.* Female slaves were used as concubines, wet nurses, and maids in the house, who worked next to the housewife and under her direction.

Then, adding to the decline of the peasant class, came *debt slavery*.

As early as the sixth century, these circumstances led to *revolutions* in Greece.

The ruined peasant class rebelled and called for new *allocations of land and soil*, a utopian demand to turn back the wheel of history. Although this call during the Solonian Revolution[1] of 594 would die away without being heard, the rebellion precipitated one thing: the *abolition of debt slavery*. (See "Ploetz.")[2] (Solon was the legislator, the Solonian Revolution is to be understood here as upheaval.)

The remarkable course of Greek history can be explained by these circumstances, where class domination took on the original form of *domination by the city over the land*.

Slavery *and trade* evolved at the same time as the aristocracy.

After slavery was initially adopted for personal service, the aristocracy reached the point where, in order to keep up with the increase in its living standards, it had to buy slaves in order to create products for exchange. For the first time, in Greece, we see workshops that are established specifically for slaves to produce goods for exchange. The use of slaves in oil and wine plantations and the massive use of slaves in mines. The slaves became direct competitors to the proletarianized peasants, and they eventually could be used by the aristocracy in their larger enterprises. In the mines, free labor was displaced *completely* by slave labor. Initially peasants doing compulsory labor carried out artisanal labor for the aristocracy. As the needs of the aristocrats became more refined, however, the peasants were no longer adequate. Specialists emerged who could do much more refined work in their craft. In the end, the free artisans were largely replaced by slaves.

Thus we see in Greece, namely in Attica, that wealthy Greeks established *entire workshops* in which slaves manufactured products for exchange.

Demosthenes, the father of the famous orator, had a workshop in which thirty slaves worked under supervision as sword sharpeners and armorers.

As a result of the Solonian Revolution, not only was debt slavery abolished, but military obligations also came to affect the peasantry. They became, so to speak, full citizens. Under the circumstances, however, this contributed to an even more rapid disintegration of the peasantry. As a result of the development of trade, which in Greece was comprised of sea trade, a merchant fleet and a navy emerged. Thus there was a large military burden upon the entire people. The burden of the navy was one of the greatest burdens on the peasantry.

After debt slavery had been abolished, *prisoners of war* increasingly became *material for slavery*. Later, in the seventh century, slaves were increasingly *purchased*. The purchased slaves were the peoples who lived around the perimeter of the Black Sea. Some of them also came from less civilized regions in the West such as what is today Spain, contemporary Gaul. The Greeks kept *colonies* all around this region. *Colonization* was one of the causes of the disintegration of the peasantry. Wherever a group of Greeks conquered a speck of land, usually along the shoreline of the sea, they established themselves there with their facilities and it became a Greek city. This was the case with Chios, an island and a Greek colony, where there was a large slave market.

The slave trading economy was especially large in centers where the large mines and plantations were concentrated, such as Sicily and Attica (Attica is Athens with a certain perimeter), in Corinth and elsewhere.

Thus, after the Solonian Revolution, there were slaves who were *captured, purchased* and who were *born into the household*.

## INDICATIONS OF THE SCOPE OF SLAVERY

The question of the size of the slave trade in Greece and in the ancient world is generally a point of contention among scholars, economists and historians.

Rodbertus[3] made himself well known for the portrayal of the ancient Greek *oikos* economy (*oikos* is the house, the family, together with the bondsmen, maidservants, and slaves). With this description, he created the impression that the whole of economic life in the ancient world rested upon slavery. This view was accepted by Professor Bücher,[4] for whom the first phase of economic development is the closed, household economy, based on slave labor. According to Bücher, this domestic economy predominated up to the Middle Ages.

*Recently, Professor Eduard Meyer has strongly contradicted this view.* Two works by him can be recommended:

1. *The Economic Development of the Ancient World. A Lecture*, 1895.
2. *Slavery in the Ancient World*, 1898.

The first work was cited heavily by Kautsky in *The Origin of Christianity*. There are also numerous articles on Professor Eduard Meyer and his views (under "Population in Ancient Times") published in the *Handwörterbuch der Staatswissenschaften*.

Unfortunately, Professor Eduard Meyer advocates the opposite extreme. He mainly demonstrates that *slavery played a rather marginal role in antiquity* and he bases his assessment on the fact that the number of slaves was either the same or smaller than the number of free laborers (with the exception of a few periods).

His rationale does not hold water. In contemporary society, capitalist production is dominant. Within it are the industrial workers. The farm laborers, the small craftsmen, the layers of educated professionals, etc., do not belong to it. But they, the industrial workers, stamp the conditions of their existence on the other classes. Contemporary society is formed by them although they are in fact a minority in the population.

It follows that the slaves may have been a minority of the population and yet all of the economic life in antiquity could have rested on them. It is not the numbers that are definitive, but the sum total of the tendencies that result from them that is definitive.

([…][5] Eduard Bernstein came up with the idea, after the census of 1905, that there were thus so and so many craftsmen, tradesmen, etc. But that in no way disproves the fact that the proletariat is the foundation of today's society. It is not possible to arrive at that with numbers.)

The first detailed evidence concerning slave labor comes from the fifth century, the time of Pericles, who lived between 444 and 429. He was prominent in Attica and had a great influence. According to the Beloch's[6] latest figures, in Attica, there were 130,000–150,000 freemen, a hundred thousand slaves at that time. The total population of Greece amounted to 2,250,000. Among them, Beloch counted 850,000 slaves in the same Periclean period.

Professor Meyer revised the numbers further. According to him, in the year 431, in the time of Pericles, there were 170,000 freemen, forty thousand *metics* [resident aliens], descendants of mixed marriages of slaves and citizens, and 150,000 slaves. (Contemporary […] Greece has over two million inhabitants, remaining more or less stable.)

Afterwards, the worsening of conditions in Greece, after the turning point of Pericles' time. 431–404 B.C., the *Peloponnesian War* between Sparta and

Athens. In this war, a sizable number of free peasants perished because they formed the infantry. Later, slavery increased even further. For Attica in the 4th century, 317–307, the following statistics: ninety thousand free citizens, forty thousand *metics*, and 400,000 slaves.

Professor Meyer does not dispute these numbers. They prove that after the war the number of slaves exceeded that of the rest of the population. He only claims that this was not the case before and, even then, not in all of Greece, but in a few centers. Furthermore, Professor Meyer speaks of industry and factories in Greece, a typically bourgeois bias.

Thus, where slaves predominated, they were not only used in crafts, mines, and on plantations, but also *very much in personal services*. Slaves were seen as belonging to the estate of a free citizen. Certain citizens owned fifty, and others had a thousand. It became fashionable in the forth century for free citizens to set foot in the city only with a drove of slaves in front and in back of them. When dandies appeared in Athens, slaves carried chairs for the dandies, letting the master sit down every few steps to shoo away the heat with fans.

Through Aristotle (born 384 B.C., died 322 B.C.), we have a strong impression of the circumstances of this period. In his *Politics*, which comprises eight books, he writes: "It is a complete household only if it contains slaves and freemen" [1255b1].

From Book I of *Politics*: "The essence of the science of being a master has to do with using his slaves correctly. He is the master, not because he is the owner of a person, but because he avails himself of it. The slave comprises a part of the wealth of the family" [1255b4].

From Book III of *Politics*: "Nature itself created slavery. Animals divide into male and female. The male is the more perfect one, it dominates. The female is imperfect, it obeys. Now, there are individuals in humankind who are just as subordinate to others, like the body to the soul, like the animal to man. These are beings that are only good for manual labor, and are not suited for anything more perfect than that. These individuals are destined by nature to be slaves because there is nothing better for them than to obey. Is there then, in fact, any real difference between slaves and animals? Their services are similar to one another; they are only useful to us through their bodies. From these principles we can conclude that nature created people for freedom and others for slavery, so that it is beneficial and just that the slave obeys" [1254b1].

There is a complete split between mental and manual labor. According to Aristotle, nature created slaves and physical labor, the basis of production, is according to him, the basis for bondage.

The free peasants were both members of society and citizens, and they took part in many aspects of public affairs.

With time, it transpired that every *aristocrat* lived in the city and his *main concern* became dealing with *affairs of state*, aside from the concern with science, art, and military service. *The peasants were proletarianized*, were unable to find work, since there were slaves everywhere. They became superfluous, did not count.

As a foreigner, the slave had no opportunity at all to take part in public life. He had no public obligations. Therefore, the master had the complete right to dispose of him, since there were no citizenship rights, no protection by the state.

Even if the slaves were the smaller group, they were nevertheless the principal focus. They proletarianized the peasants. The separation of intellectual life from the production process.

These are the fruits of slavery. This resulted in the disintegration of Greek society as well as the Roman one.

### CONCLUSIONS

In Greece, slavery led to the *separation of knowledge from the process of production*. Before this, knowledge was not separate from productive labor. *Knowledge was collective and concentrated in production. Everyone* worked, and everyone worked *together*. Knowledge remained necessary. In order to cut a stone, in order to manufacture tools; for that, scientific understanding was necessary. In order to undertake the organization of the mark, quite a bit of knowledge was required.

The *next form* is that knowledge rested with the *priests*. As in India, they were not allowed to work in the fields. Because of this, they acquired time for extensive mental labor. This was necessary, for example, in the Orient, since organizing the construction of the large waterworks came to be carried out not only by the mark, but also by many others as well. The priests were in intimate contact with nature, because they had to support the cult, which at that time was a nature cult.

The *next form* in which knowledge was disconnected from production was *slavery*. And in fact, within slavery, total separation of manual and mental labor likewise took place.

This benefited science and art. Free from being bound to production, they could now float freely in the air, hurry ahead of time. Art succeeded in blossoming in Greece to a point that has not been reached in our time. Aristotle would not have been capable of becoming what he was without slavery. Everything that exists today is bound up with the ancient Greek world, with Aristotle. In this sense we could even say: *without slavery, there would be no socialism.*

Knowledge was also beneficial to the production process.

The exclusion of slaves from mental life led of course to *the rulers creating laws* that benefited their own interests, yet these also had to be honored by the slaves, although they did not take part in their enactment. It is not much different today. There were laws and a dominant class that did not take part in the production process. Those who created all the assets had to submit to them.

In the socialist society, knowledge will be the common property of everyone. All working people will have knowledge.

# 4—Martinique

EDITORS' NOTE: This article, written shortly after a massive volcanic eruption in May 1902 at the port of St. Pierre in the Caribbean island of Martinique, reflects Luxemburg's intense interest in events outside of Europe and her fervent opposition to European colonialism. It was first published in the *Leipziger Volkszeitung* of May 15, 1902. The translation is by David Wolff.

Mountains of smoking ruins, heaps of mangled corpses, a steaming, smoking sea of fire wherever you turn, mud and ashes—that is all that remains of the flourishing little city which perched on the rocky slope of the volcano like a fluttering swallow. For some time the angry giant had been heard to rumble and rage against this human presumption, the blind self-conceit of the two-legged dwarfs. Great-hearted even in his wrath, a true giant, he warned the reckless creatures that crawled at his feet. He smoked, spewed out fiery clouds, in his bosom there was seething and boiling and explosions like rifle volleys and cannon thunder. But the lords of the earth, those who ordain human destiny, remained with faith unshaken—in their own wisdom.

On [May] 7th, the commission dispatched by the government announced to the anxious people of St. Pierre that all was in order in heaven and on earth. All is in order, no cause for alarm!—as they said on the eve of the Oath of the Tennis Court in the dance-intoxicated halls of Louis XVI, while in the crater of the revolutionary volcano fiery lava was gathering for the fearful eruption. All is in order, peace and quiet everywhere!—as they said in Vienna and Berlin on the eve of the March eruption fifty years ago.[1] The old, long-suffering titan of Martinique paid no heed to the reports of the honorable commission: after the people had been reassured by the governor on the 7th, he erupted in the early hours of the 8th and buried in a few minutes the governor, the commission, the people, houses, streets and ships under the fiery exhalation of his indignant heart.

The work was radically thorough. Forty thousand human lives mowed down, a handful of trembling refugees rescued—the old giant can rumble and

bubble in peace, he has shown his might, he has fearfully avenged the slight
to his primordial power.

And now in the ruins of the annihilated city on Martinique a new guest
arrives, unknown, never seen before—the human being. Not lords and bondsmen, not blacks and whites, not rich and poor, not plantation owners and
wage slaves—human beings have appeared on the tiny shattered island,
human beings who feel only the pain and see only the disaster, who only want
to help and succor. Old Mt. Pelee has worked a miracle! Forgotten are the days
of Fashoda,[2] forgotten the conflict over Cuba, forgotten "la Revanche"—the
French and the English, the Tsar and the Senate of Washington, Germany and
Holland donate money, send telegrams, extend the helping hand. A brotherhood of peoples against nature's burning hatred, a resurrection of humanism
on the ruins of human culture. The price of recalling their humanity was high,
but thundering Mt. Pelee had a voice to catch their ear.

France weeps over the tiny island's forty thousand corpses, and the whole
world hastens to dry the tears of the Mother Republic. But how was it then,
centuries ago, when France spilled blood in torrents for the Lesser and
Greater Antilles? In the sea off the east coast of Africa lies a volcanic island—
Madagascar: fifty years ago there we saw the disconsolate Republic who
weeps for her lost children today, how she bowed the obstinate native people
to her yoke with chains and the sword. No volcano opened its crater there:
the mouths of French cannons spewed out death and annihilation; French
artillery fire swept thousands of flowering human lives from the face of the
earth until a free people lay prostrate on the ground, until the brown queen of
the "savages" was dragged off as a trophy to the "City of Light."

On the Asiatic coast, washed by the waves of the ocean, lie the smiling
Philippines. Six years ago we saw the benevolent Yankees, we saw the Washington Senate at work there.[3] Not fire-spewing mountains—there, American
rifles mowed down human lives in heaps; the sugar cartel Senate today sends
golden dollars to Martinique, thousands upon thousands, to coax life back
from the ruins, sent cannon upon cannon, warship upon warship, golden
dollars millions upon millions to Cuba, to sow death and devastation.

Yesterday, today, far off in the African south, where only a few years ago a
tranquil little people lived by their labor and in peace, there we saw how the
English wreak havoc, these same Englishmen who in Martinique save the
mother her children and the children their parents: there we saw them stamp
on human bodies, on children's corpses with brutal soldiers boots, wading in
pools of blood, death and misery before them and behind.

Ah, and the Russians, the rescuing, helping, weeping Tsar of All the Russians—an old acquaintance! We have seen you on the ramparts of Praga, where warm Polish, blood flowed in streams and turned the sky red with its steam.[4] But those were the old days. No! Now, only a few weeks ago, we have seen you benevolent Russians on your dusty highways, in ruined Russian villages eye to eye with the ragged, wildly agitated, grumbling mob; gunfire rattled, gasping muzhiks fell to the earth, red peasant blood mingled with the dust of the highway. They must die, they must fall because their bodies doubled up with hunger, because they cried out for bread, for bread!

And we have seen you too, Oh Mother Republic, you tear-distiller. It was on May 23 of 1871: the glorious spring sun shone down on Paris; thousands of pale human beings in working clothes stood packed together in the streets, in prison courtyard, body to body and head to head; through loopholes in the walls, mitrailleuses thrust their bloodthirsty muzzles. No volcano erupted, no lava stream poured down. Your cannons, Mother Republic, were turned on the tight-packed crowd, screams of pain rent the air—over twenty thousand corpses covered the pavements of Paris![5]

And all of you—whether French and English, Russians and Germans, Italians and Americans—we have seen you all together once before in brotherly accord, united in a great league of nations, helping and guiding each other: it was in China. There too you forgot all quarrels among yourselves, there too you made a peace of peoples—for mutual murder and the torch. Ha, how the pigtails fell in rows before your bullets, like a ripe grainfield lashed by the hail! Ha, how the wailing women plunged into the water, their dead in their cold arms, fleeing the tortures of your ardent embraces!

And now they have all turned to Martinique, all one heart and one mind again; they help, rescue, dry the tears and curse the havoc-wreaking volcano. Mt. Pelee, great-hearted giant, you can laugh; you can look down in loathing at these benevolent murderers, at these weeping carnivores, at these beasts in Samaritan's clothing. But a day will come when another volcano lifts its voice of thunder: a volcano that is seething and boiling, whether you need it or not, and will sweep the whole sanctimonious, blood-splattered culture from the face of the earth. And only on its ruins will the nations come together in true humanity, which will know but one deadly foe—blind, dead nature.

# PART TWO

The Politics of Revolution:
Critique of Reformism,
Theory of the Mass Strike,
Writings on Women

# 5 — Social Reform or Revolution

EDITORS' NOTE: *Social Reform or Revolution*, Luxemburg's famous critique of Eduard Bernstein's revisionism, first appeared as a series of articles in *Leipziger Volkszeitung* in September 1898 and April 1899. Bernstein (1850–1932) was a leading figure in the German socialist movement who had been named Marx's literary executor by Frederick Engels while in exile in England in the 1890s. Bernstein's advocacy of revisionist views after Engels' death stunned many at the time, given his leading role in the Second International. The controversy was initiated by Bernstein's publication of several essays during the years 1896–98 under the title "Problems of Socialism" in *Neue Zeit*, the main theoretical journal of German Social Democracy. Bernstein called for a reappraisal of many of Marx's concepts in light of the presumed stability of capitalism and the growth of Social Democracy, earning him the appellation "revisionist." Though Luxemburg was not the first to attack Bernstein's effort to revise the basic tenets of Marxism, her analysis was the most comprehensive and her critique of Bernstein established her as a major figure in German Social Democracy and the Second International as a whole.

Luxemburg's critique of Bernstein, part of which first appeared in *Leipziger Volkszeitung,* was reprinted in book form as Part I of *Social Reform or Revolution* in 1899, along with a Part II that critiqued Bernstein's book *Voraussetzungen des Sozialismus und die Aufgaben der Sozialdemokratie*, published earlier in 1899. (Bernstein's book is available in English under the title *Evolutionary Socialism.*) A second edition of *Reform or Revolution*, which contained a number of revisions and corrections by Luxemburg, was published in 1908. This translation by Dick Howard follows the text of the 1899 edition, but incorporates changes from the second edition. Passages eliminated in the second edition are in brackets; passages added to the second edition are in the endnotes.

## PREFACE

At first view, the title of this work may be surprising. Social reform *or* revolution? Can Social Democracy be *against* social reforms? Can it *oppose* social revolution, the transformation of the existing order, its final goal, to social reforms? Certainly not. The practical daily struggle for reforms, for the amelioration of the condition of the workers within the framework of the existing social order, and for democratic institutions, offers Social Democracy the only means of engaging in the proletarian class struggle and working in the direction of the final goal—the conquest of political power and the suppression of wage labor. For Social Democracy there exists an indissoluble tie between social reforms and revolution. The struggle for reforms is its *means*; the social revolution, its *goal*.

It is in Eduard Bernstein's theory, presented in his articles on "Problems of Socialism," in the *Neue Zeit* of 1897–1898, and especially in his book, *Die Voraussetzungen des Sozialismus und die Aufgaben der Sozialdemokratie* [The Presuppositions of Socialism and the Tasks of Social Democracy],[1] that we find, for the first time, the opposition of the two moments of the labor movement. His theory tends to counsel the renunciation of the social transformation, the final goal of Social Democracy, and, inversely, to make social reforms, which are the *means* of the class struggle, into its *end*. Bernstein himself formulated this viewpoint very clearly and precisely when he wrote: "The final goal, whatever it may be, is nothing to me; the movement is everything."

But since the final goal of socialism is the only decisive factor distinguishing the Social Democratic movement from bourgeois democracy and from bourgeois radicalism, the only factor transforming the entire labor movement from a vain effort to repair the capitalist order into a class struggle *against* this order, for the suppression of this order—the question "Reform or Revolution?" as it is posed by Bernstein is, for Social Democracy, the same as the question "To be or not to be?" In the controversy with Bernstein and his followers, everybody in the Party ought to understand clearly that it is not a question of this or that method of struggle, or of the use of this or that *tactic*, but of the very *existence* of the Social Democratic movement.

[From a casual consideration of Bernstein's theory, this may appear to be an exaggeration. Does he not continually mention Social Democracy and its aims? Does he not repeat again and again, and explicitly, that he too strives toward the final goal of socialism, but in another way? Does he not stress particularly that he fully approves of the present practice of Social Democracy? That is all true, to be sure. But it is also true that every new movement, when it first elaborates its theory and policy, begins by finding support in the preceding movement, though it may be in direct contradiction with the latter. It begins by suiting itself to the forms already at hand, and by speaking the language which was spoken. In time, the new grain breaks through the old husk, and the new movement finds its own forms and its own language.

To expect an opposition against scientific socialism at its beginning to express itself clearly, fully, and to the last consequence; to expect it to *deny* openly and bluntly the theoretical basis of Social Democracy—would be to underrate the power of scientific socialism. Today, he who would pass as a socialist, and at the same time would declare war on the Marxian doctrine, the most stupendous product of the human mind in this century, must begin with involuntary esteem for Marxism. He must begin by acknowledging himself its disciple, by seeking in Marx's own teachings the points of support for an attack on them, representing this attack as a further development of Marxian doctrine. For this reason, unconcerned by its outer forms, one must pick out the sheathed kernel of Bernstein's theory. This is a matter of urgent necessity for the broad strata of the industrial proletariat in our party.

No coarser insult, no baser defamation, can be thrown against the workers than the remark "Theoretical controversies are only for intellectuals." Lassalle[2] once said: "Only when science and the workers, these opposed poles of society, become one will they crush in their arms of steel all obstacles to culture." The entire strength of the modern labor movement rests on theoretical knowledge.

But this knowledge is doubly important for the workers in the present case, because it is precisely they and their influence in the movement that are in the balance here. It is their skin that is being brought to market. The opportunist current in the Party, whose theory is formulated by Bernstein, is nothing but an unconscious attempt to assure the predominance of the petty-bourgeois elements that have entered our Party, to change the policy and aims of our Party in their direction. The question of reform and revolution, of the final goal and the movement, is, in another form, the question of the *petty-bourgeois or proletarian character of the labor movement.*

It is, therefore, in the interest of the proletarian mass of the Party to become acquainted, actively and in detail, with the present theoretical controversy with opportunism. As long as theoretical knowledge remains the privilege of a handful of "intellectuals" in the Party, it will face the danger of going astray. Only when the great mass of workers take in their own hands the keen and dependable weapons of scientific socialism will all the petty-bourgeois inclinations, all the opportunist currents, come to naught. The movement will then find itself on sure and firm ground. "Quantity will do it."]

## 1. THE OPPORTUNIST METHOD

If it is true that theories are reflections in the human consciousness of the phenomena of the external world, then it must be added, concerning Eduard Bernstein's theory, that these theories are sometimes inverted images. Think of a theory of instituting socialism by means of social reform in face of the complete stagnation of the reform movement in Germany. Think of a theory of trade-union control over production in face of the defeat of the metal workers in England. Consider the theory of winning a majority in parliament after the revision of the constitution of Saxony and the most recent attempts against universal suffrage. However, in our opinion, the pivotal point of Bernstein's system is not located in his conception of the practical tasks of Social Democracy. It is found in what he says about the course of the objective development of capitalist society which, of course, is closely bound to his conception of the practical tasks of Social Democracy.

According to Bernstein, a general breakdown of capitalism is increasingly improbable because, on the one hand, capitalism shows a greater capacity of adaptation and, on the other hand, capitalist production becomes more and more varied. The capacity of capitalism to adapt itself, says Bernstein, is manifested, first, in the disappearance of general crises thanks to the development of the credit system, employers' organizations,[3] wider means of communication and informational services. It shows itself, secondly, in the tenacity of the middle classes, which follows from the continual differentiation of the branches of production and the elevation of vast strata of the proletariat into the middle class. It is furthermore proved, argues Bernstein, by the amelioration of the economic and political situation of the proletariat as a result of the trade-union struggle.

From this is derived the following general conclusion about the practical struggle of Social Democracy. It must not direct its activity toward the conquest of political power but toward the improvement of the condition of the working class. It must not expect to institute socialism as a result of a political and social crisis but by means of the progressive extension of social control and the gradual application of the principle of cooperation.

Bernstein himself sees nothing new in his theories. On the contrary, he believes them to be in agreement with certain declarations of Marx and Engels, as well as with the general direction of Social Democracy up to the present. Nevertheless, it seems to us that it is difficult to deny that they are in fundamental contradiction with the conceptions of scientific socialism.

If Bernstein's revisionism consisted only in affirming that the march of capitalist development is slower than was thought before, he would merely be presenting an argument for adjourning the conquest of power by the proletariat on which up to now everybody agreed. Its only practical consequence would be a slowing down of the pace of the struggle.

But that is not the case. What Bernstein questions is not the rapidity of the development of capitalist society but the path of the development itself and, consequently, the transition to socialism.

Socialist theory up to now declared that the point of departure for a transformation to socialism would be a general and catastrophic crisis. We must distinguish two things in this theory: the fundamental idea and its external form. The fundamental idea consists in the affirmation that, as a result of its own inner contradictions, capitalism moves toward a point when it will be unbalanced, when it will simply become impossible. There were good reasons for thinking of that juncture in the form of a catastrophic general commercial crisis. But, nonetheless, that is of secondary importance and inessential to the fundamental idea.

As is well known, the scientific basis of socialism rests on *three* results of capitalist development. First, and most important, on the growing *anarchy* of the capitalist economy, leading inevitably to its ruin. Second, on the progressive *socialization* of the process of production, which creates the germs of the future social order. And third, on the growing *organization and class consciousness* of the proletariat, which constitutes the active factor in the coming revolution.

Bernstein eliminates the first of the three fundamental supports of scientific socialism. He says that capitalist development does not lead to a general economic collapse.

He does not merely reject a certain form of the collapse but the collapse itself. He says, textually: "One could object that by collapse of the present society is meant something else than a general commercial crisis worse than all others, namely, a complete collapse of the capitalist system brought about as a result of its own contradictions." And to this he replies: "With the growing development of society, a complete and almost general collapse of the present system of production becomes not more but less probable because capitalist development increases, on the one hand, the capacity of adaptation and, on the other—that is, at the same time—the differentiation of industry."4

But then the important question arises: Why and how shall we attain the final goal of our efforts? From the standpoint of scientific socialism, the historical necessity of the socialist revolution manifests itself above all in the growing anarchy of capitalism which drives the system into an impasse. But if one admits, with Bernstein, that capitalist development does not move in the direction of its own ruin, then socialism ceases to be *objectively necessary.* There remain only the other two mainstays of the scientific explanation of socialism, which are also consequences of the capitalist order: the socialization of the process of production and the class consciousness of the proletariat. It is these that Bernstein has in mind when he says that with the elimination of the breakdown theory "the socialist doctrine loses nothing of its power of persuasion. For, examined closely, what are all the factors enumerated by us that make for the suppression or the modification of the former crises? Nothing else, in fact, than the preconditions, or even in part the germs, of the socialization of production and exchange."5

Very little reflection is needed to see that this too is a false conclusion. Where does the importance of all the phenomena which Bernstein says are the means of capitalist adaptation—cartels, the credit system, the development of means of communication, the amelioration of the situation of the working class, etc.—lie? Obviously in that they eliminate or, at least, attenuate the internal contradictions of capitalist economy, and stop the development or the aggravation of these contradictions. Thus the elimination of crises means the suppression of the antagonism between production and exchange on the capitalist base. The amelioration of the situation of the working class, or the penetration of certain fractions of that class into the middle layers, means the attenuation of the antagonism between capital and labor. But if the cartels, credit system, trade unions, etc., suppress the capitalist contradictions and consequently save the system from ruin; if they enable capitalism to maintain itself—and that is why Bernstein calls them "means of adaptation"—how can they be at the same time "the preconditions and even in part the germs" of socialism? Obviously only in the sense that they express more clearly the social character of production. But, inversely, by maintaining it in its capitalist form, the same factors render superfluous in equal measure the transformation of this socialized production into socialist production. That is why they can be the germs or preconditions of a socialist order only in a conceptual sense and not in an historical sense. They are phenomena which, in the light of our conception of socialism, we *know* to be related to socialism but which, in fact, not only do not lead to a socialist revolution but, on the contrary, render it superfluous. There remains only one foundation of socialism—the class consciousness of the proletariat. But it, too, is in the given case not the simple intellectual reflection of the ever growing contradictions of capitalism and its approaching decline—for this decline is prevented by the means of adaptation. It is now a mere ideal whose force of persuasion rests only on the perfections attributed to it.

What we have here, in brief, is the foundation of the socialist program by means of "pure reason." We have here, to use simpler language, an idealist explanation of socialism. The objective necessity of socialism, the explanation of socialism as the result of the material development of society, falls away.

Revisionist theory stands before an Either/Or. Either the socialist transformation is, as was admitted up to now, the consequence of the internal contradictions of the capitalist order—then with this order will develop its contradictions, resulting inevitably, at some point, in its collapse. In this case, however, the "means of adaptation" are ineffective, and the breakdown theory is correct. Or, the "means of adaptation" are really capable of stopping the breakdown of the capitalist system and thereby enable capitalism to maintain itself by suppressing its own contradictions. In that case, *socialism* ceases to be an historical necessity. It then becomes anything you want to call it, except the result of the material development of society.

This dilemma leads to another. Either revisionism is correct concerning the course of capitalist development, and therefore the socialist transformation of society becomes a utopia. Or socialism is not a utopia; and therefore the theory of the "means of adaptation" is false. "*Das ist die Frage*, that is the question."

### THE ADAPTATION OF CAPITALISM

According to Bernstein, the credit system, the improved means of communication and the new employers' organizations are the important means that bring about the adaptation of the capitalist economy.

Let us begin with credit. Credit has diverse functions in the capitalist economy. Its two most important functions, as is well known, are to increase the capacity to expand production and to facilitate exchange. When the inner tendency of capitalist production to expand limitlessly strikes against the barrier of private property (the limited size of private capital), credit appears as a means of surmounting these limits in a capitalist manner. Through stock companies, credit combines in one mass a large number of individual capitals. It makes available to each capitalist the use of other capitalists' money—in the form of industrial credit. Further, as commercial credit, it accelerates the exchange of commodities and therefore the return of capital into production, and thus aids the entire cycle of the process of production.

The effect of these two principal functions of credit on the formation of crises is quite obvious. If it is true that crises appear as a result of the contradiction between the capacity for expansion, the tendency of production to increase, and the restricted consumption capacity, then in view of what was stated above, credit is precisely the specific means of making this contradiction break out as often as possible. First of all, it immensely increases the capacity for the expansion of production, and thus constitutes an inner driving force that constantly pushes production to exceed the limits of the market. But credit strikes from two sides. After having (as a factor of the process of production) provoked overproduction, credit (as mediator of the process of exchange) destroys, during the crisis, the very productive forces it itself created. At the first symptom of the stagnation, credit melts away. It abandons the exchange process just when it is still indispensable, and where it still exists, it shows itself instead ineffective and useless, and thus during the crisis it reduces the consumption capacity of the market to a minimum.

Besides these two principal results, credit also influences the formation of crises in many other ways. It offers not only the technical means of making available to an entrepreneur the capital of other owners, but at the same time stimulates bold and unscrupulous utilization of the property of others. That is, it leads to reckless speculation. Not only does credit aggravate the crisis in its capacity as a dissembled means of exchange; it also helps to bring on and extend the crisis by transforming all exchange into an extremely complex and artificial mechanism which, having a minimum of metallic money as a real base, is easily disarranged at the slightest occasion.

Thus, far from being a means for the elimination or the attenuation of crises, credit is, on the contrary, a particularly powerful factor in the formation of crises. This could not possibly be otherwise. Speaking very generally, the specific function of credit is nothing but the elimination of the remaining rigidity of capitalist relationships. It introduces everywhere the greatest elasticity possible. It renders all capitalist forces extendable, relative, and sensitive to the highest degree. Doing this, it facilitates and aggravates crises, which are nothing but the periodic collisions of the contradictory forces of the capitalist economy.

This leads, at the same time, to another question. How can credit generally have the appearance of a "means of adaptation" of capitalism? No matter in what context or form this "adaptation" is conceived, its essence can obviously only be that one of the several antagonistic relations of capitalist economy is smoothed over, that one of its contradictions is suppressed or weakened, and that thus liberty of movement is assured, at one point or another, to the otherwise fettered productive forces. In fact, it is precisely credit that aggravates these contradictions to the highest degree. It aggravates the antagonism between the *mode of production* and the *mode of exchange* by stretching production to the limit and at the same time paralyzing exchange on the smallest pretext. It increases the contradiction between the *mode of production* and the *mode of appropriation* by separating production from ownership, that is, by transforming the capital employed in production into "social" capital and at the same time transforming a part of the profit, in the form of interest on capital, into a simple title of ownership. It increases the contradiction between the *property relations* and the *relations of production* by putting immense productive forces into a small number of hands, and expropriating a large number of small capitalists. It increases the contradiction between the social character of production and capitalist *private ownership* by rendering necessary the intervention of the state in production (stock companies).

In short, credit reproduces all the fundamental contradictions of the capitalist world. It accentuates them. It precipitates their development and thus pushes the capitalist world forward to its own destruction—the breakdown. The prime act of capitalist adaptation, as far as credit is concerned, should really consist in breaking and *suppressing* credit. In fact, credit is far from being a means of capitalist adaptation. On the contrary, as it presently exists, it is a means of destruction of the most extreme revolutionary significance. Has not precisely this revolutionary character which leads the credit system beyond capitalism actually inspired plans of "socialist" reform? As such, it has had some distinguished proponents, some of whom (Isaac Pereire[6] in France) were, as Marx put it, half prophets, half rogues.

On closer examination, the second "means of adaptation," *employers' organizations*, appears just as fragile. According to Bernstein, such organizations will put an end to anarchy of production and do away with crises through the regulation of production. It is true that the multiple economic repercussions of the development of cartels and trusts have not been studied too carefully up to now. But they represent a problem which can only be solved with the aid of Marxist theory.

One thing, at least, is certain. We could speak of a damming of capitalist anarchy by capitalist employers' organizations only in the measure that cartels, trusts, etc., become, even approximately, the dominant form of production. But such a possibility is excluded by the very nature of the cartels. The final economic aim and result of employers' organizations is the following.

Through the elimination of competition in a given branch of production, the distribution of the mass of profit realized on the market is influenced in such a manner that there is an increase in the share going to this branch of industry. Such organization can only increase the rate of profit in one branch of industry at the expense of another. That is precisely why it cannot be generalized; for when it is extended to all important branches of industry, this tendency cancels its own influence.

But even within the limits of their practical application, the result of employers' organizations is the very opposite of the elimination of industrial anarchy. Cartels ordinarily succeed in obtaining an increase of the rate of profit in the internal market at the cost of having to sell the product of the excess portion of their capital—that which couldn't be absorbed by the internal market—on foreign markets at a much lower rate of profit. That is to say, they sell abroad cheaper than at home. The result is the sharpening of competition abroad and an increased anarchy on the world market—the very opposite of what is intended. This is well demonstrated by the history of the international sugar industry.

Generally speaking, employers' organizations, as a manifestation of the capitalist mode of production, can only be considered a definite phase of capitalist development. In effect, cartels are fundamentally nothing but a means resorted to by the capitalist mode of production to hold back the fatal fall of the rate of profit in certain branches of production. What method do cartels employ to this end? It is, essentially, that of keeping inactive a part of the accumulated capital. That is, they use the same method which, in another form, comes into play during crises. The remedy and the illness resemble each other like two drops of water, and the former can be considered the lesser evil only up to a certain point. When the market outlets begin to shrink because the world market has been extended to its limit and has been exhausted by the competition of the capitalist countries—and it cannot be denied that sooner or later this is bound to occur—then the forced partial idleness of capital will reach such dimensions that the remedy will itself be transformed into an illness, and capital, already pretty much "socialized" through organization, will tend to revert again to the form of private capital. In the face of the increased difficulties of finding even a tiny place, each individual portion will prefer to take its chances alone. At that time, the [employers'] organizations will burst like soap bubbles and give way to free competition in an aggravated form.7

On the whole, cartels, just like credit, appear therefore as a determined phase of capitalist development which, in the last analysis, only aggravates the anarchy of the capitalist world, expressing and ripening its internal contradictions. Cartels aggravate the contradiction between the mode of production and the mode of exchange by sharpening the struggle between producer and consumer, as is the case especially in the United States. Furthermore, they aggravate the contradiction between the mode of production and the mode of appropriation by opposing the superior force of organized capital to the working class in the most brutal fashion, and thus increasing the antagonism between capital and labor. Finally, capitalist cartels aggravate the contradiction between the international character of the capitalist world economy and the national character of the capitalist state insofar as they are always accompanied by a general tariff war which sharpens the differences among the capitalist states. We must add to this the decidedly revolutionary influence exercised by cartels on the concentration of production, technical progress, etc.

Thus, when evaluated from the angle of their final effect on the capitalist economy, cartels and trusts fail as "means of adaptation." They fail to attenuate the contradictions of capitalism. On the contrary, they appear to be a means which itself leads to greater anarchy. They encourage the further development of the internal contradictions of capitalism and accelerate the coming of a general decline of capitalism. . . .

There remains still another phenomenon which, says Bernstein, contradicts the course of capitalist development indicated above. In the "steadfast phalanx" of middle-size enterprises, Bernstein sees a sign that the development of large industry does not move in such a revolutionary direction, and is not as effective from the angle of the concentration of industry as was expected by the "breakdown theory." He is here, however, the victim of his own misunderstanding. To see the progressive disappearance of the middle-size enterprise as a necessary result of the development of large industry is, in effect, to misunderstand the nature of this process.

According to Marxist theory, small capitalists play the role of pioneers of technical revolution in the general course of capitalist development. They play that role in a double sense. They initiate new methods of production in old, well-established branches of industry, as well as being instrumental in the creation of new branches of production not yet exploited by the big capitalist. It is false to imagine that the history of the middle-size capitalist establishment proceeds unequivocally in the direction of their progressive disappearance. The course of their development is rather a purely dialectical one, and moves constantly among contradictions. The middle capitalist layers, just like the workers, find themselves under the influence of two antagonistic tendencies, one ascendant and the other descendent. In this case, the descendent tendency is the continued rise in the scale of production which periodically overflows the dimensions of the average-size capital and removes it repeatedly from the competitive terrain. The ascendant tendency is, first, the periodic depreciation of the existing capital which again lowers, for a certain time, the scale of production in proportion to the value of the necessary minimum amount of capital. It is also represented by the penetration of capitalist production into new spheres. The struggle of the average-size enterprise against big capital cannot be considered a regularly proceeding battle in which the troops of the weaker party continue to melt away directly and quantitatively. It should rather be regarded as a periodic mowing down of small capital, which rapidly grows up again only to be mowed down once more by large industry. The two tendencies play catch with the middle capitalist layers. As opposed to the development of the working class, the descending tendency must win, in the end. The victory of the descending tendency need not necessarily show itself in an absolute numerical diminution of the middle-size enterprises. It shows itself, first, in the progressive increase of the minimum amount of capital necessary for the functioning of the enterprises in the old branches of production; second, in the constant diminution of the interval of time during which the small capitalists conserve the opportunity to exploit the new branches of production. The result, as far as the small capitalist is concerned, is a progressively shorter duration of his economic life and an ever more rapid change in the methods of production and of investment; and, for the class as a whole, a more and more rapid acceleration of the social metabolism.

Bernstein knows this perfectly well; he himself comments on it. But what he seems to forget is that this very thing is the law of movement of the average capitalist enterprise. If small capitalists are the pioneers of technical progress, and if technical progress is the vital pulse of the capitalist economy, then it is manifest that small capitalists are an integral part of capitalist development. The progressive disappearance of the middle-size enterprise—in the absolute sense considered by Bernstein—would not mean, as he thinks, the revolutionary advance of capitalist development, but precisely the contrary, the cessation, the slowing down of this development. "The rate of profit, that is to say, the relative increase of capital," said Marx, "is important first of all for new investors of capital grouping themselves independently. And as soon as the formation of capital falls exclusively into the hands of a few big capitalists, the revivifying fire of production is extinguished. It dies away."[8]

[The Bernsteinian means of adaptation thus show themselves to be ineffective, and the phenomena which he considers to be symptoms of the adaptation must be pushed back to other causes. . . .]

## PRACTICAL CONSEQUENCES AND GENERAL CHARACTER
### OF REVISIONISM

In the first chapter, we attempted to show that Bernstein's theory lifts the program of the socialist movement off its material base and places it on an idealist basis. This concerns its theoretical foundation. How does this theory appear when translated into practice?

First, and formally, it does not differ in the least from the practice followed by Social Democracy up to now. Trade unions, the struggle for social reform and for the democratization of the political institutions are precisely that which constitutes the formal content of the activity of the Social Democratic Party. The difference is not in the *what* but in the *how*. At present, the trade-union and the parliamentary struggles are considered as means of gradually guiding and educating the proletariat for the taking of political power. From the revisionist standpoint, this conquest of power is impossible and useless; therefore, trade-union and parliamentary activity are to be carried on only for their immediate results, that is, the bettering of the material situation of the workers, the gradual reduction of capitalist exploitation and the extension of social control.

If we ignore the immediate amelioration of the workers' condition—an objective shared by the Party program and revisionism—the difference between the two conceptions is, in brief, the following. According to the current conception, the socialist significance of trade-union and parliamentary activity is that it prepares the proletariat—that is, the *subjective* factor of the socialist transformation—for the task of realizing socialism. According to Bernstein, the trade-union and political struggles gradually reduce capitalist exploitation itself, remove from capitalist society its capitalist character, and give it a socialist one. In a word, the two forms of struggle are said to realize the socialist transformation *in an objective sense*. Examined more closely, the two conceptions are diametrically opposed. In the current conception of our party, the proletariat becomes convinced of the impossibility of accomplishing fundamental social change as a result of its trade-union and parliamentary struggles and arrives at the conviction that these struggles cannot basically change its situation, and that the conquest of power is unavoidable. Bernstein's theory, however, begins by presupposing that the conquest of power is impossible, and it concludes by affirming that the socialist order can only be introduced as a result of the trade-union struggle and parliamentary activity.

As seen by Bernstein, trade-union and parliamentary action has a socialist character because it exercises a progressively socializing influence on the capitalist economy. We tried to show that this influence is purely imaginary. The structures of capitalist property and the capitalist state develop in entirely opposed directions. But, in the last analysis, this means that the daily practical activity of Social Democracy loses all connection with socialism. The great socialist significance of the trade-union and parliamentary struggles is that through them the *awareness*, the consciousness, of the proletariat becomes socialist, and it is organized as a class. But if they are considered as instruments for the direct socialization of the capitalist economy, they lose not only their supposed effectiveness, but also cease to be a means of preparing the working class for the proletarian conquest of power.

Eduard Bernstein and Konrad Schmidt[9] suffer from a complete misunderstanding when they console themselves with the belief that even though the program of the Party is reduced to work for social reforms and ordinary trade-union work, the final objective of the labor movement is not therefore lost, because each forward step reaches beyond the given immediate aim, and the socialist goal is implied as a tendency in the movement. This is certainly fully true of the present tactic of German Social Democracy in which a firm and conscious effort toward the conquest of political power precedes the trade-union struggle and the work for social reforms. But if this presupposed effort is separated from the movement , and social reforms are then made an end in themselves, such activity not only does not lead to the realization of socialism as the ultimate goal, but moves in precisely the opposite direction.

Konrad Schmidt simply falls back on a so to speak mechanical movement which, once started, cannot stop by itself. He justifies this with the saying "One's appetite grows with eating," and the working class will not content itself with reforms as long as the final socialist transformation is not realized. The last presupposition is quite true, as the insufficiency of capitalist social reforms themselves shows. But the conclusion drawn from it could only be true if it were possible to construct an unbroken chain of continually growing reforms leading from the present social order to socialism. This is, however, a fantasy. In accordance with the nature of things, the chain breaks quickly, and the paths that the movement can take from that point are many and varied.

The most probable immediate result of this is, then, a tactical shift toward using all means to make possible the practical results, the social reforms. As soon as immediate practical results become the principal aim, the clear-cut, irreconcilable class standpoint, which has meaning only insofar as it proposes to take power, will be found more and more an obstacle. The direct consequence of this will be the adoption by the Party of a "policy of compensation," a policy of horse-trading, and an attitude of sage diplomatic conciliation.[10] But the movement cannot remain immobile for long. Since social reforms in the capitalist world are and remain an empty promise no matter what tactics one uses, the next logical step is necessarily disillusionment in social reform. One ends up in the calm harbor where Professor Schmoller and Co.[11] have dropped anchor after having navigated the waters of social reform, finally letting the course of things proceed as God wills.[12]

It is not true that socialism will arise automatically and under all circumstances from the daily struggle of the working class. Socialism will be the consequence only of the ever growing contradictions of capitalist economy and the comprehension by the working class of the unavoidability of the suppression of these contradictions through a social transformation. When the first condition is denied and the second rejected, as is the case with revisionism, the labor movement is reduced to a simple cooperative and reformist movement, and moves in a straight line toward the total abandonment of the class standpoint.

These consequences also become clear when we regard revisionism from another side, and ask what is the general character of revisionism. It is obvious that revisionism does not defend capitalist relations. It does not join the bourgeois economists in denying the existence of the contradictions of capitalism. Rather, its theory is based on the presupposition of the existence of these contradictions, just like the Marxist conception. But, on the other hand, what constitutes precisely the essential kernel of revisionism and distinguishes it fundamentally from the attitude taken by Social Democracy up to now is that it does not base its theory on the suppression of these contradictions as a result of their logical internal development.

The theory of revisionism occupies an intermediate place between two extremes. Revisionism does not want to see the contradictions of capitalism mature, to *suppress* these contradictions through a revolutionary transformation. Rather, it wants to lessen, to *attenuate* the capitalist contradictions. Thus, the antagonism between production and exchange is to be attenuated by the cessation of crises and the formation of capitalist employers' organizations; the antagonism between capital and labor is to be adjusted by bettering the situation of the workers and by conserving the middle classes; and the contradiction between the class state and society is to be lessened through increased control and democracy.

Of course, the present tactic of Social Democracy does not consist in *waiting* for the antagonisms of capitalism to develop to their most extreme point and only then transforming them. On the contrary, the essence of revolutionary tactics is to recognize the *direction* of this development and then, in the political struggle, to push its consequences to the extreme. Thus, Social Democracy has combatted protectionism and militarism without waiting for their reactionary character to become fully evident. Bernstein's tactics, however, are not guided by a consideration of the development and the aggravation of the contradictions of capitalism but by the prospect of the attenuation of these contradictions. He shows this most clearly when he speaks of the "adaptation" of capitalist economy. Now, when could such a conception be correct? All the contradictions of modern society are simply the results of the capitalist process of production. If it is true that capitalism will continue to develop in the direction it has taken until the present, then the unavoidable consequence is that its contradictions must necessarily become sharper and more aggravated instead of lessening. The possibility of the attenuation of the contradictions of capitalism presupposes that the capitalist mode of production itself will stop its progress. In short, the general presupposition of Bernstein's theory is the *cessation of capitalist development*. In this way, however, his theory condemns itself in a twofold manner. In the first place, it manifests its *utopian* character in its stand on the establishment of socialism. It is *a priori* clear that a defective capitalist development cannot lead to a socialist transformation. This proves the correctness of our presentation of the practical consequences of the theory. In the second place, Bernstein's theory reveals its *reactionary* character when it is related to the actual rapid capitalist development. This poses the question: given the real development of capitalism, how can we explain or rather characterize Bernstein's position?

In the first chapter, we demonstrated the untenability of the economic preconditions on which Bernstein builds his analysis of existing social relationships (his theory of the "means of adaptation"). We have seen that neither the credit system nor cartels can be said to be "means of adaptation" of the capitalist economy. Neither the temporary cessation of crises nor the survival of the middle class can be regarded as symptoms of capitalist adaptation. But, aside from their incorrectness, there is a common characteristic in all of the above details of the theory of the means of adaptation. This theory does not seize these manifestations of contemporary economic life as they appear in their organic relationship with the whole of capitalist development, with the complete economic mechanism of capitalism. The theory pulls these details out of their living economic context, treating them as the *disjecta membra* of a lifeless machine. Consider, for example, the conception of the adaptive effect of *credit*. If we consider credit as a higher natural stage of the process of exchange and, therefore, as tied to all the contradictions inherent in capitalist exchange, we cannot possibly see it, at the same time, as a mechanical means of adaptation existing outside of the process of exchange any more than we could consider money, commodities, or capital as "means of adaptation" of capitalism. But, no less than money, commodities, and capital, credit is an organic link of capitalist economy at a certain stage of its development. Like them, it is an indispensable gear in the mechanism of the capitalist economy and, at the same time, an instrument of destruction, since it aggravates the internal contradictions of capitalism. The same thing is true of cartels and the perfected means of communication.

The same mechanical and undialectical conception is seen in the way that Bernstein describes the cessation of crises as a symptom of the "adaptation" of the capitalist economy. For him, crises are simply derangements of the economic mechanism. With their cessation, he thinks, the mechanism could function smoothly. But the fact is that crises are not "derangements"—or, rather, they are "derangements" without which the capitalist economy as a whole could not develop at all. If, in a word, crises constitute the only method possible in capitalism—and therefore the normal method—of periodically solving the conflict between the unlimited extension of production and the narrow limits of the market, then crises are an organic phenomenon, inseparable from the capitalist economy.

In an "undisturbed" advance of capitalist production lurks a threat to capitalism that is much greater than crises. It is not the threat resulting from the contradiction between production and exchange, but from the growth of the productivity of labor itself, which leads to a constantly falling rate of profit. The fall in the rate of profit has the extremely dangerous tendency of rendering impossible the production of small and middle-size capitals, and thus limiting the new formation and therefore the extension of placements for capital. It is precisely crises which constitute the other consequence of the same process. The result of crises is the periodic *depreciation* of capital, a fall in the prices of the means of production, a paralysis of a part of the active capital, and, in time, the increase of profits. Crises thus create the possibilities of new investment and therefore of the advance of production. Hence, they appear to be the instrument for rekindling the fire of capitalist development. Their cessation—not temporary cessation but their total disappearance—would not lead to the further development of the capitalist economy, as Bernstein thinks. Rather, it would drive capitalism into the swamps.

True to the mechanical view of his theory of adaptation, Bernstein forgets the necessity of crises as well as the necessity of new placements of small and middle-size capitals. And that is why, among other things, the constant reappearance of small capital seems to him to be a sign of the cessation of capitalist development though it is, in fact, a sign of normal capitalist development.

There is, of course, one viewpoint from which all of the above-mentioned phenomena are seen exactly as they have been presented by the theory of "adaptation." It is the viewpoint of the *individual* capitalist who reflects in his mind the economic facts around him just as they appear when deformed by the laws of competition. The individual capitalist sees each organic part of the totality of our economy as a whole, an independent entity. Further, he sees them as they act on him, the individual capitalist; and he therefore considers these facts to be simple "derangements" or simple "means of adaptation." For the individual capitalist, crises are really simple "derangements" or "means of adaptation"; the cessation of crises accords him a longer existence. As far as he is concerned, credit is only a means of "adapting" his insufficient productive forces to the needs of the market. And it seems to him that the cartel of which he becomes a member really suppresses industrial anarchy.

In a word, Bernstein's theory of adaptation is nothing but a theoretical generalization of the conception of the individual capitalist. What is this viewpoint theoretically if not the essential and characteristic aspect of bourgeois vulgar economics? All the economic errors of this school rest precisely on the conception that mistakes the phenomena of competition, as seen from the angle of the individual capitalist, for the phenomena of the whole of capitalist economy. Just as Bernstein considers credit to be a means of "adaptation," so vulgar economy considers *money* to be a judicious means of "adaptation" to the needs of exchange. Vulgar economy, too, tries to find the antidote against the ills of capitalism in the phenomena of capitalism itself. Like Bernstein, it believes in the *possibility* of regulating the capitalist economy. And, still in the manner of Bernstein, it arrives in time at the desire to *palliate* the contradictions of capitalism, that is, at the belief in the possibility of patching up the sores of capitalism. In other words, it ends up with a reactionary and not a revolutionary program, and thus in a utopia.

The revisionist theory can therefore be characterized in the following way: it is a theory of socialist standstill justified through a vulgar economic theory of capitalist standstill.

## PART TWO: ECONOMIC DEVELOPMENT AND SOCIALISM[13]

The greatest conquest in the development of the proletarian class struggle was the discovery that the point of departure for the realization of socialism lies in the *economic relations* of capitalist society. As a result, socialism was changed from an "ideal" dreamed by humanity for thousands of years to an *historical necessity*.

Bernstein denies the existence of these economic presuppositions of socialism in the society of today. In this, his reasoning has undergone an interesting evolution. At first, in the *Neue Zeit*, he only contested the rapidity of the process of concentration taking place in industry, basing his position on a comparison of the occupational statistics of Germany in 1882 and 1895. In order to use these figures for his purpose, he was obliged to have recourse to an entirely summary and mechanical procedure. But even in the most favorable case, his reference to the persistence of middle-size enterprises could not in the least weaken the Marxian analysis, because the latter does not presuppose, as a condition for the realization of socialism, either a definite *rate* of concentration of industry—that is, a definite *delay* of the realization of the socialist goal—or, as we have already shown, the *absolute disappearance* of small capitals, or the disappearance of the petty bourgeoisie.

In the further development of his ideas in his book, Bernstein furnishes us new proofs: *the statistics of shareholding societies*. These statistics are supposed to prove that the number of shareholders increases constantly and, as a result, the capitalist class does not become smaller but grows continually larger. It is surprising that Bernstein has so little acquaintance with his material, and how poorly he knows how to use the data in his own behalf.

If he wanted to disprove the Marxian law of industrial development by referring to the condition of shareholding societies, he should have resorted to entirely different figures. Namely, anybody who is acquainted with the history of shareholding societies in Germany knows that their average foundation capital has *diminished* almost constantly. Thus, while before 1871 the average foundation capital reached the figure of 10.8 million marks, it was only 4.01 million in 1871, 3.8 million in 1873, less than a million from 1882 to 1887, 0.56 million in 1891, and only 0.62 million in 1892. After this date, the figures oscillated around 1 million marks, falling from 1.78 million in 1895 to 1.19 million in the course of the first half of 1897.[14]

Surprising figures! Bernstein probably hoped to use them to construct the existence of an anti-Marxian tendency, that of the transition of large enterprises back into small ones. But, in this case, everyone can answer him: If you are to prove anything by means of these statistics, you must first of all show that they refer to the same branches of industry, that the small enterprises really replace large ones, and that they do not appear only where, previously, individual enterprises, artisan industry, or miniature industry were the rule. This, however, you cannot show. The passage of immense shareholding societies to middle-size and small enterprises can only be explained by the fact that the system of shareholding companies continues to penetrate new branches of production. Before, only a small number of large enterprises were organized as shareholding societies. Gradually shareholding organization has won middle-size and even small enterprises. (Today we can observe shareholding societies with a capital of less than 1,000 marks.)

But what is the economic significance of the ever greater extension of the system of shareholding societies? It signifies the growing socialization of production within the capitalist form—socialization not only of large but also of middle-size and even small production. Therefore, the extension of shareholding does not contradict Marxist theory but, on the contrary, confirms it emphatically.

N.b

In effect, what does the economic phenomenon of a shareholding society actually amount to? On the one hand, the unification of a number of small fortunes into one large productive capital; on the other hand, the separation of production from capitalist ownership. That is, it signifies a double victory over the capitalist mode of production—but still on the capitalist base. In view of this, what is the meaning of the statistics cited by Bernstein concerning the large number of shareholders participating in capitalist enterprises? These statistics demonstrate precisely that at present one capitalist enterprise does not correspond, as hitherto, to a single proprietor of capital but to a whole group, an ever increasing number of capitalists. Consequently, the economic concept "capitalist" no longer signifies an isolated individual. The industrial capitalist of today is a collective person, composed of hundreds and even of thousands of individuals. Within the framework of capitalist society, the category "capitalist" has itself become a social category; it has been *socialized*.

How can Bernstein's belief that the phenomenon of shareholding societies stands for the dispersion and not the concentration of capital be explained in view of the above? Why goes he see the extension of capitalist property where Marx sees the "suppression of capitalist property"? This is a simple, vulgar economic error. By "capitalist" Bernstein does not mean a category of production but of property rights; not an economic unit but a fiscal unit; not a totality of production but simply a certain quantity of money. That is why in his English thread trust he does not see the fusion of 12,300 persons into one, but fully 12,300 different capitalists. That is why the engineer Schulze, whose wife's dowry brought him "a large number of shares" from stockholder Müller, is also a capitalist for Bernstein (p. 53). That is why, for Bernstein, the whole world seems to swarm with capitalists.[15]

Here as usual, the theoretical base of Bernstein's vulgar economic error is his "popularization" of socialism. By transporting the concept "capitalist" from the relations of production to property relations, and by speaking of "men instead of speaking of entrepreneurs" (p. 52), he moves the question of socialism from the realm of production into the realm of relations of fortune—from the relation between capital and labor to the relation between rich and poor.

In this manner, we are merrily led from Marx and Engels to the author of the *Evangel of the Poor Fisherman*, only with the difference that Weitling,[16] with the sure instinct of the proletarian, recognized in the opposition between the poor and the rich the class antagonisms in their primitive form, and wanted to make of them a lever of the socialist movement, while Bernstein, on the other hand, sees the prospects of socialism in making the poor rich, that is, in the attenuation of class antagonisms. For this reason, Bernstein is engaged in a petty-bourgeois course.

True, Bernstein does not limit himself to income statistics. He furnishes statistics of economic enterprises, and from many countries: Germany, France, England, Switzerland, Austria, and the United States. But what kind of statistics are these? They are not the comparative figures of *different periods* in each country but of each period in different countries. Thus, with the exception of Germany, where he reprints the old contrast between 1895 and 1882, he does not compare the statistics of enterprises of a given country at different epochs but only the *absolute* figures for different countries: England in 1891, France in 1894, the United States in 1890, etc. He reaches the following conclusion: "If large exploitation is already supreme in industry today, it nevertheless represents, including the enterprises dependent on it, even in a country as developed as Prussia, at most *half* of the population occupied in production" (p. 98). This is also true of Germany, England, Belgium, etc.

What he proves in this way is obviously not the existence of this or that tendency of economic development but merely the absolute relation of forces of different forms of enterprise or of the various professional classes. If this is supposed to prove the impossibility of realizing socialism, the reasoning must rest on the theory according to which the result of social efforts is decided by the relation of the numerical physical forces of the elements in the struggle—that is, by the mere factor of *violence*. Here Bernstein, who always thunders against Blanquism, himself falls into the grossest Blanquist misunderstanding. There is, of course, the difference that the Blanquists as a socialist and revolutionary tendency presupposed as obvious the possibility of the economic realization of socialism and built the chances of a violent revolution—even by a small minority—on this possibility. Bernstein, on the contrary, infers from the numerical insufficiency of a majority of the people the impossibility of the economic realization of socialism. Social Democracy does not, however, expect to attain its aim either as a result of the victorious violence of a minority or through the numerical superiority of a majority. It sees socialism as a result of economic necessity—and the comprehension of that necessity—leading to the suppression of capitalism by the masses of the people. This necessity manifests itself above all in the *anarchy of capitalism*.

Concerning the decisive question of anarchy in capitalist economy, Bernstein denies only the great general crises, not the partial and national crises. Thus, he denies that there is a great deal of anarchy; at the same time, he admits the existence of a little anarchy. Concerning the capitalist economy, he is—to use Marx's illustration—like the foolish virgin who had a child "who was only very small." But the misfortune is that in matters like anarchy, little and much are equally bad. If Bernstein recognizes the existence of a little anarchy, then by the mechanism of commodity economy, this anarchy will be extended to unheard-of proportions—to the breakdown. But if Bernstein hopes, while maintaining the system of commodity production, to gradually transform the bit of anarchy into order and harmony, he again falls into one of the fundamental errors of bourgeois vulgar economics in that he treats the mode of exchange as independent of the mode of production.[17]

This is not the correct place for a detailed demonstration of Bernstein's surprising confusion concerning the most elementary principles of political economy. But one point, to which we are led by the fundamental question of capitalist anarchy, must be briefly clarified.

Bernstein declares that Marx's labor theory of value is a mere abstraction, a term which for him, in political economy, obviously constitutes an insult.

But if the labor theory of value is only an abstraction, if it is only a "mental construct" (p. 38)—then every normal citizen who has done military duty and pays his taxes has the same right as Karl Marx to fashion his favorite nonsense into such a "mental construct," to make his own law of value. "Marx has just as much right to neglect the properties of commodities until the latter are no more than the incarnation of quantities of simple human labor as have the economists of the Böhm-Jevons school to abstract all the qualities of commodities other than their utility" (p. 34).[18]

Thus, Marx's social labor and Menger's abstract utility are, for Bernstein, quite similar—pure abstractions. In this, Bernstein forgets completely that Marx's abstraction is not an invention but a discovery. It does not exist in Marx's head but in the commodity economy. It has not an imaginary but a real social existence, so real that it can be cut, hammered, weighed, and coined. The abstract human labor discovered by Marx is, in its developed form, none other than money. That is precisely one of Marx's most brilliant discoveries, while for all bourgeois political economists, from the first of the mercantilists to the last of the classicists, the essence of money has remained a book with seven seals.

The Böhm-Jevons abstract utility is, on the contrary, a mere mental construct or, rather, it is a construct of intellectual emptiness, a private absurdity for which neither capitalism nor any other society can be made responsible but only vulgar bourgeois economics itself. With this "mental construct," Bernstein, Böhm, and Jevons, and the entire subjective fraternity, can remain twenty more years before the mystery of money without arriving at a solution any different from the one reached by any cobbler—namely, that money is also a "useful" thing.

Thus, Bernstein has fully lost all comprehension of Marx's law of value. However, anybody with a small understanding of Marxian economics can see that without the law of value, Marx's whole system is incomprehensible. Or, to speak more concretely, without an understanding of the nature of the commodity and its exchange, the entire economy of capitalism, with all its concatenations, must remain an enigma.

But, what precisely is the magic key which enabled Marx to open the door to the deepest secrets of all capitalist phenomena and solve, as if at play, problems that were not even suspected by the greatest minds of classical bourgeois political economy, such as Smith and Ricardo? Nothing other than his conception of the whole capitalist economy as an historical phenomenon—not merely, as in the best of cases with the classical economists, concerning the feudal past of capitalism, but also concerning the socialist future. The secret of Marx's theory of value, of his analysis of money, his theory of capital, his theory of the rate of profit, and consequently of the whole existing economic system is—the transitory nature of the capitalist economy, its collapse: thus—and this is only another aspect of the same phenomenon—the final goal, socialism. And precisely because, *a priori*, Marx looked at capitalism from the socialist's viewpoint, that is, from the historical viewpoint, he was enabled to decipher the hieroglyphics of capitalist economy. And because he took the socialist viewpoint as a point of departure for his analyses of bourgeois society, he was in a position to give a scientific base to socialism.

This is the measure by which we evaluate Bernstein's remarks at the end of his book where he complains of the "dualism" found "everywhere in Marx's monumental work" [*Capital*—D.H.]. "The dualism is found in that the work wishes to be a scientific study and prove, at the same time, a thesis which was completely elaborated a long time before; it is based on a schema that already contains the result to which he wants to lead. The return to the *Communist Manifesto* (that is, to the socialist goal!—R.L.) proves the existence of vestiges of utopianism in Marx's system" (p. 210).

Marx's "dualism," however, is nothing but the dualism of the socialist future and the capitalist present, of capital and labor, of the bourgeoisie and the proletariat. It is the monumental scientific reflection of the dualism existing in bourgeois society, the dualism of the bourgeois class antagonisms.

When Bernstein sees this theoretical dualism in Marx as "a survival of utopianism," this is only his naïve avowal that he denies the historical dualism of bourgeois society, the existence of class antagonisms in capitalism, that for him socialism itself has become only a "survival of utopianism." Bernstein's "monism"—that is, his unity—is but the unity of the eternalized capitalist order, the unity of the socialist who has renounced his aim and has decided to see in bourgeois society, one and immutable, the goal of human development.

However, if Bernstein does not see in the economic structure of capitalism the duality, the development that leads to socialism, then in order to preserve the socialist program, at least in form, he is obliged to take refuge in an idealist construction lying outside of the economic development. He is obliged to transform socialism itself from a definite historical phase of social development into an abstract "principle." That is why the "cooperative principle"—the meager decantation of socialism with which Bernstein wishes to garnish the capitalist economy—appears not as a concession of his bourgeois theory to the socialist future of society but to Bernstein's own socialist past.

## TRADE UNIONS, COOPERATIVES, AND POLITICAL DEMOCRACY

...According to Bernstein, democracy is an inevitable stage in the development of modern society. To him, as to the bourgeois theoreticians of liberalism, democracy is the great fundamental law of historical development in general whose realization must be served by all of the active forces of political life. However, presented in such absolute form, this is totally false; it is a petty-bourgeois and superficial schematization of the results of a very short peak of bourgeois development, roughly the last twenty-five or thirty years. We reach entirely different conclusions when we examine more closely the historical development of democracy and at the same time the general political history of capitalism.

Concerning the former, democracy has been found in the most dissimilar social formations: in primitive communist societies, in the slave states of antiquity, and in the medieval city-communes. Similarly, absolutism and constitutional monarchy are found in the most varied economic contexts. On the other hand, at its beginnings—as commodity production—capitalism calls into being a democratic constitution in the city-communes of the Middle Ages. Later, in its more developed form, as manufacturing, capitalism found its corresponding political form in the absolute monarchy. Finally, as a developed industrial economy, it brought into being in France alternatively the democratic Republic (1793), the absolute monarchy of Napoleon I, the nobles' monarchy of the Restoration Period (1815–1830), the bourgeois constitutional monarchy of Louis-Philippe, then again the democratic Republic, and again the monarchy of Napoleon III, and finally, for the third time, the Republic. In Germany, the only truly democratic institution—universal suffrage—is not a conquest of bourgeois liberalism. Universal suffrage in Germany was an instrument for the fusion of the small states, and it is only in this sense that it has any importance for the development of the German bourgeoisie, which otherwise is quite satisfied with a semi-feudal constitutional monarchy. In Russia, capitalism prospered for a long time under the regime of Oriental personal rule without the bourgeoisie manifesting the least desire for democracy. In Austria, universal suffrage was above all a life line thrown to a decomposing monarchy [and how little it is actually tied together with true democracy is shown by the domination of Paragraph 14].[19] Finally, in Belgium, the conquest of universal suffrage by the labor movement was undoubtedly due to the weakness of militarism, consequently to the particular geographic and political situation of the country; and, above all, it is a "bit of democracy" that has been won not *by* the bourgeoisie but *against* it.

On closer examination, the uninterrupted ascent of democracy, which to our revisionism, as well as to bourgeois liberalism, appears as a great fundamental law of human history and, at the very least, of modern history, is shown to be a phantom. No absolute and universal relation can be constructed between capitalist development and democracy. The political form is always the result of the whole sum of political factors, domestic as well as foreign. Within its boundaries it admits all variations of the scale, from absolute monarchy to the democratic republic.

We must therefore abandon all hope of establishing a general law of the historical development of democracy even within the framework of modern society. Turning to the present phase of bourgeois history, we also see here factors in the political situation which, instead of assuring the realization of Bernstein's schema, lead rather to the abandonment by bourgeois society of the democratic conquests won up to the present.

On the one hand—and this is of the greatest importance—the democratic institutions have largely played out their role as aids in the bourgeois development. Insofar as they were necessary to bring about the fusion of small states and the creation of large modern states (Germany, Italy), they have become dispensable. Economic development has meanwhile effected an internal organic healing [and the surgical dressing, political democracy, can thus be taken off without any danger for the organism of bourgeois society!]

The same thing is true of the transformation of the entire political and administrative machinery of the state from a feudal or semi-feudal mechanism to a capitalist one. While this transformation has been historically inseparable from the development of democracy, today it has been achieved to such an extent that the purely democratic ingredients of society, such as universal suffrage and the republican form of the state, may be eliminated without the administration, the state finances, or the military organization, etc., finding it necessary to return to the pre-March forms.[20]

If liberalism as such is now essentially useless to bourgeois society, on the other hand, in important respects it has become a direct impediment. Two factors completely dominate the political life of contemporary states: *world politics* and the labor movement. Each is only a different aspect of the present phase of capitalist development.

As a result of the development of the world economy and the aggravation and generalization of competition on the world market, militarism and marinism[21] as instruments of world politics have become a decisive factor in the internal as well as in the external life of the great states. If it is true that world politics and militarism represent a *rising* tendency in the present phase, then bourgeois democracy must logically move in a *descending* line. [The most striking example: the North American union since the Spanish war. In France, the Republic owes its existence mainly to the international situation which provisionally makes a war impossible. If a war did come and, as everything leads one to believe, France were not up to the test, then the answer to the first French defeat would be—the proclamation of the monarchy in Paris. In Germany, the new era of great armaments (1893) and that of world politics which began with Kiao-Cheou[22] were paid for with two sacrifices of bourgeois democracy: the decomposition of the liberals and the change of the Center Party.][23]

If foreign policy pushes the bourgeoisie into the arms of reaction, this is no less true of domestic politics—thanks to the rise of the working class. Bernstein shows that he recognizes this when he makes the "legend" of Social Democracy which "wants to swallow everything"—in other words, the socialist efforts of the working class—responsible for the desertion of the liberal bourgeoisie [from a possible alliance with Social Democracy—D.H.]. In this connection, he advises the proletariat to disavow its socialist aim so that the mortally frightened liberals might come out of the mousehole of reaction. In thus making the abandonment of the socialist labor movement an essential condition and a social presupposition for the preservation of bourgeois democracy today, he proves in a striking manner that this democracy is in complete contradiction with the inner tendency of development of modern society. At the same time, he proves that the socialist labor movement itself is *a direct product* of this tendency.

In this way, however, he proves still another thing. By making the renunciation of the socialist goal an essential presupposition and condition of the resurrection of bourgeois democracy, he shows, conversely, how inexact is the claim that bourgeois democracy is an indispensable condition of the socialist movement and the victory of socialism. Bernstein's reasoning exhausts itself in a vicious circle; his conclusion swallows his premises.

The exit from this circle is quite simple. In view of the fact that bourgeois liberalism has sold its soul from fear of the growing labor movement and its final aim, it follows that the socialist labor movement today is and can be the *only* support of democracy. The fate of the socialist movement is not bound to bourgeois democracy; but the fate of democracy, on the contrary, is bound to the socialist movement. Democracy does not acquire greater chances of life in the measure that the working class renounces the struggle for its emancipation;

on the contrary, democracy acquires greater chances of survival as the socialist movement becomes sufficiently strong to struggle against the reactionary consequences of world politics and the bourgeois desertion of democracy. He who would strengthen democracy must also want to strengthen and not weaken the socialist movement; and with the renunciation of the struggle for socialism goes that of both the labor movement and democracy.

[At the end of his "Answer" to Kautsky[24] in *Vörwarts* (March 26, 1899), Bernstein explains that he is completely in agreement with the practical part of the Social Democratic program; his objections were only to the theoretical parts of that program. Aside from that, he obviously believes that he can march with full rights in the ranks of the Party, for how "important" is it "if there is a proposition in the theoretical part which no longer agrees with one's conception of the course of development"? This explanation shows best of all how completely Bernstein has lost the sense of the connection of the practical activity of Social Democracy with its general principles, how much the same words have ceased to mean the same thing for Bernstein and the Party. In effect, Bernstein's own theory, as we have seen, leads to the most elementary Social Democratic understanding—that without the fundamental basis, the practical struggle too is worthless and aimless, that with the giving up of the *ultimate goal*, the *movement* itself must be lost.]

## THE CONQUEST OF POLITICAL POWER

As we have seen, the fate of democracy is bound up with the fate of the labor movement. But does the development of democracy, in the best of cases, render superfluous or impossible a proletarian revolution in the sense of the seizure of state power, the conquest of political power?

Bernstein settles the question by minutely weighing the good and bad sides of legal reform and revolution in almost the same manner in which cinnamon or pepper is weighed out in a consumers' cooperative store. He sees the legal course of development as the action of the intellect, while the revolutionary course is the action of feeling. Reformist work is seen as a slow method of historical progress; revolution as a rapid method. In legislation, he sees a methodical force; in revolution, an elemental force (p. 218).

We have known for a long time that the petty-bourgeois reformer finds "good" and "bad" sides in everything; he nibbles a bit at all grasses.[25] But we have known for just as long that the real course of events is little affected by such petty-bourgeois combinations, and that the carefully gathered little pile of the "good sides" of all things possible blows away at the first wind of history. Historically, legislative reform and the revolutionary method function in accordance with influences that are more profound than the consideration of the advantages or inconveniences of this or that method.

In the history of bourgeois society, legislative reform served generally to strengthen the rising class until the latter felt sufficiently strong to seize political power, to overturn the existing juridical system and to construct a new one. Bernstein, thundering against the conquest of political power as a Blanquist theory of violence, has the misfortune to label as a Blanquist error that which has been for centuries the pivot and motive force of human history. As long as class societies have existed, and the class struggle has constituted the essential content of their history, the conquest of political power has continually been the aim of all rising classes and the beginning and end of every historical period. This can be seen in the long struggle of the peasantry against the financiers and nobility in ancient Rome; in the struggles of the medieval nobility against the bishops, and the artisans against the nobles in the cities of the Middle Ages; and in modern times, in the struggle of the bourgeoisie against feudalism.

Legal reform and revolution are not different methods of historical progress that can be picked out at pleasure from the counter of history, just as one chooses hot or cold sausages. They are different *moments* in the development of class society which condition and complement each other, and at the same time exclude each other reciprocally as, e.g., the north and south poles, the bourgeoisie and the proletariat.

In effect, every legal constitution is the *product* of a revolution. In the history of classes, revolution is the act of political creation while legislation is the political expression of the life of a society that has already come into being. Work for legal reforms does not itself contain its own driving force independent from revolution. During every historical period, work for reforms is carried on only in the direction given it by the impetus of the last revolution, and continues as long as that impulsion continues to make itself felt. Or, to put it more concretely, it is carried on only in the *framework* of the social form created by the last revolution. Precisely here is the kernel of the problem.

It is absolutely false and totally unhistorical to represent work for reforms as a drawn-out revolution, and revolution as a condensed series of reforms. A social transformation and a legislative reform do not differ according to their *duration* but according to their *essence*. The whole secret of historical transformations through the utilization of political power consists precisely in the change of simple quantitative modification into a new quality, or to speak more concretely, in the transition from one historical period, one social order, to another.

He who pronounces himself in favor of the method of legal reforms *in place of and as opposed to* the conquest of political power and social revolution does not really choose a more tranquil, surer and slower road to the *same* goal. He chooses a *different* goal. Instead of taking a stand for the establishment of a new social order, he takes a stand for surface modifications of the old order. Thus, the political views of revisionism lead to the same conclusion as the economic theories of revisionism: not to the realization of the *socialist* order, but to the reform of *capitalism*, not to the suppression of the wage system, but to the diminution of exploitation; in a word, to the elimination of the abuses of capitalism instead of to that of capitalism itself....

In a word, democracy is indispensable not because it renders *superfluous* the conquest of political power by the proletariat but, on the contrary, because it renders this conquest of power both *necessary* as well as *possible*. When Engels, in his Preface to *Class Struggles in France*, revised the tactics of the modern labor movement and opposed the legal struggle to the barricades, he did not have in mind—*this comes out in every line of the Preface*—the question of the final conquest of political power, but the modern daily struggle; not the attitude of the proletariat *opposed to* the capitalist state at the moment of the seizure of state power, but its attitude within the *bounds* of the capitalist state. In a word, Engels gave directions to the *oppressed* proletariat, not to the victorious proletariat.[26]

On the other hand, Marx's well-known declaration concerning the agrarian question in England, on which Bernstein leans heavily—"We would probably succeed more easily by buying out the landlords"—does not refer to the attitude of the proletariat *before* but *after* its victory. For, obviously, it can only be a question of buying out the old dominant class when the working class is in power. The possibility envisaged by Marx is that of the *peaceful exercise of the dictatorship of the proletariat* and not the replacement of the dictatorship by capitalist social reforms.

The necessity of the proletariat's seizing power was always unquestionable for Marx and Engels. It is left to Bernstein to consider the henhouse of bourgeois parliamentarism as the correct organ by means of which the most formidable social transformation in history, the passage of society from the *capitalist* to the *socialist* form, is to be completed.

Bernstein, however, introduces his theory with fear and warnings against the danger of the proletariat's acquiring power too *early*! That is, according to Bernstein, the proletariat ought to leave bourgeois society in its present conditions and itself suffer a frightful defeat. What follows clearly from this fear is that if circumstances led the proletariat to power, it could draw from Bernstein's theory the following "practical" conclusion: to go to sleep.[27] In this way, the theory judges itself, it is a conception which, at the most decisive moments of the struggle, condemns the proletariat to inactivity, and thus to a passive betrayal of its own cause.

In effect, our program would be a miserable scrap of paper if it could not serve us in *all* eventualities, at *all* moments of the struggle, and serve precisely by its *application* and not by its nonapplication. If our program is the formulation of the historical development of society from capitalism to socialism, obviously it must also formulate, in all their fundamental lines, all the transitory phases of this development, and consequently at every moment it should be able to indicate to the proletariat what ought to be its correct behavior in order to move toward socialism. It follows generally that there can be *no time* when the proletariat will be obliged to abandon its program, or be abandoned by it.

This is manifested practically in the fact that there can be no time when the proletariat, brought to power by the force of circumstances, is not in the condition, or is not morally obliged, to take certain measures for the realization of its program, transitory measures in the direction of socialism. Behind the belief that the socialist program could break down at any moment during the political domination of the proletariat, and give no directions for its realization, lies, unconsciously, the other belief, that *the socialist program is generally and at all times, unrealizable.*

And what if the transitory measures are premature? The question hides a whole slew of misunderstandings concerning the real course of social transformations.

Above all, the seizure of state power by the proletariat, i.e., by a large popular class, is not produced artificially. It presupposes (with the exception of cases like the Paris Commune when power was not attained after a conscious struggle for its goal, but, exceptionally, fell into the proletariat's hands like an object abandoned by everybody else) a definite degree of maturity of economic and political relations. Here we have the essential difference between Blanquist[28] coups d'état by a "resolute minority," bursting out at any moment like a pistol shot, and for this very reason, always inopportunely, and the conquest of political power by a large and class-conscious popular mass. Such a mass itself can only be the product of the beginning of the collapse of bourgeois society, and therefore bears in itself the economic and political legitimation of its opportune appearance.

If, therefore, from the standpoint of the social *presuppositions*, the conquest of political power by the working class cannot occur "too early," then from the standpoint of political effect—of *conservation* of power—it is necessarily "too early." The premature revolution, the thought of which keeps Bernstein awake, menaces us like a sword of Damocles. Against it neither prayers nor supplication, scares nor anguish, are of avail. And this, for two very simple reasons.

In the first place, it is impossible to imagine that a transformation as formidable as the passage from capitalist society to socialist society can be realized in one act, by a victorious blow of the proletariat. To consider that as possible is again to lend credence to pure Blanquist conceptions. The socialist transformation presupposes a long and stubborn struggle in the course of which, quite probably, the proletariat will be repulsed more than once, so that, from the viewpoint of the final outcome of the struggle, it will have necessarily come to power "too early" the first time.

In the second place, however, it will also be impossible to avoid the "premature" seizure of state power precisely because these "premature" attacks of the proletariat constitute a factor, and indeed a very important factor, creating the *political* conditions of the final victory. In the course of the political crisis accompanying its seizure of power, in the fire of long and stubborn struggles, the proletariat will acquire the degree of political maturity permitting it to obtain the definitive victory of the revolution. Thus these "premature" attacks of the proletariat on the state power are in themselves important historical moments helping to provoke and determine the *point* of the final victory. Considered from *this* point of view, the idea of a "premature" conquest of political power by the laboring class appears to be a political absurdity, derived from a mechanical conception of social development, and positing for the victory of the class struggle a *time* fixed *outside* and *independent* of the class struggle.

Since the proletariat is not in the position to seize political power in any other way than "prematurely"; since the proletariat is absolutely obliged to seize power "too early" once or several times before it can enduringly maintain itself in power, the objection to the "*premature*" seizure of power is nothing other than a *general opposition to the aspiration of the proletariat to take state power*.

Just as all roads lead to Rome, so, too, we logically arrive at the conclusion that the revisionist proposal to abandon the ultimate goal of socialism is really a recommendation to renounce the socialist *movement* itself [, that its advice to Social Democracy, "to go to sleep" in the case of the conquest of power, is identical with the advice: *to go to sleep now and forever, i.e., to give up the class struggle*].

### THE BREAKDOWN

Bernstein began his revision of Social Democracy by abandoning the theory of capitalist breakdown. The latter, however, is the cornerstone of scientific socialism, and with the removal of this cornerstone, Bernstein must also reject the whole socialist doctrine. In the course of his discussion, he abandons, one after another, the positions of socialism in order to be able to maintain his first affirmation.

Without the breakdown of capitalism, the expropriation of the capitalist class is impossible. Bernstein therefore renounces expropriation and chooses a progressive realization of the "cooperative principle" as the goal of the labor movement.

But cooperation cannot be realized within capitalist production. Bernstein therefore renounces the socialization of production and proposes to reform commerce and to develop consumers' cooperatives.

But the transformation of society through consumers' cooperatives, even together with the trade unions, is incompatible with the real material development of capitalist society. Bernstein therefore abandons the materialist conception of history.

But his conception of the course of economic development is incompatible with the Marxist theory of surplus value. Bernstein therefore abandons the theory of value and of surplus value and, in this way, the whole economic theory of Karl Marx.

But the class struggle of the proletariat cannot be carried on without a definite final aim and without an economic base in the existing society. Bernstein therefore abandons the class struggle and proclaims the reconciliation with bourgeois liberalism.

But in a class society, the class struggle is a fully natural and unavoidable phenomenon. Bernstein therefore contests even the existence of classes in society: for him, the working class is a mass of individuals, divided not only politically and intellectually, but also economically. And, according to him, the bourgeoisie does not group itself politically in accordance with its inner economic interest, but only because of external pressure, from above and below.

But if there is no economic base for the class struggle and if, too, there actually are no classes, then not only the future, but even the past struggles of the proletariat against the bourgeoisie appear impossible, and Social Democracy and its successes seem absolutely incomprehensible. On the other hand, from this point of view, the latter can be understood only as the results of political pressure by the government—that is, not as the natural consequences of historical development but as the fortuitous consequences of the policy of the Hohenzollern; not as the legitimate offspring of capitalist society, but as the bastard children of reaction. Thus, with rigorous logic, Bernstein passes from the materialist conception of history to the outlook of the *Frankfurter Zeitung* and the *Vossische Zeitung*.[29]

After rejecting the whole socialist criticism of capitalist society, the only thing that remains is to find that, on the whole, the present state of affairs is satisfactory. Here too, Bernstein does not hesitate. He finds that at present the reaction is not very strong in Germany, that "we do not see much of political reaction in the countries of Western Europe," and that in nearly all the countries of the West "the attitude of the bourgeois classes toward the socialist movement is at most an attitude of defense but not one of oppression" (*Vörwarts*, March 26, 1899). Far from becoming worse, the situation of the workers is getting better; the bourgeoisie is politically progressive and even morally healthy; we see little of either reaction or oppression—and it is all for the best in the best of all possible worlds . . .

Bernstein thus travels in a logical sequence from A to Z. He began by abandoning the *final aim* in favor of the movement. But as there can be no socialist movement without the socialist aim, he necessarily ends by renouncing the *movement* itself.

Thus Bernstein's conception of socialism collapses entirely. With him, the proud and admirable symmetric construction of the Marxist system becomes a pile of rubbish in which the debris of all systems, the pieces of thought of various great and small minds, find a common grave. Marx and Proudhon, Leon von Buch and Franz Oppenheimer, Friedrich Albert Lange and Kant, Herr Prokopovich and Dr. Ritter von Neupauer, Herkner and Schulze-Gaevenitz, Lassalle and Professor Julius Wolf: all contribute their bit to Bernstein's system, and he takes a little from each. This is not astonishing. When he abandoned the class standpoint, he lost the political compass, when he abandoned scientific socialism, he lost the axis of intellectual crystallization around which isolated facts group themselves in the organic whole of a coherent conception of the world.

On first consideration, his doctrine, composed of bits of all possible systems, seems to be completely free from prejudices. Bernstein does not like to talk of "party science," or to be more exact, of class science, any more than he likes to talk of class liberalism or class morality. He thinks he succeeds in representing a universal human abstract science, abstract liberalism, abstract morality. But since the actual society is made up of classes which have diametrically opposed interests, aspirations, and conceptions, a universal human science in social questions, an abstract liberalism, an abstract morality, are at present illusions, a self-deception. What Bernstein considers his universal human science, democracy, and morality, is merely the dominant science, dominant democracy, and dominant morality—that is, bourgeois science, bourgeois democracy, bourgeois morality.

In effect, when Bernstein denies the Marxist economic system in order to swear by the teachings of Brentano, Böhm-Jevons, Say, and Julius Wolf, what does he do but exchange the scientific base of the emancipation of the working class for the apologetics of the bourgeoisie? When he speaks of the universal human character of liberalism, and transforms socialism into a variety of liberalism, what does he do but deprive the socialist movement of its class character and, consequently, of its historical content and, consequently, of all content in general, while conversely making the historical bearer of liberalism, the bourgeoisie, the champion of the universal interests of humanity?

And when he condemns the "raising of the material factors to the rank of an all-powerful force of development"; when he protests against the "contempt for the ideal" in Social Democracy; when he presumes to talk for idealism, for morals, but at the same time inveighs against the only source of the moral rebirth of the proletariat, the revolutionary class struggle—what does he actually do but preach to the working class the quintessence of the morality of the bourgeoisie, that is, the reconciliation with the existing order and the transfer of hope to the beyond of an ethical ideal-world.

When he directs his keenest arrows against the dialectic, what does he do but attack the specific mode of thought of the rising class-conscious proletariat. Isn't the dialectic the sword that has helped the proletariat pierce the darkness of its historical future, the intellectual weapon with which the proletariat, though materially still in the yoke, triumphs over the bourgeoisie, proving to the bourgeoisie its transitory character, showing it the inevitability of the proletarian victory? Hasn't the dialectic already realized a revolution in the domain of thought? In that Bernstein takes leave of the dialectic and resorts instead to the intellectual seesaw of the "on the one hand—on the other hand," "yes—but," "although—however," "more—less," he quite logically lapses into the historically conditioned mode of thought of the declining bourgeoisie, a mode of thought which is the faithful intellectual reflection of its social existence and political activity. The political "on the one hand—on the other hand," "yes—but" of the bourgeoisie of today exactly resembles Bernstein's manner of thinking. This is the sharpest and surest symptom of his bourgeois conception of the world.

But for Bernstein, the word "bourgeois" itself is not a class expression but a universal social notion. Logical to the last dot on the last *i*, he has also exchanged the historical language of the proletariat, together with its science, politics, morals, and mode of thought, for that of the bourgeoisie. When he uses, without distinction, the term "citizen" in reference to the bourgeois as well as to the proletarian, thus intending to refer to man in general, he in fact identifies man in general with the bourgeois, and human society with bourgeois society.

[If at the beginning of the discussion with Bernstein, one still hoped to convince him, to be able to give him back to the movement, by means of arguments from the scientific arsenal of Social Democracy, that hope must now be fully abandoned. Now the same words no longer express the same concepts, and the concepts no longer express the same social facts for both sides. The discussion with Bernstein has become an argument of two world views, of two classes, of two social forms. Today, Bernstein and Social Democracy stand on wholly different terrain.]

### OPPORTUNISM IN THEORY AND PRACTICE

Bernstein's book is of great historical importance to the German and the international labor movement. This was the first attempt to give a theoretical base to the opportunist currents in Social Democracy.

If we take into consideration sporadic manifestations, such as the question of subsidies for steamships,[30] the opportunist currents in our movement have existed for a long time. But it is only since the beginning of the 1890s, with the suppression of the antisocialist laws and the reconquest of the terrain of legality, that we have had an explicit, unitary opportunist current. Vollmar's "state socialism," the vote on the Bavarian budget, the "agrarian socialism" of South Germany, Heine's policy of compensation, Schippel's stand on tariffs and militarism, are the high points in the development of the opportunist practice.[31]

What, above all, is the external characteristic of these practices? Hostility to "theory." This is quite understandable, for our "theory," i.e., the principles of scientific socialism, imposes clearly marked limitations to practical activity—concerning the *aims* of this activity, the *means* of struggle applied, and the *method* of struggle. It is thus natural for those who only run after practical results to want to free their hands, i.e., to split our practice from "theory," to make it independent of theory.

But at every practical effort, this theory hits them on the head. State socialism, agrarian socialism, the policy of compensation, the militia question, all constitute defeats of opportunism. It is clear that if this current is to affirm itself against our principles it must, logically, come to the point of attacking the theory itself, the principles, and rather than ignore them, it must try to shake them and to construct its own theory. Bernstein's book is precisely an effort in that direction. That is why, at the Stuttgart Party Congress [in 1898], the opportunist elements in our Party immediately grouped themselves about Bernstein's banner. If, on the one hand, opportunist currents in practical activity are an entirely natural phenomenon which can be explained in the light of the conditions of our activity and its growth, Bernstein's theory, on the other hand, is a no less natural attempt to group these currents into a general theoretical expression, to discover their proper theoretical presuppositions, and to break with scientific socialism. Bernstein's theory is thus the theoretical ordeal by fire for opportunism, its first scientific legitimation.

How did this test turn out? We have seen the result. Opportunism is not capable of constructing a positive theory capable of withstanding criticism. All it can do is to attack various isolated theses of the Marxist doctrine and, because Marxist doctrine constitutes one solidly constructed edifice, to destroy the entire system from the top to its foundations. This shows that, in its essence, its bases, opportunist practice is irreconcilable with Marxism.

But it is thus further shown that opportunism is incompatible with socialism in general, that its internal tendency is to push the labor movement into bourgeois paths, i.e., to completely paralyze the proletarian class struggle. Considered historically, the proletarian class struggle is obviously not identical with the Marxist system. Before Marx and independent of him, there also existed a labor movement and various socialist systems, each of which, corresponding to the conditions of the time, was in its way the theoretical expression of the working-class struggle for emancipation. The basing of socialism on the moral notion of justice, on a struggle against the mode of distribution instead of against the mode of production; the conception of class antagonism

as an antagonism between the poor and the rich; the effort to graft the "cooperative principle" on capitalist economy—all of what we find in Bernstein's
system—already existed before him. And, *in their time*, these theories, in spite
of their insufficiency, were actual theories of the proletarian class struggle;
they were the children's seven-league boots, thanks to which the proletariat
learned to walk upon the scene of history.

But *after* the development of the class struggle itself and its social conditions had led to the abandonment of these theories and to the formulation of
the principles of scientific socialism, at least in Germany, there can be no
socialism outside of Marxist socialism, and no socialist class struggle outside
of Social Democracy. From then on, socialism and Marxism, the proletarian
struggle for emancipation and Social Democracy, are identical. Therefore,
the return to pre-Marxist socialist theories today does not in the least signify
a return to the seven-league boots of the childhood of the proletariat. No, it is
a return to the puny, worn-out slippers of the bourgeoisie.

Bernstein's theory was the *first*, but also, at the same time, the *last* attempt to
give a theoretical base to opportunism. We say "the last," because in Bernstein's
system, opportunism has gone so far—both negatively, through its renunciation
of scientific socialism, and positively, through its jumbling together of every bit
of theoretical confusion available—that nothing remains to be done. Through
Bernstein's book, opportunism has completed its theoretical development [just
as it completed its practical development in the position taken by Schippel on
the question of militarism], and has drawn its ultimate conclusion.

Not only can Marxist doctrine refute opportunism theoretically; it alone
is able to *explain* opportunism as an historical phenomenon in the development of the Party. The world-historical forward march of the proletariat to its
final victory is, indeed, not "so simple a thing." The original character of this
movement consists in the fact that here, for the first time in history, the popular masses themselves, *in opposition* to all ruling classes, impose their will.
But they must posit this will outside of and beyond the present society. The
masses can only form this *will* in a constant struggle against the existing
order, only within its framework. The unification of the broad popular masses with an aim reaching beyond the whole existing social order, of the daily
struggle with the great world transformation—that is the task of the Social
Democratic movement, which must successfully work forward on its road to
development between two reefs: abandonment of the mass character or abandonment of the final aim; the fall back to sectarianism or the fall into bourgeois reformism; anarchism or opportunism.

Of course, more than a half a century ago the theoretical arsenal of Marxist doctrine already furnished arms that are effective against both of these extremes. But precisely because our movement is a mass movement and the dangers menacing it are not born in the human brain but in social conditions, Marxist doctrine could not assure us, in advance and once and for all, against the anarchist and opportunist deviations. Once they have taken on flesh in practice, they can be overcome only by the movement itself, though of course only with the help of the arms furnished us by Marx. Social Democracy has already overcome the lesser danger, the anarchist streak of childishness, with the "movement of the independents."[32] It is presently in the process of overcoming the greater danger—opportunist dropsy.

With the enormous expansion of the movement in the last years, and the complexity of the conditions in which, and the objectives for which, the struggle must take place, it was inevitable that the moment come in which skepticism concerning the reaching of the great final goal, and hesitations concerning the theoretical aspect of the movement, made themselves felt. Thus, and only thus, can and must the great proletarian movement progress; the instants of vacillation and hesitation are far from a surprise for the Marxist doctrine: Marx predicted them long ago:

"Bourgeois revolutions," wrote Marx a half-century ago in his *Eighteenth Brumaire of Louis Napoleon*, "like those of the eighteenth century, rush onward rapidly from success to success; their dramatic effects surpass one another; men and things seem to be set in flaming diamonds; ecstasy is the prevailing spirit. But they are short-lived; they reach their climax quickly, and then society relapses into a long hangover before it soberly learns how to appropriate the fruits of its period of storm and stress. Proletarian revolutions, on the contrary, such as those of the nineteenth century, criticize themselves continually; constantly interrupt themselves in their own course; come back to what seems to have been accomplished in order to start anew; scorn with cruel thoroughness the half-measures, weaknesses, and wretchedness of their first attempts; seem to throw down their adversary only to enable him to draw fresh strength from the earth and again to rise up against them, still more gigantically; continually recoil in fear before the undefined enormity of their own goals—until the situation is created which renders all retreat impossible, and the conditions themselves cry out: '*Hic Rhodus, hic salta!*' Here is the rose. Dance here!"[33]

This has remained true even after the elaboration of the doctrine of scientific socialism. The proletarian movement has not as yet, all at once, become Social Democratic—even in Germany. But it is *becoming* more Social Democratic

daily because and inasmuch as it continuously surmounts the extreme deviations of anarchism and opportunism, both of which are only moments of the
movement of Social Democracy considered as a *process*.

For these reasons, the surprising thing is not the appearance of the opportunist current but rather its weakness. As long as it showed itself in isolated
single cases concerning the practical activity of the Party, one could still suppose that it had behind it some serious theoretical base. But now that it has
come to full expression in Bernstein's book, one cannot help exclaiming with
astonishment: What? Is that all you have to say? Not a shadow of an original
thought! Not a single idea that was not refuted, crushed, ridiculed, and
reduced to dust by Marxism decades ago!

It was sufficient for opportunism to speak in order to prove that it had
nothing to say. That is the only significance of Bernstein's book in the history
of the Party.

And thus, while saying goodbye to the mode of thought of the revolutionary proletariat, to the dialectic, and to the materialist conception of history,
Bernstein can thank them for the attenuating circumstances that they provide
for his conversion. For only the dialectic and the materialist conception of
history, magnanimous as they are, could make Bernstein appear as a predes-
tined but unconscious instrument by means of which the rising working class
expresses its momentary weakness in order, contemptuously and with pride,
to throw it aside when it sees it in the light.

[We said that the movement *becomes* Social Democratic because and inasmuch as it overcomes the anarchistic and opportunistic deviations which
arise necessarily with its growth. But overcome does not mean to let everything pass peacefully as it pleases God. *To overcome the present opportunist
current means to reject it.*

Bernstein concludes his book by advising the Party that it should dare to
appear as what it is: a democratic socialist reform party. In our opinion, the
Party—that is, its highest organ, the Party congress—must follow this advice
by proposing to Bernstein that he too appear formally as what he is: a petty-
bourgeois democratic progressive.]

# 6 — The Mass Strike, the Political Party, and the Trade Unions

EDITORS' NOTE: One of Luxemburg's most important writings, *The Mass Strike, the Political Party, and the Trade Unions* contains her analysis the 1905 Russian Revolution, in which she participated, and reflects her effort to project the significance of the mass strike for future revolutionary developments. It contains the fullest elaboration of her theory of spontaneity as a key element in class struggle. Luxemburg kept developing the concepts contained in this work until the end of her life. She wrote the pamphlet in the summer of 1906, at the request of the Social Democratic organization in Hamburg, while staying in Koktula, Finland, where she had extensive discussions on the subject of the mass strike and the Russian Revolution with Lenin. *The Mass Strike* was first published as a pamphlet in Hamburg in the fall of 1906. It was translated by Patrick Lavan and first published by the Marxist Educational Society in Detroit in 1925. Here we include chapters 2, 3, and 4.

## THE MASS STRIKE: AN HISTORICAL AND NOT AN ARTIFICIAL PRODUCT

The first revision of the question of the mass strike which results from the experience of Russia relates to the general conception of the problem. Till the present time the zealous advocates of an "attempt with the mass strike" in Germany of the stamp of Bernstein, Eisner,[1] etc., and also the strongest opponents of such an attempt as represented in the trade union camp by, for example, Bomelburg, stand, when all is said and done, on the same conception, and that is the Anarchist one. The apparent polar opposites do not mutually exclude each other but, as always, condition, and at the same time supplement each other. For the Anarchist mode of thought is direct speculation on the "great Kladderadatsch,"[2] on the social revolution merely as an external and inessential characteristic. According to it, what is essential is the whole abstract, unhistorical view of the mass strike and of all the conditions of the proletarian struggle generally. For the Anarchist there exist only two things as material suppositions of his "revolutionary" speculations—first imagination, and second goodwill and courage to rescue humanity from the existing capitalist vale of tears. This fanciful mode of reasoning sixty years ago gave the result that the mass strike was the shortest, surest and easiest means of springing into the better social future. The same mode of reasoning recently gave the result that the trade-union struggle was the only real "direct action of the masses" and also the only real revolutionary struggle—which, as is well known, is the latest notion of the French and Italian "Syndicalists." The fatal thing for Anarchism has always been that the methods of struggle improvised in the air were not only a reckoning without their host, that is, they were purely Utopian, but that they, while not reckoning in the least with the despised evil reality, unexpectedly became in this evil reality, practical helps to the reaction, where previously they had only been, for the most part, revolutionary speculations.

On the same ground of abstract, unhistorical methods of observation stand those today who would, in the manner of a board of directors, put the mass strike in Germany on the calendar on an appointed day, and those who, like the participants in the trade-union congress at Cologne,[3] would by a prohibition of "propaganda" eliminate the problem of the mass strike from the face of the earth. Both tendencies proceed on the common purely Anarchistic assumption that the mass strike is a purely technical means of struggle, which can be "decided" at pleasure and strictly according to conscience, or "forbidden"—a kind of pocketknife which can be kept in the pocket clasped "ready for any emergency," and according to decision, can be unclasped and used. The opponents of the mass strike do indeed claim for themselves the merit of taking into consideration the historical groundwork and the material conditions of the present situation in Germany in opposition to the "revolutionary romanticists," who hover in the air, and do not at any point reckon with the hard realities and their possibilities and impossibilities. "Facts and figures; figures and facts!" they cry, like Mr. Gradgrind in Dickens' *Hard Times*. When the trade-union opponent of the mass strike understands by the "historical basis" and "material conditions" is two things—on the one hand the weakness of the proletariat, and on the other hand, the strength of Prussian–German militarism. The inadequate organization of the workers and the imposing Prussian bayonet—these are the facts and figures upon which these trade-union leaders base their practical policy in the given case. Now while it is quite true that the trade-union cash box and the Prussian bayonet are material and very historical phenomena, the conception based upon them is not historical materialism in Marx's sense but a policeman-like materialism in the sense of Puttkammer.[4] The representatives of the capitalist police state reckon much, and indeed, exclusively with the occasional real power of the organized proletariat as well as with the material might of the bayonet, and from the comparative example of these two rows of figures the comforting conclusion is always drawn, that the revolutionary labor movement is produced by individual demagogues and agitators; and that therefore there is in the prisons and bayonets an adequate means of subduing the unpleasant "passing phenomena."

The class-conscious German workers have at last grasped the humor of the policeman-like theory that the whole modern labor movement is an artificial, arbitrary product of a handful of conscienceless "demagogues and agitators."

It is exactly the same conception, however, that finds expression when two or three worthy comrades unite in a voluntary column of nightwatchmen in order to warn the German working class against the dangerous agitation of a few "revolutionary romanticists" and their "propaganda of the mass strike"; or when, on the other side, a noisy indignation campaign is engineered by those who, by means of "confidential" agreements between the executive of the party and the general commission of the trade unions, believe they can prevent the outbreak of the mass strike in Germany. If it depended on the inflammatory "propaganda" of revolutionary romanticists or on confidential or public decisions of the party direction, then we should not even yet have had in Russia a single serious mass strike. In no country in the world—as I pointed out in March 1905 in the *Sachische Arbeiterzeitun*[5]— was the mass strike so little "propagated" or even "discussed" as in Russia. And the isolated examples of decisions and agreements of the Russian party executive which really sought to proclaim the mass strike of their own accord—as, for example, the last attempt in August of this year after the dissolution of the Duma[6]—are almost valueless. If, therefore, the Russian revolution teaches us anything, it teaches above all that the mass strike is not artificially "made," not "decided" at random, not "propagated," but that it is an historical phenomenon which, at a given moment, results from social conditions with historical inevitability. It is not therefore by abstract speculations on the possibility or impossibility, the utility or the injuriousness of the mass strike, but only by an examination of those factors and social conditions out of which the mass strike grows in the present phase of the class struggle—in other words, it is not by *subjective criticism* of the mass strike from the standpoint of what is desirable, but only by *objective investigation* of the sources of the mass strike from the standpoint of what is historically inevitable, that the problem can be grasped or even discussed.

In the unreal sphere of abstract logical analysis, it can be shown with exactly the same force on either side that the mass strike is absolutely impossible and sure to be defeated, and that it is possible and that its triumph cannot be questioned. And therefore the value of the evidence shown on each side is exactly the same—and that is nil. Therefore the fear of the "propagation" of the mass strike which has even led to formal anathemas against the persons alleged to be guilty of this crime, is solely the product of the droll confusion of persons. It is just as impossible to "propagate" the mass strike as an abstract means of struggle as it is to propagate the "revolution." "Revolution" like "mass strike" signifies nothing but an external form of the class struggle which can have sense and meaning only in connection with definite political situations.

If anyone were to undertake to make the mass strike generally as a form of proletarian action the object of methodical agitation, and to go house-to-house canvassing with this "idea" in order to gradually win the working class to it, it would be as idle and profitless and absurd an occupation as it would be to seek to make the idea of the revolution or of the fight at the barricades the object of a special agitation. The mass strike has now become the center of the lively interest of the German and the international working class because it is a new form of struggle, and as such is the sure symptom of a thoroughgoing internal revolution in the relations of the classes and in the conditions of the class struggle. It is a testimony to the sound revolutionary instinct and to the quick intelligence of the mass of the German proletariat that, in spite of the obstinate resistance of their trade-union leaders, they are applying themselves to this new problem with such keen interest. But it does not meet the case, in the presence of this interest and of this fine, intellectual thirst and desire for revolutionary deeds on the part of the workers, to treat them to abstract mental gymnastics on the possibility or impossibility of the mass strike; *they* should be enlightened on the development of the Russian revolution, the international significance of that revolution, the sharpening of class antagonisms in Western Europe, the wider political perspectives of the class struggle in Germany, and the role and the tasks of the masses in the coming struggles. Only in this form will the discussion on the mass strike lead to the widening of the intellectual horizon of the proletariat, to the sharpening of their way of thinking, and to the steeling of their energy.

Viewed from this standpoint however, the criminal proceedings desired by the enemies of "revolutionary romanticism" appear in all their absurdity because, in treating of the problem, one does not adhere strictly to the text of the Jena resolution.7 The "practical politicians" agree to this resolution if need be because they couple the mass strike chiefly with the fate of universal suffrage, from which it follows that they can believe two things—first, that the mass strike is of a purely defensive character, and second, that the mass strike is even subordinate to parliamentarianism, that is, has been turned into a mere appendage of parliamentarianism. But the real kernel of the Jena resolution in this connection is that in the present position of Germany an attempt on the part of the prevailing reaction on the parliamentary vote would in all probability be the moment for the introduction of, and the signal for, a period of stormy political struggles in which the mass strike as a means of struggle in Germany might well come into use for the first time. But to seek to narrow and to artificially smother the social importance and to limit the historical scope of the mass strike as a phenomenon and as a problem of the class struggle by the wording of a congress resolution, is an undertaking which for shortsightedness can only be compared with the veto on discussion of the trade union congress at Cologne. In the resolution of the Jena Congress German Social Democracy has officially taken notice of the fundamental change which the Russian revolution has effected in the international conditions of the proletarian class struggle, and its capacity for revolutionary development and its power of adaptability to the new demands of the coming phase of the class struggle. Therein lies the significance of the Jena resolution. As for the practical application of the mass strike in Germany, history will decide that as it decided it in Russia—history in which German Social Democracy with its decisions is, it is true, an important factor, but at the same time, only *one* factor amongst many.

## DEVELOPMENT OF THE MASS STRIKE MOVEMENT IN RUSSIA

The mass strike, as it appears for the most part in the discussion in Germany, is a very clear and simply thought out, sharply sketched, isolated phenomenon. It is the political mass strike exclusively that is spoken of. What is meant by it is a single grand rising of the industrial proletariat springing from some political motive of the highest importance, undertaken on the basis of an opportune and mutual understanding on the part of the controlling authorities of the party and of the trade unions, carried through in the spirit of party discipline and in perfect order, and in still more perfect order brought to the directing committees at a signal given at the proper time, by which committees the regulation of support, the cost, the sacrifice—in a word, the whole material balance of the mass strike—is exactly determined in advance.

Now, when we compare this theoretical scheme with the real mass strike as it appeared in Russia five years ago, we are compelled to say that this representation which, in the German discussion occupies the central position, hardly corresponds to a single one of the many mass strikes that have taken place, and on the other hand that the mass strike in Russia displays such a multiplicity of the most varied forms of action that it is altogether impossible to speak of "the" mass strike, of an abstract schematic mass strike. All the factors of the mass strike, as well as its character, are not only different in the different towns and districts of the country, but its general character has often changed in the course of the revolution. The mass strike has passed through a definite history in Russia, and is passing still further through it. Who, therefore, speaks of the mass strike in Russia must, above all things, keep its history before his eyes.

The present official period, so to speak, of the Russian revolution is justly dated from the rising of the proletariat on January 22, 1905, when the demonstration of two hundred thousand workers ended in a frightful bloodbath before the Tsar's palace. The bloody massacre in St. Petersburg was, as is well known, the signal for the outbreak of the first gigantic series of mass strikes which spread over the whole of Russia within a few days and which carried the call to action of the revolution from St. Petersburg to every corner of the Empire and among the widest sections of the proletariat. But the St. Petersburg rising of January 22 was only the critical moment of a mass strike which the proletariat of the Tsarist capital had previously entered upon in January 1905. This January mass strike was without doubt carried through under the immediate influence of the gigantic general strike which in December 1904 broke out in the Caucasus, in Baku, and for a long time kept the whole of Russia in suspense. The events of December in Baku were on their part only the last and powerful ramification of those tremendous mass strikes which, like a periodical earthquake, shook the whole of south Russia, and whose prologue was the mass strike in Batum in the Caucasus in March 1902. This first mass strike movement in the continuous series of present revolutionary eruptions is, finally, separated by five or six years from the great general strike of the textile workers in St. Petersburg in 1896 and 1897, and if this movement is apparently separated from the present revolution by a few years of apparent stagnation and strong reaction, every one who knows the inner political development of the Russian proletariat to their present stage of class consciousness and revolutionary energy will realize that the history of the present period of the mass struggles begins with those general strikes in St. Petersburg. They are therefore important for the problems of the mass strike because they already contain, in the germ, all the principal factors of later mass strikes.

Again, the St. Petersburg general strike of 1896 appears as a purely economic partial wage struggle. Its causes were the intolerable working conditions of the spinners and weavers in St. Petersburg: a working day of thirteen, fourteen or fifteen hours, miserable piece-work rates, and a whole series of contemptible chicaneries on the part of the employers. This condition of things, however, was patiently endured by the workers for a long time until an apparently trivial circumstance filled the cup to overflowing. The coronation of the present Tsar, Nicholas II, which had been postponed for two years through fear of the revolutionaries, was celebrated in May 1896, and on that occasion the St. Petersburg employers displayed their patriotic zeal by giving their workers three days compulsory holidays, for which, curious to relate, they did not desire to pay their employees. The workers, angered at this, began to move. After a conference of about three hundred of the intelligent workers in the Ekaterinhof Garden a strike was decided upon, and the following demands were formulated: first, payment of wages for the coronation holidays, second, a working day of ten hours; third, increased rates for piece-work. This happened on May 24th. In a week every weaving and spinning establishment was at a standstill, and 40,000 workers were in the general strike. Today this event, measured by the gigantic mass strike of the revolution may appear a little thing. In the political polar rigidity of the Russia of that time a general strike was something unheard of; it was even a complete revolution in miniature. There began, of course, the most brutal persecution. About one thousand workers were arrested and the general strike was suppressed.

Here already we see all the fundamental characteristics of the later mass strikes. The next occasion of the movement was wholly accidental, even unimportant, its outbreak elementary; but in the success of the movement the fruits of the agitation extending over several years of the Social Democracy were seen, and in the course of the general strike the Social Democratic agitators stood at the head of the movement, directed it, and used it to stir up revolutionary agitation. Further the strike was outwardly a mere economic struggle for wages, but the attitude of the government and the agitation of the Social Democracy made it a political phenomenon of the first rank. The strike was suppressed; the workers suffered a "defeat." But in January of the following year the textile workers of St. Petersburg repeated the general strike once more and achieved this time a remarkable success: the legal introduction of a

1896

working day of eleven hours throughout the whole of Russia. What was nevertheless a much more important result was this: since that first general strike of 1896 which was entered upon without a trace of organization or of strike funds, an intensive trade union fight began in Russia proper which spread from St. Petersburg to the other parts of the country and opened up entirely new vistas to Social Democratic agitation and organization, and by which in the apparently death-like peace of the following period the revolution was prepared by underground work.

The outbreak of the Caucasian strike in March 1902 was apparently as accidental and as much due to purely economic [partial] causes (although produced by quite other factors) as that of 1896. It was connected with the serious industrial and commercial crisis which in Russia was the precursor of the Japanese war[8] and which, together with it, was the most powerful factor of the nascent revolutionary ferment. The crisis produced an enormous mass of unemployment which nourished the agitation among the proletarian masses, and therefore the government, to restore tranquility amongst the workers, undertook to transport the "superfluous hands" in batches to their respective home districts. One such measure, which was to affect about four hundred petroleum workers called forth a mass protest in Batum, which led to demonstrations, arrests, a massacre, and finally to a political trial in which the purely economic and [partial] affair suddenly became a political and revolutionary event. The reverberation of the wholly "fruitless" expiring and suppressed strike in Batum was a series of revolutionary mass demonstrations of workers in Nizni Novgorod, Saratov and other towns, and therefore a mighty surge forward of the general wave of the revolutionary movement.

Already in November 1902 the first genuine revolutionary echo followed in the shape of a general strike at Rostov-on-Don. Disputes about the rates of pay in the workshops of the Vladicaucasus Railway gave the impetus to this movement. The management sought to reduce wages and therefore the Don Committee of the Social Democracy issued a proclamation with a summons to strike for the following demands: a nine-hour day, increase of wages, abolition of fines, dismissal of obnoxious engineers, etc. Entire railway workshops participated in the strike. Presently all other industries joined in and suddenly an unprecedented state of affairs prevailed in Rostov: all industrial work was at a standstill, and every day mammoth meetings of from 15,000 to 20,000 were held in the open air, sometimes surrounded by a cordon of Cossacks, at which for the first time Social Democratic popular speakers appeared publicly, inflammatory speeches on socialism and political freedom were delivered and received with immense enthusiasm, and revolutionary appeals were distributed by tens of thousands of copies. In the midst of rigid absolutist Russia the proletariat of Rostov won for the first time the right of assembly, and freedom of speech by storm. It goes without saying that there was a massacre here. The disputes over wages in the Vladicaucasus Railway workshops grew in a few days into a political general strike and a revolutionary street battle. As an echo to this there followed immediately a general strike at the station of Tichoretzkaia on the same railway. Here also a massacre took place and also a trial, and thus even Tichoretzkaia has taken its place in the indissoluble chain of the factors of the revolution.

The spring of 1903 gave the answer to the defeated strikes in Rostov and Tichoretzkaia; the whole of South Russia in May, June, and July was aflame. Baku, Tiflis, Batum, Elizavetgrad, Odessa, Kiev, Nicholaiev and Ekaterinoslav were in a general strike in the literal meaning of those words. But here again the movement did not arise on any preconceived plan from one to another; it flowed together from individual points in each one from a different cause and in a different form. The beginning was made by Baku where several partial wage struggles in individual factories and departments culminated in a general strike. In Tiflis the strike was begun by two thousand commercial employees who had a working day of from six o'clock in the morning to eleven at night. On the fourth of July they all left their shops and made a circuit of the town to demand from the proprietors of the shops that they close their premises. The victory was complete; the commercial employees won a working day of from eight in the morning to eight in the evening, and they were immediately joined by all the factories, workshops and offices, etc. The newspapers did not appear, and tramway traffic could not be carried on under military protection. In Elisavetgrad on July 4 a strike began in all the factories with purely economic demands. These were mostly conceded, and the strike ended on the 14th. Two weeks later however it broke out again. The bakers this time gave the word and they were joined by the bricklayers, the joiners, the dyers, the mill workers, and finally all factory workers. In Odessa the movement began with a wage struggle in the course of which the "legal" workers' union, founded by government agents according to the program of the famous gendarme Zubatov,9 was developed. Historical dialectics had again seized the occasion to play one of its malicious little pranks. The economic struggles of the earlier period (among them the great St. Petersburg general strike of 1896) had misled Russian Social Democracy into exaggerating the importance of so-called "economics," and in this way the ground had been prepared among the workers for the demagogic activities of Zubatov. After a time, however, the great revolutionary stream turned round the little ship with the false flag, and compelled it to ride right at the head of the revolutionary proletarian flotilla. The Zubatovian unions gave the signal for the great general strike in Odessa in the spring of 1904, as for the general strike in St. Petersburg in January 1905. The workers in Odessa, who were not to be deceived by the appearance of friendliness on the part of the government for the workers, and of its sympathy with purely economic strikes, suddenly demanded proof by example, and compelled the Zubatovian "workers union" in a factory to declare a strike for very moderate demands. They were immediately thrown on the streets, and when they demanded the protection of the authorities which was promised them by their leader, the gentleman vanished and left the workers in the wildest excitement. The Social Democrats at once placed themselves at the head of affairs, and the strike movement extended to other factories. On July 1, 2,500 dockers struck work for an increase of wages from eighty kopeks to two roubles, and the shortening of the working day by half an hour. On July 16th the seamen joined the movement. On the 13th the tramway staff began a strike. Then a meeting took place of all the strikers, seven or eight thousand men; they formed a procession which went from factory to factory, growing like an avalanche, and presently a crowd of from 40,000 to 50,000 betook themselves to the docks in order to bring all work there to a standstill. A general strike soon reigned throughout the whole city. In Kiev a strike began in the railway workshops on July 21. Here also the immediate cause was miserable conditions of labor, and wage demands were presented. On the following day the foundry men followed the example. On July 23 an incident occurred which gave the signal for the general strike. During the night two delegates of the railwaymen were arrested. The strikers immediately demanded their release, and as this was not conceded, they decided not to allow trains to leave the town. At the station all the strikers with their wives and families sat down on the railway track—a sea of human beings. They were threatened with rifle salvoes. The workers bared their breasts and cried "Shoot"! A salvo was fired into the defenseless seated crowd, and thirty to forty corpses, among them those of women and children, remained on the ground. When this became known the whole town of Kiev went on strike immediately. The corpses of the murdered workers were raised on high by the crowd and carried round in a mass demonstration. Meetings, speeches, arrests, isolated street fights—Kiev was in the midst of the revolution. The movement was soon at an end. But the printers had won a shortening of the working day of one hour and a wage increase of one rouble; in a yeast factory the eight-hour day was introduced; the railway workshops were closed by order of the Ministry; other departments continued partial strikes for their demands. In Nicholaiev the general strike broke out under the immediate influence of the news from Odessa, Baku, Batum and Tiflis, in spite of the opposition of the Social Democratic Committee who wanted to postpone the outbreak of the movement till the time came when the military should have left the town for manoeuvres. The masses refused to hold back; one factory made a beginning, the strikes went from one workshop to another, the resistance of the military only poured oil on the fire. Mass processions with revolutionary songs were formed which were taken part in by all workers, employees, tramways officials, men and women. The cessation of work was complete. In Ekaterinoslav the bakers came out on strike on August 5, the men in the railway workshops on the 7th, and then all the other factories on August 8. Tramway traffic stopped, and the newspapers did not appear. Thus the colossal general strike in south Russia came into being in the summer of 1903. By many small channels of partial economic struggles and little "accidental" occurrences it flowed rapidly to a raging sea, and changed the entire south of the Tsarist empire for some weeks into a bizarre revolutionary workers' republic. "Brotherly embraces, cries of delight and of enthusiasm, songs of freedom, merry laughter, humor and joy, were seen and heard in the crowd of many thousands of persons which surged through the town from morning till evening. The mood was exalted; one could almost believe that a new, better life was beginning on the earth. A most solemn and at the same time an idyllic, moving spectacle." . . . So wrote at the time the correspondent of the Liberal *Osvoboshdenye* of Peter Struve.

The year 1904 brought with it war, and for a time, an interval of quiet in the mass strike movement. At first a troubled wave of "patriotic" demonstrations arranged by the police authorities spread over the country. The "liberal" bourgeois society was for the time being struck to the ground by the Tsarist official chauvinism. But soon the Social Democrats took possession of the arena; revolutionary workers' demonstrations were opposed to the demonstrations of the patriotic lumpenproletariat which were organized under police patronage. At last the shameful defeats of the Tsarist army woke the liberal society from its lethargy; then began the era of democratic congresses, banquets, speeches, addresses and manifestos. Absolutism, temporarily suppressed through the disgrace of the war, gave full scope to these gentlemen, and by and by they saw everything in rosy colors. For six months bourgeois liberalism occupied the center of the stage, and the proletariat remained in the shadows. But after a long depression absolutism again roused itself, the camarilla gathered all its strength and by a single powerful movement of the Cossack's heel the whole liberal movement was driven into a corner. Banquets, speeches and congresses were prohibited out of hand as "intolerable presumption," and liberalism suddenly found itself at the end of its tether. But exactly at the point where liberalism was exhausted, the action of the proletariat began. In December 1904 the great general strike, due to unemployment, broke out in Baku; the working class was again on the field of battle. Action began as speech was forbidden and rendered impossible. In Baku for some weeks in the midst of the general strike the Social Democrats ruled as absolute masters of the situation; and the peculiar events of December in the Caucasus would have caused an immense sensation if they had not been so quickly put in the shade by the rising tide of the revolution which they had themselves set in motion. The fantastic confused news of the general strike in Baku had not reached all parts of the Tsarist empire when in January 1905 the mass strike in St. Petersburg broke out.

Here also as is well known, the immediate cause was trivial. Two men employed at the Putilov works were discharged on account of their membership in the legal Zubatovian union. This measure called forth a solidarity strike on January 16 of the whole of the 12,000 employees in this works. The Social Democrats seized the occasion of the strike to begin a lively agitation for the extension of the demands and set forth demands for the eight-hour day, the right of combination, freedom of speech and of the press, etc. The unrest among the Putilov workers communicated itself quickly to the remainder of the proletariat, and in a few days 140,000 workers were on strike. Joint conferences and stormy discussions led to the proletarian charter of bourgeois freedom, with the eight-hour day at its head, with which 200,000 workers led by Father Gapon on January 22nd marched to the Tsar's palace. The conflict of the two Putilov workers who had been subjected to disciplinary punishment had changed within a week into the prologue of the most violent revolution of modern times.

The events that followed upon this are well known; the bloodbath in St. Petersburg called forth gigantic mass strikes and a general strike in the months of January and February in all the industrial centers and towns in Russia. Poland, Lithuania, the Baltic provinces, the Caucasus, Siberia, from north to south and east to west. On closer inspection, however, it can be seen that the mass strike was appearing in other forms than those of the previous period. Everywhere at that time the Social Democratic organizations went ahead with appeals; everywhere revolutionary solidarity with the St. Petersburg proletariat was expressly stated as the cause and aim of the general strike; everywhere, at the same time, there were demonstrations, speeches, conflicts with the military. But even here there was no predetermined plan, no organized action, because the appeals of the parties could scarcely keep pace with the spontaneous risings of the masses; the leaders had scarcely time to formulate the watchwords of the onrushing crowd of the proletariat. Further, the earlier mass and general strikes had originated from coalescing wage struggles which, in the general temper of the revolutionary situation and under the influence of the Social Democratic agitation, rapidly became political demonstrations; the economic factor and the scattered condition of trade unionism were the starting point, all-embracing class action and political direction the result. The movement was now reversed. The general strikes of January and February broke out as unified revolutionary actions to begin with under the direction of the Social Democrats; but this action soon fell into an unending series of local [partial] economic strikes in separate districts, towns, departments and factories. Throughout the spring of 1905 and into the middle of the summer there fermented throughout the whole of the immense empire an uninterrupted economic strike of almost the entire proletariat against capital—a struggle which caught on the one hand all the petit-bourgeois and liberal professions (commercial employees, technicians, actors, and members of artistic professions), and on the other hand penetrated to the domestic servants, the minor police officials and even to the stratum of the lumpenproletariat, and simultaneously surged from the towns to the country districts and even knocked at the iron gates of the military barracks.

This is a gigantic, many-colored picture of a general arrangement of labor and capital which reflects all the complexity of social organization and of the political consciousness of every section and of every district. The whole long scale runs from the regular trade-union struggle of a picked and tested troop of the proletariat drawn from large-scale industry, to the formless protest of a handful of rural proletarians, and to the first slight stirrings of an agitated military garrison; from the well-educated and elegant revolt in cuffs and white collars in the counting house of a bank to the shy-bold murmurings of a clumsy meeting of dissatisfied policemen in a smoke-grimed, dark, and dirty guardroom.

According to the theory of the lovers of "orderly and well-disciplined" struggles, according to plan and scheme, according to those especially who always ought to know better from afar "how it should have been done," the decay of the great political general strike of January 1905 into a number of economic struggles was probably "a great mistake" which crippled that action and changed it into a "straw fire."[10] But Social Democracy in Russia, which had taken part in the revolution but had not "made" it, and which had even to learn its law from its course itself, was at the first glance put out of countenance for a time by the apparently fruitless ebb of the storm-flood of the general strike. History, however, which had made that "great mistake" thereby accomplished, heedless of the reasonings of its officious schoolmaster, a gigantic work for the revolution which was as inevitable as it was, in its consequences, incalculable.

The sudden general rising of the proletariat in January under the powerful impetus of the St. Petersburg events was outwardly a political act of the revolutionary declaration of war on absolutism. But this first general direct action reacted inwardly all the more powerfully as it for the first time awoke class feeling and class consciousness in millions upon millions as if by an electric shock. And this awakening of class feeling expressed itself forthwith in the circumstances that the proletarian mass, counted by millions, quite suddenly and sharply came to realize how intolerable was that social and economic existence which they had patiently endured for decades in the chains of capitalism. Thereupon there began a spontaneous general shaking of and tugging at these chains. All the innumerable sufferings of the modern proletariat reminded them of the old bleeding wounds. Here was the eight-hour day fought for, there piece work was resisted, here were brutal foremen "driven off" in a sack on a handcar. At another place infamous systems of fines were fought against, everywhere better wages were striven for and here and there the abolition of homework. Backward degraded occupations in large towns, small provincial towns, which had hitherto dreamed in an idyllic sleep, the village with its legacy from feudalism—all these, suddenly awakened by the January lightning, bethought themselves of their rights and now sought feverishly to make up for their previous neglect. The economic struggle was not really a decay here, or a dissipation of action, but merely change of front, a sudden and natural alteration of the first general engagement with absolutism, in a general reckoning with capital, which in keeping with its character, assumed the form of individual, scattered wage struggles. Political class action was not broken in January by the decay of the general strike into economic strikes, but the reverse; after the possible content of political action in the given situation and at the given stage of the revolution was exhausted, it broke, or rather changed, into economic action.

In point of fact, what more could the general strike in January have achieved? Only complete thoughtlessness could expect that absolutism could be destroyed at one blow by a single "long-drawn" general strike after the Anarchist plan. Absolutism in Russia must be overthrown by the proletariat. But in order to he able to overthrow it the proletariat require a high degree of political education, of class consciousness and organization. All these conditions cannot be fulfilled by pamphlets and leaflets, but only by the living political school, by the fight and in the fight, in the continuous course of the revolution. Further, absolutism cannot be overthrown at any desired moment in which only adequate "exertion" and "endurance" are necessary. The fall of absolutism is merely the outer expression of the inner social and class development of Russian society. Before absolutism can, and may be overthrown, the bourgeois Russia must he formed in its interior, in its modern class divisions. That requires the drawing together of the various social layers and interests, besides the education of the proletarian revolutionary parties, and not less of the liberal, radical, petit-bourgeois, conservative and reactionary parties; it requires self-consciousness, self-knowledge and the class consciousness not merely of the layers of the people, but also of the layers of the bourgeoisie. But this also can be achieved and come to fruition in no way but in the struggle, in the process of the revolution itself, through the actual school of experience, in collision with the proletariat as well as with one another, in incessant mutual friction. This class division and class maturity of bourgeois society, as well as its action in the struggle against absolutism, is on the one hand, hampered and made difficult by the peculiar leading role of the proletariat and on the other hand, is spurred on and accelerated. The various undercurrents of the social process of the revolution cross one another, check one another, and increase the internal contradictions of the revolution, but in the end accelerate and thereby render still more violent its eruptions.

This apparently simple and purely mechanical problem may therefore be stated thus: the overthrow of absolutism is a long, continuous social process, and its solution demands a complete undermining of the soil of society; the uppermost part be placed lowest and the lowermost part highest, the apparent "order" must be changed to a chaos, and the apparently "anarchistic" chaos must be changed into a new order. Now in this process of the social transformation of the old Russia, not only the January lightning of the first general strike but also the spring and summer thunderstorms that followed it, played an indispensable part. The embittered general relations of wage labor and capital contributed in equal measure to the drawing together of the various layers of the people and those of the bourgeoisie, to the class consciousness of the revolutionary proletariat and to that of the liberal and conservative bourgeoisie. And just as the urban wage struggle contributed to the formation of a strong monarchist industrial party in Moscow, so the conflagration of the violent rural rising in Livonia led to the rapid liquidation of the famous aristocratic-agrarian Zemstvo-Liberalism.[11]

But at the same time, the period of the economic struggles of the spring and summer of 1905 made it possible for the urban proletariat, by means of active Social Democratic agitation and direction, to assimilate later all the lessons of the January prologue and to grasp clearly all the further tasks of the revolution. There was connected with this too, another circumstance of an enduring social character: *a general raising of the standard of life of the proletariat,* economic, social and intellectual. The January strikes of 1905 ended victoriously almost throughout. As proof of this, some data from the enormous, and still for the most part inaccessible, mass of material may be cited here relating to a few of the most important strikes carried through in War-saw alone by the Social Democrats of Poland and Lithuania. In the great factories of the metal industry of Warsaw: Lilpop Ltd., Ran & Lowenstein, Rudzki and Co., Borman, Schwede and Co., Handtke, Gerlach and Pulst, Geisler Bros., Eberherd, Wolski and Co., Konrad and Yarnuszkiewicz Ltd., Weber and Daehu, Ewizdzinski and Co., Wolonoski Wire Works, Gostynski and Co. Ltd., Rrun and Son, Frage Norblin, Werner, Buch, Kenneberg Bros., Labor, Dittunar Lamp Factory, Serkowski, Weszk—twenty-two factories in all the workers won, after a strike of from four to five weeks (from January 25 and 26) a nine-hour day, a 25 percent increase of wages, and obtained various smaller concessions. In the large workshops of the timber industry of Warsaw, namely Karmanski, Damieki, Gromel, Szerbinskik, Tremerowski, Horn, Devensee, Tworkowski, Daab and Martens—twelve workshops in all—the strikes had won the nine-hour day by February 23; they were not satisfied with this, but insisted upon the eight-hour day, which they also won, together with an increase of wages, after a further strike of a week. The entire bricklaying industry began a strike on February 27 and demanded, in conformity with the watchword of Social Democracy, the eight-hour day; they won the ten-hour day on March 11 together with an increase of wages for all categories, regular payment of wages weekly, etc. The painters, the cartwrights, the saddlers and the smiths all won the eight-hour day without decrease of wages. The telephone workshops struck for ten days and won the eight-hour day and an increase of wages of from 10 to 15 percent. The large linen-weaving establishment of Hielle and

Dietrich (10,000 workers) after a strike lasting nine weeks, obtained a decrease of the working day of one hour and a wage increase of from 5 to 10 percent. And similar results in endless variation were to be seen in all the older branches of industry in Warsaw, Lodz and Sosnovitz.

In Russia proper the eight-hour day was won in December 1904 by a few categories of oil workers in Baku; in May 1905 by the sugar workers of the Kiev district; in January 1905 in all the printing works in Samara (where at the same time an increase of piece-work rates was obtained and fines were abolished), in February in the factory in which medical instruments for the army are manufactured, in a furniture factory and in the cartridge factory in St. Petersburg. Further, the eight-hour day was introduced in the mines at Vladivostock, in March in the government mechanical workshops dealing with government stock, and in May among the employees of the Tiflis electric town railway. In the same month a working day of eight and a half hours was introduced in the large cotton-weaving factory of Morosov (and at the same time the abolition of night work and a wage increase of 8 percent were won); in June an eight-hour day in a few oil works in St. Petersburg and Moscow; in July a working day of eight-and-a-half hours among the smiths at the St. Petersburg docks; and in November in all the private printing establishments of the town of Orel (and at the same time an increase of time rates of 20 percent and piece-work rates of 100 percent, as well as the setting up a conciliation board in which workers and employer were equally represented).

The nine-hour day was obtained in all the railway workshops (in February), in many government, military and naval workshops, in most of the factories of the town of Berdiansk, in all the printing works of the towns of Poltava and Musk; nine and a half hours in the shipyards, mechanical workshops and foundries in the town of Nicholayev in June, after a general strike of waiters in Warsaw in many restaurants and cafes (and at the same time a wage increase of from 20 to 40 percent, with a two-week holiday every year).

The ten-hour day won in almost all the factories of the towns of Lodz, Sosnovitz, Riga, Kovno, Oval, Dorfat, Minsk, Kharkov, in the bakeries of Odessa, among the mechanics in Kishinev, at a few smelting works in St. Petersburg, in the match factories of Kovno (with an increase of wages of 10 percent), in all the government marine workshops, and among all the dockers.

The wage increases were in general smaller than the shortening of hours but always more significant: in Warsaw in the middle of March 1905 a general increase of wages of 15 percent was fixed by thee municipal factories department; in the center of the textile industry, Ivanovo-Vosnosensk, the wage increase amounted to from 7 to 15 percent, in Kovno the increase affected 73 percent of the workers. A fixed minimum wage was introduced in some of the bakeries in Odessa, in the Neva shipbuilding yards in St. Petersburg, etc.

It goes without saying that these concessions were withdrawn again, here and there. This however, was only the cause of renewed strife and led to still more bitter struggles for revenge, and thus the strike period of the spring of 1905 has of itself become the prologue to an endless series of everspreading and interlacing economic struggles which have lasted to the present day. In the period of the outward stagnation of the revolution, when the telegraph carried no sensational news from the Russian theatre of war to the outside world, and when the West European laid aside his newspaper in disappointment with the remark that there "was nothing doing" in Russia, the great underground work of the revolution was in reality being carried on without cessation, day by day and hour by hour in the very heart of the empire. The incessant intensive economic struggle effected, by rapid and abbreviated methods, the transition of capitalism from the stage of primitive accumulation and of patriarchal unmethodical methods of working, to a highly modern, civilized one. At the present time the actual working day in Russian industry leaves behind not only Russian factory legislation (that is the legal working day of eleven hours) but even the actual conditions of Germany. In most departments of large-scale industry in Russia the ten-hour day prevails, which in Germany is declared in social legislation to be an unattainable goal. And what is more, that longed-for "industrial constitutionalism," for which there is so much enthusiasm in Germany, and for the sake of which the advocates of opportunist tactics would keep every keen wind from the stagnant waters of their all-suffering parliamentarianism, has already been born, together with political "constitutionalism," in the midst of the revolutionary storm, from the revolution itself! In actual fact it is not merely a general raising of the standard of life, or of the cultural level of the working class that has taken place. The material standard of life as a permanent stage of well-being has no place in the revolution. Full of contradictions and contrasts it brings simultaneously surprising economic victories, and the most brutal acts of revenge on the part of the capitalists; today the eight-hour day, and tomorrow wholesale lockouts and actual starvation for the millions. The most precious, because lasting, thing in this rapid ebb and flow of the wave is its mental sediment: the intellectual, cultural growth of the proletariat, which proceeds by fits and starts, and which offers an inviolable guarantee of their further irresistible progress in the economic as in the political struggle. And not only that. Even the relations of the worker to the employer are turned round; since the January general strike and the strikes of 1905 which followed upon it, the principle of the capitalist "mastery of the house" is de facto abolished. In the large factories of all important industrial centers the establishment of workers' committees has, as if by itself, taken place, with which alone the employer negotiates and which decide all disputes. And finally another thing the apparently "chaotic" strikes and the "disorganized" revolutionary action after the January general strike is becoming the starting point of a feverish *work of organization*. Dame History, from afar, smilingly hoaxes the bureaucratic lay figures who keep grim watch at the gate over the fate of the German trade unions. The firm organizations, which as the indispensable hypothesis for an eventual German mass strike should be fortified like an impregnable citadel—these organizations are in Russia, on the contrary, already born from the mass strike. And while the guardians of the German trade unions for the most part fear that the organizations will fall in pieces in a revolutionary whirlwind like rare porcelain, the Russian revolution shows us the exactly opposite picture; from the whirlwind and the storm, out of the fire and glow of the mass strike and the street fighting rise again, like Venus from the foam, fresh, young, powerful, buoyant trade unions.

Here again a little example however, which is typical of the whole empire. At the second conference of the Russian trade unions which took place at the end of February 1906 in St. Petersburg, the representative of the Petersburg trade unions, in his report on the development of trade union organizations of the Tsarist capital said:

> January 22, 1905, which washed away the Gapon union, was a turning point. The workers in large numbers have learned by experience to appreciate and understand the importance of organization, and that only they themselves can create these organizations. The first trade union—that of the printers—originated in direct connection with the January movement. The commission appointed to work out the tariffs framed the statutes, and on July 19 the union began its existence. Just about this time the union of office workers and bookkeepers was called into existence. In addition to those organizations, which existed almost openly, there arose from January to October 1906 semi-legal and illegal trade unions. To the former belonged, for example, the union of chemists' assistants and commercial employees. Among the illegal unions special attention must be drawn to the watchmakers' union, whose first secret session was held on April 24. All attempts to convene a general open meeting were shattered on the obstinate resistance of

the police and the employers in the form of the Chamber of Commerce. This mis-chance has not prevented the existence of the union. It held secret meetings of members on June 9 and August 14, apart from the sessions of the executive of the union. The tailors' and tailoresses' union was founded in 1905 at a meeting in a wood at which seventy tailors were present. After the question of forming the union was discussed a commission was appointed which was entrusted with the task of working out the statutes. All attempts of the commission to obtain a legal existence for the union were unsuccessful. Its activities were confined to agitation and the enrolling of new members in the individual workshops. A similar fate was in store for the shoemakers' union. In July a secret night meeting was convened in a wood near the city. Over one hundred shoemakers attended; a report was read on the importance of trade unionism, on its history in Western Europe and its tasks in Russia. It was then decided to form a trade union; a commission of twelve was appointed to work out the statutes and call a general meeting of shoemakers. The statutes were drawn up, but in the meantime it had not been found possible to print them nor had the general meeting been convened.

These were the first difficult beginnings. Then came the October days, the second general strike, the Tsar's manifesto of October 30 and the brief "con-stitution period."[12] The workers threw themselves with fiery zeal into the waves of political freedom in order to use it forthwith for the purpose of the work of organization. Besides daily political meetings, debates and the for-mation of clubs, the development of trade unionism was immediately taken in hand. In October and November *forty* new trade unions appeared in St. Petersburg. Presently a "central bureau," that is a trade union council, was established, various trade union papers appeared, and since November a central organ has also been published, *The Trade Union*. What was reported above concerning Petersburg was also true on the whole of Moscow and Odessa, Kiev and Nichola, Saratov and Voronezh, Samara and Nizhni-Nov-gorod, and all the larger towns of Russia, and in still higher degree of Poland. The trade unions of different towns seek contact with one another and con-ferences are held. The end of the "constitution period," and the return to reaction in December 1905, put a stop for the time being to the open wide-spread activity of the trade unions, but did not, however, altogether extin-guish them. They operate as organizations in secret and occasionally carry on quite open wage struggles. A peculiar mixture of the legal and illegal con-dition of trade union life is being built up, corresponding to the highly con-tradictory revolutionary situation. But in the midst of the struggle the work of organization is being more widely extended, in a thoroughgoing, not to say pedantic fashion. The trade unions of the Social Democracy of Poland and Lithuania, for example, which at the last congress (in July 1906) were represented by five delegates from a membership of 10,000 are furnished with the usual statutes, printed membership cards, adhesive stamps, etc. And the same bakers and shoemakers, engineers and printers of Warsaw and Lodz who in June 1905 stood on the barricades and in December only awaited the word from Petersburg to begin street fighting, find time and are eager, between one mass strike and another, between prison and lockout, and under the conditions of a siege, to go into their trade union statutes and discuss them earnestly. These barricade fighters of yesterday and tomorrow have indeed more than once at meetings severely reprimanded their leaders and threatened them with withdrawal from the party because the unlucky trade union membership cards could not be printed quickly enough in secret printing works under incessant police persecution. This zeal and this earnestness continue to this day. For example, in the first two weeks of July 1906 fifteen new trade unions appeared in Ekaterinoslav, six in Kostroma, several in Kiev, Poltava, Smolensk, Tscherkassy, Proskurvo, down to the most significant provincial towns. In the session of the Moscow trade union council of June 4 this year, after the acceptance of the reports of individual trade union delegates, it was decided "that the trade unions should discipline their members and restrain from street rioting because the time is not considered opportune for the mass strike. In the face of possible provocation on the part of the government care should be taken that the masses do not stream out in the streets." Finally, the Council decided that if at any time one trade union began a strike the others should hold back from any wages movement. Most of the economic struggles are now directed by the trade unions.[13]

Thus the great economic struggle which proceeded from the January general strike and which has not ceased to the present day, has formed a broad background of the revolution from which, in ceaseless reciprocal action with the political agitation and the external events of the revolution there ever arise here and there now isolated explosions, and now great general actions of the proletariat. Thus there flame up against this background the following events one after the other; at the May Day demonstration there was an unprecedented, absolute general strike in Warsaw which ended in a bloody encounter between the defenseless crowd and the soldiers. At Lodz, in June a mass outing which was scattered by the soldiers led to a demonstration of 100,000 workers at the funeral of some of the victims of the brutal soldiery and to a renewed encounter with the military, and finally, on June 23, 24, and 25, passed into the first barricade fight in the Tsarist empire. Similarly in June the first great revolt of the sailors of the Black Sea Fleet exploded in the harbor at Odessa from a trifling incident on board the armored vessel *Potemkin* which reacted immediately on Odessa and Nicholaiev in the form of a violent mass strike. As a further echo, the mass strike and the sailors' revolts followed in Kronstadt, Libau and Vladivostok.

In the month of October the grandiose experiment of St. Petersburg was made with the introduction of the eight-hour day. The general council of workers delegates decided to achieve the eight-hour day in a revolutionary manner. That means that on the appointed day all the workers of Petersburg should inform their employers that they were not willing to work more than eight hours a day, and should leave their places of work at the end of eight hours. The idea was the occasion of lively agitation, was accepted by the proletariat with enthusiasm and carried out, but very great sacrifices were not thereby avoided. Thus for example, the eight-hour day meant an enormous fall in wages for the textile workers who had hitherto worked eleven hours and that on a system of piece work. This, however, they willingly accepted. *Within a week the eight-hour day prevailed in every factory and workshop in Petersburg,* and the joy of the workers knew no bounds. Soon, however, the employers, stupefied at first, prepared their defenses; everywhere they threatened to close their factories. Some of the workers consented to negotiate and obtained here a working day of ten hours and there one of nine hours. The elite of the Petersburg proletariat, however, the workers in the large government engineering estab-lishments, remained unshaken, and a lockout ensued which threw from 45,000 to 50,000 men on the streets for a month. At the settlement the eight-hour day movement was carried into the general strike of December which the great lockout had hampered to a great extent.

Meanwhile, however, the second tremendous general strike throughout the whole empire followed in October as a reply to the project of the Bulygin Duma[14]—the strike to which the railwaymen gave the summons. This second great action of the proletariat already bears a character essentially different from that of the first one in January. The element of political consciousness already plays a much bigger role. Here also, to be sure the immediate occasion for the outbreak of the mass strike was a subordinate and apparently accidental thing: the conflict of the railwaymen with the management over the pension fund. But the general rising of the industrial proletariat which followed upon it was conducted in accordance with clear political ideas. The prologue of the January strike was a procession to the Tsar to ask for political freedom: the watchword of the October strike ran away with the constitutional comedy of Tsarism! And thanks to the immediate success of the general strike, to the Tsar's manifesto of October 30, the movement does not flow back on itself (as in January) but rushes over outwardly in the eager activity of newly acquired political freedom. Demonstrations, meetings, a young press, public discussions and bloody massacres as the end of the story, and thereupon new mass strikes and demonstrations—such is the stormy picture of the November and December days. In November, at the instance of the Social Democrats in Petersburg the first demonstrative mass strike is arranged as a protest demonstration against the bloody deeds and the proclamation of a state of siege in Poland and Livonia. The fermentation after the brief constitutional period and the gruesome awakening finally leads in December to the outbreak of the third general mass strike throughout the empire. This time its course and its outcome are altogether different from those in the two earlier cases. Political action does not change into economic action (as in January), but it no longer achieves a rapid victory (as in October). The attempts of the Tsarist camarilla with real political freedom are no longer made, and revolutionary action therewith, for the first time, and along its whole length, knocked against the strong wall of the physical violence of absolutism. By the logical internal development of progressive experience the mass strike this time changes into an open insurrection, to armed barricades, and street fighting in Moscow. The December days in Moscow close the first eventful year of the revolution as the highest point in the ascending line of political action and of the mass strike movement.

The Moscow events show a typical picture of the logical development and at the same time of the future of the revolutionary movement on the whole: their inevitable close in a general open insurrection, which again on its part cannot come in any other way than through the school of a series of preparatory partial insurrections, which therefore meantime end in partial outward "defeats" and considered individually, may appear to be "premature."

The year 1906 brings the elections to the Duma and the Duma incidents. The proletariat, from a strong revolutionary instinct and clear knowledge of the situation, boycotts the whole Tsarist constitutional farce; and liberalism again occupies the center of the stage for a few months. The situation of 1904 appears to have come again, a period of speeches instead of acts, and the proletariat for a time walk in the shadow in order to devote themselves the more diligently to the trade union struggle and the work of organization. The mass strikes are no longer spoken of, while the clattering rockets of liberal rhetoric are fired off day after day. At last the iron curtain is torn down, the actors are dispersed, and nothing remains of the liberal rockets but smoke and vapor. An attempt of the Central Committee of the Russian Social Democracy to call forth a mass strike as a demonstration for the Duma and the reopening of the period of liberal speechmaking falls absolutely flat. The role of the political mass strike alone is exhausted, but at the same time, the transition of the mass strike into a general popular rising is not yet ac-complished. The liberal episode is past, the proletarian episode is not yet begun. The stage remains empty for the time being.

## THE INTERACTION OF THE POLITICAL
## AND THE ECONOMIC STRUGGLE

We have attempted in the foregoing to sketch the history of the mass strike in Russia in a few strokes. Even a fleeting glance at this history shows us a picture which in no way resembles that usually formed by the discussions in Germany on the mass strike. Instead of the rigid and hollow scheme of an arid political action carried out by the decision of the highest committees and furnished with a plan and panorama, we see a bit of pulsating life of flesh and blood, which cannot be cut out of the large frame of the revolution but is connected with all parts of the revolution by a thousand veins.

The mass strike, as the Russian revolution shows it to us, is such a changeable phenomenon that it reflects all phases of the political and economic struggle, all stages and factors of the revolution. Its adaptability, its efficiency, the factors of its origin are constantly changing. It suddenly opens new and wide perspectives of the revolution when it appears to have already arrived in a narrow pass and where it is impossible for anyone to reckon upon it with any degree of certainty. It flows now like a broad billow over the whole kingdom, and now divides into a gigantic network of narrow streams; now it bubbles forth from under the ground like a fresh spring and now is completely lost under the earth. Political and economic strikes, mass strikes and partial strikes, demonstrative strikes and fighting strikes, general strikes of individual branches of industry and general strikes in individual towns, peaceful wage struggles and street massacres, barricade fighting—all these run through one another, run side by side, cross one another, flow in and over one another—it is ceaselessly moving, a changing sea of phenomena. And the law of motion for these phenomena is clear: it does not lie in the mass strike itself nor in its technical details, but in the political and social proportions of the forces of the revolution. The mass strike is merely the form of the revolutionary struggle and every disarrangement of the relations of the contending powers, in party development and in class division, in the position of the counterrevolution—all this immediately influences the action of the strike in a thousand invisible and scarcely controllable ways. But strike action itself does not cease for a single moment. It merely alters its forms, its dimensions, its effect. It is the living pulse-beat of the revolution and at the same time its most powerful driving wheel. In a word, the mass strike, as shown to us in the Russian revolution, is not a crafty method discovered by subtle reasoning for the purpose of making the proletarian struggle more effective, *but the method of motion of the proletarian mass,* the phenomenal form of the proletarian struggle in the revolution.

Some general aspects may now be examined which may assist us in forming a correct estimate of the problem of the mass strike.

1) It is absurd to think of the mass strike as one act, one isolated action. The mass strike is rather the indication, the rallying idea, of a whole period of the class struggle lasting for years, perhaps for decades. Of the innumerable and highly varied mass strikes which have taken place in Russia during the last four years the scheme of the mass strike was a purely political movement, begun and ended after a cut and dried plan, a short single act of one variety only and that a subordinate variety—pure demonstration strike. In the whole course of the five-year period we see in Russia only a few demonstration strikes which, be it noted, were generally confined to single towns. Thus the annual May Day general strike in Warsaw and Lodz in Russia proper on the First of May has not yet been celebrated to any appreciable extent by abstention from work—the mass strike in Warsaw on September 11, 1905, as a memorial service in honor of the executed Martin Kasprzak;[15] the Petersburg protest demonstration against the declaration of a state of siege in Poland and Livonia in November 1905; that of January 22, 1906, in Warsaw, Lodz, Czentochon and in the Dombrowa coal basin, as well as, in part, those in a few Russian towns as anniversary celebrations of the Petersburg bloodbath; in addition, in July 1906 a general strike in Tiflis as demonstration of sympathy with soldiers sentenced by court-martial on account of the military revolt; and finally from the same cause in September 1906, during the deliberations of the court-martial in Reval. All the above great and partial mass strikes and general strikes were not demonstration strikes but fighting strikes, and as such they originated for the most part spontaneously, in every case from specific local accidental causes, without plan and undesignedly, and grew with elemental power into great movements, and then they did not begin an

"orderly retreat," but turned now into economic struggles, now into street fighting, and now collapsed of themselves.

In this general picture the purely political demonstration strike plays quite a subordinate role—isolated small points in the midst of a mighty expanse. Thereby, temporarily considered, the following characteristic discloses itself: the demonstration strikes which, in contradistinction to the fighting strikes, exhibit the greatest mass of party discipline, conscious direction and political thought, and therefore must appear as the highest and most mature form of the mass strike, play in reality the greatest part in the *beginnings* of the movement. Thus for example, the absolute cessation of work on May 1, 1905, in Warsaw as the first instance of a decision of the Social Democrats carried throughout in such an astonishing fashion, was an experience of great importance for the proletarian movement in Poland. In the same way the sympathetic strike of the same year in Petersburg made a great impression as the first experiment on conscious systematic-mass action in Russia. Similarly the "trial mass strike" of the Hamburg comrades on January 17, 1906,[16] will play a prominent part in the history of the future German mass strike as the first vigorous attempt with the much disputed weapon, and also a very successful and convincingly striking test of the fighting temper and the lust for battle of the Hamburg working class. And just as surely will the period. of the mass strike in Germany, when it has once begun in real earnest, lead itself to a real, general cessation of work on May First. The May Day festival may naturally be raised to a position of honor as the first great demonstration under the aegis of the mass struggle. In this sense the "lame horse," as the May Day festival was termed at the trade-union congress at Cologne, has still a great future before it and an important part to play in the proletarian class struggle in Germany. But with the development of the earnest revolutionary struggle the importance of such demonstration diminishes rapidly. It is precisely those factors which objectively facilitate the realization of the demonstration strike after a preconceived plan and at the party's word of command—namely, the growth of political consciousness and the training of the proletariat—make this kind of mass strike impossible; today the proletariat in Russia, the most capable vanguard of the masses, does not want to know about mass strikes; the workers are no longer in a mood for jesting and will now think only of a serious struggle with all its consequences. And when, in the first great mass strike in January 1905,[17] the demonstrative element, not indeed in an intentional but more in an instinctive spontaneous form, still played a great part, on the other hand, the attempt of the central committee of the Russian Social Democrats to call a mass strike in August as a demonstration for the dissolved Duma, was shattered by, among other things, the positive disinclination of the educated proletariat to engage in weak half-actions and mere demonstrations.

2) When, however, we have in view the less important strike of the demonstrative kind, instead of the fighting strike as it represents in Russia today the actual vehicle of proletarian ac-tion, we see still more clearly that it is impossible to separate the economic and the political factors from one another. Here also the reality deviates from the theoretical scheme, and the pedantic representation in which the pure political mass strike is logically derived from the trade union general strike as the ripest and highest stage, but at the same time is kept distinct from it, is shown to be absolutely false. This is expressed not merely in the fact that the mass strikes, from that first great wage struggle of the Petersburg textile workers in 1896–97 to the last great mass strike in December 1905, passed imperceptibly from the economic field to the political, so that it is almost impossible to draw a dividing line between them. Again, every one of the great mass strikes repeats, so to speak, on a small scale, the entire history of the Russian mass strike, and begins with a pure economic, or at all events, a partial trade union conflict, and runs through all the stages to the political demonstration. The great thunderstorm of mass strikes in South Russia in 1902 and 1903 originated, as we have seen, in Baku from a conflict arising from the disciplinary punishment of the unemployed, in Rostov from disputes about wages in the railway workshops, in Tiflis from a struggle of the commercial employees for reduction of working hours, in Odessa from a wage dispute in one single small factory. The January mass strike of 1905 developed from an internal conflict in the Putilov works, the October strike from the struggle of the railway workers for a pension fund, and finally the December strike from the struggle of the postal and telegraph employees for the right of combination. The progress of the movement on the whole is not expressed in the circumstances that the economic initial stage is omitted, but much more in the rapidity with which all the stages to the political demonstration are run through and in the extremity of the point to which the strike moves forward.

But the movement on the whole does not proceed from the economic to the political struggle, not even the reverse. Every great political mass, action, after it has attained its political highest point, breaks up into a mass of economic strikes. And that applies not merely to each of the great mass strikes, but also to the revolution as a whole. With the spreading, clarifying and involution of the political struggle the economic struggle not merely does not recede, but extends, organizes and becomes involved in equal measure. Between the two there is the most complete reciprocal action.

Every new onset and every fresh victory of the political struggle is transformed into a powerful impetus for the economic struggle extending at the same time its external possibilities and intensifying the inner urge of the workers to better their position, and their desire to struggle. After every foaming wave of political action a fructifying deposit remains behind from which a thousand stalks of economic struggle shoot forth. And conversely, the workers' condition of ceaseless economic struggle with the capitalists keeps their fighting energy alive in every political interval; it forms, so to speak, the permanent fresh reservoir of the strength of the proletarian classes, from which the political fight ever renews its strength and at the same time leads the indefatigable economic sappers of the proletariat at all times, now here and now there, to isolated sharp conflicts, out of which political conflicts on a large scale unexpectedly explode.

In a word, the economic struggle is the transmitter from one political center to another; the political struggle is the periodic fertilization of the soil for the economic struggle. Cause and effect here continually change places; and thus the economic and the political factor in the period of the mass strike, now widely removed, completely separated or even mutually exclusive, as the theoretical plan would have them, merely form the two interlacing sides of the proletarian class struggle in Russia. And, *their unity* is precisely the mass strike. If the sophisticated theory purposes to make a clever logical dissection of the mass strike for the purpose of getting at the "purely political mass strike," it will by this dissection, as with any other, not perceive the phenomenon in its living essence, but will kill it altogether.

3) Finally, the events in Russia show us that the mass strike is inseparable from the revolution. The history of the Russian mass strikes is the history of the Russian revolution. When, to be sure, the representatives of our German opportunism hear of "revolution," they immediately think of bloodshed, street fighting or powder and shot, and the logical conclusion thereof is: the mass strike leads inevitably to the revolution, therefore we dare not have it. In actual fact we see in Russia that almost every mass strike in the long run leads to an encounter with the armed guardians of Tsarist order, and therein the so-called political strikes exactly resemble the larger economic struggle. The revolution, however, is something other and something more than bloodshed. In contradiction to the police interpretation, which views the revolution exclusively from the standpoint of street disturbances and rioting, that is, from the standpoint of "disorder," the interpretation of scientific socialism sees in the

revolution above all a thoroughgoing internal reversal of social class relations. And from this standpoint an altogether different connection exists between revolution and mass strike in Russia from that contained in the commonplace conception that the mass strike generally ends in bloodshed.

We have seen above the inner mechanism of the Russian mass strike which depends upon the ceaseless reciprocal action of the political and economic struggles. But this reciprocal action is conditioned during the revolutionary period. Only in the sultry air of the period of revolution can any [partial] little conflict between labor and capital grow into a general explosion. In Germany the most violent, most brutal collisions between the workers and employers take place every year and every day without the struggle overleaping the bounds of the individual departments or individual towns concerned, or even those of the individual factories. Punishment of organized workers in Petersburg and unemployment as in Baku, wage struggles as in Odessa; struggles for the right of combination as in Moscow, are the order of the day in Germany. No single one of these cases however, changes suddenly into a common class action. And when they grow into isolated mass strikes, which have without question a political coloring, they do not bring about a general storm. The general strike of the Dutch railwaymen, which died away in spite of the warmest sympathy, in the midst of the complete impassivity of the proletariat of the country, affords a striking proof of this.

And conversely, only in the period of the revolution, when the social foundations and the walls of the class society are shaken and subjected to a constant process of disarrangement, any political class action of the proletariat can arouse from their passive condition in a few hours whole sections of the working class who have hitherto remained unaffected, and this is immediately and naturally expressed in a stormy economic struggle. The worker, suddenly aroused to activity by the electric shock of political action, immediately seizes the weapon lying nearest his hand for the fight against his condition of economic slavery: the stormy gesture of the political struggle causes him to feel with unexpected intensity the weight and the pressure of his economic chains. And while, for example, the most violent political struggle in Germany—the electoral struggle or the Parliamentary struggle on the customs tariff—exercised a scarcely perceptible direct influence upon the course and the intensity of the wage struggles being conducted at the same time in Germany, every political action of the proletariat in Russia immediately expresses itself in the extension of the area and the deepening of the intensity of the economic struggle.

The revolution thus first creates the social conditions in which this sudden change of the economic struggle into the political and of the political struggle into the economic is possible, a change which finds its expression in the mass strike. And if the vulgar scheme sees the connection between mass strike and revolution only in bloody street encounters with which the mass strikes conclude, a somewhat deeper look into the Russian events shows an exactly opposite connection: in reality the mass strike does not produce the revolution, but the revolution produces the mass strike.

4) It is sufficient, in order to comprehend the foregoing, to obtain an explanation of the question of the conscious direction and initiative in the mass strike. If the mass strike is not an isolated act but a whole period of the class struggle, and if this period is identical with a period of revolution, it is clear that the mass strike cannot be called at will, even when the decision to do so may come from the highest committee of the strongest Social Democratic party. As long as the Social Democracy has not the power to stage and countermand revolutions according to its fancy, even the greatest enthusiasm and impatience of the Social Democratic troops will not suffice to call into being a real period of mass strike as a living, powerful movement of the people. On the basis of a decision of the party leadership and of party discipline a single short demonstration may well be arranged similar to the Swedish mass strike, or to the latest Austrian strike, or even to the Hamburg mass strike of January 17. These demonstrations, however, differ from an actual period of revolutionary mass strikes in exactly the same way that the well-known demonstrations in foreign ports during a period of strained diplomatic relations differ from a naval war. A mass strike born of pure discipline and enthusiasm will, at best, merely play the role of an episode, of a symptom of the fighting mood of the working class upon which, however, the conditions of a peaceful period are reflected. Of course, even during the revolution mass strikes do not exactly fall from heaven. They must be brought about in some way or another by the workers. The resolution and determination of the workers also play a part and indeed the initiative and the wider direction naturally fall to the share of the organized and most enlightened kernel of the proletariat. But the scope of this initiative and this direction, for the most part, is confined to application to individual acts, to individual strikes, when the revolutionary period is already begun, and indeed, in most cases, is confined within the boundaries of a single town. Thus, for example, we have seen that the Social Democrats have already on several occasions successfully issued a direct summons for a mass strike in Baku, in Warsaw, in Lodz and in Petersburg. But this succeeds much less frequently when applied to general

movements of the whole proletariat. Further, there are quite definite limits set to
initiative and conscious direction. During the revolution it is extremely difficult
for any directing organ of the proletarian movement to foresee and to calculate
which occasions and factors can lead to explosions and which cannot. Here
also initiative and direction do not consist in issuing commands according to
one's inclinations, but in the most adroit adaptability to the given situation, and
the closest possible contact with the mood of the masses. The element of spontaneity, as we have seen, plays a great part in all Russian mass strikes without
exception, be it as a driving force or as a restraining influence. This does not
occur in Russia, however, because Social Democracy is still young or weak, but
because in every individual act of the struggle so very many important economic, political and social, general and local, material and psychical, factors react
upon one another in such a way that no single act can be arranged and resolved
as if it were a mathematical problem. The revolution, even when the proletariat
with the Social Democrats at their head appear in the leading role, is not a
maneuver of the proletariat in the open field, but a fight in the midst of the
incessant crashing, displacing, and crumbling of the social foundation. In
short, in the mass strikes in Russia the element of spontaneity plays such a predominant part, not because the Russian proletariat are "uneducated," but
because revolutions do not allow anyone to play the schoolmaster with them.

On the other hand, we see in Russia that the same revolution which rendered the Social Democrats' command of the mass strike so difficult, and
which struck the conductor's baton from, or pressed it into, their hand at all
times in such a comical fashion—we see that it resolved of itself all those
difficulties of the mass strike which, in the theoretical scheme of German discussion, are regarded as the chief concern of the "directing body": the question of "provisioning," "discovery of cost," and "sacrifice." It goes without
saying that it does not resolve them in the way that they would be resolved in a
quiet, confidential discussion between the higher directing committees of the
labor movement, the members sitting pencil in hand. The "regulation" of all
these questions consists in the circumstance that the revolution brings such
an enormous mass of people upon the stage that any computation or regulation of the cost of the movement such as can be effected in a civil process,
appears to be an altogether hopeless undertaking. The leading organizations
in Russia certainly attempt to support the direct victims to the best of their
ability. Thus, for example, the brave victims of the gigantic lockout in St.
Petersburg, which followed upon the eight-hour day campaign, were supported for weeks. But all these measures are, in the enormous balance of the revo-

lution, but as a drop in the ocean. At the moment that a real, earnest period of mass strikes begins, all these "calculations" of "cost" become merely projects for exhausting the ocean with a tumbler. And it is a veritable ocean of frightful privations and sufferings which is brought by every revolution to the proletarian masses. And the solution which a revolutionary period makes of this apparently invincible difficulty consists in the circumstance that such an immense volume of mass idealism is simultaneously released that the masses are insensible to the bitterest sufferings. With the psychology of a trade unionist who will not stay off his work on May Day unless he is assured in advance of a definite amount of support in the event of his being victimized, neither revolution nor mass strike can be made. But in the storm of the revolutionary period even the proletarian is transformed from a provident paterfamilias demanding support into a "revolutionary romanticist," for whom even the highest good, life itself, to say nothing of material well-being, possesses but little in comparison with the ideals of the struggle.

If, however, the direction of the mass strike in the sense of command over its origin, and in the sense of the calculating and reckoning of the cost, is a matter of the revolutionary period itself, the directing of the mass strike becomes, in an altogether different sense, the duty of Social Democracy and its leading organs. Instead of puzzling their heads with the technical side, with the mechanism of the mass strike, the Social Democrats are called upon to assume *political* leadership in the midst of the revolutionary period.

To give the cue for and the direction to the fight; to so regulate the tactics of the political struggle in its every phase and at its every moment that the entire sum of the available power of the proletariat which is already released and active will find expression in the battle array of the party; to see that the tactics of the Social Democrats are decided according to their resoluteness and acuteness, and that they never fall below the level demanded by the actual relations of forces, but rather rise above it—that is the most important task of the directing body in a period of mass strikes. And this direction changes of itself, to a certain extent, into technical direction. Consistent, resolute, progressive tactics on the part of the Social Democrats produces in the masses a feeling of security, self-confidence and desire for struggle; vacillating weak  tactics, based on an underestimation of the proletariat, has a crippling and confusing effect upon the masses. In the first case mass strikes break out "of themselves" and "opportunely"; in the second case they remain ineffective amid direct summonses of the directing body to mass strikes. And of both the Russian revolution affords striking examples.

# 7—Address to the Fifth Congress of the Russian Social-Democratic Labor Party

EDITORS' NOTE: The fifth Congress of the Russian Social-Democratic Labor Party (RSDLP) was held in London from May 13 to June 1, 1907 (May 1–20 by the old Russian calendar). Luxemburg played a major role at the conference, where she sought to concretize the lessons of the 1905 Russian Revolution, especially the actuality of the mass strike, to emerging international developments. She attended as a delegate from both the Social Democracy of the Kingdom of Poland and Lithuania (SDKPiL) and the Central Committee of the SPD. The following remarks, made at the seventh evening session of the conference on May 16, evaluate the various political tendencies in Russia in light of both the experience of the revolution and Marx's theory of revolution. The session was chaired by Lenin. The translation is by Raya Dunayevskaya, from *Pyati Londonskii S'ezd RDRLP, April-May 1907 goda. Prokoly* (Moscow: Institute of Marxism-Leninism, 1963), pp. 97–104). It was first published as an appendix to Dunayevskaya's *Rosa Luxemburg, Women's Liberation, and Marx's Philosophy of Revolution* (Urbana and Chicago: University of Illinois Press, 1991).

Comrades! The Central Committee of the German Social-Democratic Party, having known about my intention to participate in your Congress, decided to take advantage of this opportunity and delegated me to bring you fraternal greetings and wishes for the greatest success. The multimillions of class-conscious German proletariat have followed with lively sympathy and the closest attentiveness the revolutionary struggle of their Russian brothers, and have already demonstrated in deed that they are ready to draw for themselves fruitful lessons from the rich treasures of the experiences of the Russian Social-Democracy. At the very beginning of 1905, when the first thunderstorm of the revolution erupted in Petersburg with the emergence of the proletariat on 9 January, a revival stirred in the ranks of the German Social-Democracy. From it flowed heated debates on the question of tactics, and the Resolution on the general strike at the Jena Congress[1] was the first important result which our Party drew from the struggle of the Russian proletariat. It is true that thus far this decision has had no practical application, and it will hardly become a reality in the near future. Nevertheless, its principal significance is beyond doubt.

Up until 1905 a very negative attitude to the general strike prevailed in the ranks of the German Social-Democratic Party; it was thought to be a purely anarchistic, which meant reactionary slogan, a harmful utopia. But as soon as the German proletariat saw in the general strike of the Russian proletariat a new form of struggle, not in opposition to the political struggle, but as a weapon in that struggle, not as a miraculous remedy to achieve a sudden leap to a socialist order, but rather as a weapon of class struggle for the winning of the most elementary freedoms from the modern class state, it hastened fundamentally to change its attitude to the general strike, acknowledging its possible application in Germany under certain conditions.

Comrades! I consider it necessary to turn your attention to the fact—to the great honor of the German proletariat—that it did change its attitude to the general strike, not at all influenced by the marks of any formal successes of this method of struggle, which impressed even bourgeois politicians. The Resolution at the Jena Congress was passed more than a month before the first, and, at the time, only great victory of the revolution, before the memorable October Days that wrested from absolutism the first constitutional concessions in the form of the October 17th Manifesto.[2] Still, Russia suffered only defeat, and already the German proletariat, with true class instinct, felt that in these outward defeats lies hidden a never-before-seen proletarian strength, a genuine ground for future victories. The fact remains that the German proletariat, before the Russian proletariat achieved any formal victories, hurried to pay tribute to this experience. They incorporated this new tactical slogan into earlier forms of their struggles, aimed not at parliamentary action, but at involvement of the broadest proletarian masses.

Further events in Russia—the October and November days and especially the high point the revolutionary storm reached in Russia, the December crisis in Moscow[3]—were reflected in Germany in a great awakening of spirit in Social-Democratic ranks. In December and January—after the massive demonstrations in Austria for general electoral rights—there began in Germany a new spirited debate on the question of whether it wasn't time to apply some form of a general strike in connection with the electoral struggle in Prussia, in Saxony, and in Hamburg. The question was decided negatively:

the idea of artificially creating a mass movement was rejected. However, on January 17, 1906, it was tested for the first time with a brilliantly executed half-day general work stoppage in Hamburg. This further enhanced the daring and consciousness-of-power of the working masses in the major center of the German Social-Democracy.

At first glance, last year, 1906, appears one of defeat for the Russian Revolution. In Germany, too, it ended with an apparent defeat of the German Social-Democracy. You are acquainted with the fact that in the first democratic general elections in January (January 25), the German Social-Democracy lost nearly half of their delegates. But this electoral defeat comes at the very time when it is in closest connection to the Russian Revolution. For those who understand the interdependence of the position of the Party in the last election, there was no doubt that the Russian Revolution was for it the most important point, the determining factor in the results of the electoral campaign. There is no doubt that the stamp of the events in Russia, and the fear with which this filled the bourgeois classes in Germany, was one of the factors that united and rallied all layers of bourgeois society and the bourgeois parties, with the exception of the Center, under one reactionary slogan: Down with the class representatives of the class-conscious German proletariat, down with Social-Democracy! Never before was Lassalle's formulation that the bourgeoisie was "one reactionary mass" realized in so palpable a manner as in this election. But for that reason the result of the election compelled the German proletariat to turn, with redoubled attention, to the revolutionary struggle of their Russian brothers.

If one could, in a few words, sum up the political and historical results of the last elections to the Reichstag, then it would be necessary to say that, after January 25 and February 5, 1907, Germany showed itself to be the only modern country in which not a trace of bourgeois liberalism and bourgeois democracy remained in the strict sense of the word. Bourgeois liberalism and democracy definitively and irrevocably took their stand on the side of reaction in the struggle against the revolutionary proletariat. It is, precisely, the treason of liberalism, above all, which delivered us directly into the hands of Junker reaction in the last elections. And, although presently the liberals in the Reichstag increased their representation, they nevertheless are nothing but the liberal cover-up for the pathetic toadies of reaction.

A question arose in our ranks in relation to this situation which, to an ever-greater degree, concerns you, our Russian comrades. To the extent to which I am aware, one of the circumstances which is playing a fundamental role in the determination of tactics of the Russian comrades is the view that the proletariat in Russia faces a very special task wrought with great inner contradiction: to create, at one and the same time, the first political conditions of the bourgeois order and yet to carry on the class struggle against the bourgeoisie. This struggle appears fundamentally different from that of the proletariat in Germany and all of West Europe.

Comrades! I think that such a conception is a purely formalistic expression of the question. We, too, to a certain degree, are finding ourselves in just such a difficult position. To us in Germany this became graphically clear in the last elections—the proletariat is the only true fighter and defender even of bourgeois democratic rights in a bourgeois state.

Even were we not to speak of the fact that there is no universal suffrage in the majority of the electoral districts in Germany, it is still a fact that we suffer from many leftovers of medieval feudalism; even the few freedoms we do enjoy, like general electoral rights for election to the Reichstag, the right to strike, to form trade unions, freedom of assembly—these are not seriously guaranteed and are subject to constant attack from the side of reaction. And in all these instances bourgeois liberalism has definitely proven to be a treacherous ally. Under all these circumstances, the class-conscious proletariat is the only durable bulwark for democratic development in Germany.

The question that surfaced in connection with the last electoral defeat was the relationship to bourgeois liberalism. Voices—true, not many—were heard bewailing the premature death of liberalism. In connection with this also came advice from France to take into consideration in one's tactics the weak position of bourgeois liberalism, in order to spare its remains so that we could use it as an ally in the struggle against reaction and for the defense of the general foundation of democratic development.

Comrades! I can testify to the fact that these voices that lamented the political development of Germany were sharply rejected by the class-conscious German proletariat. I can gladly testify to the fact that in this case there were no differences in the Party between the various factions, and the whole Party with a single voice declared: "We may be saddened by the electoral results of this historic development, but we will not take a single step backward toward liberalism, nor by a single iota retreat from our principled political tactics." The conscious German proletariat drew very different conclusions from these last elections to the Reichstag: if bourgeois liberalism and bourgeois democracy are proving themselves so brittle and shaky that with each energetic gesture of the class struggle of the proletariat, they are willing to sink into the abyss of reaction, then they get what they deserve!

Under the impact of the elections of January 25, it has become clear to ever broader layers of the German proletariat that, in view of the disintegration of liberalism, it is necessary for the proletariat to free itself of all illusions and hopes of any help from liberalism in the struggle against reaction, and at the present time more than at any other time, to count only on itself in the struggle for its class interests as well as in the struggle against reactionary attacks upon the democratic development. In the light of these electoral defeats, a greater clarity than even before was achieved regarding class antagonisms. The internal development of Germany has reached a point of maturity that the most optimistic could not have dreamed before. Marx's analysis of the development of bourgeois society had, once again, reached its highest and most brilliant confirmation. But along with this it is clear to all that this development, this sharpening of class contradictions, not just sooner or later, but inevitably, would lead to the period of the stormiest political struggle also in Germany. And, in connection with this, questions of different forms and phases of the class struggle are followed by us with very special interest.

For that reason, the German workers presently fix their gaze with redoubled attention on the struggle of their Russian brothers as the more advanced fighters, the vanguard of the international working class. From my experience in the electoral campaign, I can testify that in all electoral meetings—and I had the opportunity to appear in meetings of two to three thousand people—the workers resounded in a single voice: "Tell us about the Russian Revolution!" And in this is reflected not only their sympathy flowing from instinctive class solidarity with their struggling brothers. It also reflects their recognition that the interests of the Russian Revolution are indeed their cause as well. What the German proletariat expects most from the Russian is the deepening and enrichment of proletarian tactics, the application of the principles of class struggle under new historic conditions. Indeed, that Social-Democracy tactic which is being applied in the present time by the proletarian class in Germany and to which we owe our victories is primarily adapted to parliamentary struggles, a struggle within the framework of bourgeois parliamentarism.

The Russian Social-Democracy is the first to whom has fallen the difficult but honorable task of applying the principles of Marx's teaching not in a period of quiet parliamentary course in the life of the state, but in a stormy revolutionary period. The only experience that scientific socialism had previously in practical politics during a revolutionary period was the activity of Marx himself in the 1848 revolution. The course itself of the 1848 revolution, however, cannot be a model for the present revolution in Russia. From it we can only learn how not to act in a revolution. Here was the schema of this revolution: the proletariat fights with its usual heroism but is unable to utilize its victories; the bourgeoisie drives the proletariat back in order to usurp the fruits of its struggle; finally, absolutism pushes the bourgeoisie aside in order to crush the proletariat as well as defeat the revolution.

The class independence of the proletariat was still in a most embryonic state. It is true that it already had the *Communist Manifesto*—that great charter of class struggle. It is true that Karl Marx participated in the revolution as a practical fighter. But precisely as a result of the particular historic conditions, he had to express, not socialist politics, but that of the extreme left position of bourgeois democracy. The *Neue Rheinische Zeitung*[4] was not so much an organ of class struggle as the organ of the extreme left wing of the bourgeois revolutionary camp. True, there was not in Germany the kind of democracy for which the *NRZ* could have become ideological spokesman. But this is precisely the politics that Marx had to carry out with indefatigable consistency during the first year of the revolution. Doubtless, his politics consisted in this, that Marx had to support with all means the struggle of the bourgeois democracy against absolutism.

But in what did the support consist? In this, that from the first to the last he mercilessly, relentlessly, lashed out against the halfway measures, inconsistency, weakness, cowardice of bourgeois politics. Without the slightest vacillation he supported and defended every action of the proletarian masses—not only the eruption which was the first fleeting sign of victory—March 18—but also the memorable storming of the Berlin Armory on June 14, which then and later the bourgeoisie obstinately claimed was a trap reaction laid for the proletariat, and the September and October uprisings in Vienna—these last attempts of the proletariat to save the revolution from perishing from the wobbliness and treachery of the bourgeoisie.

Marx supported the national struggles of 1848, holding that they were allies of the revolution. The politics of Marx consisted in this, that he pushed the bourgeoisie every moment to the limits of the revolutionary situation. Yes, Marx supported the bourgeoisie in the struggle against absolutism, but he supported it with whips and kicks. Marx considered it an inexcusable mistake that the proletariat allowed, after its first short-lived victory of March 18, the formation of a responsible bourgeois ministry of Camphausen-Hansemann.[5] But once the bourgeoisie got power, Marx demanded from the very first moment that it should actualize the revolutionary dictatorship. He categorically demanded, in the *NRZ*, that the transitional period after each revolution demanded the most energetic dictatorship. Marx very clearly understood the total impotence of the German "Duma," the Frankfurt National Assembly.[6] But he saw this, not as a mitigating circumstance, but the contrary. He showed that the only way out of the impotent situation was through winning actual power in open battle against the old power, and in this, depending on the revolutionary national masses.

But, comrades, how did the politics of Marx end? The following year Marx had to abandon this position of extreme bourgeois democracy—a position completely isolated and hopeless—and go over to pure class-struggle politics. In the autumn of 1849, Marx with his co-thinkers left the bourgeois democratic union and decided to establish an independent organization of the proletariat. They also wished to participate in a projected all-German workers' congress, an idea which emerged from the ranks of the proletariat of East Prussia. But when Marx wanted to change the course of his politics, the revolution was living out its last days and before he succeeded in carrying out the new, pure proletarian tactics, the *NRZ* became the first victim of triumphant reaction.

Clearly comrades, you in Russia at the present time have to begin, not where Marx began, but where Marx ended in 1849, with a clearly expressed, independent proletarian class policy. Presently the Russian proletariat finds itself, not in the position of the embryonic state that characterized the German proletariat in 1848, but representing a cohesive and conscious political proletarian force. The Russian workers need not feel themselves isolated, but rather part of the all-world international army of the proletariat. They cannot forget that the present revolutionary struggle is not an isolated skirmish, but one of the greatest battles in the entire course of the international class struggle.

It is clear that in Germany, sooner or later, in accordance with the maturing class relations, the proletarian struggle will inescapably flow out into mass collisions with the ruling classes, and the German proletariat will need to utilize the experience, not of the 1848 bourgeois revolution, but of the Russian proletariat in the current revolution. Therefore, comrades, you are carrying responsibility to the whole international proletariat. And the Russian proletariat will attain its height in this task only if, in the range of the tactics in its own struggles, it shows the decisiveness, the clear consciousness of its goal, and that it has learned the results of the international development in its entirety, has achieved the degree of maturity that the whole capitalistic society has reached.

The Russian proletariat, in its actions, must show that between 1848 and 1907, in the more than half-century of capitalist development, and from the point of this development taken as a whole, we are not at the beginning but at the end of this development. It must show that the Russian Revolution is not just the last act in a series of bourgeois revolutions of the nineteenth century, but rather the forerunner of a new series of future proletarian revolutions in which the conscious proletariat and its vanguard, the Social-Democracy, are destined for the historic role of leader. The German worker expects from you not only victory over absolutism, not only a new foothold for the liberation movement in Europe, but also the widening and deepening of the perspectives of the proletarian tactic: he wishes to learn from you how to step into this period of open revolutionary struggle.

However, in order to carry out this role, it is necessary for the Russian Social-Democracy to learn one important condition. This condition is the unity of the Party, not just a formal, purely mechanical unity, but an inner cohesion, an inner strength which genuinely will result from clear, correct tactics corresponding to this inner unity of the class struggle of the proletariat. The extent to which the German Social-Democracy counts on the unity of the Russian Party you can see from the letter which the Central Committee of the German Social-Democracy has authorized me to deliver to you. At the start of my talk I delivered the fraternal greetings which the Central Committee sent to all the representatives of the Social-Democracy. The rest of this letter reads:

> The German Social-Democracy has fervently followed the struggle of the Russian brothers against absolutism and against plutocracy striving to share power with it.
>
> The victory which you have achieved in the elections to the Duma, despite the rigged electoral system, has delighted us. It showed that, no matter what the obstacles, the spontaneous triumphant force of socialism is irresistible.
>
> As the bourgeoisie tries everywhere, so the Russian bourgeoisie is attempting, to conclude peace with its rulers. It wants to stop the victorious forward march of the Russian proletariat. It tries also in Russia to steal the fruit of the proletariat's unyielding struggle. Therefore the role of leader in the liberation movement falls to the Russian Social-Democracy.
>
> The necessary condition for carrying out this emancipation struggle is unity and cohesion of the Russian Social-Democratic Party. What we expect to hear from the representatives of our Russian brothers is that the deliberations and decisions of their Congress have fulfilled our expectations and wishes for the realization of the unity and cohesion of the Russian Social-Democracy.
>
> In this spirit we are sending our fraternal greetings to your Congress.

# 8 — Theory and Practice

EDITORS' NOTE: Published in *Neue Zeit* in 1910, "Theory and Practice" marks Luxemburg's open break from Karl Kautsky, the leading theoretician of the Second International. Early in 1910 Kautsky refused to publish an essay on the mass strike by Luxemburg (entitled "What Next?") on the grounds that its call for a republic did not accord with the SPD program. After a bitter exchange of letters between them, Kautsky defended his position in "A New Strategy" (*Neue Zeit*, June 12–24, 1910), in which he argued that the SPD should follow a "strategy of attrition" rather than risk a frontal assault on the government. Luxemburg's retort to Kautsky, of which the first four sections are published here, demonstrates her projection of a new relation of spontaneity and organization in the face of growing opposition from SPD leaders. Her dispute with Kautsky in 1910 foreshadowed the crisis which openly tore apart the Second International at the start of World War I. The translation is by David Wolff.

## I

The first question which the interest of party circles demands in our present dispute is this: whether discussion of the mass strike was obstructed in the party press, namely in *Vorwärts* and the *Neue Zeit*. Comrade Kautsky denies this, asserting that it would "naturally never have occurred to him to wish to 'forbid' discussion of the mass strike."[1] Comrade Kautsky wishes to misunderstand me. We are obviously not concerned with a veto of Comrade Kautsky's—a single editor cannot "forbid" anything—but with a veto by the "high command" of his original acceptance of my article, which was obeyed by Comrade Kautsky in his sphere of influence, the *Neue Zeit*.

As for the other question—propaganda for a republic—here Comrade Kautsky also denies that he obstructed me. "That would never have occurred to him." All that was involved was one passage about a republic in my mass strike article, "whose wording seemed inexpedient" to the editors of the *Neue Zeit*. I myself then had my article published in the Dortmund *Arbeiter-Zeitung*.[2] "*But in vain will one search this article for that passage about a*

208

*republic.*" Comrade Kautsky has "not noticed" that I had published this passage somewhere else. "The cowardly veiling of principles with which Comrade Luxemburg reproaches us," he concludes, "is therefore reduced to this: that we objected to one passage in her article, which she herself has voluntarily dropped since then. Such strategy is no piece of heroism, Octavia!"

In this representation of the facts, which places me in such a ridiculous light, Comrade Kautsky has fallen victim to singular errors. In reality it was not at all a question of "one passage" and the possible danger of its "wording": it was a question of the <u>content, of the slogan of a republic and the agitation for it</u>—and Comrade Kautsky must excuse me, in the precarious position in which his presentation of the case has left me, if I call upon him as chief witness and rescuer in my greatest need. Comrade Kautsky wrote me this after he received my mass strike article:

> Your article is very beautiful and very important, I am not in agreement with everything and reserve the right to polemicize against it. Today I don't have time to do so in writing. Enough, I gladly accept the article if you delete pages 29 to the end. Under no circumstances could I print this. Even your point of departure is false. There is not one word in our program about a republic. Not out of oversight, not because of editorial caprice, but on well-considered grounds. Likewise the Gotha Program said nothing of a republic, and Marx, as much as he condemned this program, acknowledged in his letter that it wouldn't do to openly demand a republic (*Neue Zeit*, IX, 1, P. 573).[3] Engels spoke on the same matter regarding the Erfurt Program (*Neue Zeit*, XX, 1, p. 11).[4]
>
> I don't have time to set forth to you the grounds which Marx and Engels, Bebel[5] and Liebknecht[6] acknowledged to be sound. Enough, that what you want is an entirely new agitation which until now has always been rejected. This new agitation, however, is the sort we have no business discussing so openly. With your article you want to proclaim on your own hook, as a single individual, an entirely new agitation which the party has always rejected. We cannot and will not proceed in this manner. A single personality, however high she may stand, cannot pull off a fait accompli on her own hook which can have unforeseeable consequences for the party.

It goes on in the same vein for about another two pages.

The "entirely new agitation," which could have "unforeseeable consequences" for the party, had the following wording:

Universal, equal, direct suffrage for all adults, without distinction of sex, is the immediate goal which ensures us the enthusiastic agreement of the broadest strata at the present moment. But this goal is not the only one which we must now preach. As long as we answer the infamous electoral reform bungling of the government and the bourgeois parties by proclaiming the slogan of a truly democratic electoral system, we still find ourselves—taking the political situation as a whole—on the defensive. In accord with the good old principle of every real battle tactic, that a powerful blow is the best defense, we must answer the ever more insolent provocations of the reigning reaction by turning the tables in our agitation and going over to a sharp attack all along the line. This can be done in the most visible, clear, and so to speak lapidary form if our agitation clearly champions the following demand, which the first point of our political program leads to: *the demand for a republic.*

Up till now the watchword republic has played a limited role in our agitation. There were good reasons for this: our party wished to save the German working class from those bourgeois, or rather petty bourgeois republican illusions which were (for example) so disastrous in the history of French socialism, and still are today. From the beginning, the proletarian struggle in Germany was consistently and resolutely directed not against this or that form and excrescence of class society in particular, but against class society as such; instead of splintering into anti-militarism, anti-monarchism, and other petty bourgeois "isms," it constantly built itself as anticapitalism, mortal enemy of the existing order in all its excrescences and forms, whether under the cloak of monarchy or republic. And through forty years' radical labor of enlightenment, we have succeeded in making this conviction the enduring possession of the awakened German proletariat: that the best bourgeois republic is no less a class state and bulwark of capitalist exploitation than the present monarchy, and that only the abolition of the wage system and class rule in every form, and not the outward show of "popular sovereignty" in a bourgeois republic, can materially alter the condition of the proletariat.

Well then, it is just because the forty-year labor of Social Democracy has been such a fundamental prophylaxis against the dangers of republican petty bourgeois illusions in Germany that today we can calmly make a place in our agitation for the foremost principle of our political program, a place that is its due by right. By pushing forward the republican character of Social Democracy we win, above all, one more opportunity to illustrate in a palpable, popular fashion our principled opposition as a *class party of the proletariat* to the united camp of *all bourgeois parties.* For the frightening downfall of bourgeois liberalism in Germany is revealed most drastically in its Byzantine genuflection to the monarchy, in which liberal burgerdom runs only a nose behind conservative Junkerdom.

But this is not enough. The general state of Germany's domestic and foreign politics in recent years points to the monarchy as the center, or at least the outward, visible head of the reigning reaction. The semi-absolute monarchy with its personal authority has formed for a quarter century, and with every year more so, the stronghold of militarism, the driving force of battleship diplomacy, the leading spirit of geopolitical adventure, just as it has been the shield of Junkerdom in Prussia and the bulwark of the ascendancy of Prussia's political backwardness in the entire Reich: it is finally, so to speak, the personal sworn foe of the working class and Social Democracy.

In Germany, *the slogan of a republic* is thus infinitely more than the expression of a beautiful dream of democratic "peoples' government," or political doctrinairism floating in the clouds: it is a practical war cry against militarism, navalism, colonialism, geopolitics, Junker rule, the Prussianization of Germany; it is only a consequence and drastic summation of our daily battle against all individual manifestations of the reigning reaction. In particular, the most recent events point straight in the same direction: Junkerdom's threats in the Reichstag of an absolutist coup d'état and the Reich Chancellor's insolent attacks on Reichstag voting rights in the Prussian *Landtag*, as well as the redemption of the "royal pledge" on the question of Prussian suffrage through the Bethmann reform bill.

With a clear conscience I can here set forth this "entirely new agitation," as it has already appeared in print without causing the party the slightest injury in body and soul. Although I had agreed (with a sigh, to be sure, but with resignation) to delete the section on the republic, Comrade Kautsky finally returned the whole mass strike article to me. Without altering a word I published the interdicted pages "29 to the end," furnished with an introduction and conclusion, as a self-sufficient article in the Breslau *Volkswacht* of March 25 under the title "A Time for Sowing": whereupon it was reprinted by a string of party papers—to my recollection in Dortmund, Bremen, Halle, Elberfeld, Königsberg, and in Thuringian papers. That is certainly no piece of heroism on my part: it's just my tough luck that Comrade Kautsky's reading of the party press at that time was as desultory as his consideration of the party's position regarding the slogan of a republic. If he had, let us say, more maturely considered the subject, he could not possibly have mobilized Marx and Engels against me on the question of a republic. Engels' article to which Kautsky refers is the critique of the party leadership's draft of the Erfurt Program of 1891. Here Engels says in Section II, "Political Demands":

The draft's political demands have one great flaw. What actually should have been said *is not there*. If all these ten demands were conceded we would indeed have diverse further means to carry the main political point, but in no way the main point itself.

Engels substantiates the urgent need to clarify this "main point" of Social Democracy's political demands with an allusion to the "opportunism prevalent in a great part of the Social Democratic press." Then he continues:

What then are these ticklish, but very essential points?

*First.* If anything is certain, it is this: that our party and the working class can only come to power under the form of a democratic republic. This is even the specific form for the dictatorship of the proletariat, as the great French Revolution has already shown. It is surely unthinkable that our best people should, like Miquel, become ministers under a Kaiser. At present it seems that legally, it won't do to set a demand for a republic directly in the program—although this was admissible even under Louis Philippe in France, just as it now is in Italy. But the fact that one cannot even draw up an openly republican party program in Germany proves how colossal the illusion is, that we can genially, peacefully install a republic there—and not only a republic, but communist society.

In any case, for the time being we can sidestep the question of a republic. But in my opinion, what should and can be included is the demand for *concentration of all political power in the hands of the people's representatives*. And for the present that would be sufficient, if one can go no further.

*Second.* The reconstitution of Germany....

So, then, a unified republic....

On all these subjects, not much can be said in the program. I call this to your attention chiefly to characterize both the situation in Germany, where it will not do to say such things, and the self-delusion that would transform this situation into a communist society by legal means. And further, to remind the party executive that there are still more weighty political questions besides direct legislation by the people and the free administration of justice before we reach the end. With the universal instability, any of these questions could catch fire overnight: and what then, if we have never discussed, never come to an understanding on them?

We see that Engels perceives "one great flaw" in the party program: that it does not include the demand for a republic, solely on the basis of categorical representations from Germany that, for political reasons, such things were out of the question. With visible discomfort and various misgivings, he decides to bite the sour apple and "in any case" to "sidestep" the demand for a republic. But what he unqualifiedly declares to be essential is *discussion of the slogan of a republic in the party press*:

> You there can judge better than I can here, whether it is possible to further formulate the above-mentioned points as program demands. But it would be desirable *that these questions be debated within the party before it is too late.*[7]

*This* "political testament" of Friedrich Engels was, let us say, peculiarly interpreted by Comrade Kautsky when he banned discussion of the necessity of agitation for a republic from the *Neue Zeit* as an "entirely new agitation" which allegedly "until now has always been rejected by the party."

As for Marx, in his critique of the Gotha Program he went so far as to declare that if it were not possible to openly advance a republic as the program's foremost political demand, then all the demands for democratic details should have been omitted as well. He wrote, regarding the Gotha Program:

> Its political demands include nothing beyond the old, well-known democratic litany: universal suffrage, direct legislation, human rights, a people's militia, etc. . .
>
> But one thing has been forgotten. Since the German workers' party expressly declares that it acts within "the present nation state," and hence *its own* state, the Prusso-German Empire . . . , it should not have forgotten the main point: that all these pretty little things rest on recognition of the so-called "popular sovereignty," that they are therefore only appropriate to a *democratic republic*. Since you do not feel yourselves in the position—and wisely, for the circumstances demand caution [*nota bene*, Marx wrote this thirty-five years ago in the era of Tessendorf,[8]under the advancing shadow of the oncoming Anti-Socialist Law[9]—R.L.]—to demand a democratic republic as the French workers' programs did under Louis Philippe and Louis Napoleon, you should not have tried to hide behind the . . . dodge [the dots are substituted for a boisterous adjective of Marx's—R.L.] of demanding things which only make sense in a democratic republic, from a state which is nothing but a military despotism embellished with parliamentary forms, alloyed with a feudal admixture, obviously influenced by the bourgeoisie, shored up with a bureaucracy, and watched over by the police.
>
> Even vulgar democracy which sees the millennium in the democratic republic and has no suspicion, that it is in just this last state form of bourgeois society that the class struggle will be fought out to the end—even it towers mountain-high

over this sort of democratism within the limits of the police-permitted and the logically impermissible.[10]

Thus, Marx too spoke an entirely different language *in puncto* republic. Shortly before and after the Anti-Socialist law was in effect, Marx, like Engels, allowed—on the strength of assurances from Germany—that perhaps it wouldn't do, to formally advance the demand for a republic in the *program*. But that today, a quarter century later, this demand in the agitation (and that is all we are concerned with here) should pass for something "entirely new" and unheard of—that is surely something which neither of them could have dreamed.

To be sure, Comrade Kautsky points out that he has already propagandized for a republic in *Neue Zeit*, in a manner "totally different" from that in which I, in my harmless way, do so now. He must know more about it than I: in this case my memory seems to fail me. But is more conclusive proof required than the most recent events, that in this matter the essential thing, the follow-up in practice, was not done? The increase of the Prussian civil list[11] offered once again the most splendid opportunity imaginable, and at the same time laid the undeniable duty on the party to sound the slogan of a republic loud and clear, and to look to its propaganda. The insolent challenge of this government bill, following the ignominious end of the suffrage bill, should have been unconditionally answered by unfolding the political function of the monarchy and its personal authority in Prusso-Germany; by emphasizing its connection with militarism, navalism, and the social-political stasis; by recalling the famous "discourses" and "remarks" on the "rabble of the people" and the "compote dish"; by recalling the "penitentiary bill";[12] by revealing the monarchy as the visible expression of the entire imperial German reaction.

The pathetic unanimity of all bourgeois parties in their Byzantine handling of the bill drastically shows once again, that in today's Germany the slogan of a republic has become the shibboleth of class division, the watchword of class struggle. Of all this, nothing in the *Neue Zeit* or in *Vorwärts*. The increase of the civil list is not approached from the political side; it is treated chiefly as a fiscal question, as a question of the Hohenzollern family income, and this is dilated upon with more or less wit. But not one syllable in our two leading organs has championed the slogan of a republic.

Comrade Kautsky is a more qualified Marxian scholar than I: he should know better, what pointed adjective Marx would have applied to *this* "dodge" and *this* sort of republicanism "within the limits of the police-permitted and logically impermissible."

Thus Comrade Kautsky is in error when he says I "bewail myself" of being "badly handled" by the editors of the *Neue Zeit*. I find only that Comrade Kautsky has handled himself badly.


## II

And now to the mass strike. To explain his unexpected stand against the slogan of the mass strike in the latest Prussian voting rights campaign, Comrade Kautsky created a whole theory of two strategies: the "strategy of overthrow" and the "strategy of attrition." Now Comrade Kautsky goes a step farther, and constructs ad hoc yet another whole new theory of the conditions for political mass strikes in Russia and in Germany.

He begins with general reflections on the deceptiveness of historical examples, and how plausibly one can, with insufficient caution, find appropriate justification in history for all strategies, methods, aims, institutions, and earthly things in general. These observations, of a harmless nature in their initial breadth and generality, soon show their less than harmless tendency and purpose in this formulation: that it is "especially dangerous to appeal to revolutionary examples." These warnings, in spirit somewhat reminiscent of Comrade Frohme's[13] fatherly admonitions, are directed specifically against the Russian Revolution [of 1905]. Thereupon follows a theory intended to show and prove the total antithesis of Russia and Germany: Russia, where conditions for the mass strike exist and Germany, where they do not.

In Russia we have the weakest government in the world, in Germany the strongest; in Russia an unsuccessful war with a small Asian land, in Germany the "glory of almost a century of continuous victories over the strongest great powers in the world." In Russia we have economic backwardness and a peasantry which, until 1905, believed in the Tsar like a god; in Germany we have the highest economic development, and with it the concentrated might of the cartels which suppresses the working masses through the most ruthless terrorism. In Russia we have the total absence of political freedom; in Germany we have political freedom which provides the workers various "safe" forms for their protest and struggle, and hence they "are totally preoccupied with organizations, meetings, the press, and elections of all sorts." And the result of these contrasts is this: in Russia the strike was the only possible form of proletarian struggle, and therefore the strike was in itself a victory, even though it was planless and ineffectual—and further, because strikes were forbidden, every strike was in itself a political act. On the other hand, in Western

Europe—here the German schema is extended to all of Western Europe—such "amorphous, primitive strikes" have long been outmoded: here one only strikes when a positive result can be expected.

The moral of all this is that the long revolutionary period of mass strikes, in which economic and political action, demonstration and fighting strikes continuously alternate and are transformed one into the other, is a specific product of Russian backwardness. In Western Europe, and especially in Germany, even a demonstration mass strike like the Russian ones would be extremely difficult, almost impossible, "not in spite, but because of the half-century old socialist movement." As a means of struggle, the political mass strike could only be employed here in a single, final battle "to the death"—and therefore only when the question, for the proletariat, was to conquer or die.

In passing only, I wish to point out that Comrade Kautsky's depiction of the Russian situation is, in the most important points, an almost total reversal of the truth. For example, the Russian peasantry did not suddenly begin to rebel in 1905. From the so-called emancipation of the serfs in 1861, with a single pause between 1885 and 1895, peasant uprisings run like a red thread through the internal history of Russia; uprisings against the landowners as well as violent resistance to the organs of government. It is this which occasioned the Minister of Interior's well-known circular letter of 1898 which placed the entire Russian peasantry under martial law. The new and exceptional in 1905 was simply that, for the first time, the peasant masses' chronic rebellion took on political and revolutionary meaning as concomitant and totalization of the urban proletariat's goal-conscious, revolutionary class action.

Even more turned around, if this is possible, is Comrade Kautsky's conception of the question's main point—the strike and mass strike actions of the Russian proletariat. The picture of chaotic, "amorphous, primitive strikes" by the Russian workers—who strike out of bewilderment, simply to strike, without goal or plan, without demands and "definite successes"—is a blooming fantasy. The Russian strikes of the revolutionary period effected a very respectable raise in wages, but above all they succeeded in almost universally shortening the working day to ten hours, and in many cases to nine. With the most tenacious struggle, they were able to uphold the eight-hour day for many weeks in St. Petersburg. They won the right to organize not only for the workers, but for the state's postal and railroad employees as well: and until the counterrevolution gained the upper hand, they defended this right from all attacks. They broke the overlordship of the employers, and in many of the larger enterprises they created workers' committees to regulate working conditions. They undertook the task of abolishing piecework, household work, night work, factory penalties, and of forcing strict observance of Sundays off.

These strikes, from which promising union organizations rapidly sprouted in almost all industries with vigorous life, and with solid leadership, treasuries, constitutions, and an imposing union press—these strikes, from which as bold a creation as the famous St. Petersburg Council of Workers' Delegates was born for unified leadership of the entire movement in the giant empire— these Russian strikes and mass strikes were so far from being "amorphous and primitive" that in boldness, strength, class solidarity, tenacity, material gains, progressive aims and organizational results, they could safely be set alongside any "West European" union movement. Granted, since the revolution's defeat most of the economic gains, together with the political ones, have little by little been lost. But this plainly does not alter the character which the strikes had as long as the revolution lasted.

Not "organized" and hence "planless," these economic, partial, and local conflicts continuously, "spontaneously" grew into general political and revolutionary mass strikes—from which, in turn, further local actions sprouted up thanks to the revolutionary situation and the potential energy of the masses' class solidarity. The course and immediate outcome of such a general political-revolutionary action was also not "organized" and elemental—as will always be the case in mass movements and stormy times. But if, like Comrade Kautsky, one wishes to measure the progressive character of strikes and "rational strike leadership" by their immediate successes, the great period of strikes in Russia achieved relatively greater economic and social-political successes in a few years of revolution than the German union movement has in the four decades of its existence. And all this is due to neither a special heroism, nor a special genius of the Russian proletariat: it is simply the measure of a revolutionary period's quickstep, against the leisurely gait of peaceful development within the framework of bourgeois parliamentarianism.

As Comrade Kautsky said in his *Social Revolution*, 2nd edition, p. 63:

> There remains only one objection which can be, and hence all the more frequently will be raised to this "revolutionary romanticism": that the situation in Russia proves nothing for us in Western Europe because our circumstances are fundamentally different.
>
> Naturally, I am not unaware of the differences in circumstances: but they should not, on the other hand, be exaggerated. Our Comrade Luxemburg's latest pamphlet clearly demonstrates that the Russian working class has not fallen as

low and achieved as little as is generally accepted. Just as the English workers must break themselves of looking down on the German proletariat as a backward class, so we in Germany must give up viewing the Russians in the same way.

And further on:

> As a political factor, the English workers today stand even lower than the workers of the economically most backward and politically least free of European states: Russia. It is their living revolutionary Reason that gives the Russians their great practical strength; and it was their renunciation of revolution and self-limitation to immediate interests, their so-called "political realism," that made the English a zero in real politics.[14]

But for the present, let us set aside the Russian situation and turn to Comrade Kautsky's depiction of the Prusso-German situation. Strange to say, here too we learn of marvels. For example, it has been until now the prerogative of East Elbian Junkerdom to live by the ennobling conviction that Prussia possesses "the strongest contemporary government." How Social Democracy, on the other hand, should in all seriousness come to acknowledge a government to be "the strongest" which "is nothing but a military despotism embellished with parliamentary forms, alloyed with a feudal admixture, obviously influenced by the bourgeoisie, shored up with a bureaucracy, and watched over by the police"—I find that somewhat hard to grasp. That foolish picture of misery, the Bethmann-Hollweg "cabinet": a government reactionary to the bone and therefore without a plan or political direction, with lackeys and bureaucrats instead of statesmen, with a whimsical zig-zag course; internally the football of a vulgar Junker clique and the insolent intrigues of a courtly rabble; in its foreign policy, the football of a personal authority accountable to none; only a few years ago the contemptible shoeshine boy of the "weakest government in the world," Russian Tsarism; propped up by an army which to an enormous extent consists of Social Democrats, with the stupidest drill, the most infamous mistreatment of soldiers in the world—this is the "strongest contemporary government"! In any case, a unique contribution to the materialist conception of history, which until now has not deduced the "strength" of a government from its backwardness, hatred of culture, "slavish obedience," and police spirit.

Besides, Comrade Kautsky has done yet more for this "strongest government": he has even wooed her with the "glory of almost a century of continuous victories over the strongest great powers in the world." In the veterans' associations they have lived, until now, solely on the "glorious campaign" of 1870. To construe his "century" of Prussian glory, Comrade Kautsky has apparently added in the Battle of Jena—as well as the Hunn Campaign in China led by our Count Waldersee,[15]and Trotha's victory over the Hottentot women and children in the Kalahari.[16]

But as it says in Comrade Kautsky's beautiful article of December 1906, "The State of the Reich," at the end of a long and detailed description:

> Comparing the Reich's shining outward state at its beginning with the present sit-
> uation, one must confess that never has a more splendid inheritance of might and
> prestige been more rashly squandered . . . , never in its history has the German
> Reich's position in the world been weaker, and never has a German government
> more thoughtlessly and willfully played with fire than at the present time.[17]

Of course, at that time the main thing was to paint the shining electoral victory that awaited us in the 1907 elections[18] and the overwhelming catastrophes which, according to Comrade Kautsky, would inevitably follow it—with the same inevitability with which he now has them follow the next Reichstag election.

On the other hand, from his depiction of economic and political conditions in Germany and Western Europe, Comrade Kautsky constructs a strike policy which—measured against reality—is a downright astonishing fantasy. "The worker," Comrade Kautsky assures us, "in Germany—and throughout Western Europe as a whole—takes up the strike as a means of struggle only when he has the prospect of attaining *definite successes* with it. If these successes fail to appear, the strike has failed its purpose." With this discovery, Comrade Kautsky has pronounced a harsh judgment on the practice of German and "West European" unions. For what do the strike statistics in Germany show us? Of the 19,766 strikes and lockouts we have had, in all, from 1890 to 1908, an entire quarter (25.2 percent) were wholly unsuccessful; almost another quarter (22.5 percent) were only partly successful; and less than half (49.5 percent) were totally successful.[19]

These statistics just as crassly contradict the theory of Comrade Kautsky that because of the effective development of the workers' organizations as well as the cartels, "the struggles between these organizations likewise grow ever more centralized and concentrated" and on this account "ever more *infrequent.*" In the decade 1890 through 1899, we had a total of 3,722 strikes and lockouts in Germany; in the nine years 1900 through 1908, the time of greatest growth for both cartels and unions, we had 15,994. So little are

NB

strikes growing "ever more infrequent" that they have rather grown four times as numerous in the last decade. And while in the previous decade 425,142 workers took part in strikes, in the last nine years 1,709,415 did: once again four times as many, and thus on the average approximately the same number per strike.

According to the schema of Comrade Kautsky, one quarter to one half of all these union struggles in Germany have "failed their purpose." But every union agitator knows very well that "definite successes" in the form of material gains absolutely are not and cannot be the sole purpose, the sole determining aspect in economic struggles. Instead, union organizations "in Western Europe" are forced step by step into a position which compels them to take up the struggle with limited prospects of "definite successes": as specifically shown by the statistics of purely defensive strikes, of which a whole 32.5 percent turned out completely unsuccessful. That such "unsuccessful" strikes have, nevertheless, not "failed their purpose"; that on the contrary they are a direct condition of life for the defense of the workers' standard of living, for sustaining the workers' fighting spirit, for impeding future onslaughts by the employers: these are the elementary ground rules of German union practice.

And further, it is generally known that besides a "definite success" in material gains, and indeed *without* this success, strikes "in Western Europe" have perhaps their most important effect as beginning points of union *organization*: and it is specifically in backward places and hard-to-organize branches of labor that such "unsuccessful" and "ill-advised" strikes are most common, from which over and over arise the foundations of union organization. The history of the Vogtland textile workers' struggles and sufferings, whose most famous chapter is the great Crimmitschau strike,[20] is but a single testimony to this. The "strategy" which Comrade Kautsky has now set forth is not merely incapable of directing a great political mass action, but even a normal union movement.

But the above-mentioned schema for "West European" strikes has yet another gaping hole—just at the point, in fact, where the economic struggle brings the question of the mass strike, and thus our own proper theme, into consideration. That is, this schema entirely excludes the fact that it is just "in Western Europe" where ever longer, more violent strikes without much "plan" break like an elemental storm over those regions where a great exploited mass of proletarians stands opposed to the concentrated ruling power of capital or the capitalistic state: strikes which grow not "ever more infrequent" but ever more frequent; which mostly end without any "definite successes" at all—but in spite, or rather just because of this are of greater significance as explosions of a deep inner contradiction which spills over into the realm of politics. These are the periodic giant strikes of the *miners* in Germany, in England, in France, in America; these are the spontaneous mass strikes of the *farm workers*, as they have occurred in Italy and in Galicia. and further, the mass strikes of the *railroad workers* which break out now in this state, now in that one.

As it says in Comrade Kautsky's excellent article on "The Lessons of the Miners' Strike" of 1905 in the Ruhr district:

> In this way alone can substantial advances be realized for the miners. The strike against the mine owners has become hopeless: from now on the strike must step forward as *political*; its demands, its tactics must be calculated to set legislation in motion . . .

And Comrade Kautsky continues:

> This new union tactic of the *political strike*, of uniting union and political action, is in fact the only one which remains possible for the miners; and it is the only one certain to reanimate union as well as parliamentary action, and to give heightened aggressive strength to both.

It could appear, perhaps, that here under "political action" we are to understand parliamentary action and not political mass strikes. Comrade Kautsky destroys every doubt, declaring point-blank:

> But the great decisive actions of the struggling proletariat will be fought out more and more through various sorts of political strikes. And here practice strides forward faster than theory. For while we discuss the political strike and search for its theoretical formulation and confirmation, one mighty political mass strike after another flames up through the spontaneous combustion of the masses—or rather every mass strike becomes a political action, every great political test of strength climaxes in a mass strike, whether among the miners, the proletariat of Russia, the Italian farm workers and railroad workers, etc.[21]

So wrote Comrade Kautsky on March 11, 1905.

Here we have "the spontaneous combustion of the masses" and the union leadership, economic struggle and political struggle, mass strikes and revolution, Russia and Western Europe in the most beautiful confusion, all rubrics of the schema fused together in the living interconnection of a great period of fierce social storms.

It seems that "theory" does not merely "stride forward" more slowly than practice: alas, from time to time it also goes tumbling backwards.

### III

We have briefly examined the factual basis of Comrade Kautsky's newest theory on Russia and Western Europe. But the most important thing about this latest creation is its general tendency, which runs on to construct an absolute contradiction between revolutionary Russia and parliamentary "Western Europe," and sets down the prominent role played by the political mass strike in the Russian revolution as a product of Russia's economic and political *backwardness*.

But here Comrade Kautsky finds himself in the disagreeable position of having proved much too much. In this case, somewhat less would have been decidedly more.

Above all, Comrade Kautsky has not noticed that his current theory destroys his earlier theory of the "strategy of attrition." At the center of the "strategy of attrition" stands an allusion to the coming Reichstag elections. My inexcusable error lay in this: I held that the mass strike was already called for in the present struggle for Prussian voting rights, while Comrade Kautsky declared that our overwhelming victory-to-come in next year's Reichstag elections would create the "entirely new situation" which might make the mass strike necessary and appropriate. But now Comrade Kautsky has demonstrated with all desirable clarity that conditions for a period of political mass strikes in Germany—indeed, in all of Western Europe—are lacking after all. "Because of the half-century old socialist movement, Social Democratic organization and political freedom," even simple demonstration mass strikes of the extent and momentum of the Russian ones have become almost impossible in Western Europe.

Yet if this is so, then prospects for the mass strike after Reichstag elections seem fairly problematic. It is clear that all the conditions which make the mass strike absolutely impossible in Germany—the strongest contemporary government and its glittering prestige, the slavish obedience of the state employees, the unshakable opposing might of the cartels, the political isolation of the proletariat—that all this will not suddenly disappear after next year. If the reasons which speak against the political mass strike no longer lie in the situation of the moment, as the "strategy of attrition" would have it, but in the direct results of "half a century of socialist enlightenment and political freedom," in the highly developed level of "Western Europe's" economic and political life—then postponement of expectations for a mass strike until the year after the Reichstag elections turns out to be no more than a modest fig leaf covering the "strategy of attrition's" only real content: the commendation of Reichstag elections. In my first reply[22] I tried to show that in reality the "strategy of attrition" amounted to "Nothing-But-Parliamentarianism." Now Comrade Kautsky himself confirms this in elaborating his theories.

Yet more. Comrade Kautsky has, to be sure, postponed the great mass action until after the Reichstag elections: but at the same time he must admit that in the present situation, the political mass strike could become necessary "at any moment"—for "never in the history of the German Reich were the social, political, and international contradictions under such tension as now."[23] But if in general the social conditions and historic ripeness of "Western Europe," and specifically of Germany, make a mass strike action impossible now, how can such an action suddenly "at any moment" be set in motion? A brutal provocation by the police, a massacre at a demonstration could greatly heighten the masses' agitation and sharpen the situations yet it obviously could not be that "great occasion" which would abruptly overturn the entire economic and political structure of Germany.

But Comrade Kautsky has proved yet another superfluous thing. If the general economic and political conditions in Germany are such as to make a mass strike action like the Russian one impossible, and if the extension which the mass strike underwent in the Russian Revolution [of 1905] is the specific product of Russian *backwardness*, then not only is the use of the mass strike in the Prussian voting rights struggle called into question, but the Jena resolution as well. Until now, the resolution of the Jena party convention [of 1905— Tr.] was regarded both here and abroad as such a highly significant announcement because it officially borrowed the mass strike from the arsenal of the Russian Revolution, and incorporated it among the tactics of German Social Democracy as a means of political struggle. Admittedly this resolution was formally so composed, and by many exclusively interpreted so that Social Democracy seemed to declare it would only turn to the mass strike in case of an attack on Reichstag voting rights. But once, in any case, Comrade Kautsky did not belong to those formalists; indeed, in 1904 he emphatically wrote:

> If we learn one thing from the Belgian example, it is that it would be a fatal error for us in Germany to commit ourselves to a specific time for proclaiming the political strike—*for example, in the event of an attack on the present Reichstag voting rights*.[24]

The chief significance, the essential content of the Jena resolution lay not in this formalistic "commitment," but in the fact of German Social Democracy's principled acceptance of the lessons and example of the Russian Revolution. It was the spirit of the Russian Revolution which ruled the convention of our party in Jena. And now when Comrade Kautsky directly derives the role of the mass strike in the Russian Revolution from Russian *backwardness*, thereby constructing a contradiction between revolutionary Russia and parliamentary "Western Europe"; when he emphatically warns against the examples and methods of revolution—yes, when by implication even the proletariat's defeat in the Russian Revolution is debited in his account to the grandiose mass strike action, through which the proletariat "must eventually be exhausted"—in short, when Comrade Kautsky declares point-blank "but be that as it may, the schema of the Russian mass strike before and during the revolution does not fit German conditions": then from this standpoint it seems an incredible blunder, that German Social Democracy officially borrowed the mass strike directly from the Russian Revolution as a new means of struggle. At bottom, Comrade Kautsky's current theory is a frightfully fundamental revision of the Jena resolution.

To justify his individual, cockeyed stand in the last Prussian voting rights campaign, Comrade Kautsky step-by-step sells out the lessons of the Russian Revolution—the most significant extension and enrichment of proletarian tactics in the last decade.

IV

In light of the conclusions which follow from Comrade Kautsky's newest theory, it now becomes clear how very false, from the ground up, this theory is. To derive the mass strike action of the Russian proletariat, unparalleled in the history of modern class struggle, from Russia's social backwardness—in other words; to explain the outstanding importance and leading role of the urban industrial proletariat in the Russian Revolution as Russian "backwardness"—is to stand things right on their heads.

It was not economic retardation, but precisely the high development of capitalism, modern industry, and commerce in Russia which made that grandiose mass strike action possible, and which caused it. It was just because the urban industrial proletariat was already so numerous, concentrated in the great centers, and so strongly moved by class consciousness, just because the genuine modern capitalist contradiction had progressed so far,

that the struggle for political freedom could be decisively led by this proletariat alone. But because of this it could be no purely constitutional struggle
after the liberal formula, but a genuine modern class struggle in all its breadth
and depth, fighting for the economic as well as the political interests of the
workers—against capital as well as Tsarism, for the eight-hour day as well as a
democratic constitution. And only because capitalist industry and the modern means of commerce bound to it had become a condition of existence for
the state's economic life, could the mass strikes of the proletariat in Russia
realize such a staggering, decisive effect: that the revolution celebrated its victories with them, and with them went down in defeat and grew silent.

At this moment I can think of no more exact formulation of the factors
in question here, than that which I gave in my pamphlet on the mass strike
in 1906:

We have seen that the mass strike in Russia represents not the synthetic product
of a deliberate Social Democratic tactic, but a natural historic figure on the
ground of the present revolution. What are the forces in Russia now which have
brought forth this new manifestation of revolution?

The immediate task of the Russian Revolution is putting an end to absolutism
and establishing a modern bourgeois parliamentary constitutional state. Formally,
this is exactly the same task faced by the March Revolution in Germany and by
the Great Revolution in France at the end of the eighteenth century. But the circumstances, the historic milieu in which these formally analogous revolutions
took place, are fundamentally different from those of today's Russia. The difference in circumstances is the entire cycle of capitalist development which has run
between those bourgeois revolutions in the West and the present bourgeois revolution in the East. That is, this development has not seized the Western European
lands alone, but absolutist Russia as well. Large scale industry with all its consequences—the modern class division, the glaring social contrasts, modern metro-
politan life and the modern proletariat—has become the leading form of
production in Russia (i.e., the decisive one for its social development).

But from this has resulted a strange, contradictory historical situation: that a
revolution whose formal objectives are bourgeois will be carried out under the
leadership of a modern, class-conscious proletariat, and in an international milieu
which stands under the sign of bourgeois democracy's downfall. Now the bourgeoisie is not the leading revolutionary element it was in the earlier revolutions of
the West, when the proletarian mass, dissolved in the petty bourgeoisie, served as
its military levies. All is reversed: the class-conscious proletariat is the leading,

driving element; the big bourgeois strata are in part directly counterrevolutionary, in part weakly liberal; only the rural petty bourgeoisie, along with the urban petty bourgeois intelligensia, are decidedly oppositional, indeed revolutionary minded. But the Russian proletariat, so clearly destined for the leading role in the bourgeois revolution, is itself free from all illusions about bourgeois democracy—and therefore it enters the struggle with a strongly developed consciousness of its own specific class interests in the acutely sharpened opposition of capital and labor.

This contradictory state of affairs is expressed in the fact that in this formally bourgeois revolution, bourgeois society's opposition to absolutism will be commanded by the proletariat's opposition to bourgeois society; that the proletariat's struggle will be simultaneously directed, with equal force, against absolutism and capitalist exploitation; that the program of revolutionary struggle is directed, with equal emphasis, toward political freedom and the eight-hour day, as well as a material existence for the proletariat worthy of humanity. *This two-fold character of the Russian Revolution manifests itself in that inner unity and reciprocal action of economic and political struggle in which we have been instructed by the events in Russia, and which finds its natural expression in the mass strike. . . .*

So the mass strike shows itself to be no specifically Russian product, arising from absolutism, but *a universal form of proletarian class struggle resulting from the present stage of capitalist development and class relations.* From this standpoint, the three bourgeois revolutions—the Great French Revolution, the German March Revolution, and the present Russian one—form an onrunning chain of development in which the prosperity and the end of the capitalist century are reflected. . . .

The present revolution realizes, in the special circumstances of absolutist Russia, the universal results of international capitalist development: and in this *it seems less a final descendant of the old bourgeois revolutions than a forerunner of a new series of proletarian revolutions in the West.* Just because it has so inexcusably delayed its bourgeois revolution, the most backward land *shows ways and methods of extended class struggle for the proletariat of Germany and the most advanced capitalist lands.*[25]

Earlier, Comrade Kautsky also viewed the Russian Revolution in the same historical perspective. In December 1906, in complete agreement with my interpretation, he wrote:

We may most speedily master the lessons of the Russian Revolution and the tasks which it sets us, if we regard it as neither a bourgeois revolution in the traditional sense nor a socialist one, but as a wholly unique process taking place on the border

line between bourgeois and socialist society it demands dissolution of the one, prepares for the formation of the other, and in either case brings all of humanity under
capitalist civilization a mighty step forward in its march of development.[26]

If thus one grasps the real social and historical conditions which lie at the
root of the Russian Revolution's specific new form of struggle, the mass
strike action—and another interpretation is not very well possible without
phantasizing the *actual* course of this action out of thin air, as Comrade Kautsky now does with his "amorphous, primitive strikes"—then it is clear that
mass strikes as the form of the proletariat's revolutionary struggle come into
consideration even more for Western Europe than in Russia, to the extent
which capitalism (in Germany, for example) is much more highly developed.

In fact, all the conditions which Comrade Kautsky mobilizes against the
political mass strike are just so many forces which must make the mass strike
action in Germany even more inevitable, extensive, and powerful.

The opposing might of the cartels which Comrade Kautsky invokes,
"searching" in vain "for its like," the slavish obedience in which the enormous category of German state employees is sunken—these are the very
things which make a peaceful, profitable union action ever more difficult for
the bulk of the German proletariat. They feed ever mightier trials of strength
and explosions in the economic sphere, whose elemental character and mass
extension take on more and more political meaning the longer they continue.

It is just the political isolation of the proletariat in Germany to which
Comrade Kautsky refers, just the fact that the united bourgeoisie down to the
last petty bourgeois stands behind the government like a wall, that shapes
every great political struggle against the government into a struggle against
the bourgeoisie, against exploitation. And the same circumstances guarantee
that every energetic revolutionary mass action in Germany will not take parliamentary forms of liberalism or the previous form of the revolutionary petty
bourgeoisie's struggle, the brief barricade battle, but the classic proletarian
form of the mass strike.

And finally: it is just because we in Germany have "a half century of
socialist enlightenment and political freedom" behind us, that as soon as the
situation has so ripened that the masses take to the field, the action of the proletariat set in motion by every political struggle will roll together all ancient
reckonings against private and state exploitation, and unite the political with
an economic mass struggle. For, as Comrade Kautsky wrote in 1907:

We have not the slightest ground to assume that the degree of exploitation of the German proletariat is less than that in Russia. On the contrary, we have seen that with the advance of capitalism the exploi-tation of the proletariat increases. If the German worker is in a somewhat better position than the Russian, the productivi-ty of his labor is also much greater, and his needs in relation to the general nation-al standard of living are much higher: so that the German worker finds the capitalist yoke perhaps even more galling than the Russian does.[27]

Comrade Kautsky, who paints in such splendid colors how the German worker is "totally preoccupied with organizations, meetings, and elections of all sorts," has for the moment forgotten the quite enormous slave herds of Prusso-German state employees, railroad workers and postal workers, as well as the farm workers, who unfortunately enjoy very limited measure of that contented preoccupation with "organizations, meetings, and options of all sorts" as long as the right to organize is legally or practically denied them. He has forgotten that in the midst of royal Prussian freedom these enormous cat-egories live politically as well as economically in genuine "Russian" condi-tions, and that therefore these very categories—not to mention the miners—will find it impossible, in the midst of a political convulsion, to maintain their slavish obedience or to refrain from presenting their special bill of reckoning in the form of giant mass strikes.

But let us look at "Western Europe." In disputing all this, Comrade Kaut-sky has yet another opponent besides myself to deal with: reality. Specifically, what do we see here when we only direct our attention to the most important mass strikes of the last ten years?

The great Belgian mass strikes which won universal suffrage stand by themselves in the '90s as a bold experiment. Nevertheless, what depth and multidimensionality!

In 1900 the mass strike by the miners in Pennsylvania which, according to the testimony of American comrades, did more to spread socialist ideas than ten years of agitation; also in 1900, mass strike by the miners in Austria; 1902, mass strike by the miners in France; 1902, general strike by all production workers in Barcelona in support of the struggling metal workers; 1902, demonstration mass strike in Sweden for universal, equal suffrage; 1902, mass strike in Belgium for universal, equal suffrage; 1902, mass strike by the farm workers in all east Galicia (over 200,000 taking part) in defense of the right to organize; 1903, in January and April, two mass strikes by the railroad workers in Holland; 1904, mass strike by the railroad workers in Hungary;

1904, demonstration mass strike in Italy protesting the massacres in Sardinia; in January 1905, mass strike by the miners in the Ruhr district; in October 1905, demonstration mass strike in and around Prague (by 100,000 workers) for universal, equal suffrage in Bohemian Landtag elections; in October 1905, demonstration mass strike in Lemburg for universal, equal suffrage in Galician Landtag elections; in November 1905, demonstration mass strike in all of Austria for, universal, equal suffrage in Reichsrat elections; 1905 mass strike by the Italian workers; 1905, mass strike by the Italian railroad workers; 1906, demonstration mass strike in Trieste for universal, equal suffrage in Landtag elections *which victoriously forced the reform through*; 1906, mass strike by the foundry workers in Witkowitz (Mähren) in support of 400 shop stewards fired because of the May Day celebration—victoriously concluded; 1909, mass strike in Sweden in defense of the right to organize; 1909, mass strike by the postal workers in France; in October 1909, demonstration mass strike by all workers in Trient and Rovereto protesting the political persecution of Social Democracy; 1910, mass strike in Philadelphia in support of the streetcar workers' struggle for the right to organize; and at this moment, preparations for a mass strike by the railroad workers in France.

This is the "impossibility" of "West European" mass strikes, especially demonstration mass strikes, which Comrade Kautsky has so beautifully demonstrated in black and white. Comrade Kautsky has theoretically proved the obvious impossibility of mixing political and economic strikes, the impossibility of impressive, general demonstration mass strikes, the impossibility of mass strikes being a *period* of repeated hand-to-hand combat. He has forgotten that for the last ten years we have lived in a period of economic, political, fighting and demonstration strikes: a period which has extended, with striking unity, over almost all "West European lands" as well as the United States; over the capitalistically most backward like Spain, and the most advanced like North America; over lands with the weakest union movements like France, and those with strapping Social Democratic unions like Austria; over agrarian Galicia and highly industrialized Bohemia; over half-feudal states like the Hapsburg monarchy, republics like France, and absolutist states like Russia. And of course, in addition to the above-enumerated stands Russia's grandiose mass strike action from 1902 to 1906, which has shown how the significance and extent of the mass strike initially grow together with the revolutionary situation and the political action of the proletariat.

For while we discuss the political strike and search for its theoretical formulation and confirmation, one mighty political mass strike after another flames up through the spontaneous combustion of the masses—or rather every mass strike becomes a political action, every great political test of strength climaxes in a mass strike, whether among the miners, the proletariat of Russia, the Italian farm workers and railroad workers, etc.[28]

From this it almost seems as if Comrade Kautsky, through his newest theory of the impossibility of a period of political mass strikes in Germany, has demonstrated not so much a contradiction between Russia and Western Europe as a contradiction between Germany and the rest of the world—Western Europe and Russia thrown in together. Prussia must in fact be the exception among all capitalist lands, if what Comrade Kautsky has worked out on the impossibility of even short general demonstration mass strikes in Prussia is true. It would be "entirely unthinkable that in a demonstration strike against the government here, commuter railways, streetcars, and gas works come to a standstill," that we in Germany experience a demonstration strike which "alters the entire landscape, and in so doing makes the deepest impression on the entire bourgeois world as well as the most indifferent strata of the proletariat." But then what is "unthinkable" in Germany must be what has already proved itself possible in Galicia, in Bohemia, in Italy, in Trieste and Trento, in Spain, and in Sweden. In all these lands and cities, splendid demonstration strikes have taken place which completely altered "the landscape." In Bohemia on November 20, 1905, an absolute, general work stoppage reigned which extended even to *agriculture*—a thing they have not yet experienced in Russia. In Italy in September 1904 the farm workers, streetcars, electric and gas works took a holiday, and even the daily press had to stop publication. "It has indeed become the most total general strike," wrote the *Neue Zeit*, "that history knows of: for three whole days the city of Genoa was left without light and bread and meat; all economic life was paralyzed."[29] In Sweden's capital Stockholm, in 1902 as well as 1909, all means of communication and commerce—streetcars, cabs, wagons, municipal services—were shut down in the first week. In Barcelona in 1902, all economic life rested for many days.

And so in Prusso-Germany—with its "strongest contemporary government," and its special "German conditions" which supposedly show proletarian methods of struggle, possible in all the rest of the world, to be all sorts of impossibilities—we have finally acquired an unexpected counterpart to those special "Bavarian" and "south German" conditions which Comrade

Kautsky once so heartily derided with us. But in particular, these German "impossibilities" plume themselves on the fact that precisely in Germany we have the strongest party, the strongest unions, the best organization, the greatest discipline, the most enlightened proletariat, and the greatest influence of Marxism. By this method we would come, in fact, to the singular conclusion that the stronger Social Democracy is, the more powerless the proletariat. But I believe that to say mass strikes and demonstration strikes which were possible in various other lands are impossible today in Germany, is to fix a brand of incapacity on the German proletariat which it has as yet done nothing to deserve.

# 9 — Writings on Women, 1902-14

EDITORS' NOTE: While Luxemburg was a strong supporter of emancipatory working women's movements throughout her life, much of her involvement in women's issues was obscured by the fact that she usually worked behind the scenes, through her close friend Clara Zetkin, who was the leader of the German Social Democratic Women's Movement and the editor of *Gleichheit* (Equality), its widely circulated newspaper. This chapter begins with "A Tactical Question," Luxemburg's stinging 1902 attack on the reformist-dominated Belgian Social Democrats for having agreed to drop their call for women's suffrage at the demand of the Liberals, with whom they were in an electoral coalition. In this article, she writes that taking up women's suffrage would shake up not only society as a whole, but also a "suffocating" sexism that existed among both the leaders and rank and file of the Social Democratic movement. The 1907 Address to the International Socialist Women's Conference advocated that the women's association keep its headquarters in Stuttgart, where it could maintain an independent existence that it would have lost had it moved to Brussels, the seat of the International Socialist Bureau. The 1912 speech on "Women's Suffrage and Class Struggle" makes a strong argument for the continuation of a working women's movement independent of the middle-class German women's associations. Finally, the 1914 article, "Proletarian Women," written for International Women's Day, offers a moving sociohistorical sketch of working women's oppression and resistance, both in the industrialized lands and in Africa and Latin America, where women were struggling for their very lives against colonialist and capitalist barbarism. The published articles originally appeared in *Leipziger Volkszeitung* (April 4, 1902); *Vorwärts* (August 18, 1907); and *Sozialdemokratische Korrespondenz* (March 5, 1914). The 1912 article is the only selection from this chapter that has previously appeared in English, and is translated by Rosmarie Waldrop. The others have been translated by Ashley Passmore and Kevin B. Anderson from Luxemburg's *Gesammelte Werke*.

## 9A. A TACTICAL QUESTION

A few years ago, when the question of alliances with bourgeois parties became the subject of an especially lively debate with our ranks, the defenders of political alliances were careful to point to the example of the Belgian [Social Democratic] Workers' Party. Its alliance with the Liberals during the long struggle for universal suffrage was supposed to serve as an example of how coalitions between Social Democracy and bourgeois democracy were occasionally necessary and politically harmless.

Their evidence had already fallen apart. Only those who were unaware of the constant vacillations and the repeated betrayals on the part of the Belgian Liberals towards their proletarian comrades-in-arms could be brought away from the deepest pessimism regarding bourgeois democracy's support of the working class. Today, the resolutions of the most recent Party Conference of the Belgian Social Democracy[1] provide us with a new and very important aid for assessing this question.

As we know, the Belgian proletariat is facing an important turning point in the struggle for universal suffrage that they have fought with the utmost tenacity for fifteen years. It is preparing to take up a renewed attack against the clerical leadership and the plural voting system.[2] Under pressure from a resolute working class, a worn-out liberal bourgeoisie is pulling itself together for action and is offering its hand to Social Democracy for a joint campaign.

This time, however, the alliance is being brokered like a downright barter. The Liberals are dispensing with the plural voting system and will accept universal, *equal* suffrage (one man, one vote). In exchange, Social Democracy shall accept the proportional voting system as a constitutionally valid voting method and will dispense with the demand for *women's right to vote* and with *revolutionary methods* in the struggle for voting rights. The Brussels Federation of the Workers' Party had already accepted the terms and conditions of the Liberals on the main points. The Easter Conference of the Belgian Social Democrats completed the political deal by giving its approval.

It is therefore clear, and this simple fact cannot be argued away, that the alliance, or more correctly, the compromise with the Liberals by the Social Democrats, led to the abandonment of one of the basic tenets of their program. Of course, the Belgian comrades assure us that they have only set aside the demand for women's right to vote "*for the time being*" in order to resume it after winning universal suffrage for men. Yet, up to now, this concept that their program can serve as a kind of menu, wherein each dish can only be eaten one after the other, is something new to Social Democracy in all nations. And even if the particular political situation entails the Workers' Party temporarily placing more weight on agitating for specific demands in its program rather than other ones, the *entirety* of our demands continue to remain the permanent foundation of our political struggle. Between the temporary, diminished emphasis on an item in the program and the explicit, though temporary, sacrifice of it as the price for another demand in the program, there lies quite a distance separating the principled struggle of Social Democracy from the political manipulations of bourgeois parties.

It is true that, in the case of women's right to vote in Belgium, we are dealing with a *sacrifice*. Indeed, the resolution accepted by the Brussels Congress states laconically: "The next constitutional appeal shall be limited to universal suffrage for men." Yet, it is to be expected that the clerics will bring in a formal bill for women's right to vote during the appeal, just to throw a bone of contention between the Liberals and the Social Democrats. And in this case, the Brussels Resolution recommends that the delegates of the Workers' Party should "foil this maneuver and *uphold* the alliance of supporters of universal suffrage." Translated, this means they should vote *against* women's suffrage!

Riding high on principles is indeed a nasty affair, and we would never conceive of requiring any Workers' Party to forgo imminent practical gains for the sake of an abstract programmatic schema. Yet, as always, principles are here being sacrificed to mere *illusions,* rather than actual, practical gains. As usual, upon closer inspection of this case, it is simply a *fantasy* that adherence to our political principles has been a barrier to our practical success.

Indeed! It has been argued that if the Belgian Social Democrats were to insist upon their demand for women's right to vote, this would lead to a break with the Liberals and would endanger the entire campaign. Yet, the small extent to which the Workers' Party takes the Federal Coalition of Liberals and their conditions seriously can be seen in the silent shrug with which they acquiesced to the third condition of the Liberals, the *abandonment of revolutionary methods.* For the Belgian Social Democracy, it seemed obvious that it would in no way allow its hand to be tied as to the method of its struggle. And yet, it allowed itself to be diverted from the one true certainty—that the intrinsic power of the struggle, the secure guarantee of victory, lies *not* in supporting doddering liberal mayors and senators, but in the combat readiness of the proletarian masses, not in parliament, but *on the streets*.

It would also be rather strange if the Belgian Workers' Party harbored even the slightest doubt about this point, after owing their earlier victory, the partial suppression of the plural voting system, to the noteworthy mass strike and the threat of street demonstrations by the working class. Just as before, however, the first bold stirrings by the Belgian proletariat will explode like a thunderclap over the "liberal" bourgeoisie, after which the "allies" of Social Democracy will scurry off with predictable speed to their rat-hole of parliamentary betrayal and they will leave universal suffrage to the workers. Even this attractive prospect is nothing less than a mystery to the Belgian Workers' Party.

If, despite all of this, it quietly brushes the third condition of the pact with the Liberals under the table and prepares itself openly for every eventuality, then it will clearly show that it takes the "Liberal support" for what it truly is: a contingent and transitory comradeship for a stretch of the same road, which one accepts while on the march, but for which one would not deviate a single step from his one's path.

This logically proves that even the supposed "practical gain" for which one sacrificed women's right to vote is a mere bugbear. And it thus turns out that every time foolish projects for compromise arise that cost us our basic principles, something that can be observed here at home as well as abroad, it is never in actuality a matter of the imagined "practical accomplishments," but rather a sacrifice of programmatic demands. To our "practical politicians," who are, at heart, Hecubas[3] *in principle*, these are merely formalistic rubbish that has been carted out and parroted so often that it no longer retains any practical meaning.

Women's right to vote has not only been continuously and universally recognized by Belgian Social Democracy, but the workers' representatives in parliament also voted for it *unanimously* in 1895. Indeed, up to now this demand has had no prospect at all of being realized in Belgium or in other European countries. Today, it threatens to become an issue on the political agenda for the first time, and now it suddenly is becoming apparent that not just *one* opinion about the old programmatic demand holds sway inside the ranks in the Workers' Party. Even better, according to the statement by Dewinne[4] at the Brussels Congress: "the whole Party has adopted a negative attitude toward the question of women's suffrage!"

This surprising drama displays the Belgian Social Democrats' *rationale* against women's suffrage. These are the exact same arguments used by Russian Tsarism, the same arguments formerly used by the German doctrine of divine right in order to justify political injustice: "The public is not mature enough to exercise the right to vote." As if there were some other school of political maturity for members of the public than simply *exercising* these rights themselves! As if the male working class had also not already learned to gradually use the ballot as a weapon to defend its class interests and must still learn this!

To the contrary, every clear-thinking individual must anticipate, sooner or later, nothing less than a powerful upswing for the workers' movement with the inclusion of proletarian women in political life. This perspective not only opens up an enormous new field for the agitational work of Social Democracy. In its political and social life as well, a strong, fresh wind would blow in with the political emancipation of women, which would clear out the suffocating air of the current, philistine family life that rubs itself off so unmistakably, even on our Party members, workers and leaders alike.

Admittedly, in the beginning, there could be very disagreeable political results, such as the strengthening of clerical authority as a consequence of women's suffrage in Belgium. The entire organization and agitation of the Workers' Party would also have to be thoroughly revamped. In a word, the political equality of women is a *bold and grand political experiment.*

Yet strangely, all of those who have the greatest admiration for "experiments" in the style of *Millerand*[5] and cannot praise the *boldness* of these experiments highly enough, do not utter a single word of rebuke toward the Belgian comrades who shrink at the enfranchisement of women. Yes, even the Belgian leader, Anseele,[6] who was quick at the time to be the first to offer his congratulations to "Comrade" Millerand for his "bold" ministerial experiment is today the one most resolutely opposed to all efforts to bring about women's right to vote in his own country. Here again we have, among other things, evidence of just what sort of "boldness" it is that our "practical politicians" recommend to us from time to time. Apparently, it is merely the boldness to undertake opportunistic experiments at the expense of Social Democratic principles. However, when it concerns the bold *implementation* of our programmatic demands, these same politicians do not demonstrate the least bit of interest in impressing us with their boldness, and they are much more likely to search for pretexts to abandon this particular programmatic item "for the time being" and "with great pain."

## 9B. ADDRESS TO THE INTERNATIONAL
## SOCIALIST WOMEN'S CONFERENCE (1907)[7]

The wish has been expressed that the international women's movement affiliate with the International Socialist Bureau in Brussels. Since I am myself a member, and indeed, I am the only member of the fairer sex (cheers) in this Bureau, I feel inclined to say a few things about it. I must tell you frankly that probably only those comrades who have felt the influence of the International Bureau from afar have such a high admiration of it. (Cheers). We have become convinced that we are unable to achieve a center for the international socialist workers' movement through purely mechanical means. The times of the International, when *Marx himself* was the actual center of the international proletarian movement, are over. Today, we have little more than periodic gatherings of representatives from various countries in Brussels, which are always a very unpleasant duty for these representatives. Because each time, we have the feeling that we cannot accomplish even one-hundredth of the real tasks of the Bureau. This says nothing about our good intentions, or anything about the inadequate skills of the current Secretary. But again and again, the complaint resurfaces that the International Bureau is being, as it were, completely ignored by the affiliated national parties. Not even short reports about movements that have taken place are sent in. Only when we are fortunate and become a center of moral authority, which is capable of awakening sufficient interest within the affiliated countries, will we have a more viable and more active center for the socialist movement. But it will be you who will be in this fortunate position if you accept the proposal of the German women comrades. I want to confide yet another secret to you. (Cheers.) Once we had, in Amsterdam,[8] four years of painful disappointment with the activity of the International Bureau in Brussels behind us, it was already clear in our minds that we could only have a true International Bureau, firstly, if we relocated to Germany; secondly, to Stuttgart; and thirdly into the editorial office of *Gleichheit*. But the Party Executive waved the [idea of placing] the International Bureau in Germany aside with a gesture of the hand as short as it was significant, and thus we had to forgo this ideal. You, however, will resurrect this moral center of the International, and I can only marvel at Comrade Zetkin that she too will still shoulder this workload. The wish to relocate the International Socialist Women's Bureau to Brussels can only emanate from an ignorance of the situation.[9] Do not believe that by declining this thought you lose something. Do not say, "It would have been so nice, it did not have to be."[10] (Loud cheers and applause.)

## 9C. WOMEN'S SUFFRAGE AND CLASS STRUGGLE

"Why are there no organizations for working women in Germany? Why do we hear so little about the working women's movement?" With these questions, Emma Ihrer,[11] one of the founders of the proletarian women's movement of Germany, introduced her 1898 essay, "Working Women in the Class

Struggle." Hardly fourteen years have passed since, but they have seen a great expansion of the proletarian women's movement. More than a hundred fifty thousand women are organized in unions and are among the most active troops in the economic struggle of the proletariat. Many thousands of politically organized women have rallied to the banner of Social Democracy: the Social Democratic women's paper [*Die Gleichheit*, edited by Clara Zetkin][12] has more than 100,000 subscribers; women's suffrage is one of the vital issues on the platform of Social Democracy.

Exactly these facts might lead you to underrate the importance of the fight for women's suffrage. You might think: even without equal political rights for women we have made enormous progress in educating and organizing women. Hence, women's suffrage is not urgently necessary. If you think so, you are deceived. The political and syndical awakening of the masses of the female proletariat during the last fifteen years has been magnificent. But it has been possible only because working women took a lively interest in the political and parliamentary struggles of their class in spite of being deprived of their rights. So far, proletarian women are sustained by male suffrage, which they indeed take part in, though only indirectly. Large masses of both men and women of the working class already consider the election campaigns a cause they share in common. In all Social Democratic electoral meetings, women make up a large segment, sometimes the majority. They are always interested and passionately involved. In all districts where there is a firm Social Democratic organization, women help with the campaign. And it is women who have done invaluable work distributing leaflets and getting subscribers to the Social Democratic press, this most important weapon in the campaign.

The capitalist state has not been able to keep women from taking on all these duties and efforts of political life. Step by step, the state has indeed been forced to grant and guarantee them this possibility by allowing them union and assembly rights. Only the last political right is denied women: the right to vote, to decide directly on the people's representatives in legislature and administration, to be an elected member of these bodies. But here, as in all other areas of society, the motto is: "Don't let things get started!" But things have been started. The present state gave in to the women of the proletariat when it admitted them to public assemblies, to political associations. And the state did not grant this voluntarily, but out of necessity, under the irresistible pressure of the rising working class. It was not least the passionate pushing ahead of the proletarian women themselves which forced the Prusso-German police state to give up the famous "women's section"[13] in gatherings of political associations and to open wide the doors of political organizations to women. This really set the ball rolling. The irresistible progress of the proletarian class struggle has swept working women right into the whirlpool of political life. Using their right of union and assembly, proletarian women have taken a most active part in parliamentary life and in election campaigns. It is only the inevitable consequence, only the logical result of the movement that today millions of proletarian women call defiantly and with self-confidence: *Let us have suffrage!*

Once upon a time, in the beautiful era of pre-1848 absolutism, the whole working class was said not to be "mature enough" to exercise political rights. This cannot be said about proletarian women today, because they have demonstrated their political maturity. Everybody knows that without them, without the enthusiastic help of proletarian women, the Social Democratic Party would not have won the glorious victory of January 12 [1912], would not have obtained four and a quarter million votes. At any rate, the working class has always had to prove its maturity for political freedom by a successful revolutionary uprising of the masses. Only when Divine Right on the throne and the best and noblest men of the nation actually felt the calloused fist of the proletariat on their eyes and its knee on their chests, only then did they feel confidence in the political "maturity" of the people, and felt it with the speed of lightning. Today, it is the proletarian woman's turn to make the capitalist state conscious of her maturity. This is done through a constant, powerful mass movement which has to use all the means of proletarian struggle and pressure.

Women's suffrage is the goal. But the mass movement to bring it about is not a job for women alone, but is a common class concern for women and men of the proletariat. Germany's present lack of rights for women is only one link in the chain of the reaction that shackles the people's lives. And it is closely connected with the other pillar of the reaction: the monarchy. In advanced capitalist, highly industrialized, twentieth-century Germany, in the age of electricity and airplanes, the absence of women's political rights is as much a reactionary remnant of the dead past as the reign by Divine Right on the throne. Both phenomena—the instrument of heaven as the leading political power, and woman, demure by the fireside, unconcerned with the storms of public life, with politics and class struggle—both phenomena have their roots in the rotten circumstances of the past, in the times of serfdom in the country and guilds in the towns. In those times, they were justifiable and necessary. But both monarchy and women's lack of rights have been uprooted by the development of modern capitalism, have become ridiculous caricatures.

They continue to exist in our modern society, not just because people forgot to abolish them, not just because of the persistence and inertia of circumstances. No, they still exist because both—monarchy as well as women without rights—have become powerful tools of interests inimical to the people. The worst and most brutal advocates of the exploitation and enslavement of the proletariat are entrenched behind throne and altar as well as behind the political enslavement of women. Monarchy and women's lack of rights have become the most important tools of the ruling capitalist class.

In truth, our state is interested in keeping the vote from working women and from them alone. It rightly fears they will threaten the traditional institutions of class rule, for instance militarism (of which no thinking proletarian woman can help being a deadly enemy), monarchy, the systematic robbery of duties and taxes on groceries, etc. Women's suffrage is a horror and abomination for the present capitalist state because behind it stand millions of women who would strengthen the enemy within, i.e., revolutionary Social Democracy. If it were a matter of bourgeois ladies voting, the capitalist state could expect nothing but effective support for the reaction. Most of those bourgeois women who act like lionesses in the struggle against "male prerogatives" would trot like docile lambs in the camp of conservative and clerical reaction if they had suffrage. Indeed, they would certainly be a good deal more reactionary than the male part of their class. Aside from the few who have jobs or professions, the women of the bourgeoisie do not take part in social production. They are nothing but co-consumers of the surplus value their men extort from the proletariat. They are parasites of the parasites of the social body. And co-consumers are usually even more rabid and cruel in defending their "right" to a parasite's life than the direct agents of class rule and exploitation. The history of all great revolutionary struggles confirms this in a horrible way. Take the great French Revolution. After the fall of the Jacobins, when Robespierre was driven in chains to the place of execution the naked whores of the victory-drunk bourgeoisie danced in the streets, danced a shameless dance of joy around the fallen hero of the Revolution. And in 1871, in Paris, when the heroic workers' Commune was defeated by machine guns, the raving bourgeois females surpassed even their bestial men in their bloody revenge against the suppressed proletariat. The women of the property-owning classes will always fanatically defend the exploitation and enslavement of the working people by which they indirectly receive the means for their socially useless existence.

Economically and socially, the women of the exploiting classes are not an independent segment of the population. Their only social function is to be tools of the natural propagation of the ruling classes. By contrast, the women of the proletariat are economically independent. They are productive for society like the men. By this I do not mean their bringing up children or their housework which helps men support their families on scanty wages. This kind of work is not productive in the sense of the present capitalist economy no matter how enormous an achievement the sacrifices and energy spent, the thousand little efforts add up to. This is but the private affair of the worker, his happiness and blessing, and for this reason nonexistent for our present society. As long as capitalism and the wage system rule, only that kind of work is considered productive which produces surplus value, which creates capitalist profit. From this point of view, the music-hall dancer whose legs sweep profit into her employer's pocket is a productive worker, whereas all the toil of the proletarian women and mothers in the four walls of their homes is considered unproductive. This sounds brutal and insane, but corresponds exactly to the brutality and insanity of our present capitalist economy. And seeing this brutal reality clearly and sharply is the proletarian woman's first task.

For, exactly from this point of view, the proletarian women's claim to equal political rights is anchored in firm economic ground. Today, millions of proletarian women create capitalist profit like men—in factories, workshops, on farms, in home industry, offices, stores. They *are* therefore productive in the strictest scientific sense of our present society. Every day enlarges the hosts of women exploited by capitalism. Every new progress in industry or technology creates new places for women in the machinery of capitalist profiteering. And thus, every day and every step of industrial progress adds a new stone to the firm foundation of women's equal political rights. Female education and intelligence have become necessary for the economic mechanism itself. The narrow, secluded woman of the patriarchal "family circle" answers the needs of industry and commerce as little as those of politics. It is true, the capitalist state has neglected its duty even in this respect. So far, it is the unions and the Social Democratic organizations that have done most to awaken the minds and moral sense of women. Even decades ago, the Social Democrats were known as the most capable and intelligent German workers. Likewise, unions and Social Democracy have today lifted the women of the proletariat out of their stuffy, narrow existence, out of the miserable and petty mindlessness of household managing. The proletarian class struggle has widened their horizons, made their minds flexible, developed their thinking, shown them great goals for their efforts. Socialism has brought about the mental rebirth of the mass of proletarian women—and thereby has no doubt also made them capable productive workers for capital.

Considering all this, the proletarian woman's lack of political rights is a vile injustice, and the more so for being by now at least half a lie. After all, masses of women take an active part in political life. However, Social Democracy does not use the argument of "injustice." This is the basic difference between us and the earlier sentimental, utopian socialism. We do not depend on the justice of the ruling classes, but solely on the revolutionary power of the working masses and on the course of social development which prepares the ground for this power. Thus, injustice by itself is certainly not an argument with which to overthrow reactionary institutions. If, however, there is a feeling of injustice in large segments of society—says Friedrich Engels, the co-founder of scientific socialism—it is always a sure sign that the economic bases of the society have shifted considerably, that the present conditions contradict the march of development. The present forceful movement of millions of proletarian women who consider their lack of political rights a crying wrong is such an infallible sign, a sign that the social bases of the reigning system are rotten and that its days are numbered.

A hundred years ago, the Frenchman Charles Fourier,[14] one of the first great prophets of socialist ideals, wrote these memorable words: In any society, the degree of female emancipation is the natural measure of the general emancipation.[15] This is completely true for our present society. The current mass struggle for women's political rights is only an expression and a part of the proletariat's general struggle for liberation. In this lies its strength and its future. Because of the female proletariat, general, equal, direct suffrage for women would immensely advance and intensify the proletarian class struggle. This is why bourgeois society abhors and fears women's suffrage. And this is why we want and will achieve it. Fighting for women's suffrage, we will also hasten the coming of the hour when the present society falls in ruins under the hammer strokes of the revolutionary proletariat.

## 9D. THE PROLETARIAN WOMAN (1914)

Proletarian Women's Day inaugurates the "Week of Social Democracy."[16] The party of the disinherited places its female columns in the front lines by sending them into the heat of battle for eight days, in order to spread the seeds of socialism onto new fields. *And the call for the political equality of women is the first one* they make, as they prepare to win over new supporters for the working class as a whole.

Today, the modern female wage-earning proletarian appears on the public stage as a female pioneer of the working class and, at the same time, of the female gender, the first female pioneer in centuries.

*The woman of the people has always worked hard.* In the savage horde, she carried heavy loads, collected food; in the primitive village, she planted grains and ground them, and she made pottery; in ancient times, as a slave, she served the masters and suckled their offspring at her breast; in the Middle Ages, she labored in the spinning room for the feudal lord. But since the establishment of private property, the woman of the people has, for the most part, worked separately from the great workshop of social production, and therefore also of culture, cooped up in the domestic constriction of a miserable familial existence. Capitalism was the first to rip her out of the family and put her under the yoke of social production, forced into others' fields, into workshops, into buildings, into offices, factories, and warehouses. As a bourgeois woman, the female is a parasite on society; her function consists in sharing in the consumption of the fruits of exploitation. As a petty-bourgeois woman, she is a workhorse for the family. As a modern female proletarian, the woman becomes a human being for the first time, *since the [proletarian] struggle is the first to prepare human beings to make a contribution to culture, to the history of humanity.*

For the property-owning bourgeois woman, her house is the world. *For the proletarian woman, the whole world is her house,* the world with its sorrow and joy, with its cold cruelty and its raw size. The proletarian woman marches with the tunnel workers from Italy to Switzerland, camps in barracks and whistles as she dries diapers next to cliffs exploding into the air with blasts of dynamite. As a seasonal agricultural worker, she sits in springtime amidst the commotion of train stations on her modest bundle, a scarf covering her plainly parted hair, and waits patiently to be hauled from east to west. Among the many-tongued masses of starving proletarians on the middle deck of an ocean liner, she migrates from Europe to America with each wave that flushes away the misery stemming from the crisis. In this way, should an American crisis well up as a countercurrent in the direction of her original misery in Europe, she will return, to new hopes and disappointments, to a new hunt for work and bread.

The *bourgeois woman* has no real interest in political rights, because she does not exercise any economic function in society, because she enjoys the finished products of class domination. The call for women's equality, when it does well up among bourgeois women, is the pure ideology of a few feeble groups without material roots, a phantom of the antagonism between man and woman, a quirk. Thus, the farcical nature of the suffragette movement.

*The proletarian woman needs political rights* because she exercises the same economic function, slaves away for capital in the same way, maintains the state in the same way, and is bled dry and suppressed by it in the same way as the male proletarian. She has the same interests and takes up the same weapons to defend them. Her political demands are rooted deep in the social abyss that separates the class of the exploited from the class of the exploiters, not in the antagonism between man and woman but in the antagonism between capital and labor.

At a formal level, women's political rights conform quite harmoniously with the bourgeois state. The examples of Finland, of American states, of a few municipalities, all show that a policy of equal rights for women has not yet overturned the state; it does not encroach upon the domination of capital. Yet, since the political rights of women today are actually merely a proletarian class demand, for today's capitalist Germany, it is akin to the last trump. Like the *republic,* like the *militia,* like the *eight-hour workday, women's suffrage* can only succeed or fail together with the proletarian class struggle as a whole; it can only be defended by proletarian methods of struggle and forcible means.

*Bourgeois advocates of women's rights want to secure political rights* in order then to assume a role in political life. The proletarian woman can only follow the path of the workers' struggle, the opposite to winning an inch of real power through primarily legal statutes. *At the beginning of every social advance, there was the deed.* Proletarian women must gain solid ground in political life, through their activity in all areas; in this way alone will they secure a foundation for their rights. The ruling society denies them entry into their temples of law, but another great power throws open the gates for them—the *Social Democratic Party.* Here, in the rank and file of the organization, an expansive field of political work and political power opens up for the proletarian woman. Here alone the woman is a factor on equal footing. Through Social Democracy, she will be introduced into the workshop of history. And here, where cyclopean forces are hammering, she will be fighting for truly equal rights, despite the lack of a written statute in a bourgeois constitution. Here, the working woman shakes the pillars of the existing social order next to the men, and before it grants her the illusion of her rights, she will help to bury this social order under rubble.

The workshop of the future requires many hands and hearts. A world of female misery is waiting for relief. The wife of the peasant moans as she nearly collapses under life's burdens. In German Africa, in the Kalahari Desert, the bones of defenseless Herero women are bleaching in the sun, those who were hunted down by a band of German soldiers and subjected to a horrific death of hunger and thirst.[17] On the other side of the ocean, in the high cliffs of Putumayo, the death cries of martyred Indian women, ignored by the world, fade away in the rubber plantations of the international capitalists.[18]

Proletarian women, the poorest of the poor, the most disempowered of the disempowered, hurry to join the struggle for the emancipation of women and of humankind from the horrors of capitalist domination! Social Democracy has assigned to you a place of honor. Hurry to the front lines, into the trenches!

# PART THREE

Spontaneity, Organization, and Democracy
in the Disputes with Lenin

# 10 — Organizational Questions of Russian Social Democracy

EDITORS' NOTE: By 1904 Rosa Luxemburg had become recognized as a leading expert on Polish and Russian affairs for the Second International as a whole. It was in this capacity that she was asked by the editors of *Iskra*, a Menshevik-dominated journal of Russian Marxism, to analyze the split between the Mensheviks and Bolsheviks in the Russian Social-Democratic Party in 1903. She published her analysis in German in *Neue Zeit* in 1904 in German under the title "Organizational Questions of Russian Social Democracy." The essay contains one of her most important criticisms of Lenin's theory of organization. Though Lenin later responded to her critique, it is unclear if Luxemburg ever saw it, since Kautsky refused to publish Lenin's reply in *Neue Zeit*. Despite Luxemburg's sharp criticism of Lenin's organizational "centralism," she worked closely with him at a number of junctures throughout the rest of her life, especially in the aftermath of the 1905 Revolution. The translation is by Richard Taylor.

A unique task that is without parallel in the history of socialism has fallen to Russian social democracy: it is to work out a social democratic tactic suited to the class struggle of the proletariat in an autocratic state. The customary comparison between conditions in Russia today and those in Germany at the time of the Anti-Socialist Law is untenable insofar as it views Russian conditions from the police, and not from the political standpoint. The *obstacles* that the lack of democratic freedoms creates for the mass movement are, relatively speaking, of secondary importance: even in Russia the mass movement has managed to overrun the barriers of the autocratic "constitution" and create for itself an albeit crippled "constitution" of "street disorders." It will continue along these lines until it has achieved its final victory over the autocracy. The principal difficulty facing the social democratic struggle in Russia consists in the fact that the class domination of the bourgeoisie is veiled by the domination of autocratic coercion; this domination by the autocracy necessarily gives the socialist doctrine of class struggle an abstract propagandistic character, and immediate political agitation a predominantly revolutionary democratic one. The Anti-Socialist Law was intended only to place the working class beyond the bounds of the constitution and to do this in a highly developed bourgeois society where class antagonisms had been laid bare and fully exposed in parliamentarism; herein lay the insanity, the absurdity of Bismarck's venture. In Russia the inverse experiment must be accomplished: social democracy must be created in the absence of the direct political domination of the bourgeoisie.

This has a unique bearing not only on the question of transplanting socialist doctrine to Russian soil, not only on the question of *agitation*, but also on that of *organization*.

For the social democratic movement even *organization*, as distinct from the earlier utopian experiments of socialism, is viewed not as an artificial product of propaganda but as a historical product of the class struggle, to which social democracy merely brings political consciousness. Under normal circumstances, i.e. where the fully developed political class domination of the bourgeoisie precedes the social democratic movement, it is the bourgeoisie itself that to a considerable extent takes care of the initial political merger of the workers. "At this stage," says *The Manifesto of the Communist Party*, "the mass solidarity of the workers results not from their own unity but from the unity of the bourgeoisie."[1] In Russia it is the task of social democracy to miss out a stage in the historical process through deliberate intervention and to lead the proletariat straight from the political atomization that forms the basis of the autocratic regime to the highest form of organization—a class that is conscious of its aims and fights for them. As a result the question of organization poses particular problems for Russian social democracy, not just because it has to create an organization in the absence of any of the formal devices of bourgeois democracy, but above all because to some extent it has to create this organization like Almighty God "from nothing," in a void, without the political raw material that is elsewhere prepared by bourgeois society.

The problem that has already exercised Russian social democracy for some years is that of the transition from the type of splintered and completely autonomous organization at circle and local level, a type of organization that suited the preparatory, predominantly propagandist phase of the movement, to the kind of organization necessary for concerted political action by the mass throughout the state. But, as splintering, complete autonomy, and self-government for local organizations were the distinguishing feature of the burdensome and politically outmoded old organizational forms, the rallying cry for the new phase—that of the large-scale prepared organizational structure—is naturally *centralism*. The affirmation of the centralist idea was the *leitmotiv* of the brilliant three-year campaign waged by *Iskra* in preparation for the last party congress, which was in fact the founding one; and the same idea has preoccupied the whole of the younger generation of Social Democrats in Russia. It soon became apparent at the congress,[2] and even more apparent afterwards, that centralism is a slogan that nowhere nearly covers the historical content and the peculiarities of the social democratic type of organization; it has once more been demonstrated that the Marxist conception of socialism cannot be fitted into rigid formulas in any field, not even in the field of organizational questions.

The book before us, *One Step Forward, Two Steps Back* by Comrade Lenin,[3] one of the distinguished leaders and militants of *Iskra* in its campaign of preparation for the Russian party congress, is a systematic exposition of the views of the *ultracentralist* tendency in the Russian party. The point of view that finds forceful and exhaustive expression here is that of uncompromising centralism: its essential principle consists, on the one hand, in the rigid separation and isolation of the organized elements of outright and active revolutionaries from their, albeit unorganized, revolutionary activist milieu, and, on the other hand, in the strict discipline and the direct, decisive and definite intervention of the central authority in all the signs of life of local party organizations. Suffice it to note that in this view the Central Committee has, for instance, the right to organize all the local committees of the party and thus also to determine the membership of every individual Russian local organization from Geneva and Liège to Tomsk and Irkutsk, to provide them with a ready-made local statute, to dissolve and reconstitute them by *fiat* and hence also to exert indirect influence on the composition of the highest party organ, the congress. Thus the Central Committee emerges as the real active nucleus of the party; all the remaining organizations are merely its executive instruments.

It is in precisely this combination of the strictest organizational centralism and the social democratic mass movement that Lenin sees a specifically revolutionary Marxist principle and he can marshal a whole series of facts to support his point of view. But let us look at the matter more closely.

There is no doubt that a strong inclination toward centralism is inherent in social democracy as a whole. Growing in the economic soil of capitalism, with its centralist tendencies, and depending in its struggle on the political framework of the large centralized bourgeois state, social democracy is by nature an outright opponent of all forms of particularism or national federalism. Called upon within the framework of a particular state to represent the general interests of the proletariat as a class, as opposed to all the particular and group interests of the proletariat, it everywhere has the natural desire to weld all the national, religious and professional groups within the working class into a single party; it is only in special, abnormal circumstances such as those in Austria, for instance, where it has to make an exception, a concession to the federalist principle.4

In this respect there was, and is, no question, for Russian social democracy either, that it should form a federative conglomerate of a multiplicity of special national and local organizations rather than a homogeneous and compact party for the Russian Empire. The question of a greater or lesser degree of centralization and of its precise *nature* within a united and homogeneous Russian social democracy is, however, a quite different one.

From the standpoint of the formal tasks of social democracy as a party of struggle, it appears from the outset that the party's battle-readiness and its energy are directly dependent on the realization of centralism in its organization. But in this context the specific historical conditions of the proletariat's struggle are far more important than the standpoints of the formal requirements of any organization of struggle.

The social democratic movement is the first movement in the history of class societies to be premised in its every aspect and in its whole development on the organization and the independent direct action of the mass.

In this sense social democracy creates a completely different type of organization from earlier socialist movements, e.g. those of the Jacobin–Blanquist type.

It appears that Lenin underestimates this when he writes in his book that the revolutionary Social Democrat is really nothing but "the Jacobin indissolubly linked to the *organization* of the *class conscious* proletariat." It is in the organization and class consciousness of the proletariat, as opposed to the conspiracy of a small minority, that Lenin sees the exhaustive distinctions between social democracy and Blanquism. He forgets that this implies a complete reappraisal of our organizational concepts, a completely new concept of centralism, a completely new notion of the mutual relationship between organization and struggle.

Blanquism was not premised on the direct class activity of the masses and did not therefore require a mass organization. On the contrary, as the broad popular masses were supposed to emerge onto the battlefield only at the actual moment of revolution, while the preliminary activity consisted in the preparation of a revolutionary coup by a small minority, a rigid distinction between the people appointed to this specific task and the popular mass was directly necessary for the success of their mission. But it was also possible and attainable because there was no inherent connection between the conspiratorial activity of the Blanquist organization and the everyday life of the popular mass.[5]

At the same time both the tactics and the precise tasks of activity were worked out in advance in the minutest detail, determined and prescribed as a definite plan, because they were improvised off the cuff and at will, with no connection with the elemental class struggle. As a result the active members of the organization were naturally transformed into the purely executive organs of a will that had been predetermined outside their own field of activity, into the *instruments* of a central committee. This also gave rise to the second characteristic of conspiratorial centralism: the absolute blind submission of the individual organs of the party to their central authority and the extension of the latter's powers right to the very periphery of the party organization.

The conditions for social democratic activity are radically different. This derives historically from the elemental class struggle. It operates within the dialectical contradiction that here it is only in the struggle itself that the proletarian army is itself recruited and only in the struggle that it becomes conscious of the purpose of the struggle. Organization, enlightenment and struggle are here not separate moments mechanically divided in time, as in a Blanquist movement, they are merely different facets of the same process. On the one hand, apart from the general basic principles of struggle, there is no ready-made predetermined and detailed tactic of struggle that the Central Committee could drill into the social democratic membership. On the other hand, the process of struggle that creates the organization stipulates a constant fluctuation in the sphere of influence of social democracy.

From this it follows that social democratic centralization cannot be based either on blind obedience or on the mechanical submission of the party's militants to their central authority and, further, that an impenetrable wall can never be erected between the nucleus of the class conscious proletariat that is already organized into tightly knit party cadres and those in the surrounding stratum who have already been caught up in the class struggle and are in the process of developing class consciousness. The establishment of centralization in social democracy on these two principles—on the blind submission of all party organizations and their activity, down to the smallest detail, to a central authority that alone thinks, acts and decides for everyone, and also on the strict separation of the organized nucleus of the party from its surrounding revolutionary milieu, as Lenin advocates—therefore seems to us to be a mechanical transposition of the organizational principles of the Blanquist movement of conspiratorial circles to the social democratic movement of the working masses. And Lenin characterizes this point of view, perhaps more astutely than any of his opponents could, when he defines his "revolutionary Social Democrat" as a "Jacobin *linked* to the organization of the class conscious work." In fact, however, social democracy is not linked to the organization of the working class; it is the working class's own movement. Social democratic centralism must therefore have an essentially different character from Blanquist centralism. It be none other than the authoritative expression of the will of the conscious and militant vanguard of the workers, vis-à-vis the separate groups and individuals among them; it is, as it were, a "self-centralism" of the leading stratum of the proletariat, the rule of its majority within the confines of its own party organization.

From our examination of the real content of social democratic centralism it is already becoming clear that the necessary conditions for it could not yet be said to exist in full measure in Russia at the present time. These conditions are: the presence of a significant stratum of the proletariat that has already been schooled in political struggle and the opportunity to express their battle-readiness through the exercise of direct influence (in public party congresses, in the party press, etc.).

The latter condition can obviously only be realized in Russia in conditions of political liberty, but the former—the creation of a judicious and class conscious proletarian vanguard—is only now in the process of emerging and should be regarded as the principal theme of immediate agitational and organizational work.

All the more surprising is Lenin's inverse conviction that all the preconditions for the realization of a large and highly centralized workers' party are already to hand in Russia. When he optimistically exclaims that it is now "not the proletariat but certain intellectuals in Russian social democracy who are lacking in self-education in the spirit of organization and discipline," and when he praises the educational significance of the factory for the proletariat in making it completely ripe for "discipline and organization," this once again betrays an over-mechanistic conception of social democratic organization. The "discipline" that Lenin has in mind is instilled into the proletariat not just by the factory but also by the *barracks* and by modern bureaucracy— in a word, by the entire mechanism of the centralized bourgeois state. It is quite simply a misuse of the catchword simultaneously to characterize as "discipline" two such opposing concepts as the lack of will and thought in a body with many arms and legs that moves mechanically to the baton and the voluntary coordination of the conscious political actions of a social stratum; such concepts as the blind obedience of an oppressed class and the organized rebellion of a class that is struggling for its emancipation. It is not through the discipline instilled in the proletariat by the capitalist state, with the straightforward transfer of the baton from the bourgeoisie to a social democratic Central Committee, but only the defying and uprooting this spirit of servile discipline that the proletarian can be educated for the new discipline, the voluntary self-discipline of social democracy.

Furthermore, it is clear from the same consideration that centralism in the social democratic sense is by no means an absolute concept existing in equal measure at every stage in the workers' movement; rather it should be regarded more as a *tendency*, which is increasingly realized in accordance with the developing consciousness and political education of the working mass in the process of its struggle.

Of course the insufficient presence of the most important preconditions for the complete realization of centralism in the Russian movement can present a tremendous obstacle. But it seems to us perverse to think that the as yet unrealizable rule of the majority of the conscious workers within their own party organization may be "temporarily" replaced by the "delegated" sole power of the central party authority, and that the absence of public control by the working masses over what the party organs do and do not do might equally well be replaced by the inverse control by a Central Committee over the activity of the revolutionary workers.

The very history of the Russian movement furnishes many proofs of the doubtful value of centralism in this latter sense. An all-powerful central institution, with the almost unlimited right of intervention and control that Lenin envisages, would obviously be a nonsense if it had to confine its power exclusively to the purely *technical* aspect of social democracy, to the regulation of the day-to-day methods and expedients of agitation such as the supply of party literature and the appropriate distribution of agitational and financial resources. It would have an appreciable political purpose only if it were to use its power to organize a tactic of struggle and launch a great political action in Russia. But what do we see in the changes that the Russian movement has so far undergone? The most important and profitable changes of the last decade were not "invented" by any of the movement's leaders, let alone the leading organizations, but were in every case the spontaneous product of the unfettered movement. This applies to the first stage of the truly proletarian movement in Russia, which began with the spontaneous outbreak of the colossal St. Petersburg strike of 1896 and which first inaugurated the mass economic activity of the Russian proletariat. The same applies to the second phase, that of political street demonstrations, which began completely spontaneously with the student unrest in St Petersburg in March 1901. The next significant turning-point in tactics that pointed the way to new horizons was the mass strike that broke out "of its own accord" in Rostov-on-Don, with its improvised *ad hoc* street agitation, open air popular assemblies and public addresses, all of which would have seemed, only a few years before, like a fantasy, like something unthinkable, even to the most enthusiastic Social Democrat. In all these cases, "in the beginning was the deed."[6] The *initiative* and conscious leadership of social democratic organizations played an extremely insignificant role. This arose, however, not so much from the inadequate preparedness of these special organizations for their role (although this point may have had considerable influence) and still less from the absence at that time from Russian social democracy of an allpowerful central authority in the spirit of Lenin's plan. On the contrary, such an authority would very probably only have increased the indecision of the individual party committees and provoked a split between the tempestuous mass and temporizing social democracy. It is rather the case that this same phenomenon—the insignificant role of a conscious initiative by the party leadership in shaping tactics—can be observed in Germany and elsewhere. The main features of the social democratic tactic of struggle are on the whole not "invented": on the contrary, they are the consequence of a continuing series of great creative acts of experimental, often of spontaneous, class struggle. Here too the unconscious precedes the conscious, the logic of the objective historical process precedes the subjective logic of its agents. The role of the social democratic leadership in all this has an essentially conservative character because, as experience demonstrates, once they have won new terrain for the struggle, they will work it over thoroughly and soon turn it into a bulwark against further innovation on a greater scale. The current tactics of German social democracy, for instance, are everywhere admired for their remarkable diversity, their flexibility and, at the same time, for their assuredness. But this means only that, in its everyday struggle, our party has adapted itself admirably well to contemporary parliamentary conditions down to the smallest detail, that it can make full use of the whole field of battle that parliamentarism has to offer and master it according to its own rules. However this particular tactical formulation conceals the broader horizons so effectively that there plainly emerges a considerable tendency to perpetuate the parliamentary tactic and to view it as *the* tendency for the social democratic struggle. Characteristic of this mood is, for instance, the hopelessness of Parvus'[7] long-standing efforts to provoke a discussion in the party press of the change in tactics that would be appropriate in the event of the abolition of universal suffrage, despite the fact that the party leaders view such an eventuality with deadly seriousness. This inertia is to a great extent explained by the fact that it is very difficult to present the contours and tangible forms of an as yet non-existent and, therefore, imaginary political situation in a void of abstract speculation. The important thing for social democracy as well is never to predict and prepare a ready-made plan for future tactics but to keep alive within the party the correct historical evaluation of the forms of struggle that dominate at a particular moment and a living sense of the relativity of a particular phase in the struggle and of the necessary increase in revolutionary momentum from the standpoint of the final goal of the class struggle of the proletariat.

But to grant the party leadership the kind of absolute powers of a *negative* character that Lenin does means to strengthen, artificially and to a very dangerous degree, the conservatism that springs inevitably from its very essence. If social democratic tactics are the creation, not of a Central Committee, but of the party as a whole—or, more accurately, of the movement as a whole—then individual party organizations will need the elbow room that alone gives them the opportunity to make full use of the means to further the struggle furnished by the particular situation and to develop revolutionary initiative. The ultra-centralism that Lenin advocates seems to us, in its whole essence, to be imbued, not with a positive creative spirit, but with the sterile spirit of the night-watchman state.[8] His line of thought is concerned principally with the control of party activity and not with its fertilization, with *narrowing* and not with *broadening*, with *tying the movement up* and not with *drawing it together*.

It seems doubly risky for Russian social democracy to indulge in an experiment of this kind at precisely this moment. It stands on the eve of great revolutionary battles for the overthrow of the autocracy, before, or rather in, a period of the most intensive creative activity in the tactical field and—as goes without saying in a revolutionary epoch—a period of feverish and spasmodic expansion and contraction in its sphere of influence. To try and restrict the initiative for party thought and erect a barbed-wire fence around the party's capacity for sudden expansion is by that very fact to render social democracy to a considerable extent unfit from the outset for the great tasks of the movement.

We cannot yet, of course, derive a concrete draft of the paragraphs of an organizational statute for the Russian party from the general observations we have made on the characteristic features of social democratic centralism. This draft naturally depends in the final analysis on the concrete conditions in which activity proceeds at a particular period and, because in Russia it is a question of the first attempt to build up a large proletarian party organization, [a statute of this kind] cannot lay advance claims to infallibility; rather it must in any case first undergo the trial by fire of practice. However, what we can deduce from our general conception of the social democratic type of organization are its principal features, the *spirit* of its organization, and this means, especially in the initial stages of the mass movement, predominantly the coordinating and rallying, and not the regulating and excluding, character of social democratic centralism. But, if this spirit of political flexibility, combined with firm loyalty to the principles of the movement and its unity, takes root in the ranks of the party, then the bumps in any organizational statute, even a badly drafted one, will very soon be ironed out by practice itself. It is not the letter of the statute, but the sense and spirit instilled into it by the active militants that determine the value of an organizational form.

## II

So far we have looked at the question of centralism from the point of view of the general principles of social democracy and, partly, of the current conditions in Russia. But the night-watchman spirit that informs the ultracentralism advocated by Lenin and his friends is not just a chance product of errors: it is related to an hostility towards opportunism that is carried to the minutest detail of organizational questions.

"It is a matter," says Lenin, "*of forging a more or less pointed weapon through the paragraphs of the organizational statute.* The deeper the sources of opportunism, the sharper the point must be."9

Similarly, Lenin regards the absolute power of the Central Committee and the strict statutory restriction of the party as an effective barrier against the opportunist tendency, whose specific characteristics he defines as the innate preference of the intellectual for autonomism and disorganization and his horror at strict party discipline at any form of "bureaucratism" in the life of the party. In Lenin's view, it is only the socialist "man of letters" who, because of his innate confusion and individualism, could oppose such unbridled powers for the Central Committee; a true proletarian, on the other hand, must, because of his revolutionary class instinct, feel a certain delight in the strictness, severity and resolve of his supreme party organ, and submit, with his eyes cheerfully closed, to all the rough operations of "party discipline." "*Bureaucratism* versus democratism," says Lenin, "*is the organizational principle of revolutionary social democracy* versus the organizational principle of the opportunist."[10] He emphasizes that a similar conflict between the centralist and the autonomist conception manifests itself in the social democracy of every country where the revolutionary and reformist or revisionist tendencies stand in opposition to one another. He points in particular to recent events in the German party and to the discussion that has begun on the question of the autonomy of the electoral district.[11] For this reason alone a re-examination of the parallels drawn by Lenin should not be without interest and profit.

First of all we should note that there is nothing inherently "revolutionary Marxist" in the strong emphasis on the innate capacities of the proletarians for social democratic organization and in the suspicion against the "intellectual" elements in the social democratic movement; on the contrary it is just as easy to discern in them an affinity with opportunist views. The antagonism between the purely proletarian element and the non-proletarian socialist intelligentsia is the common ideological banner beneath which the French semi-anarchist pure trade-unionist, with his old call, "Méfiez-vous de politiciens!,"[12] joins hands with the mistrust of English trade-unionism for the socialist "visionary," and lastly, if we have been correctly informed, with the pure "economism" of the former Petersburg *Rabochaya Mysl* (the newspaper *Labor Thought*),[13] with its translation of trade-unionist narrow-mindedness to autocratic Russia.

Of course, we can detect in the hitherto existing practice of Western European social democracy an undeniable connection between opportunism and the intellectual element as well as between opportunism and decentralizing tendencies in organizational questions. But anyone who separates these phenomena, which have arisen on concrete historical foundations, from this context in order to hold them up as abstract models of universal and absolute value is committing a grave sin against the "Holy Spirit" of Marxism, namely against its historical–dialectical mode of thought.

Taken in the abstract, one can only state that the "intellectual" as a social element that, stemming from the bourgeoisie, is by origin alien to the proletariat, cannot come to socialism in a manner consonant with his own sense of class identity but only by overcoming that sense by taking the ideological path. For this reason he is more predisposed to opportunistic aberration than is the class conscious proletarian whose immediate class instinct, insofar as he has not lost the living link with his native social milieu and with the proletarian mass, gives him firm revolutionary backbone. However, the concrete form that this inclination on the part of the intellectual towards opportunism takes and, in particular, the tangible shape that it acquires in organizational tendencies, depend in every case on the concrete social milieu of the society in question.

The phenomena in the life of German, French and Italian social democracy to which Lenin refers have arisen on a very definite social basis, namely that of *bourgeois parliamentarism*. As this is the specific breeding-ground for the present opportunist current in the social democratic movement in Western Europe, so the particular tendencies of opportunism towards disorganization have grown out of it.

Parliamentarism not only supports all the well-known illusions of current opportunism as we have come to know it in France, Italy and Germany: the overrating of reform, of collaboration between classes and parties and of peaceful development, etc. It also prepares the ground in which these illusions can work in practice because, even within social democracy, it separates intellectuals as parliamentarians from, and to a certain extent raises them above, the proletarian mass. Lastly, as the workers' movement grows, this same parliamentarism molds it into a springboard for political careerism, which is why it makes it into an easy refuge for ambitious castaways from the bourgeoisie.

All these factors also give rise to the definite inclination of the opportunistic intellectual of Western European social democracy towards disorganization and lack of discipline. The second specific condition for the present opportunist current is the presence of an already highly developed socialist movement and thus also of an influential social democratic party organization. The latter now serves as the bastion of the revolutionary class movement against bourgeois-parliamentary tendencies, one that will have to be dismantled and destroyed if the compact and active nucleus of the proletariat is to be dissolved in an amorphous mass electorate. This is how the "autonomist" and decentralizing tendencies of modern opportunism arose. They were historically well-founded and very well-suited to particular political aims and can therefore be explained, not by the innate disorderliness or effeteness of the "intellectual," as Lenin supposes, but by the needs of the bourgeois parliamentarian, not by the *psychology* of the intellectual, but by the *politics* of the opportunist.

All these conditions look significantly different in autocratic Russia, however, where opportunism in the workers' movement is by no means a product of the strong growth in social democracy, of the disintegration of bourgeois society, as in the West, but, on the contrary, of its political backwardness.

It is understandable that the Russian intelligentsia, from which the social-ist intellectual is recruited, has a much less well-defined class character, is to a far greater extent declassed, in the precise sense of the word, than the West-ern European intelligentsia. This, combined with the infancy of the proletari-an movement in Russia, certainly results in general in a far greater scope for theoretical instability and opportunistic vacillation which sometimes turns into a complete denial of the political side of the workers' movement and sometimes into the quite opposite belief in terror as the only salvation, and which finally comes to rest in the quagmires of liberalism in the political sphere or Kantian idealism in the "philosophical."[14]

In our view the Russian social democratic intellectual lacks not only the positive experience of bourgeois parliamentarism to encourage a specifically *active* tendency towards disorganization but also the corresponding socio-psychological milieu. The modern Western European man of letters, who devotes himself to the cult of his reputed "ego" and even drags this "master-race morality" into the world of socialist thought and struggle, is not typical of the bourgeois intelligentsia in general but of a particular phase of its exis-tence; in other words it is the product of a decadent, putrefied bourgeoisie that has already become entwined in the vicious circles of its own class hege-mony. The utopian and opportunist fantasies of the Russian socialist intellec-tual tend, on the contrary and for good reason, rather to an acceptance of the inverse theoretical form of self-denial and self-deprecation. Surely the one-time movement of "going to the people,"[15] i.e. the obligatory masquerading of the intellectual as a peasant, was for the old Narodniks just a despairing invention by that same intellectual, in the same way that the recent crude cult of the "calloused hand" is for the disciples of pure "Economism."

If we try to solve the question of organizational forms, not by mechanisti-cally transferring rigid patterns from Western Europe to Russia but by examining the particular concrete conditions in Russia itself, we achieve a quite different result. To attribute to opportunism, as Lenin does, general enthusiasm for any particular form of organization, such as decentralization, is to misapprehend its inner nature. Opportunist as it is, opportunism has, even in questions of organization, only one principle and that is lack of prin-ciple. It always selects its methods in accordance with circumstances, as long as they suit its ends. But if, like Lenin, we define opportunism as the desire to cripple the independent revolutionary class movement of the pro-letariat to make it an instrument of the bourgeois intelligentsia's longing for domination, then we must also admit that in the *initial stages* of the workers' movement this end is best achieved not through decentralization but through rigid *centralism* which puts the still indistinct proletarian movement at the mercy of a handful of intellectual leaders. It is characteristic that in Germany too in the *initial* stages of the movement, before a strong nucleus of conscious proletarians and a proven social democratic tactic existed, both organizational tendencies were represented: extreme centralism through Lassalle's General German Workers' Union,[16] and "autonomism" through the Eisenachers. It was this tactic of the Eisenachers which, despite all its admitted confusion of principle, provoked a significantly greater active participation of the proletarian element in the intellectual life of the party, a greater spirit of initiative amongst the workers themselves—among other things, the rapid development of a substantial provincial press by this group provides proof of this—and caused a much stronger and healthier *broadening* of the movement than the Lassalleans, who naturally had increasingly pathetic results with their "dictators."

In general it can easily be demonstrated that, in conditions where the revolutionary part of the working mass is still unorganized and the movement itself wavering, in short in conditions similar to those in Russia now, it is precisely strict despotic centralism that emerges as the organizational tendency favored by the opportunist academic. Just as on the other hand in a later stage—against a parliamentary background and in the face of a strong united workers' party—on the other hand *decentralization* becomes the corresponding tendency of the opportunist intellectual.

It is precisely from the standpoint of Lenin's fears of the dangerous influences exerted by the intelligentsia on the proletarian movement that his own concept of organization presents the greatest danger to Russian social democracy.

In fact nothing will more easily and more surely deliver up a still young proletarian movement to the power-hungry intellectuals than forcing the movement into the straitjacket of a bureaucratic centralism that reduces the militant workers to a docile instrument of a "committee." On the other hand, nothing will more surely protect the workers from any opportunist abuse committee by an ambitious intelligentsia than the spontaneous revolutionary activity of the workers, the heightening of their sense of political responsibility.

What Lenin sees as a specter today may very easily become tangible reality tomorrow.

Let us not forget that the revolution imminent in Russia is not a proletarian but a bourgeois revolution that will radically alter the whole setting for the social democratic struggle. Then the Russian intelligentsia too will very soon acquire the clear stamp of its bourgeois class composition. If social democracy is currently the only leader of the Russian working mass, on the morrow of the revolution the bourgeoisie, and above all of course its intelligentsia, will want the mass to form the pedestal for its parliamentary hegemony. The less the spontaneous activity, the free initiative, the political sense of the most aware stratum of the workers is released, the more it is politically dragooned and drilled by a social democratic central committee, the easier the game of the bourgeois demagogues will be in the new Russia, and the more the harvest of today's social democratic labors will find its way into the haylofts of the bourgeoisie.

Above all, however, the whole basic approach of the ultra-centralist view, which culminates in the idea of protecting the workers' movement from opportunism through an organizational statute, is false. Under the immediate influence of recent events in French, Italian and German social democracy, a tendency has clearly emerged among the Russian Social Democrats also to view opportunism in general as an ingredient that is alien to the proletarian movement and that has only been brought into the workers' movement from outside, together with the elements of bourgeois democracy. Were this correct, statutory organizational limitations would in themselves prove to be quite ineffective against the pressure of the opportunist element. If the massive influx of non-proletarian elements into social democracy arises from such deep-seated causes as the rapid economic collapse of the petty bourgeoisie and the even more rapid political collapse of bourgeois liberalism, the extinction of bourgeois democracy, then it is a naive illusion to imagine that this tidal wave could be held back by a particular version of the paragraphs of the party statute. Paragraphs only regulate the existence of small sects or private societies—the currents of history have always known how to set themselves above the subtlest paragraph. Furthermore, it is quite wrong to think that it is only in the interest of the workers' movement to fend off the massive influx of the elements released by the progressive disintegration of bourgeois society. The idea that social democracy, a class representative of the proletariat, is at the same time the representative of all the progressive interests in society and of all the oppressed victims of the bourgeois social order, is not to be understood merely in the sense that in the program of social democracy all these interests are brought together as an ideal. This idea becomes reality in the course of the process of historical development, in which social democracy, as a *political party*, increasingly becomes the refuge for the most varied discontented elements, so that it really becomes the party of the people against a tiny minority of the dominant bourgeoisie. It depends only on its knowing how to subjugate the present afflictions of this motley crew of fellow-travelers to the final aims of the working class on a lasting basis, to merge the spirit of non-proletarian opposition into revolutionary proletarian action, in a word, to assimilate the elements that are flooding to it and to digest them. The latter is, however, only possible when, as in Germany until now, there are already powerful trained proletarian elite troops within social democracy who set the tone and are sufficiently conscious to take the declassed and petty bourgeois fellow-travelers into revolutionary tow. In this case a stricter application of the centralist conception in the organizational statute and the sterner formulation of party discipline is very expedient as a dam against the opportunist current. In these circumstances the organizational statute can undoubtedly serve as a weapon in the struggle with opportunism, just as it did in fact serve French revolutionary social democracy against the onslaught of the Jaurésist[17] confusion and just as a revision of the German party statute in this direction has now become a necessity. But even in this case the party statute should not be construed as in itself a sort of weapon of defense against opportunism, but merely an external coercive instrument for the exercise of the authoritative influence of the revolutionary proletarian majority that actually exists within the party. Where such a majority is lacking, the most rigorous paper sanctions cannot be a substitute.

However, as we have mentioned, the influx of bourgeois elements is by no means the only source of the opportunist current in social democracy. The other source is located rather in the essence of the social democratic struggle itself, in its internal contradictions. The world historical advance of the proletariat towards its victory is a process which is unique because here, for the first time in history, the popular masses are themselves carrying out their will and carrying it out in opposition to all ruling classes, but this will can only be realized above and beyond the limits of present-day society. On the other hand, however, the masses can only develop this *will* in the day-to-day struggle with the existing order and therefore only within its framework. The identification of the great popular mass with a goal that transcends the whole existing order and the identification of the day-to-day struggle with revolutionary upheaval constitute the dialectical contradiction of the social democratic movement which must, in the whole course of its development, work a way forward logically between the two pitfalls, between losing its mass character and abandoning its goal, between relapsing into sects and declining into a bourgeois reform movement.

It is therefore a quite unhistorical illusion to think that social democratic tactics in the revolutionary sense can be determined in advance once and for all, that the workers' movement can be saved once and for all from opportunist aberrations. Certainly, Marx's teaching provides devastating ammunition against all the basic types of opportunist thought. But, since the social democratic movement is a mass movement and the pitfalls that threaten it derive not from the human mind but from social conditions, no action can be taken against opportunist errors in advance: they can only be overcome, when they have taken tangible form in practice, by the movement itself, with the help, of course, of the weapons provided by Marxism. Seen from this angle, opportunism also appears as a product of the movement itself, as a necessary feature of its historical development. It is precisely in Russia, where social democracy is still young and the political conditions of the workers' movement are so abnormal, that opportunism might to a great extent arise from this source, from the unavoidable groping and experimenting in tactics, from the need to bring the present struggle in quite exceptional, unparalleled circumstances into line with basic socialist principles.

If this is so, then the idea that the emergence of opportunist currents can be prevented in the initial stages of a workers' movement by a particular version of the organizational statute seems to us all the more whimsical. The attempt to ward off opportunism by such paper means can in fact wound not opportunism but social democracy itself and, because this attempt stops the pulse of a healthy living organism, it weakens its resistance in the struggle, not just against opportunist currents, but also—and this might also be of some importance—against the existing social order. The means turn against the end.

This anxious desire of a section of the Russian Social Democrats to protect, through the tutelage of an omniscient and ever-present Central Committee, a workers' movement that is developing with such promise and vigor against making false moves, seems to us generally redolent of the same *subjectivism* that has already played more than one trick on socialist thought in Russia. The tricks that the revered human subject of history likes to perform in its own historical process are amusing. The ego, crushed and mangled by Russian autocracy, wreaks its revenge by placing itself, in its own system of thought, on the throne and declaring itself all-powerful, as a committee of conspirators in the name of a non-existent "Narodnaya Volya."[18] But the "object" proves to be stronger; the knot soon triumphs since *it* proves to be the "legitimate" expression of the particular stage of historical process. In the end an even more "legitimate" child of the historical process appears on the scene—the Russian workers' movement, which has made the most promising start in creating a real people's will for the first time in Russian history. But now the "ego" of the Russian revolutionary promptly stands on its head and once more declares itself to be an all-powerful controller of history—this time in the majestic person of a Central Committee of the social democratic workers' movement. The nimble acrobat fails to see that the only subject to whom this role of controller now falls is the *mass ego* of the working class that everywhere insists on making its own mistakes and learning the dialectic of history for itself. Finally, let us speak frankly between ourselves: the mistakes that are made by a truly revolutionary workers' movement are, historically speaking, immeasurably more fruitful and more valuable than the infallibility of the best possible "Central Committee."

# 11 — Credo: On the State of Russian Social Democracy [1]

EDITORS' NOTE: This article, handwritten in Polish and never published during Luxemburg's lifetime, is from September or early October 1911, when the split between Mensheviks and Bolsheviks was about to become irrevocable. Referred to in her private correspondence as the "Credo," it offers a broad critique of the various tendencies within Russian Marxism and an argument for party unity despite their differences. While Luxemburg makes clear her far greater affinity with Lenin and the Bolsheviks than with the Mensheviks or Trotsky, whom she attacks mercilessly, she also takes issue with Lenin's organizational methods. In this sense, the article represents her third critique of Lenin, alongside the 1904 one on organization and the 1918 one on the Russian Revolution, both of which have long been known. The period in which this was written was a particularly turbulent one for German Marxism as well. Just weeks before, in August and September 1911, Luxemburg had publicly criticized Kautsky and the SPD leadership over their failure to oppose German imperialist designs on Morocco, for which she was accused of breaking party discipline. Feliks Tych published the Credo for the first time in 1991 in a German translation, after he discovered it in the archives of Luxemburg's Polish Party in Moscow. We have drawn heavily on Tych's preface and explanatory notes in our notes below. This translation from the German by Ashley Passmore and Kevin B. Anderson has been checked against the Polish original by Urszula Wislanka. We would like to thank Albert Resis for background information.

Recently, a serious crisis has reemerged in the organizational life of the Social Democratic Party of Russia, a moment that is, to a certain extent, becoming decisive. The starting point of the current crisis was the meeting of members of the Central Committee that took place in Paris in June of this year.[2] Their resolutions formed the axis of a subsequent series of important events in the party as well as a realignment of its factions and tendencies. However, before we discuss the resolutions of this meeting more thoroughly, it is essential to consider, even if only in preliminary form, the overall situation in which the Russian Social Democratic Party found itself in the middle of this year, in order to be able to gauge the meaning of the fact that such a meeting occurred, and the meaning of the political work undertaken there.

All comrades can likely still remember the positive impression that the report on the last plenary session of the Central Committee at the beginning of 1910[3] had on the party as a whole and, without exception, on its members, irrespective of their positions. The complete unification of the party, the dissolution of the factional organizations, and the discontinuation of factional newspapers! These were announcements that one almost did not want to believe, so strongly did they contradict this woeful and abhorrent practice of endless factional bickering, which one had come to expect in the Russian party and which had continued forcefully until shortly before the commencement of the meeting of the plenary session of the Central Committee. The refreshing belief in the strength and the future of the party aroused by these resolutions of the Central Committee had an even stronger effect[4] in spite of the great difficulties and aggravated relationships that resulted from this important undertaking of organizational unity in the Russian party, enacted by means of a firm hand. Hence, one could therefore expect that we would hear in the press less about "Mensheviks" and "Bolsheviks,"[5] and less about their bickering and infighting, and instead about Russian Social Democrats, who, despite their various positions nevertheless value the unity of the party above all.

The achievement of the Central Committee appeared even more enduring, because Party unity had been established not merely mechanistically, but on a solid, ideological, and more principled foundation. The plenary session, which did not limit itself to technical and organizational measures, had also devised clear political directives, formulating the direction that party policy was to take. On the one hand, it was decided that it was necessary to use all types of legal tactics, but only insofar as they could be used—under current counter-revolutionary conditions—in accord with the principles of class struggle and the position of Social Democracy as a separate party of the revolutionary proletariat. On the other hand, the plenary session issued the rallying cry: stronger and determined struggle both against the "Liquidators," or the tendency that seeks to destroy the party as an illegal organization for the sake of a full legal existence, and against such nonsense as so-called "Ostzovism," the tendency that has demanded for some time the recall of the Social Democratic faction from the Third Duma [Parliament], supposedly in order to rip the mask of "representing the people" off this fortress of counter-revolution.[6]

After the plenary session had separated Party policy from Right and Left deviations, placing it on the solid foundation of principled class struggle, it crowned its labor with a resolution calling for a full Party Conference as soon as possible. This would, in lieu of a regular Party Congress,7 further the practical work of the party in the spirit of its stated principles, and consolidate its intellectual unity by collective and consistent practice.

Such was the course of the plenary session of the Central Committee and those were the prospects in 1910 after its completion.

Unfortunately, these were, to a certain extent, futile hopes and prospects. It soon became clear that the old factional vices and evils had won the upper hand over any consideration for the good of the party and the proletarian movement. Contrary to the clear resolution of the plenary session of the Central Committee, the organ of the Menshevik faction, *Golos,* did not cease to appear. On the contrary, practically only a day after the end of the plenary session, it began to bombard the central party institutions. Two members of the editorial board of the central organ of the party, who represent the Menshevik position, began a boycott of this organ by refusing to contribute their work,8 which did not stop them, however, from continuing to draw their editorial salaries for almost a year. Such conduct by rebels from among the "Mensheviks" naturally became the cue to begin a factional campaign from the opposite side and soon the old factional struggle was reestablished in the journals in all of its splendor, at which point even the factional organizations, which formed a *de facto* "state within a state" in the heart of the party, fortified their bunkers and fortresses even more openly.

This turn of events produced lamentable results. The Party Conference, which had been arranged by the last session of the Central Committee, did not take place. The highest party organ, the Central Committee, battered by arrests, did not meet once during a period of one and a half years, showed no vital signs, and for all practical purposes, did not exist. Total confusion reigned in the editorial office in the wake of the unremitting faction fights. In the "Foreign Commission of the Central Committee," a commission that had been appointed by the last plenary session of the Central Committee to handle various technical matters and also to call a Party Conference, the same situation prevailed: an incessant, fractious struggle. The "Mensheviks," with support from the representatives of the Bund and the Latvian Social Democracy, made use of their single-vote majority against the representatives of the Bolsheviks and the SDKPiL9 and unabashedly used this body to make the "Foreign Commission," an ancillary, technical organ of the Central Committee, into an instrument of the factional politics of "Menshevism," against the Central Committee's explicit resolutions and directives. This manifested itself most clearly and specifically in the systematic resistance that the Foreign Commission launched against convening a plenary session of the Central Committee. Because of the reigning anarchy inside the party ranks, such a session increasingly became a burning necessity. Without a Party Congress or a Conference, only the highest central organ, the Central Committee, could put out the newly ignited, factional struggles, unify the party, give the party a clear and unified direction and thrust it into practical action. It was, as it were, the cursed duty and responsibility of the Foreign Commission, an instrument of the Central Committee by designation alone, that was to convene the Central Committee as quickly as possible, even though this situation came about only because of arrests and other difficulties. Yet, in order to convene a Party Conference or even a session of the Central Committee, a difficult dispute clearly loomed between the party majority and the opportunist minority, which, as one soon discovered, did what it pleased, thanks to a fortuitous majority in the Foreign Commission, and that, with a strictly factional view, wanted to exploit what to it was the happy circumstance of the absence of the central party institutions, even though it was obvious to everyone that this situation would inevitably lead to the dissolution of the party, to chaos, to demoralization, and to the paralysis of party activities and the deterioration of the party's authority throughout the country [Russia].

Manifestations[10] of this deterioration increasingly came to the surface. The orgies of opportunism of the "Mensheviks" and their open support of the Liquidators led, as we know, to the split in the heart of their own faction and to the secession of the "party Mensheviks," led by Georgi Plekhanov. Yet in response to the crass opportunism of Menshevism, a dangerous development appeared in the midst of the Bolshevik faction. Instead of using all their powers to save the cohesion of the party, this faction, under Lenin's direction, threw itself with vehemence into the rebuilding of its own factional apparatus. The Bolsheviks constructed or renewed their factional organization with a separate factional center, with their own organ, accompanied by a separate popular newspaper for workers, and even a separate "Party School," which recruited people into the faction. However, the greatest danger to the future of the party became this organizational politics, in which Lenin and his friends took part ever more openly. This politics consisted of wanting to form a bloc only with the "party Mensheviks," i.e., the Plekhanov group,[11] yet it also meant simply shutting the Martov-Dan group, connected to the editorial staff of the *Golos* out of the Party, along with the movement of the former "Ozto-vists" aligned with the *Vperyod* newspaper,[12] and the followers of Trotsky's *Pravda*,[13] which practices a completely hypocritical politics and, with phrases extolling radicalism and the cohesion of the party, basically supports, through a benign silence, opportunism, the Liquidators, and all of their misdeeds.

Due to the facts outlined here, the state of the party became desperate. The organizational split was in fact virtually complete and would become open at any moment. The behavior of the warring factions proved that any consideration for the existence of the party as a whole was no longer able to subdue the fury that drove the factions. The dirty brochure that Martov put out against Lenin,[14] which constituted such a base and impertinent pamphlet that up to this point could have flowed only from the pens of paid scribes of reactionaries wanting to destroy the honor of the socialists and cover them with mud, was an ominous warning that it was high time to put out the fire that was splitting the Party, which had been maliciously set by the Mensheviks. On the other hand, the opposition with which the Foreign Commission of the Central Committee resisted convening a Plenum of the Central Committee caused the representative of the "Bolsheviks" to resign from the Commission and to withdraw the financial resources allocated to him from party funds. With this, the factional split within these party institutions had already become a fact, just as in the editorial staff of the central organ, due to the boycott of the Menshevik editors. Under Lenin's leadership, the Bolsheviks began conspicuously preparing to call for a factional conference of their tendency that would[15] have officially expressed and verified the split in Russian Social Democracy.

In this situation, a group of members of the Central Committee took the initiative to meet to discuss how to save the unity and cohesion of the party. Yet before we evaluate the politics carried out by this meeting, we must consider the question of the standpoint of our organization, the SDKPiL, with respect to the whole state of affairs within the Russian party.

From the beginning,[16] the position and role of the SDKPiL rested on the fact that they neither identified themselves with the Menshevik line nor with the Bolshevik faction; rather, they adopted their own position, in the spirit of the revolutionary Social Democracy of Western Europe.[17] A significant gulf separates us from the Mensheviks concerning the fundamental understanding of proletarian tactics as a whole in the Russian Empire. For their part, Martov and Dan's movement understands the revolution that began in 1905 as bourgeois in the sense that its political leadership is drawn from the liberal bourgeoisie. The sole role of the working class is to furnish them aid, to support the activities of the liberals. Our party has for a long time adopted the position that the political leadership of the masses of the Russian Empire belongs to the conscious proletariat, which alone can overthrow absolutism through independent revolutionary action and can create a new political order, but for whom the wretched bourgeois liberalism under Tsarism must be seen as the enemy and as allies of the counter-revolution. From this fundamental difference in outlook results, at every turn, a completely different tactics and a completely different estimation of the course of revolution, of its results, of the reasons for its failure, and of its future prospects, as well as completely different guidelines for the proletarian party in the current counter-revolutionary period. The Mensheviks, who were eventually disappointed by the course of events after the defeat of the revolution and were in doubt about the rekindling of independent revolutionary action, began to search for a full legal existence within the Stolypin framework,[18] consistently subordinating the politics of the proletariat to the actions of the liberal bourgeoisie. Soon the Russian opportunists rallied around the idea of a "Workers' Congress"[19]; soon they saw prospects for legal, cultural, and trade union activities by the grace of, and on the coattails of, the counter-revolution, and, since the failure of the revolution, increasingly showed an open contempt and disregard for the illegal Social Democratic organization and illegal Social Democratic activities. While they were, during the revolutionary struggle, a danger to the independent class politics of the proletariat, under the sway of the counter-revolution, they became a clear danger, to the very existence of an illegal proletarian party. They also became a factor, which consciously or unconsciously was out to liquidate Social Democracy as its own revolutionary organization and to hand over the working class as a reward to all the have-nots of the radical and liberal intelligentsia. The relentless struggle against this epidemic of opportunism and the Liquidators was, from the beginning, the pivot of the politics of the SDKPiL inside the all-Russian party.

Yet our party is also in serious opposition to the Bolshevik line. Already in 1903, shortly after the constitution of the two factional wings in the Russian Party, we felt obliged to stand up decisively against the organizational centralism of Lenin and his friends, because they wanted to secure a revolutionary direction for the proletarian movement by swaddling the party, in a purely mechanistic fashion, with an intellectual dictator from the central party Executive.[20] No sooner did this jarringly mechanistic way of understanding the nature of revolution appear during the course of the revolution of 1905 and 1906 than did Lenin's supporters rant loudly about the need to "prepare for an armed uprising." They would install "three-man" and "five-man" groups, small armed battalions, and would hold "combat" drills. At the last full Party Congress in London in 1907, our delegation consistently resisted both the opportunist corruption of the Menshevik Right and the crude, revolutionary actions of the Leninist Left. Since that time, the evolution of the Bolsheviks in the direction of a more European understanding of Social Democratic radicalism made a rapprochement possible between our party and this tendency on the basis of a collective, fundamental struggle against the plague of Liquidationism. Recently, however, since the period of the general disruption of the party illustrated above, the specific tactics of Lenin and his friends force our party to renew its decisive opposition. This time, what showed itself again to a certain extent was Lenin's inclination to resolve problems and difficulties in the development of the Russian Party mechanistically, with fists and knives, an inclination that is dangerous for the party. In view of the cynical excesses of the factional entities that side with the Liquidators Martov, Dan, & Co., Lenin and his friends began to address the question of convening a Party Conference that would exclude the *Golos* tendency. Our comrades also, who deal with the Russian Mensheviks, read their literature, and who are, to a certain extent, conversant with their practice, could come to no other conclusion than the conviction that this group is the ruin of the workers' movement. Our active worker comrades inside the country [Poland] have expressed, in an entire series of meetings, conferences and congresses of our party, the firm conviction that there is no place in the ranks of the party of the revolutionary proletariat for this Liquidator-opportunist decay. Thus, in the political estimation of the Mensheviks, there are no significant differences between our tendency and Lenin's. What does become a significant difference, however, is the method of struggle against the Martov-Dan group and against other, smaller groups. This is where the *Vperyod* group, which undoubtedly shows certain anarchistic tendencies, and whose confusion in no way contributes to the energy in the ranks of the party, comes into play. Entering into consideration here as well are the handful of followers of Trotsky's *Pravda* in the party who, without question, practice Jesuitical politics because he basically supports the *Golos* group by simply denying the danger stemming from the Liquidators and by thrusting himself into the role of patron of the Polish Liquidators, i.e., the PPS Lewica. For us, as for Lenin and friends, there is little doubt that this duplicitous brokering by Trotsky, who rants professionally about "party unity," but who in practice barks at the left wing of the party at every opportunity, basically amounts to political support for opportunism. But nevertheless, and despite all of that, the representatives of our party in the Central Committee, in the central organ, and in the Foreign Commission, could not and cannot be in agreement with the tactics employed by Lenin's group vis-à-vis all of these groups. These tactics amount to throwing out the *Golos* group, along with the *Vperyod* group and Trotsky's *Pravda*, out of the party and affiliating themselves with the Plekhanov tendency of Party Mensheviks. This tactic is undoubtedly straight as a stick, but like all sticks, it has two ends, which means it can be double-edged from the position of the interests of the party as a whole. Even though we regard the nest of Liquidators of the *Golos* group as a malignant cancer on the body of the party, of which the party should rid itself—the sooner the better—we do not see that it is possible to accomplish this operation by settling old factional scores with fists, as it were. So far, the *Golos* group still belongs to the party, and only the party as such, the party as a whole, has the power and the duty to suppress this disastrous movement or to do away with them in an organizational fashion. Therefore, the representatives of the SDKPiL must also adopt a completely different position than Lenin and his comrades. They were against the mutual exclusion of the factions and deemed it instead necessary even to call upon the *Golos* group to join in the work of collectively rebuilding the central party institutions, in order to lead an even stiffer ideological resistance within the party itself against the Liquidator epidemic, all within the scope of a restored party unity.

Our party was even less able to support the Leninist tactics used on the other remaining groups. To indiscriminately antagonize the *Vperyod* group and Trotsky's *Pravda* with the same doggedness as the Liquidators of *Golos*—these "strong-arm policies" of Lenin led directly to the artificial convergence of all of these elements, now consolidated against the left wing of the party. It was not so much kindred political views as it was being similarly, indiscriminately kicked out via the Leninist tactics that drove all these groups into a unified opposition against the Bolsheviks. This stubborn Bolshevik war against all other groups even had the result that Plekhanov's group also, made fearful by the isolation of the Leninist faction, definitively backed out from an alliance that Lenin saw as the only possibility.

If we take this situation into consideration, it becomes clear that Lenin's tactics inevitably led, on the one hand, to the splintering of the left wing of the

Party and the complete isolation of the Bolshevik faction, and on the other hand, to a coalition of some very heterogeneous elements with the right wing. In the final analysis, Lenin's radical tactics led to precisely the same result as the opportunist tactics of Martov & Co.: the breakup of the party. The two extreme wings ripped the entire party into pieces: the calculating, Liquidationist cynicism of the Mensheviks from *Golos* and the Foreign Commission, and on the other hand, the blind "mechanistic" radicalism of Lenin. Our party must stand up to save party unity against these suicidal politics with a clear and decisive program of consolidation. No exclusion of groups that belong to the party by means of factional disputes, the creation of a solid ideological core to support party unity and to combat the danger from the Liquidators within the party—this was the clear, well-defined plan that the representatives of the SDKPiL had to put forward. At the same time, this plan contained one further, very important point: the life of the party should not, for any reason, be exclusively and completely absorbed by internal disputes. If Lenin and his friends tried to proclaim the struggle against Liquidationism as the single rallying cry of party politics, then the representatives of he SDKPiL would have to bring forward the simultaneous rallying cry, struggle against the reaction; and the rallying cry, prepare for the elections of the Fourth Duma.[21] Taking the general tasks of the party into consideration, the consolidation and strengthening of the organizations for the election campaign; guiding and strengthening the trade union struggle with regard to the revival of the mass movement and the strike waves, arranging legal activities, rebuilding the centers of illegal work— all of these are burning issues for the whole party. In order to take care of these tasks, and at the same time, to revitalize the unified party and restore the Central Committee, it was essential to hold a collective Party Conference to which all organizations and movements that count themselves as part of the party were to be summoned. This is the policy that the representatives of the SDKPiL suggested, because they had become convinced of the need to act in this way alone: in the spirit of the mandate assigned to them by our party, in the spirit of the resolutions of their Party Conferences and Congresses; and in the spirit of the policies of our entire party.

The position put forward by the SDKPiL turned out to be the single foundation upon which the Central Committee meeting could rely. In the present situation, there was no other choice. It was either Lenin's tactics, which would lead to an open split within the party, which had indeed already been ushered in by the official departure of the Bolshevik representative from the Foreign Commission, or the tactics of the Polish members of the Central

Committee, which would lead to consolidation and the rebuilding of party unity on the foundation of an effective, revolutionary class struggle. This alternative was so unambiguous and the necessity of the Polish plan so clear that our comrades were able to win over a portion of the Bolshevik faction, who understood that the interests of their party and those of their own wing did not allow them to follow Lenin any longer in his impulsive campaign. Thanks to these circumstances, Comrade Tyshka [Jogiches] was successful in creating, together with the group of party Bolsheviks, a strong center in the spirit of this proposal, and the meeting of the Central Committee in Paris rested upon this new internal party constellation. Almost all of their resolutions were pushed through against the resistance of Lenin and his friends who insisted upon his policies. This was thanks to the majority that our representatives formed with the party Bolsheviks against him.

Now we come to the Paris meeting itself. It should be noted that all members of the Central Committee living abroad were invited to it. Appearing at the meeting were: three members representing the Bolsheviks, two representatives of the SDKPiL, two members of the majority of the Foreign Commission of the Central Committee (a Menshevik and a member of the Bund), along with the representative of the Latvian Social Democracy to the Central Committee. In all, therefore, eight members of the Central Committee appeared at the meeting, or more than half of this body, which consisted of fifteen members. Immediately, even before the meeting began, it became apparent that the two members of the Foreign Commission of the Central Committee, who represented the Bund and the Mensheviks, had appeared at the meeting with preformulated instructions in the spirit of Menshevik policies, determined to disrupt the meeting and to frustrate any productive work. The Liquidators operated under the pretext, which was all too transparent, where first one and then the other would leave the meeting with the usual rhetoric against the legitimacy of its resolutions, before a resolution had even been drafted. The remaining members, undeterred by these maneuvers, which were nothing more than the continuation of the tactics of the Foreign Commission, set about their work with all their energy.

Any questions about the competency of the meeting can be single-handedly answered by the character of its resolutions. The Paris meeting did not draft any new resolutions beyond those that had been conveyed by the last plenary session of the Central Committee. In particular, the latter's resolution with respect to the call for a general Party Conference represents the actual central pivot of the meeting. Solely and exclusively with the aim of carrying out this resolution, the meeting, in order to provisionally secure the existence of the party and to summon a Conference, was forced to appoint a Technical Commission, to take care of the most pressing day-to-day affairs of the party, and an Organizational Commission, whose sole and exclusive task was to call for a full Party Conference in the near future. The establishment of these provisional organizations had become absolutely necessary because of the fact that the Foreign Commission, the technical organ established by the last Plenum of the Central Committee, had become completely disloyal in its character and had openly become an organ of a faction and thus an impediment to the mission of its governing body, the Central Committee itself. Following the departure of the Bolshevik member from the Foreign Commission, the meeting confronted the issue of its breakup and had to reckon with the fact that the Foreign Commission had ceased to function as an instrument of the Central Committee. A whole series of practical, burning needs of the party, such as the publication of the central organ, transportation, etc., had to be dealt with on a day-to-day basis and were not to interrupt the existence of the party as a whole. Since it was the main task and duty of the meeting to save the unity of the party from a looming split, it was essential to maintain the daily functions of the party and therefore, to this end, to found a needed organ in place of the Foreign Commission of the Central Committee. The foundation of the Organizational Commission resulted directly from the need to carry out the resolution of the Central Committee to summon an all-Party Conference, which naturally necessitated all kinds of preparations and communications with the organizations that operated in the country [Russia], etc. Not only that. The Paris meeting established at the outset that both Commissions would have to adhere to the concrete scope of the directives and resolutions of the last plenary session. The Technical Commission was instructed to spend party funds strictly within the limits of the party budget determined by the Central Committee, to which the Foreign Commission formerly adhered.[22] However, the Organizational Commission was instructed by the meeting that, when preparing to assemble the full Party Conference, it was to follow the guidelines that had been outlined expressly for this purpose by the Plenum of the Central Committee. Beyond this, the meeting did not draft any resolutions. With the above steps carrying out the resolutions of the last plenary session of the Central Committee, the members of the Central Committee in no way overstepped their competence, but simply performed their duty for the party. This could only draw the objection of those for whom the continuation of chaos and disorder in the party, indeed even its disruption, rests within the interest of their faction. For everyone for whom salvaging the unity of the party is near to their hearts, the initiatives of the members of the Central Committee to hold the Paris meeting and the work brought about by it were a diligent exercise of duty on the part of those members, the neglect of which would have represented a punishable offense against the interests of the party at the most dangerous of moments, when the cohesiveness of the party was at stake.

The second accusation raised by the half-open and veiled followers of the Liquidators is the split that the Paris meeting allegedly caused when it established illegal and factional institutions, the Technical Commission and the Organizational Commission, in the place of "legal" party institutions. This accusation intentionally ignores the fact that the split, the paralysis of activity in the Foreign Commission of the Central Committee, had already taken place before the Paris meeting, and the latter simply confronted accomplished facts: the refusal of the Foreign Commission of the Central Committee to call a session of the Central Committee and the departure of the Bolshevik member from the same Commission; also, the persistent boycott on the part of two Menshevik members of the editorial staff of the central organ and finally, such facts as the degrading brochure by Martov, the publication of which had heralded an already completely shameless and cynical factional war on the cadaver of the unified party. Thus, the Paris meeting did not cause the split, but rather, stumbled upon it. What it did do, however, did not directly lead to the deepening of the division, but to the prevention of its further progress with the utmost resolve. The meeting declared, against the resistance of Lenin and his closest friends, the slogan of a non-factional politics of consolidation and reconciliation, the only slogan that could end the fratricidal, fractious infighting. The meeting resolved to call a full Party Conference, not a Conference for a single faction or one for the left wing alone, but one to which all party organizations were to be invited. In fact, no invitation was issued directly to the *Golos* group and the members of the Central Committee hardly felt appointed to do so, since they had resolved in their last session to discontinue this organ and to issue the rallying cry of a stiff resistance against the Liquidators, whom this organ now more or less openly supported. But although the Paris meeting did not take the responsibility upon itself to invite the editorial staff of the organ, which is an active voice of the factional rebellion against party discipline and party unity, it nevertheless allowed for the virtually guaranteed eventuality of the participation of the *Golos* group at the conference. For they decided that an invitation to this group was inevitable, in the event that another, legal conference participant would make a claim for them regarding this issue and then take it upon himself to do this. The meeting further decided to invite, apart from the national organization of the SDKPiL, the Bund and the Latvians, the *Vperyod* group, the editorial staff of *Pravda,* and naturally Plekhanov's group to the Conference; in a word, all the tendencies of the party. In conformity with this, the Technical Commission and the Organizational Commission announced explicitly that they in no way intended to conduct a factional policy, that they were far removed from factional entities such as that of Lenin and that they, in clear contrast to Lenin's politics of isolation, stood for the position of a policy of reconciliation and consolidation of the party, but that, in doing so, they would adhere closely to the tactical directives of the last Plenum of the Central Committee, i.e., to the need for intense struggle against Liquidationism, in all of its hues and manifestations.

This is the work that was achieved by the last Paris meeting: the call for a full Party Conference for the rebuilding of the Central Committee, the renovation of the remaining Party institutions and the strengthening of the party for the campaign in the pre-election period—this is the task that now appears on the agenda. The Technical Commission and the Organizational Commission have devoted all their energies to this task. The Organizational Commission resolved to relocate the center of gravity for the preparations from abroad to Russia and to appoint the party organizations active on site to set up a special committee to call the Conference. All party organizations, irrespective of their tendency, can take part in the Commission, which means that there remains not even the slightest legitimacy for any factional reproaches concerning the Conference preparations. The non-resident Organizational Commission ceded all encumbrances and all responsibility of the work of summoning the Conference into the hands of this committee established on-site, and thus reduced their own role to a minimum. It will now merely monitor compliance with the directives of the last Plenum of the Central Committee.

One would have thought that in light of the guarantees against factionalism and in light of such a loyal and steadfast compliance with the politics of reconciliation, that the work undertaken by the Paris meeting would have been met with complete approval from all sides. Unfortunately, the obstinate spirit of factionalism has, up to now, stood in the way of the best intentions and efforts to save the party. On the one side, Lenin and those following his policy of breaking up the party have, from the first moment onward, impeded the work of consolidation and preparation for a full Party Conference. On the other side, the Foreign Commission, where member and representative Comrade Tyshka of the SDKPiL filed the formal petition to make an agreement with the Organizational Commission to collaborate in the summoning of the Conference, cynically denied this petition, which only underlined once again the anti-party stance of those who aim to continue the anarchy and their disruption of the party. On the third side, Trotsky's *Pravda*, taking off the mask of an apostle of unity and party cohesion, shamelessly attacked the participants in the Paris meeting as "usurpers" and "destroyers of the party" and thereby openly moved to the side of the *Golos* Liquidator group and of the "Foreign Commission." And once the Foreign Commission saw that, despite all of the impediments, the work of the Organizational Commission was proceeding in Russia, it decided actively to thwart this effort, allegedly on the Organizational Commission's own accord, by calling for a second Party Conference. In light of the disruption by the Menshevik organization and in light of the attitude of over half of the party toward the Foreign Commission, the Conference called by the Foreign Commission, an organ of the Liquidators, is in reality never going to take place, which is something of which the *Golos* group, together with their ally Comrade Trotsky, is just as utterly convinced as all the others. For Dan and Martov's followers within the Party, therefore, the point of this affair has absolutely nothing to do with the Conference itself, but has to do with the confusion being provoked by these two parallel efforts, in order to hinder the work of party consolidation, which is being accomplished by the Organizational Commission. The intrigues spun to this end by the Foreign Commission took place lately in such a cavalier manner that the Foreign Commission did not think it necessary even once to brief Comrade Tyshka, who represents our party in the Foreign Commission, on its measures and proceedings.

Despite all of these machinations and manipulations from abroad, the work of the Organizational Commission in Russia is, without a doubt, proceeding, albeit slowly. The on-site organizations, irrespective of political tendency, greet the initiatives of the Paris meeting with pleasure and are joining the Preparatory Committee one after the other. The prospects for a full Party Conference are improving and one can only have the firm hope that the work begun can lead successfully to a positive end.

At present, the duty of all comrades is to support fully and completely these preparations for summoning a full Party Conference. Social Democracy must once again overcome disintegration from within; it must, with a firm hand, strangle both the hydra of these instincts toward factionalism, which lacerate its insides, and the cancer of opportunistic Liquidationism, which gnaws away at it. With the twofold slogan of party consolidation and the strengthening of their revolutionary class tactics, and with their subsequent designation as the site of practical action for the summoning of a full Party Conference and to bring about a political action by Social Democracy across the board, the representatives of the SDKPiL in the central party organization believe that they have lived up to their task and that they have fulfilled the duty imparted to them in the spirit of the principles and traditions of the SDKPiL since the moment of its accession into the all-Russian party.

# 12—The Russian Revolution

EDITORS' NOTE: Luxemburg wrote "The Russian Revolution" in September 1918 while she was in prison for opposing World War I. She originally intended for it to be published by her colleagues in the Spartacus League (formed in 1916 by revolutionaries opposed to the war and the capitulation of German Social Democracy), but the work was unfinished upon her release from prison in November 1918 and it was never published during her lifetime. It was published by Paul Levi, who served as her lawyer and later as a leader of the German Communist Party. Levi published it after his expulsion from the Party in 1922. "The Russian Revolution" represents Luxemburg's most comprehensive evaluation of the accomplishments and limitations of the Bolshevik revolution of 1917 and her most elaborate defense of the need for revolutionary democracy *after* the seizure of power. The entire document is reproduced here, except for chapter 7, "The Struggle Against Corruption." The following translation, by Bertram D. Wolfe, is based on the 1928 German edition published in the *Archiv für die Geschichte des Sozialismus und der Arbeiterbewegung*, the organ of the early Frankfurt School.

## THE FUNDAMENTAL SIGNIFICANCE
## OF THE RUSSIAN REVOLUTION

The Russian Revolution is the mightiest event of the World War. Its outbreak, its unexampled radicalism, its enduring consequences, constitute the clearest condemnation of the lying phrases which official Social-Democracy so zealously supplied at the beginning of the war as an ideological cover for German imperialism's campaign of conquest. I refer to the phrases concerning the mission of German bayonets, which were to overthrow Russian Tsarism and free its oppressed peoples.

The mighty sweep of the revolution in Russia, the profound results which have transformed all class relationships, raised all social and economic problems, and, with the fatality of their own inner logic developed consistently from the first phase of the bourgeois republic to ever more advanced stages, finally reducing the fall of Tsarism to the status of a mere minor episode—all these things show as plain as day that the freeing of Russia was not an achievement of the war and the military defeat of Tsarism, not some service of "German bayonets in German fists," as the *Neue Zeit* under Kautsky's editorship once promised in an editorial. They show, on the contrary, that the freeing of Russia had its roots deep in the soil of its own land and was fully matured internally. The military adventure of German imperialism under the ideological blessing of German Social-Democracy did not bring about the revolution in Russia but only served to interrupt it at first, to postpone it for a while after its first stormy rising tide in the years 1911–13, and then, after its outbreak, created for it the most difficult and abnormal conditions.

Moreover, for every thinking observer, these developments are a decisive refutation of the doctrinaire theory which Kautsky shared with the Government Social-Democrats, according to which Russia, as an economically backward and predominantly agrarian land, was supposed not to be ripe for social revolution and proletarian dictatorship. This theory, which regards only a *bourgeois* revolution as feasible in Russia, is also the theory of the opportunist wing of the Russian labor movement, of the so-called Mensheviks, under the experienced leadership of Axelrod and Dan.[1] And from this conception follow the tactics of the coalition of the socialists in Russia with bourgeois liberalism. On this basic conception of the Russian Revolution, from which follow automatically their detailed positions on questions of tactics, both the Russian and the German opportunists find themselves in agreement with the German Government Socialists. According to the opinion of all three, the Russian Revolution should have called a halt at the stage which German imperialism in its conduct of the war had set as its noble task, according to the mythology of the German Social-Democracy, i.e., it should have stopped with the overthrow of Tsarism. According to this view, if the revolution has gone beyond that point and has set as its task the dictatorship of the proletariat, this is simply a mistake of the radical wing of the Russian labor movement, the Bolsheviks. And all difficulties which the revolution has met with in its further course, and all disorders it has suffered, are pictured as purely a result of this fateful error.

*Theoretically,* this doctrine (recommended as the fruit of "Marxist thinking" by the *Vorwarts* of Stampfer[2] and by Kautsky alike) follows from the original "Marxist" discovery that the socialist revolution is a national and, so to speak, a domestic affair in each modern country taken by itself. Of course, in the blue mists of abstract formulae, a Kautsky knows very well how to trace the worldwide economic connections of capital which make of all modern countries a single integrated organism. The problems of the Russian Revolution, moreover—since it is a product of international developments plus the agrarian question—cannot possibly be solved within the limits of bourgeois society.

*Practically,* this same doctrine represents an attempt to get rid of any responsibility for the course of the Russian Revolution, so far as that responsibility concerns the international, and especially the German, proletariat, and to deny the international connections of this revolution. It is not Russia's unripeness which has been proved by the events of the war and the Russian Revolution, but the unripeness of the German proletariat for the fulfillment of its historic tasks. And to make this fully clear is the first task of a critical examination of the Russian Revolution.

The fate of the revolution in Russia depended fully upon international events. That the Bolsheviks have based their policy entirely upon the world proletarian revolution is the clearest proof of their political farsightedness and firmness of principle and of the bold scope of their policies. In it is visible the mighty advance which capitalist development has made in the last decade. The revolution of 1905–07 roused only a faint echo in Europe. Therefore, it had to remain a mere opening chapter. Continuation and conclusion were tied up with the further development of Europe.

Clearly, not uncritical apologetics but penetrating and thoughtful criticism is alone capable of bringing out the treasures of experiences and teachings. Dealing as we are with the very first experiment in proletarian dictatorship in world history (and one taking place at that under the hardest conceivable conditions, in the midst of the worldwide conflagration and chaos of the imperialist mass slaughter, caught in the coils of the most reactionary military power in Europe, and accompanied by the completest failure on the part of the international working class), it would be a crazy idea to think that every last thing done or left undone in an experiment with the dictatorship of the proletariat under such abnormal conditions represented the very pinnacle of perfection. On the contrary, elementary conceptions of socialist politics and an insight into their historically necessary prerequisites force us to understand that under such fatal conditions even the most gigantic idealism and the most storm-tested revolutionary energy are incapable of realizing democracy and socialism but only distorted attempts at either.

To make this stand out clearly in all its fundamental aspects and consequences is the elementary duty of the socialists of all countries; for only on the background of this bitter knowledge can we measure the enormous magnitude of the responsibility of the international proletariat itself for the fate of the Russian Revolution. Furthermore, it is only on this basis that the decisive importance of the resolute international action of the proletarian revolution can become effective, without which action as its necessary support, even the greatest energy and the greatest sacrifices of the proletariat in a single country must inevitably become tangled in a maze of contradiction and blunders.

There is no doubt either that the wise heads at the helm of the Russian Revolution, that Lenin and Trotsky on their thorny path beset by traps of all kinds, have taken many a decisive step only with the greatest inner hesitation and with most violent inner opposition. And surely nothing can be farther from their thoughts than to believe that all the things they have done or left undone under the conditions of bitter compulsion and necessity in the midst of the roaring whirlpool of events, should be regarded by the International as a shining example of socialist policy toward which only uncritical admiration and zealous imitation are in order.

It would be no less wrong to fear that a critical examination of the road so far taken by the Russian Revolution would serve to weaken the respect for and the attractive power of the example of the Russian Revolution, which alone can overcome the fatal inertia of the German masses. Nothing is farther from the truth. An awakening of the revolutionary energy of the working class in Germany can never again be called forth in the spirit of the guardianship methods of the German Social-Democracy of late-lamented memory. It can never again be conjured forth by any spotless authority, be it that of our own "higher committees" or that of "the Russian example." Not by the creation of a revolutionary hurrah-spirit, but quite the contrary: only by an insight into all the fearful seriousness, all the complexity of the tasks involved, only as a result of political maturity and independence of spirit, only as a result of a capacity for critical judgment on the part of the masses, which capacity was systematically killed by the Social-Democracy for decades under various pretexts, only thus can the genuine capacity for historical action be born in the German proletariat. To concern one's self with a critical analysis of the Russian Revolution in all its historical connections is the best training for the German and the international working class for the tasks which confront them as an outgrowth of the present situation.

The first period of the Russian Revolution, from its beginning in March to the October Revolution, corresponds exactly in its general outlines to the course of development of both the Great English Revolution and the Great

French Revolution. It is the typical course of every first general reckoning of the revolutionary forces begotten within the womb of bourgeois society.

Its development moves naturally in an ascending line: from moderate beginnings to ever-greater radicalization of aims and, parallel with that, from a coalition of classes and parties to the sole rule of the radical party.

At the outset in March 1917, the "Cadets," that is the liberal bourgeoisie, stood at the head of the revolution. The first general rising of the revolutionary tide swept everyone and everything along with it. The Fourth Duma, ultra-reactionary product of the ultra-reactionary four-class right of suffrage and arising out of the *coup d'état,* was suddenly converted into an organ of the revolution. All bourgeois parties, even those of the nationalistic right, suddenly formed a phalanx against absolutism. The latter fell at the first attack almost without a struggle, like an organ that had died and needed only to be touched to drop off. The brief effort, too, of the liberal bourgeoisie to save at least the throne and the dynasty collapsed within a few hours. The sweeping march of events leaped in days and hours over distances that formerly, in France, took decades to traverse. In this, it became clear that Russia was realizing the result of a century of European development, and above all, that the revolution of 1917 was a direct continuation of that of 1905–07, and not a gift of the German "liberator." The movement of March 1917 linked itself directly onto the point where, ten years earlier, its work had broken off. The democratic republic was the complete, internally ripened product of the very first onset of the revolution.

Now, however, began the second and more difficult task. From the very first moment, the driving force of the revolution was the mass of the urban proletariat. However, its demands did not limit themselves to the realization of political democracy but were concerned with the burning question of international policy—immediate peace. At the same time, the revolution embraced the mass of the army, which raised the same demand for immediate peace, and the mass of the peasants, who pushed the agrarian question into the foreground, that agrarian question which since 1905 had been the very axis of the revolution. Immediate peace and land—from these two aims the internal split in the revolutionary phalanx followed inevitably. The demand for immediate peace was in most irreconcilable opposition to the imperialist tendencies of the liberal bourgeoisie for whom Milyukov was the spokesman. On the other hand, the land question was a terrifying specter for the other wing of the bourgeoisie, the rural landowners. And, in addition, it represented an attack on the sacred principle of private property in general, a touchy point for the entire propertied class.

Thus, on the very day after the first victories of the revolution, there began an inner struggle within it over the two burning questions—peace and land. The liberal bourgeoisie entered upon the tactics of dragging out things and evading them. The laboring masses, the army, the peasantry, pressed forward ever more impetuously. There can be no doubt that with the questions of peace and land, the fate of the political democracy of the republic was linked up. The bourgeois classes, carried away by the first stormy wave of the revolution, had permitted themselves to be dragged along to the point of republican government. Now they began to seek a base of support in the rear and silently to organize a counter-revolution. The Kaledin Cossack campaign against Petersburg³ was a clear expression of this tendency. Had the attack been successful, then not only the fate of the peace and land questions would have been sealed, but the fate of the republic as well. Military dictatorship, a reign of terror against the proletariat, and then return to monarchy, would have been the inevitable results.

From this we can judge the utopian and fundamentally reactionary character of the tactics by which the Russian "Kautskyans" or Mensheviks permitted themselves to be guided. Hardened in their addiction to the myth of the bourgeois character of the Russian Revolution—for the time being, you see, Russia is not supposed to be ripe for the social revolution!—they clung desperately to a coalition with the bourgeois liberals. But this means a union of elements which had been split by the natural internal development of the revolution and had come into the sharpest conflict with each other. The Axelrods and Dans wanted to collaborate at all costs with those classes and parties from which came the greatest threat of danger to the revolution and to its first conquest, democracy.

It is especially astonishing to observe how this industrious man (Kautsky), by his tireless labor of peaceful and methodical writing during the four years of the World War, has torn one hole after another in the fabric of socialism. It is a labor from which socialism emerges riddled like a sieve, without a whole spot left in it. The uncritical indifference with which his followers regard this industrious labor of their official theoretician and swallow each of his new discoveries without so much as batting an eyelash, finds its only counterpart in the indifference with which the followers of Scheidemann and Co. look on while the latter punch socialism full of holes in practice. Indeed, the two labors completely supplement each other. Since the outbreak of the war, Kautsky, the official guardian of the temple of Marxism, has really only been doing in theory the same things which the Scheidemanns have been doing in practice, namely: 1) the International an instrument of peace; 2) disarmament, the League of Nations and nationalism; and finally 3) democracy *not* socialism.[4]

In this situation, the Bolshevik tendency performs the historic service of having proclaimed from the very beginning, and having followed with iron consistency, those tactics which alone could save democracy and drive the revolution ahead. All power exclusively in the hands of the worker and peasant masses, in the hands of the soviets—this was indeed the only way out of the difficulty into which the revolution had gotten; this was the sword stroke with which they cut the Gordian knot, freed the revolution from a narrow blind-alley and opened up for it an untrammeled path into the free and open fields.

The party of Lenin was thus the only one in Russia which grasped the true interest of the revolution in that first period. It was the element that drove the revolution forward, and, thus it was the only party which really carried on a socialist policy.

It is this which makes clear, too, why it was that the Bolsheviks, though they were at the beginning of the revolution a persecuted, slandered and hunted minority attacked on all sides, arrived within the shortest time to the head of the revolution and were able to bring under their banner all the genuine masses of the people: the urban proletariat, the army, the peasants, as well as the revolutionary elements of democracy, the left wing of the Socialist-Revolutionaries.[5]

The real situation in which the Russian Revolution found itself, narrowed down in a few months to the alternative: victory of the counter-revolution or dictatorship of the proletariat—Kaledin or Lenin. Such was the objective situation, just as it quickly presents itself in every revolution after the first intoxication is over, and as it presented itself in Russia as a result of the concrete, burning questions of peace and land, for which there was no solution within the framework of bourgeois revolution.

In this, the Russian Revolution has but confirmed the basic lesson of every great revolution, the law of its being, which decrees: either the revolution must advance at a rapid, stormy and resolute tempo, break down all barriers with an iron hand and place its goals ever farther ahead, or it is quite soon thrown backward behind its feeble point of departure and suppressed by counter-revolution. To stand still, to mark time on one spot, to be contented with the first goal it happens to reach, is never possible in revolution. And he who tries to apply the home-made wisdom derived from parliamentary battles between frogs and mice to the field of revolutionary tactics only shows thereby that the very psychology and laws of existence of revolution are alien to him and that all historical experience is to him a book sealed with seven seals.

Take the course of the English Revolution from its onset in 1642. There the logic of things made it necessary that the first feeble vacillations of the Presbyterians, whose leaders deliberately evaded a decisive battle with Charles I and victory over him, should inevitably be replaced by the Independents, who drove them out of Parliament and seized the power for themselves. And in the same way, within the army of the Independents, the lower petty-bourgeois mass of the soldiers, the Lilburnian "Levellers"[6] constituted the driving force of the entire Independent movement; just as, finally, the proletarian elements within the mass of the soldiers, the elements that went farthest, in their aspirations for social revolution and who found their expression in the Digger movement, constituted in their turn the leaven of the democratic party of the "Levellers."[7]

Without the moral influence of the revolutionary proletarian elements on the general mass of the soldiers, without the pressure of the democratic mass of the soldiers upon the bourgeois upper layers of the party of the Independents, there would have been no "purge" of the Long Parliament of its Presbyterians, nor any victorious ending to the war with the army of the Cavaliers and Scots, nor any trial and execution of Charles I, nor any abolition of the House of Lords and proclamation of a republic.

And what happened in the Great French Revolution? Here, after four years of struggle, the seizure of power by the Jacobins proved to be the only means of saving the conquests of the revolution, of achieving a republic, of smashing feudalism, of organizing a revolutionary defense against inner as well as outer foes, of suppressing the conspiracies of counter-revolution and spreading the revolutionary wave from France to all Europe.

Kautsky and his Russian coreligionists who wanted to see the Russian Revolution keep the "bourgeois character" of its first phase, are an exact counterpart of those German and English liberals of the preceding century who distinguished between the two well-known periods of the Great French Revolution: the "good" revolution of the first Girondin phase and the "bad" one after the Jacobin uprising. The liberal shallowness of this conception of history, to be sure, doesn't care to understand that, without the uprising of the "immoderate" Jacobins, even the first, timid and half-hearted achievements of the Girondin phase would soon have been buried under the ruins of the revolution, and that the real alternative to Jacobin dictatorship—as the iron course of historical development posed the question in 1793—was not "moderate" democracy, but . . . restoration of the Bourbons! The "golden mean" cannot be maintained in any revolution. The law of its nature demands a quick decision: either the locomotive drives forward full steam ahead to the most extreme point of the historical ascent, or it rolls back of its own weight again to the starting point at the bottom; and those who would keep it with their weak powers half way up the hill, it but drags down with it irredeemably into the abyss.

Thus it is clear that in every revolution only that party is capable of seizing the leadership and power which has the courage to issue the appropriate watch-words for driving the revolution ahead, and the courage to draw all the necessary conclusions from the situation. This makes clear, too, the miserable role of the Russian Mensheviks, the Dans, Tseretellis,[8] etc., who had enormous influence on the masses at the beginning, but, after their prolonged wavering and after they had fought with both hands and feet against taking over power and responsibility, were driven ignobly off the stage.

The party of Lenin was the only one which grasped the mandate and duty of a truly revolutionary party and which, by the slogan—"All power in the hands of the proletariat and peasantry"—insured the continued development of the revolution.

Thereby the Bolsheviks solved the famous problem of "winning a majority of the people," which problem has ever weighed on the German Social-Democracy like a nightmare. As bred-in-the-bone disciples of parliamentary cretinism, these German Social-Democrats have sought to apply to revolutions the home-made wisdom of the parliamentary nursery: in order to carry anything, you must first have a majority. The same, they say, applies to revolution: first let's become a "majority." The true dialectic of revolutions, however, stands this wisdom of parliamentary moles on its head: not through a majority to revolutionary tactics, but through revolutionary tactics to a majority—that is the way the road runs.

Only a party which knows how to lead, that is, to advance things, wins support in stormy times. The determination with which, at the decisive moment, Lenin and his comrades offered the only solution which could advance things ("all power in the hands of the proletariat and peasantry"), transformed them almost overnight from a persecuted, slandered, outlawed minority whose leader had to hide like Marat[9] in cellars, into the absolute master of the situation.

Moreover, the Bolsheviks immediately set as the aim of this seizure of power a complete, far-reaching revolutionary program: not the safeguarding of bourgeois democracy, but a dictatorship of the proletariat for the purpose of realizing socialism. Thereby they won for themselves the imperishable historic distinction of having for the first time proclaimed the final aim of socialism as the direct program of practical politics.

Whatever a party could offer of courage, revolutionary far-sightedness and consistency in an historic hour, Lenin, Trotsky and the other comrades have given in good measure. All the revolutionary honor and capacity which western Social-Democracy lacked was represented by the Bolsheviks. Their October uprising was not only the actual salvation of the Russian Revolution; it was also the salvation of the honor of international socialism.

### THE BOLSHEVIK LAND POLICY

The Bolsheviks are the historic heirs of the English Levellers and the French Jacobins. But the concrete task which faced them after the seizure of power was incomparably more difficult than that of their historical predecessors. (Importance of the agrarian question. Even in 1905. Then, in the Third Duma, the right-wing peasants! The peasant question and defense, the army.)

Surely the solution of the problem by the direct, immediate seizure and distribution of the land by the peasants was the shortest, simplest, most clean-cut formula to achieve two diverse things: to break down large land-ownership, and immediately to bind the peasants to the revolutionary government. As a political measure to fortify the proletarian socialist government, it was an excellent tactical move. Unfortunately, however, it had two sides to it; and the reverse side consisted in the fact that the direct seizure of the land by the peasants has in general nothing at all in common with socialist economy.

A socialist transformation of economic relationships presupposes two things so far as agrarian relationships are concerned:

In the first place, only the nationalization of the large landed estates, as the technically most advanced and most concentrated means and methods of agrarian production, can serve as the point of departure for the socialist mode of production on the land. Of course, it is not necessary to take away from the small peasant his parcel of land, and we can with confidence leave him to be won over voluntarily by the superior advantages of social production and to be persuaded of the advantages first of union in cooperatives and then finally of inclusion in the general socialized economy as a whole. Still, every socialist economic reform on the land must obviously begin with large and medium land-ownership. Here the property right must first of all be turned over to the nation, or to the state, which, with a socialist government, amounts to the same thing; for it is this alone which affords the possibility of organizing agricultural production in accord with the requirements of inter-related, large-scale socialist production.

Moreover, in the second place, it is one of the prerequisites of this transfor-mation that the separation between rural economy and industry, which is so characteristic of bourgeois society, should be ended in such a way as to bring about a mutual interpenetration and fusion of both, to clear the way for the planning of both agrarian and industrial production according to a unified point of view. Whatever individual form the practical economic arrangements may take—whether through urban communes, as some propose, or directed from a governmental center—in any event, it must be preceded by a reform introduced from the center, and that in turn must be preceded by the national-ization of the land. The nationalization of the large and middle-sized estates and the union of industry and agriculture—these are two fundamental require-ments of any socialist economic reform, without which there is no socialism.

That the Soviet government in Russia has not carried through these mighty reforms—who can reproach them for that! It would be a sorry jest indeed to demand or expect of Lenin and his comrades that, in the brief peri-od of their rule, in the center of the gripping whirlpool of domestic and for-eign struggles, ringed about by countless foes and opponents—to expect that under such circumstances they should already have solved, or even tackled, one of the most difficult tasks, indeed, we can safely say, *the* most difficult task of the socialist transformation of society! Even in the West, under the most favorable conditions, once we have come to power, we too will break many a tooth on this hard nut before we are out of the worst of the thousands of com-plicated difficulties of this gigantic task!

A socialist government which has come to power must in any event do one thing: it must take measures which lead in the direction of that funda-mental prerequisite for a later socialist reform of agriculture; it must at least avoid everything which may bar the way to those measures.

Now the slogan launched by the Bolsheviks, immediate seizure and distri-bution of the land by the peasants, necessarily tended in the opposite direc-tion. Not only is it not a socialist measure; it even cuts off the way to such measures; it piles up insurmountable obstacles to the socialist transformation of agrarian relations.

The seizure of the landed estates by the peasants according to the short and precise slogan of Lenin and his friends—"*Go and take the land for your-*

*selves"* —simply led to the sudden, chaotic conversion of large land ownership into peasant land ownership. What was created is not social property
but a new form of private property, namely, the breaking up of large estates
into medium and small estates, or relatively advanced large units of production into primitive small units which operate with technical means from the
time of the Pharaohs.

Nor is that all! Through these measures and the chaotic and purely arbitrary manner of their execution, differentiation in landed property, far from
being eliminated, was even further sharpened. Although the Bolsheviks
called upon the peasantry to form peasant committees so that the seizure of
the noble estates might, in some fashion, be made into a collective act, yet it is
clear that this general advice could not change anything in the real practice
and real relations of power on the land. With or without committees, it was
the rich peasants and usurers who made up the village bourgeoisie possess-
ing the actual power in their hands in every Russian village, that surely
became the chief beneficiaries of the agrarian revolution. Without being
there to see, any one can figure out for himself that in the course of the distribution of the land, social and economic inequality among the peasants was
not eliminated but rather increased, and that class antagonisms were further
sharpened. This shift of power, however, took place to the *disadvantage* of
the interests of the proletariat and of socialism. Formerly, there was only a
small caste of noble and capitalist landed proprietors and a small minority of
rich village bourgeoisie to oppose a socialist reform on the land. And their
expropriation by a revolutionary mass movement of the people is mere
child's play. But now, after the "seizure," as an opponent of any attempt at
socialization of agrarian production, there is an enormous, newly developed
and powerful mass of owning peasants who will defend their newly won
property with tooth and nail against every socialist attack. The question of
the future socialization of agrarian economy—that is, any socialization of production in general in Russia—has now become a question of opposition and
of struggle between the urban proletariat and the mass of the peasantry. How
sharp this antagonism has already become is shown by the peasant boycott of
the cities, in which they withhold the means of existence to carry on speculation in them, in quite the same way as the Prussian Junker does.

The French small peasant became the boldest defender of the Great French
Revolution which had given him land confiscated from the *emigrés*. As a
Napoleonic soldier, he carried the banner of France to victory, crossed all
Europe and smashed feudalism to pieces in one land after another. Lenin and

his friends might have expected a similar result from their agrarian slogan. However, now that the Russian peasant has seized the land with his own fist, he does not even dream of defending Russia and the revolution to which he owes the land. He has dug obstinately into his new possessions and abandoned the revolution to its enemies, the state to decay, the urban population to famine.

Lenin's speech on the necessity of centralization in industry, nationalization of banks, of trade and of industry. Why not of the land? Here, on the contrary, decentralization and private property.

Lenin's own agrarian program before the revolution was different. The slogan taken over from the much condemned Socialist-Revolutionaries, or rather, from the spontaneous peasant movement.

In order to introduce socialist principles into agrarian relations, the Soviet government now seeks to create agrarian communes out of proletarians, mostly city unemployed. But it is easy to see in advance that the results of these efforts must remain so insignificant as to disappear when measured against the whole scope of agrarian relations. After the most appropriate starting points for socialist economy, the large estates, have been broken up into small units, now they are trying to build up communist model production units out of petty beginnings. Under the circumstances these communes can claim to he considered only as experiments and not as a general social reform. Grain monopoly with bounties. Now, *post-festum*, they want to introduce the class war into the village!

The Leninist agrarian reform has created a new and powerful layer of popular enemies of socialism in the countryside, enemies whose resistance will be much more dangerous and stubborn than that of the noble large landowners.


## THE NATIONALITIES QUESTION

The Bolsheviks are in part responsible for the fact that the military defeat was transformed into the collapse and breakdown of Russia. Moreover, the Bolsheviks themselves have, to a great extent, sharpened the objective difficulties of this situation by a slogan which they placed in the foreground of their policies: the so-called right of self-determination of peoples, or—something which was really implicit in this slogan—the disintegration of Russia.

The formula of the right of the various nationalities of the Russian Empire to determine their fate independently "even to the point of the right of governmental separation from Russia," was proclaimed again with doctrinaire obstinacy as a special battle cry of Lenin and his comrades during their opposition against Miliukovist, and then Kerenskyan imperialism.[10] It constituted the axis of their inner policy after the October Revolution also. And it constituted the entire platform of the Bolsheviks at Brest-Litovsk,[11] all they had to oppose to the display of force by German imperialism.

One is immediately struck with the obstinacy and rigid consistency with which Lenin and his comrades stuck to this slogan, a slogan which is in sharp contradiction to their otherwise outspoken centralism in politics as well as to the attitude they have assumed toward other democratic principles. While they showed a quite cool contempt for the Constituent Assembly, universal suffrage, freedom of press and assemblage, in short, for the whole apparatus of the basic democratic liberties of the people which, taken all together, constituted the "right of self-determination" inside Russia, they treated the right of self-determination of peoples as a jewel of democratic policy for the sake of which all practical considerations of real criticism had to be stilled. While they did not permit themselves to be imposed upon in the slightest by the plebiscite for the Constituent Assembly in Russia,[12] a plebiscite on the basis of the most democratic suffrage in the world, carried out in the full freedom of a popular republic, and while they simply declared this plebiscite null and void on the basis of a very sober evaluation of its results, still they championed the "popular vote" of the foreign nationalities of Russia on the question of which land they wanted to belong to, as the true palladium of all freedom and democracy, the unadulterated quintessence of the will of the peoples and as the court of last resort in questions of the political fate of nations.

The contradiction that is so obvious here is all the harder to understand since the democratic forms of political life in each land, as we shall see, actually involve the most valuable and even indispensable foundations of socialist policy, whereas the famous "right of self-determination of nations" is nothing but hollow, petty-bourgeois phraseology and humbug.

Indeed, what is this right supposed to signify? It belongs to the ABC of socialist policy that socialism opposes every form of oppression, including also that of one nation by another.

If, despite all this, such generally sober and critical politicians as Lenin and Trotsky and their friends, who have nothing but an ironical shrug for every sort of utopian phrase such as disarmament, league of nations, etc., have in this case made a hollow phrase of exactly the same kind into their special hobby, this arose, it seems to us, as a result of some kind of policy made to order for the occasion. Lenin and his comrades clearly calculated that there was no surer method of binding the many foreign peoples within the Russian Empire to the cause of the revolution, to the cause of the socialist proletariat, than that of offering them, in the name of the revolution and of socialism, the most extreme and most unlimited freedom to determine their own fate. This was analogous to the policy of the Bolsheviks toward the Russian peasants, whose land-hunger was satisfied by the slogan of direct seizure of the noble estates and who were supposed to be bound thereby to the banner of the revolution and the proletarian government. In both cases, unfortunately, the calculation was entirely wrong.

While Lenin and his comrades clearly expected that, as champions of national freedom even to the extent of "separation," they would turn Finland, the Ukraine, Poland, Lithuania, the Baltic countries, the Caucasus, etc., into so many faithful allies of the Russian Revolution, we have witnessed the opposite spectacle. One after another, these "nations" used the freshly grant-ed freedom to ally themselves with German imperialism against the Russian Revolution as its mortal enemy, and, under German protection, to carry the banner of counter-revolution into Russia itself. The little game with the Ukraine at Brest, which caused a decisive turn of affairs in those negotiations and brought about the entire inner and outer political situation at present prevailing for the Bolsheviks, is a perfect case in point. The conduct of Fin-land, Poland, Lithuania, the Baltic lands, the peoples of the Caucasus, shows most convincingly that we are not dealing here with an exceptional case, but with a typical phenomenon.

To be sure, in all these cases, it was really not the "people" who engaged in these reactionary policies, but only the bourgeois and petty-bourgeois classes, who—in sharpest opposition to their own proletarian masses—per-verted the "national right of self-determination" into an instrument of their counter-revolutionary class policies. But—and here we come to the very heart of the question—it is in this that the utopian, petty-bourgeois character of this nationalistic slogan resides: that in the midst of the crude realities of class society and when class antagonisms are sharpened to the uttermost, it is simply converted into a means of bourgeois class rule. The Bolsheviks were to be taught, to their own great hurt and that of the revolution, that under the rule of capitalism there is no self-determination of peoples, that in a class society each class of the nation strives to "determine itself" in a different fash-ion, and that, for the bourgeois classes, the standpoint of national freedom is fully subordinated to that of class rule. The Finnish bourgeoisie, like the Ukrainian bourgeoisie, were unanimous in preferring the violent rule of Ger-many to national freedom, if the latter should be bound up with Bolshevism.

The hope of transforming these actual class relationships somehow into their opposite and of getting a majority vote for union with the Russian Revolution by depending on the revolutionary masses—if it was seriously meant by Lenin and Trotsky—represented an incomprehensible degree of optimism. And if it was only meant as a tactical flourish in the duel with the German politics of force, then it represented dangerous playing with fire. Even without German military occupation, the famous "popular plebiscite," supposing that it had come to that in the border states, would have yielded a result, in all probability, which would have given the Bolsheviks little cause for rejoicing; for we must take into consideration the psychology of the peasant masses and of great sections of the petty bourgeoisie, and the thousand ways in which the bourgeoisie could have influenced the vote. Indeed, it can be taken as an unbreakable rule in these matters of plebiscites on the national question that the ruling class will either know how to prevent them where it doesn't suit their purpose, or where they somehow occur, will know how to influence their results by all sorts of means, big and little, the same means which make it impossible to introduce socialism by a popular vote.

The mere fact that the question of national aspirations and tendencies toward separation were injected at all into the midst of the revolutionary struggle, and were even pushed into the foreground and made into the shibboleth of socialist and revolutionary policy as a result of the Brest peace, has served to bring the greatest confusion into socialist ranks and has actually destroyed the position of the proletariat in the border countries.

In Finland, so long as the socialist proletariat fought as a part of the closed Russian revolutionary phalanx, it possessed a position of dominant power: it had the majority in the Finnish parliament, in the army; it had reduced its own bourgeoisie to complete impotence, and was master of the situation within its borders.

Or take the Ukraine. At the beginning of the century, before the tomfoolery of "Ukrainian nationalism" with its silver rubles and its "Universals" and Lenin's hobby of an "independent Ukraine" had been invented, the Ukraine was the stronghold of the Russian revolutionary movement. From there, from Rostov, from Odessa, from the Donetz region, flowed out the first lava-streams of the revolution (as early as 1902–04) which kindled all South Russia into a sea of flame, thereby preparing the uprising of 1905. The same thing was repeated in the present revolution, in which the South Russian proletariat supplied the picked troops of the proletarian phalanx. Poland and the Baltic lands have been since 1905 the mightiest and most dependable hearths of revolution, and in them the socialist proletariat has played an outstanding role.

How does it happen then that in all these lands the counter-revolution suddenly triumphs? The nationalist movement, just because it tore the proletariat loose from Russia, crippled it thereby, and delivered it into the hands of the bourgeoisie of the border countries.

Instead of acting in the same spirit of genuine international class policy which they represented in other matters, instead of working for the most compact union of the revolutionary forces throughout the area of the Empire, instead of defending tooth and nail the integrity of the Russian Empire as an area of revolution and opposing to all forms of separatism the solidarity and inseparability of the proletarians in all lands within the sphere of the Russian Revolution as the highest command of politics, the Bolsheviks, by their hollow nationalistic phraseology concerning the "right of self-determination to the point of separation," have accomplished quite the contrary and supplied the bourgeoisie in all border states with the finest, the most desirable pretext, the very banner of the counter-revolutionary efforts. Instead of warning the proletariat in the border countries against all forms of separatism as mere bourgeois traps, they did nothing but confuse the masses in all the border countries by their slogan and delivered them up to the demagogy of the bourgeois classes. By this nationalistic demand they brought on the disintegration of Russia itself, pressed into the enemy's hand the knife which it was to thrust into the heart of the Russian Revolution.

To be sure, without the help of German imperialism, without "the German rifle butts in German fists," as Kautsky's *Neue Zeit* put it, the Luibynskys and other little scoundrels of the Ukraine, the Erichs and Mannerheims of Finland,[13] and the Baltic barons, would never have gotten the better of the socialist masses of the workers in their respective lands. But national separatism was the Trojan horse inside which the German "comrades," bayonet in hand, made their entrance into all those lands. The real class antagonisms and relations of military force brought about German intervention. But the Bolsheviks provided the ideology which masked this campaign of counter-revolution; they strengthened the position of the bourgeoisie and weakened that of the proletariat.

The best proof is the Ukraine, which was to play so frightful a role in the fate of the Russian Revolution. Ukrainian nationalism in Russia was something quite different from, let us say, Czech, Polish or Finnish nationalism in that the former was a mere whim, a folly of a few dozen petty-bourgeois intellectuals without the slightest roots in the economic, political or psychological relationships of the country; it was without any historical tradition, since the Ukraine never formed a nation or government, was without any national culture, except for the reactionary-romantic poems of Shevschenko. It is exactly as if, one fine day, the people living in the *Wasserkante* should want to found a new Low-German *(Plattdeutsche)* nation and government![14] And this ridiculous pose of a few university professors and students was inflated into a political force by Lenin and his comrades through their doctrinaire agitation concerning the "right of self-determination including etc." To what was at first a mere farce they lent such importance that the farce became a matter of the most deadly seriousness—not as a serious national movement for which, afterward as before, there are no roots at all, but as a shingle and rallying flag of counter-revolution! At Brest, out of this addled egg crept the German bayonets.

There are times when such phrases have a very real meaning in the history of class struggles. It is the unhappy lot of socialism that in this World War it was given to it to supply the ideological screens for counter-revolutionary policy. At the outbreak of the war, German Social-Democracy hastened to deck the predatory expedition of German imperialism with an ideological shield from the lumber-room of Marxism by declaring it to be a liberating expedition against Russian Tsarism, such as our old teachers (Marx and Engels) had longed for. And to the lot of the Bolsheviks, who were the very antipodes of our government socialists, did it fall to supply grist for the mill of counter-revolution with their phrases about self-determination of peoples; and thereby to supply not alone the ideology for the strangling of the Russian Revolution itself, but even for the plans for settling the entire crisis arising out of the World War.

We have good reason to examine very carefully the policies of the Bolsheviks in this regard. The "right of self-determination of peoples," coupled with the league of nations and disarmament by the grace of President Wilson, constitute the battle-cry under which the coming reckoning of international socialism with the bourgeoisie is to be settled. It is obvious that the phrases concerning self-determination and the entire nationalist movement, which at present constitute the greatest danger for international socialism, have experienced an extraordinary strengthening from the Russian Revolution and the Brest negotiations. We shall yet have to go into this platform thoroughly. The tragic fate of these phrases in the Russian Revolution, on the thorns of which the Bolsheviks were themselves destined to be caught and bloodily scratched, must serve the international proletariat as a warning and lesson.

And from all this there followed the dictatorship of Germany from the time of the Brest treaty to the time of the "supplementary treaty."[15] The two hundred expiatory sacrifices, in Moscow. From this situation arose the terror and the suppression of democracy.

## THE CONSTITUENT ASSEMBLY

Let us test this matter further by taking a few examples.

The well-known dissolution of the Constituent Assembly in November 1917 played an outstanding role in the policy of the Bolsheviks. This measure was decisive for their further position; to a certain extent, it represented a turning point in their tactics.

It is a fact that Lenin and his comrades were stormily demanding the calling of a Constituent Assembly up to the time of their October victory, and that the policy of dragging out this matter on the part of the Kerensky government constituted an article in the indictment of that government by the Bolsheviks and was the basis of some of their most violent attacks upon it. Indeed, Trotsky says in his interesting pamphlet, *From October to Brest-Litovsk,* that the October Revolution represented "the salvation of the Constituent Assembly" as well as of the revolution as a whole. "And when we said," he continues, "that the entrance to the Constituent Assembly could not be reached through the Preliminary Parliament of Tseretelli, but only through the seizure of power by the Soviets, we were entirely right."[16]

And then, after these declarations, Lenin's first step after the October Revolution was . . . the dissolution of this same Constituent Assembly, to which it was supposed to be an entrance. What reasons could be decisive for so astonishing a turn? Trotsky, in the above-mentioned pamphlet, discusses the matter thoroughly, and we will set down his argument here:

> While the months preceding the October Revolution were a time of leftward movement on the part of the masses and of an elemental flow of workers, soldiers and peasants toward the Bolsheviks, inside the Socialist-Revolutionary Party this process expressed itself as a strengthening of the left wing at the cost of the right. But within the list of party candidates of the Socialist-Revolutionaries, the old names of the right wing still occupied three fourths of the places. . . .
>
> Then there was the further circumstance that the elections themselves took place in the course of the first weeks after the October Revolution. The news of the change that had taken place spread rather slowly in concentric circles from the capital to the provinces and from the towns to the villages. The peasant masses in

many places had little notion of what went on in Petrograd and Moscow. They voted for "Land and Freedom," and elected as their representatives in the land committees those who stood under the banner of the *Narodniki*. Thereby, however, they voted for Kerensky and Avksentiev,[17] who had been dissolving these land committees and having their members arrested. . . . This state of affairs gives a clear idea of the extent to which the Constituent Assembly had lagged behind the development of the political struggle and the development of party groupings.

All of this is very fine and quite convincing. But one cannot help wondering how such clever people as Lenin and Trotsky failed to arrive at the conclusion which follows immediately from the above facts. Since the Constituent Assembly was elected long before the decisive turning point, the October Revolution,[18] and its composition reflected the picture of the vanished past and not of the new state of affairs, then it follows automatically that the outgrown and therefore still-born Constituent Assembly should have been annulled, and without delay, new elections to a new Constituent Assembly should have been arranged. They did not want to entrust, nor should they have entrusted, the fate of the revolution to an assemblage which reflected the Kerenskyan Russia of yesterday, of the period of vacillations and coalition with the bourgeoisie. Hence there was nothing left to do except to convoke an assembly that would issue forth out of the renewed Russia that had advanced further.

Instead of this, from the special inadequacy of the Constituent Assembly which came together in October, Trotsky draws a general conclusion concerning the inadequacy of any popular representation whatsoever which might come from universal popular elections during the revolution.

> Thanks to the open and direct struggle for governmental power, the laboring masses acquire in the shortest time an accumulation of political experience, and they climb rapidly from step to step in their political development. The bigger the country and the more rudimentary its technical apparatus, the less is the cumbersome mechanism of democratic institutions able to keep pace with this development.

Here we find the "mechanism of democratic institutions" as such called in question. To this we must at once object that in such an estimate of representative institutions there lies a somewhat rigid and schematic conception which is expressly contradicted by the historical experience of every revolutionary epoch. According to Trotsky's theory, every elected assembly reflects once and for all only the mental composition, political maturity and mood of its electorate just at the moment when the latter goes to the polling place. According to that, a democratic body is the reflection of the masses at the end of the electoral period, much as the heavens of Herschel always show us the heavenly bodies not as they are when we are looking at them but as they were at the moment they sent out their light-messages to the earth from the measureless distances of space. Any living mental connection between the representatives, once they have been elected, and the electorate, any permanent interaction between one and the other, is hereby denied.

Yet how all historical experience contradicts this! Experience demonstrates quite the contrary: namely, that the living fluid of the popular mood continuously flows around the representative bodies, penetrates them, guides them. How else would it be possible to witness, as we do at times in every bourgeois parliament, the amusing capers of the "people's representatives," who are suddenly inspired by a new "spirit" and give forth quite unexpected sounds; or to find the most dried-out mummies at times comporting themselves like youngsters and the most diverse little *Scheidemaennchen*[19] suddenly finding revolutionary tones in their breasts—whenever there is rumbling in factories and workshops and on the streets?

And is this ever-living influence of the mood and degree of political ripeness of the masses upon the elected bodies to be renounced in favor of a rigid scheme of party emblems and tickets in the very midst of revolution? Quite the contrary! It is precisely the revolution which creates by its glowing heat that delicate, vibrant, sensitive political atmosphere in which the waves of popular feeling, the pulse of popular life, work for the moment on the representative bodies in most wonderful fashion. It is on this very fact, to be sure, that the well-known moving scenes depend which invariably present themselves in the first stages of every revolution, scenes in which old reactionaries or extreme moderates, who have issued out of a parliamentary election by limited suffrage under the old regime, suddenly become the heroic and stormy spokesmen of the uprising. The classic example is provided by the famous "Long Parliament" in England, which was elected and assembled in 1642 and remained at its post for seven whole years and reflected in its internal life all alterations and displacements of popular feeling, of political ripeness, of class differentiation, of the progress of the revolution to its highest point, from the initial devout skirmishes with the Crown under a Speaker who remained on his knees, to the abolition of the House of Lords, the execution of Charles and the proclamation of the republic.

And was not the same wonderful transformation repeated in the French

Estates General, in the censorship-subjected parliament of Louis Philippe, and even—and this last, most striking example was very close to Trotsky—even in the Fourth Russian Duma which, elected in the Year of Grace 1909 under the most rigid rule of the counter-revolution, suddenly felt the glowing heat of the impending overturn and became the point of departure for the revolution?

All this shows that "the cumbersome mechanism of democratic institutions" possesses a powerful corrective—namely, the living movement of the masses, their unending pressure. And the more democratic the institutions, the livelier and stronger the pulse-beat of the political life of the masses, the more direct and complete is their influence—despite rigid party banners, outgrown tickets (electoral lists), etc. To be sure, every democratic institution has its limits and shortcomings, things which it doubtless shares with all other human institutions. But the remedy which Trotsky and Lenin have found, the elimination of democracy as such, is worse than the disease it is supposed to cure; for it stops up the very living source from which alone can come the correction of all the innate shortcomings of social institutions. That source is the active, untrammeled, energetic political life of the broadest masses of the people.

### THE QUESTION OF SUFFRAGE

Let's take another striking example: the right of suffrage as worked out by the Soviet government. It is not altogether clear what practical significance is attributed to this right of suffrage. From the critique of democratic institutions by Lenin and Trotsky, it appears that popular representation on the basis of universal suffrage is rejected by them on principle, and that they want to base themselves only on the soviets. Why, then, any general suffrage system was worked out at all is really not clear. It is also not known to us whether this right of suffrage was put in practice anywhere; nothing has been heard of any elections to any kind of popular representative body on the basis of it. More likely, it is only a theoretical product, so to speak, of diplomacy; but, as it is, it constitutes a remarkable product of the Bolshevist theory of dictatorship.

Every right of suffrage, like any political right in general, is not to be measured by some sort of abstract scheme of "justice," or in terms of any other bourgeois-democratic phrases, but by the social and economic relationships for which it is designed. The right of suffrage worked out by the Soviet government is calculated for the transition period from the bourgeois-capitalist to the socialist form of society, that is, it is calculated for the period of the proletarian dictatorship. But, according to the interpretation of this dictatorship which Lenin and Trotsky represent, the right to vote is granted only to those who live by their own labor and is denied to everybody else.

Now it is clear that such a right to vote has meaning only in a society which is in a position to make possible for all who want to work an adequate civilized life on the basis of one's own labor. Is that the case in Russia at present? Under the terrific difficulties which Russia has to contend with, cut off as she is from the world market and from her most important sources of raw materials, and under circumstances involving a terrific general uprooting of economic life and a rude overturn of productive relationships as a result of the transformation of property relationships in land and industry and trade—under such circumstances, it is clear that countless existences are quite suddenly uprooted, derailed without any objective possibility of finding any employment for their labor power within the economic mechanism. This applies not only to the capitalist and land-owning classes, but to the broad layer of the middle class also, and even to the working class itself. It is a known fact that the contraction of industry has resulted in a mass-scale return of the urban proletariat to the open country in search of a place in rural economy. Under such circumstances, a political right of suffrage on the basis of a general obligation to labor, is a quite incomprehensible measure. According to the main trend, only the exploiters are supposed to be deprived of their political rights. And, on the other hand, at the same time that productive labor powers are being uprooted on a mass scale, the Soviet government is often compelled to hand over national industry to its former owners, on lease, so to speak. In the same way, the Soviet government was forced to conclude a compromise with the bourgeois consumers cooperatives also. Further, the use of bourgeois specialists proved unavoidable. Another consequence of the same situation is that growing sections of the proletariat are maintained by the state out of public resources as Red Guardists, etc. In reality, broad and growing sections of the petty bourgeoisie and proletariat, for whom the economic mechanism provides no means of exercising the obligation to work, are rendered politically without any rights.

It makes no sense to regard the right of suffrage as a utopian product of fantasy, cut loose from social reality. And it is for this reason that it is not a serious instrument of the proletarian dictatorship. It is an anachronism, an anticipation of the juridical situation which is proper on the basis of an already completed socialist economy, but not in the transition period of the proletarian dictatorship.

As the entire middle class, the bourgeois and petty-bourgeois intelligentsia, boycotted the Soviet government for months after the October Revolution and crippled the railroad, post and telegraph, and educational and administrative apparatus, and, in this fashion, opposed the workers government, naturally enough all measures of pressure were exerted against it. These included the deprivation of political rights, of economic means of existence, etc., in order to break their resistance with an iron fist. It was precisely in this way that the socialist dictatorship expressed itself, for it cannot shrink from any use of force to secure or prevent certain measures involving the interests of the whole. But when it comes to a suffrage law which provides for the general disfranchisement of broad sections of society, whom it places politically outside the framework of society and, at the same time, is not in a position to make any place for them even economically within that framework, when it involves a deprivation of rights not as a concrete measure for a concrete purpose but as a general rule of long-standing effect, then it is not a necessity of dictatorship but a makeshift, incapable of being carried out in life. This applies alike to the soviets as the foundation, and to the Constituent Assembly and the general suffrage law.

The Bolsheviks designated the soviets as reactionary because their majority consisted of peasants (peasant and soldier delegates). After the Soviets went over to them, they became correct representatives of popular opinion. But this sudden change was connected only with the peace and land questions.[20]

But the Constituent Assembly and the suffrage law do not exhaust the matter. We did not consider above the destruction of the most important democratic guarantees of a healthy public life and of the political activity of the laboring masses: freedom of the press, the rights of association and assembly, which have been outlawed for all opponents of the Soviet regime. For these attacks (on democratic rights), the arguments of Trotsky cited above, on the cumbersome nature of democratic electoral bodies, are far from satisfactory. On the other hand, it is a well-known and indisputable fact that without a free and untrammelled press, without the unlimited right of association and assemblage, the rule of the broad mass of the people is entirely unthinkable.

### THE PROBLEM OF DICTATORSHIP

Lenin says: the bourgeois state is an instrument of oppression of the working class; the socialist state, of the bourgeoisie. To a certain extent, he says, it is only the capitalist state stood on its head. This simplified view misses the most essential thing: bourgeois class rule has no need of the political training and education of the entire mass of the people, at least not beyond certain narrow limits. But for the proletarian dictatorship that is the life element, the very air without which it is not able to exist.

"Thanks to the open and direct struggle for governmental power," writes Trotsky, "the laboring masses accumulate in the shortest time a considerable amount of political experience and advance quickly from one stage to another of their development."

Here Trotsky refutes himself and his own friends. Just because this is so, they have blocked up the fountain of political experience and the source of this rising development by their suppression of public life! Or else we would have to assume that experience and development were necessary up to the seizure of power by the Bolsheviks, and then, having reached their highest peak, became superfluous thereafter. (Lenin's speech: Russia is won for socialism!!!)

In reality, the opposite is true! It is the very giant tasks which the Bolsheviks have undertaken with courage and determination that demand the most intensive political training of the masses and the accumulation of experience.

Freedom only for the supporters of the government, only for the members of one party—however numerous they may be—is no freedom at all. Freedom is always and exclusively freedom for the one who thinks differently. Not because of any fanatical concept of "justice" but because all that is instructive, wholesome and purifying in political freedom depends on this essential characteristic, and its effectiveness vanishes when "freedom" becomes a special privilege.

The Bolsheviks themselves will not want, with hand on heart, to deny that, step by step, they have to feel out the ground, try out, experiment, test now one way now another, and that a good many of their measures do not represent priceless pearls of wisdom. Thus it must and will be with all of us when we get to the same point—even if the same difficult circumstances may not prevail everywhere.

The tacit assumption underlying the Lenin–Trotsky theory of the dictatorship is this: that the socialist transformation is something for which a ready-made formula lies completed in the pocket of the revolutionary party, which needs only to be carried out energetically in practice. This is, unfortunately—or perhaps fortunately—not the case. Far from being a sum of ready-made prescriptions which have only to be applied, the practical realization of socialism as an economic, social and juridical system is something which lies completely hidden in the mists of the future. What we possess in our program is nothing but a few main signposts which indicate the general direction in which to look for the necessary measures, and the indications are mainly negative in character at that. Thus we know more or less what we must eliminate at the outset in order to free the road for a socialist economy. But when it comes to the nature of the thousand concrete, practical measures, large and small, necessary to introduce socialist principles into economy, law and all social relationships, there is no key in any socialist party program or textbook. That is not a shortcoming but rather the very thing that makes scientific socialism superior to the utopian varieties. The socialist system of society should only be, and can only be, an historical product, born out of the school of its own experiences, born in the course of its realization, as a result of the developments of living history, which—just like organic nature of which, in the last analysis, it forms a part—has the fine habit of always producing along with any real social need the means to its satisfaction, along with the task simultaneously the solution. However, if such is the case, then it is clear that socialism by its very nature cannot be decreed or introduced by *ukase*. It has as its prerequisite a number of measures of force—against property, etc. The negative, the tearing down, can be decreed; the building up, the positive, cannot. New territory. A thousand problems. Only experience is capable of correcting and opening new ways. Only unobstructed, effervescing life falls into a thousand new forms and improvisations, brings to light creative force, itself corrects all mistaken attempts. The public life of countries with limited freedom is so poverty-stricken, so miserable, so rigid, so unfruitful, precisely because, through the exclusion of democracy, it cuts off the living sources of all spiritual riches and progress. (Proof: the year 1905 and the months from February to October 1917.) There it was political in character; the same thing applies to economic and social life also. The whole mass of the people must take part in it. Otherwise, socialism will be decreed from behind a few official desks by a dozen intellectuals.

Public control is indispensably necessary. Otherwise the exchange of experiences remains only with the closed circle of the officials of the new regime. Corruption becomes inevitable. (Lenin's words, Bulletin No. 29) Socialism in life demands a complete spiritual transformation in the masses degraded by centuries of bourgeois class rule. Social instincts in place of egotistical ones, mass initiative in place of inertia, idealism which conquers all suffering, etc., etc. No one knows this better, describes it more penetratingly; repeats it more stubbornly than Lenin. But he is completely mistaken in the means he employs. Decree, dictatorial force of the factory overseer, draconic penalties, rule by terror—all these things are but palliatives. The only way to a rebirth is the school of public life itself, the most unlimited, the broadest democracy and public opinion. It is rule by terror which demoralizes.

When all this is eliminated, what really remains? In place of the representative bodies created by general, popular elections, Lenin and Trotsky have laid down the soviets as the only true representation of the laboring masses. But with the repression of political life in the land as a whole, life in the soviets must also become more and more crippled. Without general elections, without unrestricted freedom of press and assembly, without a free struggle of opinion, life dies out in every public institution, becomes a mere semblance of life, in which only the bureaucracy remains as the active element. Public life gradually falls asleep, a few dozen party leaders of inexhaustible energy and boundless experience direct and rule. Among them, in reality only a dozen outstanding heads do the leading and an elite of the working class is invited from time to time to meetings where they are to applaud the speeches of the leaders, and to approve proposed resolutions unanimously—at bottom, then, a clique affair—a dictatorship, to be sure, not the dictatorship of the proletariat, however, but only the dictatorship of a handful of politicians, that is a dictatorship in the bourgeois sense, in the sense of the rule of the Jacobins (the postponement of the Soviet Congress from three-month periods to six-month period!) Yes, we can go even further: such conditions must inevitably cause a brutalization of public life: attempted assassinations, shooting of hostages, etc. (Lenin's speech on discipline and corruption.)

## DEMOCRACY AND DICTATORSHIP

The basic error of the Lenin–Trotsky theory is that they too, just like Kautsky, oppose dictatorship to democracy. "Dictatorship *or* democracy" is the way the question is put by Bolsheviks and Kautsky alike. The latter naturally decides in favor of "democracy," that is, of bourgeois democracy, precisely because he opposes it to the alternative of the socialist revolution. Lenin and Trotsky, on the other hand, decide in favor of dictatorship in contradistinction to democracy, and thereby, in favor of the dictatorship of a handful of persons, that is, in favor of dictatorship on the bourgeois model. They are two opposite poles, both alike being far removed from a genuine socialist policy. The proletariat, when it seizes power, can never follow the good advice of Kautsky, given on the pretext of the "unripeness of the country," the advice being to renounce the socialist revolution and devote itself to democracy. It cannot follow this advice without betraying thereby itself, the International, and the revolution. It should and must at once undertake socialist measures in the most energetic, unyielding and unhesitant fashion, in other words, exercise a dictatorship, but a dictatorship of the *class,* not of a party or of a clique—dictatorship of the class, that means in the broadest public form on the basis of the most active, unlimited participation of the mass of the people, of unlimited democracy.

"As Marxists," writes Trotsky, "we have never been idol worshippers of formal democracy." Surely, we have never been idol worshippers of formal democracy. Nor have we ever been idol worshippers of socialism or Marxism either. Does it follow from this that we may also throw socialism on the scrap-heap, á la Cunow, Lensch,[21] and Parvus, if it becomes uncomfortable for us? Trotsky and Lenin are the living refutation of this answer.

"We have never been idol worshippers of formal democracy." All that that really means is: We have always distinguished the social kernel from the political form of *bourgeois* democracy; we have always revealed the hard kernel of social inequality and lack of freedom hidden under the sweet shell of formal equality and freedom—not in order to reject the latter but to spur the working class into not being satisfied with the shell, but rather, by conquering political power, to create a socialist democracy to replace bourgeois democracy—not to eliminate democracy altogether.

But socialist democracy is not something which begins only in the promised land after the foundations of socialist economy are created; it does not come as some sort of Christmas present for the worthy people who, in the interim, have loyally supported a handful of socialist dictators. Socialist democracy begins simultaneously with the beginnings of the destruction of class rule and of the construction of socialism. It begins at the very moment of the seizure of power by the socialist party. It is the same thing as the dictatorship of the proletariat.

Yes, dictatorship! But this dictatorship consists in the *manner of applying democracy,* not in its *elimination,* in energetic, resolute attacks upon the well-entrenched rights and economic relationships of bourgeois society, without which a socialist transformation cannot be accomplished. But this dictatorship must be the work of the *class* and not of a little leading minority in the name of the class—that is, it must proceed step by step out of the active participation of the masses; it must be under their direct influence, subjected to the control of complete public activity; it must arise out of the growing political training of the mass of the people.

Doubtless the Bolsheviks would have proceeded in this very way were it not that they suffered under the frightful compulsion of the world war, the

German occupation and all the abnormal difficulties connected therewith, things which were inevitably bound to distort any socialist policy, however imbued it might be with the best intentions and the finest principles.

A crude proof of this is provided by the use of terror to so wide an extent by the Soviet government, especially in the most recent period just before the collapse of German imperialism, and just after the attempt on the life of the German ambassador. The commonplace to the effect that revolutions are not pink teas is in itself pretty inadequate.

Everything that happens in Russia is comprehensible and represents an inevitable chain of causes and effects, the starting point and end term of which are the failure of the German proletariat and the occupation of Russia by German imperialism. It would be demanding something superhuman from Lenin and his comrades if we should expect of them that under such circumstances they should conjure forth the finest democracy, the most exemplary dictatorship of the proletariat and a flourishing socialist economy. By their determined revolutionary stand, their exemplary strength in action, and their unbreakable loyalty to international socialism, they have contributed whatever could possibly be contributed under such devilishly hard conditions. The danger begins only when they make a virtue of necessity and want to freeze into a complete theoretical system all the tactics forced upon them by these fatal circumstances, and want to recommend them to the international proletariat as a model of socialist tactics. When they get in their own light in this way, and hide their genuine, unquestionable historical service under the bushel of false steps forced upon them by necessity, they render a poor service to international socialism for the sake of which they have fought and suffered; for they want to place in its storehouse as new discoveries all the distortions prescribed in Russia by necessity and compulsion—in the last analysis only by-products of the bankruptcy of international socialism in the present world war.

Let the German Government Socialists cry that the rule of the Bolsheviks in Russia is a distorted expression of the dictatorship of the proletariat. If it was or is such, that is only because it is a product of the behavior of the German proletariat, in itself a distorted expression of the socialist class struggle. All of us are subject to the laws of history, and it is only internationally that the socialist order of society can be realized. The Bolsheviks have shown that they are capable of everything that a genuine revolutionary party can contribute within the limits of the historical possibilities. They are not supposed to perform miracles. For a model and faultless proletarian revolution in an isolated land, exhausted by world war, strangled by imperialism, betrayed by the international proletariat, would be a miracle.

What is in order is to distinguish the essential from the non-essential, the kernel from the accidental excrescences in the policies of the Bolsheviks. In the present period, when we face decisive final struggles in all the world, the most important problem of socialism was and is the burning question of our time. It is not a matter of this or that secondary question of tactics, but of the capacity for action of the proletariat, the strength to act, the will to power of socialism as such. In this, Lenin and Trotsky and their friends were the *first*, those who went ahead as an example to the proletariat of the world; they are still the *only ones* up to now who can cry with Hutten: "I have dared!"

This is the essential and *enduring* in Bolshevik policy. In *this* sense theirs is the immortal historical service of having marched at the head of the international proletariat with the conquest of political power and the practical placing of the problem of the realization of socialism, and of having advanced mightily the settlement of the score between capital and labor in the entire world. In Russia the problem could only be posed. It could not be solved in Russia. And in *this* sense, the future everywhere belongs to "Bolshevism."

# PART FOUR

From Opposition to World War
to the Actuality of Revolution

# 13 — The Junius Pamphlet: The Crisis in German Social Democracy

EDITORS' NOTE: *The Crisis in German Social Democracy* was written between February and April 1915 when Luxemburg was in prison for opposing World War I. She published it under the pseudonym "Junius," evoking a name used to sign political lead articles in the German press in the 1760s. The pseudonym may also derive from Lucius Junius Brutus, a legendary figure who was said to have led the uprising that established the Roman Republic. Luxemburg had the work smuggled out of prison and it was first published in 1916 as a pamphlet in Zurich, Switzerland. Her critique of the collapse of European socialism in the face of world war proved enormously influential in reorientating the thought of those who were searching for a way to reconstitute a revolutionary Marxist perspective. Lenin, among other internationalists, favorably commented on it soon after its publication, although he also criticized it over its opposition to national self-determination. Many of the ideas in it became the basis of the political perspective of the Spartacus League and the German far left in the revolutionary upsurge of 1918–19. What follows is chapter 1 and excerpts of chapters 7 and 8 of the pamphlet, as translated by the Socialist Publication Society in New York in 1918.

## CHAPTER I

The scene has thoroughly changed. The six weeks' march to Paris has become world drama.[1] Mass murder has become a monotonous task, and yet the final solution is not one step nearer. Capitalist rule is caught in its own trap, and cannot ban the spirit that it has invoked.

Gone is the first mad delirium. Gone are the patriotic street demonstrations, the chase after suspicious looking automobiles, the false telegrams, the cholera-poisoned wells. Gone the mad stories of Russian students who hurl bombs from every bridge of Berlin, or Frenchmen flying over Nuremberg;[2] gone the excesses of a spy-hunting populace, the singing throngs, the coffee shops with their patriotic songs; gone the violent mobs, ready to denounce, ready to persecute women, ready to whip themselves into a delirious frenzy over every wild rumor; gone the atmosphere of ritual murder, the Kishinev air that left the policeman at the corner as the only remaining representative of human dignity.3

The show is over. The curtain has fallen on trains filled with reservists, as they pull out amid the joyous cries of enthusiastic maidens. We no longer see their laughing faces, smiling cheerily from the train windows upon a war-mad population. Quietly they trot through the streets, with their sacks upon their shoulders. And the public, with a fretful face, goes about its daily task.

Into the disillusioned atmosphere of pale daylight there rings a different chorus; the hoarse croak of the hawks and hyenas of the battlefield. Ten thousand tents, guaranteed according to specifications, 100,000 kilos of bacon, cocoa powder, coffee substitute—cash on immediate delivery. Shrapnel, drills, ammunition bags, marriage bureaus for war widows, leather belts, war orders—only serious propositions considered. And the cannon fodder that was loaded upon the trains in August and September is rotting on the battlefields of Belgium and the Vosges, while profits are springing, like weeds, from the fields of the dead.

Business is flourishing upon the ruins. Cities are turned into shambles, whole countries into deserts, villages into cemeteries, whole nations into beggars, churches into stables; popular rights, treaties, alliances, the holiest words and the highest authorities have been torn into scraps; every sovereign by the grace of God is called a fool, an unfaithful wretch, by his cousin on the other side;4 every diplomat calls his colleague in the enemy's country a desperate criminal; each government looks upon the other as the evil genius of its people, worthy only of the contempt of the world. Hunger revolts in Venetia, in Lisbon, in Moscow, in Singapore; pestilence in Russia, misery and desperation is everywhere.

Shamed, dishonored, wading in blood and dripping with filth, thus capitalist society stands. Not as we usually see it, playing the roles of peace and righteousness, of order, of philosophy, of ethics—but as a roaring beast, as an orgy of anarchy, as a pestilential breath, devastating culture and humanity—so it appears in all its hideous nakedness.

And in the midst of this orgy a world tragedy has occurred; the capitulation of the Social Democracy.5 To close one's eyes to *this* fact, to try to hide it, would be the most foolish, the most dangerous thing that the international proletariat could do. "The Democrat [i.e., the revolutionary middle-class],"  says Karl Marx, "emerges from the most shameful downfall as spotlessly as he went innocently into it. With the strengthened confidence that he must win, he is more than ever certain that he and his party need no new principles, that events and conditions must finally come to meet them." His mistakes are as gigantic as his problems. No firmly fixed plan, no orthodox ritual that holds good for all times shows him the path that he must travel. Historical experience is his only teacher, his Via Dolorosa[6] to freedom is covered not only with unspeakable suffering, but with countless mistakes. The goal of his journey, his final liberation, depends entirely upon the proletariat, on whether *it* understands to learn from *its* own mistakes. Self-criticism, cruel, unsparing criticism that goes to the very root of the evil is life and breath for the proletarian movement. The catastrophe into which the world has thrust the socialist proletariat is an unexampled misfortune for humanity. But socialism is lost only if the international proletariat is unable to measure the depths of the catastrophe and refuses to understand the lesson that it teaches.

The last forty-five years in the development of the labor movement are at stake. The present situation is a closing of its accounts, a summing-up of the items of half a century of work. In the grave of the Paris Commune lies buried the first phase of the European labor movement and the First International. Instead of spontaneous revolution, revolts, and barricades, after each of which the proletariat relapsed once more into its dull passiveness, there came the systematic daily struggle, the utilization of bourgeois parliamentarism, mass organization, the welding of the economic with the political struggle, of socialist ideals with the stubborn defense of most immediate interests. For the first time the cause of the proletariat and its emancipation were led by the guiding star of scientific knowledge. In place of sects and schools, Utopian undertakings and experiments in every country, each altogether and absolutely separate from each other, we found a uniform, international, theoretical basis that united the nations. The theoretical works of Marx gave to the working class of the whole world a compass by which to fix its tactics from hour to hour, in its journey toward the one unchanging goal.

The bearer, the defender, the protector of this new method was the German Social Democracy. The war of 1870[7] and the downfall of the Paris Commune had shifted the center of gravity of the European labor movement to Germany. Just as France was the classic country of the first phase of the proletarian class struggle, as Paris was the torn and bleeding heart of the European working class of that time, so the German working class became the vanguard of the second phase. By innumerable sacrifices in the form of agitational work it has built up the strongest, the model organization of the proletariat, has created the greatest press, has developed the most effective educational and propaganda methods. It has collected under its banners the most gigantic labor masses, and has elected the largest representative groups to its national parliament.

The German Social Democracy has been generally acknowledged to be the purest incarnation of Marxian Socialism. It has held and wielded a peculiar prestige as teacher and leader in the Second International: Friedrich Engels wrote in his famous foreword to Marx's *Class Struggles in France*: "Whatever may occur in other countries, the German Social Democracy occupies a particular place and, for the present at least, has therefore a particular duty to perform. The two million voters that it sends to the ballot boxes, and the young girls and women who stand behind them as non-voters, are numerically the greatest, the most compact mass, the most decisive force of the proletarian international army."[8] The German Social Democracy was, as the *Wiener Arbeiter-Zeitung* wrote on August 5, 1914, the jewel of the organization of the class-conscious proletariat.[9] In its footsteps the French, the Italian, and the Belgian Social Democracies, the labor movements of Holland, Scandinavia, Switzerland and United States followed more or less eagerly. The Slav nations, the Russians, and the Social Democrats of the Balkans looked up to the German movement in boundless, almost unquestioning admiration. In the Second International the German Social Democracy was the determining factor. In every Congress, in the meetings of the International Socialist Bureau,[10] everything waited upon the opinion of the German group.

Particularly in the fight against militarism and war the position taken by the German Social Democracy has always been decisive. "We Germans cannot accept that," was usually sufficient to determine the orientation of the International. Blindly confident, it submitted to the leadership of the much admired, mighty German Social Democracy. It was the pride of every socialist, the horror of the ruling classes of all countries.

And what happened in Germany when the great historical crisis came? The deepest fall, the mightiest cataclysm. Nowhere was the organization of the proletariat made so completely subservient to imperialism. Nowhere was the state of siege so uncomplainingly borne. Nowhere was the press so thoroughly gagged, public opinion so completely choked off; nowhere was the political and industrial class struggle of the working class so entirely abandoned as in Germany.

But the German Social Democracy was not only the strongest body, it was the thinking brain of the International as well. Therefore the process of self-analysis and appraisement must begin in its own movement, with its own case. It is in honor bound to lead the way to the rescue of international social-ism, to proceed with the unsparing criticism of its own shortcomings.

No other party, no other class in capitalist society can dare to expose its own errors, its own weaknesses before the whole world in the clear mirror of reason, for the mirror would reflect the historical fate that is hidden behind it. The working class can always look truth in the face even when this means bitterest self-accusation; for its weakness was but an error and the inexorable laws of history give it strength and assure its final victory.

This unsparing self-criticism is not only a fundamental necessity, but the highest duty of the working class as well. We have on board the highest treas-ure of humanity, and the proletariat is their ordained protector. While capi-talist society, shamed and dishonored, rushes through the bloody orgy to its doom, the international proletariat will gather the golden treasures that were allowed to sink to the bottom in the wild whirlpool of the world war in the moment of confusion and weakness.

One thing is certain. It is a foolish delusion to believe that we need only live through the war, as a rabbit hides under the bush to await the end of a thunder-storm to trot merrily off in his old accustomed gait when all is over. The world war has changed the condition of our struggle, and has changed us most of all. Not that the laws of capitalist development or the life and death conflict between capital and labor have been changed or minimized. Even now, in the midst of the war, the masks are falling, and the old well-known faces grinning at us. But evolution has received a mighty forward impetus through the outbreak of the imperialist volcano. The enormity of the tasks that tower before the socialist proletariat in the immediate future make the past struggles of the labor movement seem but a delightful idyll in comparison.

Historically the war is ordained to give to the cause of labor a mighty impetus. Marx, whose prophetic eyes foresaw so many historic events as they lay in the womb of the future, writes in *The Class Struggles in France* the fol-lowing significant passage:

> In France the middle class does what should normally be done by the industrial
> bourgeoisie [i.e., to fight for the democratic republic]; but who shall solve the
> problems of labor? They will not be solved in France. They will be proclaimed in
> France. They will nowhere be solved within national boundaries. Class war in
> France will revert into a world war. The solution will begin only when the world
> war has driven the proletariat into the leadership of that nation which controls the
> world market, to the leadership of England. The revolution that will here find, not

its end, but its organizatory beginning, is no short-lived one. The present generation is like the Jews who were led by Moses through the wilderness. Not only
must it conquer a new world, it must go down to make way for those who will be
better able to cope with its problems.[11]

This was written in 1850, at a time when England was the only capitalistically
developed nation, when the English proletariat was the best organized and
seemed destined through the industrial growth of its nation to take the leadership in the international labor movement. Read Germany instead of England, and the words of Karl Marx become an inspired prophecy of the
present world war. It is ordained to drive the German proletariat "to the leadership of the people, and thus to create the organizatory beginning of the
great international conflict between labor and capital for the political
supremacy of the world."

Have we ever had a different conception of the role to be played by the
working class in the great world war? Have we forgotten how we were wont
to describe the coming event, only a few short years ago? "Then will come
the catastrophe. All Europe will be called to arms, and sixteen to eighteen
million men, the flower of the nations, armed with the best instruments of
murder will make war upon each other. But I believe that behind this march
there looms the final crash. Not we, but they themselves will bring it. They
are driving things to the extreme, they are leading us straight into a catastrophe. They will harvest what they have sown. The *Götterdammerung*[12] of the
bourgeois world is at hand. Be sure of that. It is coming." Thus spoke Bebel,
the speaker of our group in the Reichstag in the Morocco debate.[13]

An official leaflet published by the Party, *Imperialism and Socialism*, that
was distributed in hundreds of thousands of copies only a few years ago,
closes with the words:

> Thus the struggle against militarism daily becomes more and more clearly a deci-
> sive struggle between capital and labor. War, high prices and capitalism—peace,
> happiness for all, Socialism! Yours is the choice. History is hastening onward
> toward a decision. The proletariat must work unceasingly at its world mission,
> must strengthen the power of its organization and the clearness of its understand-
> ing. Then, come what will, whether it will succeed, by its power, in saving human-
> ity from the horrible cruelties of the world war, or whether capitalism shall sink
> back into history, as it was born, in blood and violence, the historic moment will
> find the working class prepared, and preparedness is everything.

The official handbook for socialist voters in 1911, the date of the last Reichstag elections, contains the following comments on the expected world war:

> Do our rulers and our ruling classes dare to demand this awful thing of the people? Will not a cry of horror, of fury and of indignation fill the country and lead the people to put an end to this murder? Will they not ask: "For whom and for what? Are we insane that we should be treated thus or should tolerate such treatment?" He who dispassionately considers the possibility of a great European world war can come to no other conclusion.
>
> The next European war will be a game of *va-banque*,[14] whose equal the world has never seen before. It will be, in all probability, the last war.

With such words the Reichstag representatives won their 110 seats in the Reichstag.

When in the summer of 1911, the *Panther* made its spring to Agadir, and the noisy clamor of German imperialists brought Europe to the precipice of war, an international meeting in London, on the 4th of August, adopted the following resolution:

> The German, Spanish, English, Dutch and French delegates of labor organizations hereby declare their readiness to oppose every declaration of war with every means in their power. Every nationality here represented pledges itself, in accordance with the decisions of its national and international congresses to oppose all criminal machinations on the part of the ruling classes.

But when in November 1912, the International Peace Congress met at Basel, when the long train of labor representatives entered the Minster, a presentiment of the coming hour of fate made them shudder and the heroic resolve took shape in every breast.[15]

The cool, skeptical Victor Adler cried out:

> Comrades, it is most important that we here, at the common source of our strength, that we, each and every one of us take from hence the strength to do in his country what he can, through the forms and means that are at his disposal, to oppose this crime of war, and if it should be accomplished, if we should really be able to prevent war, let this be the cornerstone of our coming victory. That is the spirit that animates the whole International.
>
> And when murder and arson and pestilence sweep over civilized Europe—we can think of it only with horror and indignation, and protests ring from our

hearts. And we ask, are the proletarians of today really nothing but sheep to be led mutely to the slaughter?[16]

Troelstra spoke in the name of the small nations, in the name of the Belgians as well:[17]

> With their blood and with all that they possess the proletariat of the small nations swear their allegiance to the International in everything that it may decide to prevent war. Again we repeat that we expect, when the ruling classes of the large nations call the sons of the proletariat to arms to satiate the lust for power and the greed of their rulers, in the blood and on the lands of the small peoples, we expect that then the sons of the proletariat, under the powerful influence of their proletarian parents and of the proletarian press, will think thrice before they harm us, their friends, in the service of the enemies of culture.

And Jaures closed his speech, after the anti-war manifesto of the International Bureau had been read: "The International represents the moral forces of the world! And when the tragic hour strikes, when we must sacrifice ourselves, this knowledge will support and strengthen us. Not lightly, but from the bottom of our hearts we declare that we are ready for all sacrifices!"

It was like a Ruetli pledge.[18] The whole world looked toward the Minster of Basel, where the bells, slowly and solemnly, rang to the approaching great fight between the armies of labor and capital.

On September 3, 1912, the Social Democratic deputy, David,[19] spoke in the German Reichstag:

> That was the most beautiful hour of my life. That I here avow. When the chimes of the Minster rang in the long train of international Social Democrats, when the red flags were planted in the nave of the church about the altar, when the emissaries of the people were greeted by the peals of the organ that re-sounded the message of peace, that was an impression that I can never forget. . . .
>
> You must realize what it was that happened here. The masses have ceased to be will-less, thoughtless herds. That is new in the history of the world. Hitherto the masses have always blindly followed the lead of those who were interested in war, who drove the peoples at each other's throats to mass murder. That will stop. The masses have ceased to be the instruments, the yeomen of war profiteers.

A week before the war broke out, on July 26, 1914, the German party papers wrote:

We are no marionettes; we are fighting with all our might against a system that makes men the powerless tools of blind circumstances, against this capitalism that is preparing to change Europe, thirsty for peace, into a smoking battlefield. If destruction takes its course, if the determined will for peace of the German, of the international proletariat, that will find expression in the next few days in mighty demonstrations, should not be able to prevent the world war, then it must be at least, the last war, it must be the *Götterdammerung* of capitalism.

On July 30, 1914, the central organ of the German Social Democracy cried out:

The socialist proletariat rejects all responsibility for the events that are being precipitated by a ruling class that is blinded, and on the verge of madness. We know that for us new life will spring from the ruins. But the responsibility falls upon the rulers of today.

For them it is a question of existence!

*Die Weltgeschichte ist das Weltgericht!* [20]

And then came the awful, the incredible August 4, 1914.

Did it *have* to come? An event of such importance cannot be a mere accident. It must have its deep, significant, objective causes. But perhaps these causes may be found in the errors of the leader of the proletariat, the Social Democracy itself, in the fact that our readiness to fight has flagged, that our courage and our convictions have forsaken us. Scientific socialism has taught us to recognize the objective laws of historical development. Man does not make history of his own volition, but he makes history nevertheless. The proletariat is dependent in its actions upon the degree of righteousness to which social evolution has advanced. But again, social evolution is not a thing apart from the proletariat; it is in the same measure its driving force and its cause as well as its product and its effect. And though we can no more skip a period in our historical development than a man can jump over his shadow, it lies within our power to accelerate or to retard it.

Socialism is the first popular movement in the world that has set itself a goal and has established in the social life of a man a conscious thought, a definite plan, the free will of mankind. For this reason Friedrich Engels calls the final victory of the socialist proletariat a stride by humankind from the animal kingdom into the kingdom of liberty. This step, too, is bound by unalterable historical laws to the thousands of rungs of the ladder of the past with its tortuous sluggish growth. But it will never be accomplished, if the burning spark of the conscious will of the masses does not spring from the material conditions that have been built up by past development. Socialism will not fall as manna from heaven. It can only be won by a long chain of powerful struggles, in which the proletariat, under the leadership of the Social Democracy, will learn to take hold of the rudder of society to become instead of the powerless victim of history, its conscious guide.

Friedrich Engels once said, "Capitalist society faces a dilemma, either an advance to socialism or a reversion to barbarism."[21] What does a "reversion to barbarism" mean at the present stage of European civilization? We have read and repeated these words thoughtlessly without a conception of their terrible import. At this moment one glance about us will show us what a reversion to barbarism in capitalist society means. *This world war* means a reversion to barbarism. The triumph of imperialism leads to the destruction of culture, sporadically during a modern war, and forever, if the period of world wars that has just begun is allowed to take its damnable course to the last ultimate consequence. Thus we stand today, as Friedrich Engels prophesied more than a generation ago, before the awful proposition: Either the triumph of imperialism and the destruction of all culture, and, as in ancient Rome, depopulation, desolation, degeneration, a vast cemetery; or, the victory of socialism, that is, the conscious struggle of the international proletariat against imperialism, against its methods, against war. This is the dilemma of world history, its inevitable choice, whose scales are trembling in the balance awaiting the decision of the proletariat. Upon it depends the future of culture and humanity. In this war imperialism has been victorious. Its brutal sword of murder has dashed the scales, with overbearing brutality, down into the abyss of shame and misery. If the proletariat learns *from* this war and *in* this war to exert itself, to cast off its serfdom to the ruling classes, to become the lord of its own destiny, the shame and misery will not have been in vain.

The modern working class must pay dearly for each realization of its historic mission. The road to the Golgotha[22] of its class liberation is strewn with awful sacrifices. The June combatants,[23] the victims of the Commune, the martyrs of the Russian Revolution—an endless line of bloody shadows. They have fallen on the field of honor, as Marx wrote of the heroes of the Commune, to be enshrined forever in the great heart of the working class. Now millions of proletarians are falling on the field of dishonor, of fratricide, of self-destruction, the slave-song on their lips. And that too has not been spared us. We are like the Jews whom Moses led through the desert. But we are not lost, and we will be victorious if we have not forgotten how to learn. And if the modern leaders of the proletariat do not know how to learn, they will go down "to make room for those who will be more able to cope with the problems of a new world."

CHAPTER VII

"But since we have been unable to prevent the war, since it has come in spite of us, and our country is facing invasion, shall we leave our country defenseless! Shall we deliver it into the hands of the enemy? Does not Socialism demand the right of nations to determine their own destinies? Does it not mean that every people is justified, nay more, is in duty bound, to protect its liberties, its independence? When the house is on fire, shall we not first try to put out the blaze before stopping to ascertain the incendiary?"

These arguments have been repeated, again and again in defense of the attitude of the Social Democracy in Germany and in France.

Even in the neutral countries this argument has been used. Translated into Dutch we read for instance: "When the ship leaks must we not seek, first of all, to stop the hole?"

To be sure. Fie upon a people that capitulates before invasion and fie upon a party that capitulates before the enemy within.

But there is one thing that the fireman in the burning house has forgotten: that in the mouth of a Socialist, the phrase "defending one's fatherland" cannot mean playing the role of cannon fodder under the command of an imperialist bourgeoisie.

Is an invasion really the horror of all horrors, before which all class conflict within the country must subside as though spellbound by some supernatural witchcraft? According to the police theory of bourgeois patriotism and military rule, every evidence of the class struggle is a crime again the interests of the country because they maintain that it constitutes a weakening of the stamina of the nation. The Social Democracy has allowed itself to be perverted into this same distorted point of view. Has not the history of modern capitalist society shown that in the eyes of capitalist society, foreign invasion is by no means the unmitigated terror as it is generally painted; that on the contrary, it is a measure to which the bourgeoisie has frequently and gladly resorted as an effective weapon against the enemy within? Did not the Bourbons and the aristocrats of France invite foreign invasion against the Jacobins? Did not the Austrian counterrevolution in 1849 call out the French invaders against Rome, the Russian against Budapest? Did not the "Party of Law and Order" in France in 1850 openly threaten an invasion of the Cossacks in order to bring the National Assembly to terms?24 And was not the Bonaparte army released, and the support of the Prussian army against the Paris Commune assured, by the famous contract between Jules Favre, Thiers and Co., and Bismarck?[25] This historical evidence led Karl Marx, forty-five years ago, to expose the "national wars" of modern capitalist society as miserable frauds. In his famous address to the General Council of the International on the downfall of the Paris Commune, he said:

> That, after the greatest war of modern times the belligerent armies, the victor and the vanquished, should unite—for the mutual butchery of the proletariat—this incredible event proves, not as Bismarck would have us believe, the final overthrow of the new social power, but the complete disintegration of the old bourgeois society. The highest heroic accomplishment of which the old order is capable, is the national war. And this has now proved to be a fraud perpetrated by government for no other purpose than to put off the class struggle, a fraud that is bared as soon as the class struggle flares up in a civil war. Class rule can no longer hide behind a national uniform. The national governments are united against the proletariat.[26]

In capitalist history, invasion and class struggle are not opposites, as the official legend would have us believe, but one is the means and the expression of the other. Just as invasion is the true and tried weapon in the hands of capital against the class struggle, so on the other hand the fearless pursuit of the class struggle has always proven the most effective preventative of foreign invasions. On the brink of modern times are the examples of the Italian cities, Florence and Milan, with their century of bitter struggle against the Hohenstauffen. The stormy history of these cities, torn by inner conflicts, proves that the force and the fury of inner class struggles not only does not weaken the defensive powers of the community, but that on the contrary, from their fires shoot the only flames that are strong enough to withstand every attack from a foreign foe.

But the classic example of our own times is the great French Revolution. In Paris in 1793, the heart of France was surrounded by enemies. And yet Paris and France at that time did not succumb to the invasion of a stormy flood of European coalition; on the contrary, it welded its force in the face of the growing danger, to a more gigantic opposition. If France, at that critical time, was able to meet each new coalition of the enemy with a new miraculous and undiminished fighting spirit, it was only because of the impetuous loosening of the inmost forces of society in the great struggle of the classes of France. Today, in the perspective of a century, it is clearly discernible that only this intensification of the class struggle, that only the dictatorship of the French people and their fearless radicalism, could produce means and forces out of the soil of France, sufficient to defend and to sustain a newborn society

against a world of enemies, against the intrigues of a dynasty, against the trai-
torous machinations of the aristocrats, against the attempts of the clergy,
against the treachery of their generals, against the opposition of sixty departments and provincial capitals, and against the united armies and navies of
monarchical Europe. The centuries have proven that not the state of siege,
but relentless class struggle is the power that awakens the spirit of self-
sacrifice, the moral strength of the masses, that the class struggle is the best
protection and the best defense against a foreign enemy.

This same tragic *quid pro quo* victimized Social Democracy when it
based its attitude in this war upon the doctrine of the right of national self-
determination.

It is true that socialism gives to every people the right of independence
and the freedom of independent control of its own destinies. But it is a veritable perversion of socialism to regard present day capitalist society as the
expression of this self-determination of nations. Where is there a nation in
which the people have had the right to determine the form and conditions of
their national, political and social existence? In Germany the determination
of the people found concrete expression in the demands formulated by the
German revolutionary democrats of 1848; the first fighters of the German
proletariat, Marx, Engels, Lassalle, Bebel and Liebknecht, proclaimed and
fought for a united German Republic. For this ideal the revolutionary forces
in Berlin and in Vienna, in those tragic days of March, shed their heart's
blood upon the barricades. To carry out this program, Marx and Engels
demanded that Prussia take up arms against Tsarism. The foremost demand
made in the national program was for the liquidation of "the heap of organized decay, the Habsburg monarchy," as well as of two dozen other dwarf
monarchies within Germany itself. The overthrow of the German revolution,
the treachery of the German bourgeoisie to its own democratic ideals, led to
the Bismarck regime and to its creature, present day Greater Prussia, twenty-
five fatherlands under one helm, the German Empire. Modern Germany is
built upon the grave of the March Revolution[27] upon the wreckage of the
right of self-determination of the German people. The present war, supporting Turkey and the Hapsburg monarchy, and strengthening German military
autocracy is a second burial of the March revolutionists, and of the national
program of the German people. It is a fiendish jest of history that the Social
Democrats, the heirs of the German patriots of 1848, should go forth in this
war with the banner of "self-determination of nations" held aloft in their
hands. But, perhaps the third French Republic, with its colonial possessions

in four continents and its colonial horrors in two, is the expression of the self-determination of the French nation? Or the British nation, with its India, with its South African rule of a million whites over a population of five million colored people? Or perhaps Turkey, or the Empire of the Tsar?

Capitalist politicians, in whose eyes the rulers of the people and the ruling classes are the nation, can honestly speak of the "right of national self-determination" in connection with such colonial empires. To the Socialist, no nation is free whose national existence is based upon the enslavement of another people, for to him colonial peoples, too, are human beings, and, as such, parts of the national state. International Socialism recognizes the right of free independent nations with equal rights. But Socialism alone can create such nations, can bring self-determination of their peoples. This slogan of Socialism is like all its others, not an apology for existing conditions, but a guidepost, a spur for the revolutionary, regenerative, active policy of the proletariat. So long as capitalist states exist, i.e., so long as imperialistic world policies determine and regulate the inner and the outer life of a nation, there can be no "national self-determination" either in war or in peace.

In the present imperialistic milieu there can be no wars of national self-defense. Every socialist policy that depends upon this determining historic milieu, that is willing to fix its policies in the world whirlpool from the point  of view of a single nation is built upon a foundation of sand.

We have already attempted to show the background for the present conflict between Germany and her opponents. It was necessary to show up more clearly the actual forces and relations that constitute the motive power behind the present war, because this legend of the defense of the existence, the freedom and civilization of Germany plays an important part in the attitude of our group in the Reichstag and our Socialist press. Against this legend historical truth must be emphasized to show that this is a war that has been prepared by German militarism and its world-political ideas for years, that it was brought about in the Summer of 1914 by Austrian and German diplomacy, with a full realization of its import.

In a discussion of the general causes of the war, and of its significance, the question of the "guilty party" is completely beside the issue. Germany certainly has not the right to speak of a war of defense, but France and England have little more justification. They too, are protecting, not their national, but their world-political existence, their old imperialistic possessions, from the attacks of the German upstart. Doubtless the raids of German and Austrian imperialism in the Orient started the conflagration, but French imperialism, by devouring Morocco, and English imperialism, in its attempts to rape Mesopotamia, and all the other measures that were calculated to secure its rule of force in India, Russia's Baltic policies, aiming toward Constantinople, all of these factors have carried together and piled up, brand for brand, the firewood that feeds the conflagration. If capitalist armaments have played an important role as the mainspring that times the outbreak of the catastrophe, it was a competition of armaments in all nations. And if Germany laid the cornerstone for European competitive armaments by Bismarck's policy of 1870, this policy was furthered by that of the second Empire and by the military-colonial policies of the third Empire, by its expansions in East Asia and in Africa.

The French Socialists have some slight foundation for their illusion of "national defense," because neither the French government nor the French people entertained the slightest warlike desires in July 1914. "Today everyone in France is honestly, uprightly and without reservation for peace," insisted Jaurès in the last speech of his life, on the eve of the war when he addressed a meeting in the People's House in Brussels. This was absolutely true, and gives the psychological explanation for the indignation of the French Socialists when this criminal war was forced upon their country. But this fact was not sufficient to determine the Socialist attitude on the world war as an historic occurrence.

The events that bore the present war did not begin in July 1914 but reach back for decades. Thread by thread they have been woven together on the loom of an inexorable natural development until the firm net of imperialist world politics has encircled five continents. It is a huge historical complex of events, whose roots reach deep down into the Plutonic deeps of economic creation, whose outermost branches spread out and point away into a dimly dawning new world, events before whose all-embracing immensity, the conception of guilt and retribution, of defense and offense, sink into pale nothingness.

Imperialism is not the creation of any one or of any group of states. It is the product of a particular stage of ripeness in the world development of capital, an innately international condition, an indivisible whole, that is recognizable only in all its relations, and from which no nation can hold aloof at will. From this point of view only is it possible to understand correctly the question of "national defense" in the present war.

The national state, national unity and independence were the ideological shield under which the capitalist nations of central Europe constituted themselves in the past century. Capitalism is incompatible with economic and political divisions, with the accompanying splitting up into small states. It needs for its development large, united territories, and a state of mental and intellectual development in the nation that will lift the demands and needs of society to a plane corresponding to the prevailing stage of capitalist production, and to the mechanism of modern capitalist class rule. Before capitalism could develop, it sought to create for itself a territory sharply defined by national limitations. This program was carried out only in France at the time of the great revolution, for in the national and political heritage left to Europe by the feudal middle ages, this could be accomplished only by revolutionary measures. In the rest of Europe this nationalization, like the revolutionary movement as a whole, remained the patchwork of half-kept promises. The German empire, modern Italy, Austria-Hungary, and Turkey, the Russian Empire and the British world-empire, are all living proofs of this fact. The national program could play a historic role only so long as it represented the ideological expression of a growing bourgeoisie, lusting for power, until it had fastened its class rule, in some way or other, upon the great nations of central Europe and had created within them the necessary tools and conditions of its growth. Since then, imperialism has buried the old bourgeois democratic program completely by substituting expansionist activity irrespective of national relationships for the original program of the bourgeoisie in all nations. The national phrase, to be sure, has been preserved, but its real content, its function has been perverted into its very opposite. Today the nation is but a cloak that covers imperialistic desires, a battle cry for imperialistic rivalries, the last ideological measure with which the masses can be persuaded to play the role of cannon fodder in imperialistic wars.

This general tendency of present day capitalist policies determines the policies of the individual states as their supreme blindly operating law, just as the laws of economic competition determine the conditions under which the individual manufacturer shall produce. . . .

The great historical hour of the world war obviously demanded a unanimous political accomplishment, a broad-minded, comprehensive attitude that only the Social Democracy is destined to give. Instead, there followed on the part of the parliamentary representatives of the working class a miserable collapse. The Social Democracy did not adopt the wrong policy—it had no policy whatsoever. It has wiped itself out completely as a class partly with a world conception of its own, has delivered the country, without a word of protest, to the fate of imperialist war without to the dictatorship of the sword within. Nay more, it has taken the responsibility for the war upon its own shoulders. The declaration of the "Reichstag group" says: "We have voted only the means for our country's defense. We decline all responsibility for the war." But as a matter of fact, the truth lies in exactly the opposite direction. The means for "national defense," i.e., for imperialistic mass butchery by the armed forces of the military monarchy, were not voted by the Social Democracy. For the availability of the war credits did not in the least depend upon the Social Democracy. They, as a minority, stood against a compact three-quarters majority of the capitalist Reichstag. The Social Democratic group accomplished only one thing by voting in favor of the war credits. It placed upon the war the stamp of democratic fatherland defense, and supported and sustained the fictions that were propagated by the government concerning the actual conditions and problems of the war.

Thus the serious dilemma between the national interests and international solidarity of the proletariat, the tragic conflict that made our parliamentarians fall "with heavy heart" to the side of imperialistic warfare, was a mere figment of the imagination, a bourgeois nationalist fiction. Between the national interests and the class interests of the proletariat, in war and in peace, there is actually complete harmony. Both demand the most energetic prosecution of the class struggle, and the most determined insistence on the Social Democratic program.

But what action should the party have taken to give to our opposition to the war and to our war demands weight and emphasis? Should it have proclaimed a general strike? Should it have called upon the soldiers to refuse military service? Thus the question is generally asked. To answer with a simple yes or no, were just as ridiculous as to decide: "When war breaks out we will start a revolution." Revolutions are not "made" and great movements of the people are not produced according to technical recipes that repose in the pockets of the party leaders. Small circles of conspirators may organize a riot for a certain day and a certain hour, can give their small group of supporters the signal to begin. Mass movements in great historical crises cannot be initiated by such primitive measures. The best prepared mass strike may break down miserably at the very moment when the party leaders give the signal, may collapse completely before the first attack. The success of the great popular movements depends, aye, the very time and circumstance of their inception is decided, by a number of economic, political and psychological factors. The existing degree of tension between the classes, the degree of intelligence of the masses and the degree or ripeness of their spirit of resistance—all these factors, which are incalculable, are premises that cannot be artificially created by any party. That is the difference between the great historical upheavals, and the small show demonstrations that a well-disciplined party can carry out in times of peace, orderly, well-trained performances, responding obediently to the baton in the hands of the party leaders. The great historical hour itself creates the forms that will carry the revolutionary movements to a successful outcome, creates and improvises new weapons, enriches the arsenal of the people with weapons unknown and unheard of by the parties and their leaders.

What the Social Democracy as the advance guard of the class conscious proletariat should have been able to give was not ridiculous precepts and technical recipes, but a political slogan, clearness concerning the political problems and interests of the proletariat in times of war.

For what has been said of mass strikes in the Russian Revolution is equally applicable to every mass movement: "While the revolutionary period itself commands the creation and the computation and payment of the cost of a mass strike, the leaders of the Social Democracy have an entirely different mission to fill. Instead of concerning itself with the technical mechanism of the mass movement, it is the duty of the Social Democracy to undertake the political leadership even in the midst of a historical crisis. To give the slogan, to determine the direction of the struggle, to so direct the tactics of the political conflict that in its every phase and movement the whole sum of available and already mobilized active force of the proletariat is realized and finds expression in the attitude of the party, that the tactics of the Social Democracy in determination and vigor shall never be weaker than is justified by the actual power at its back, but shall rather hasten in advance of its actual power, that is the important problem of the party leadership in a great historical crisis. Then this leadership will become, in a sense, the technical leadership. A determined, consistent, progressive course of action on the part of the Social Democracy will create in the masses assurance, self-confidence and a fearless fighting spirit. A weakly vacillating course, based upon a low estimate of the powers of the proletariat, lames and confuses the masses. In the first case mass action will break out 'of its own accord' and 'at the right time'; in the second, even a direct call to action on the part of the leaders often remains ineffectual."

Far more important than the outward, technical form of the action is its political content. Thus the parliamentary stage, for instance, the only far reaching and internationally conspicuous platform, could have become a mighty motive power for the awakening of the people, had it been used by the Social Democratic representatives to proclaim loudly and distinctly, the interests, the problems and the demands of the working class.

"Would the masses have supported the Social Democracy in its attitude against the war?" That is a question that no one can answer. But neither is it an important one. Did our parliamentarians demand an absolute assurance of victory from the generals of the Prussian army before voting in favor of war credits? What is true of military armies is equally true of revolutionary armies. They go into the fight, wherever necessity demands it, without previous assurance of success. At the worst, the party would have been doomed, in the first few months of the war, to political ineffectuality.

Perhaps the bitterest persecutions would have been inflicted upon our party for its manly stand, as they were, in 1870, the reward of Liebknecht and Bebel. "But what does that matter," said Ignaz Auer,[28] simply, in his speech on the Sedanfeier in 1895. "A party that is to conquer the world must bear its principles aloft without counting the dangers that this may bring. To act differently is to be lost!"

"It is never easy to swim against the current," said the older Liebknecht,

and when the stream rushes on with the rapidity and the power of a Niagara it does not become easier. Our older comrades still remember the hatred of that year of greatest national shame, under the Socialist exception laws of 1878. At that time millions looked upon every Social Democrat as having played the part of a murderer and vile criminal in 1870; the Socialist had been in the eyes of the masses a traitor and an enemy. Such outbreaks of the "popular soul" are astounding, stunning, crushing in their elementary fury. One feels powerless, as before a higher power. It is a real *force majeure*. There is no tangible opponent. It is like an epidemic, in the people, in the air, everywhere.

The outbreak of 1878 cannot, however, be compared with the outbreak in 1870. This hurricane of human passions, breaking, bending, destroying all that stands in its way—and with it the terrible machinery of militarism, in fullest, most horrible activity; and we stand between the crushing iron wheels, whose touch means instant death, between iron arms, that threaten every moment to catch us. By the side of this elemental force of liberated spirits stood the most complete mechanism of the art of murder the world had hitherto seen; and all in the wildest activity, every boiler heated to the bursting point. At such a time, what is the will and the strength of the individual? Especially, when one feels that one represents a tiny minority, that one possesses no firm support in the people itself.

At that time our party was still in a period of development. We were placed before the most serious test, at a time when we did not yet possess the organization necessary to meet it. When the anti-socialist movement came in the year of shame of our enemies, in the year of honor for the Social Democracy, then we had already a strong, widespread organization. Each and every one of us was strengthened by the feeling that he possessed a mighty support in the organized movement that stood behind him, and no sane person could conceive of the downfall of the party.

So it was no small thing at that time to swim against the current. But what is to be done, must be done. And so we gritted our teeth in the face of the inevitable. There was no time for fear. . . . Certainly Bebel and I . . . never for a moment thought of the warning. We did not retreat. We had to hold our posts, come what might!

They stuck to their posts, and for forty years the Social Democracy lived upon the moral strength with which it had opposed a world of enemies.

The same thing would have happened now. At first we would perhaps have accomplished nothing but to save the honor of the proletariat and thousands upon thousands of proletarians who are dying in the trenches in mental darkness, would not have died in spiritual confusion, but with the one certainty that that which has been everything in their lives, the International, liberating Social Democracy, is more than the figment of a dream.

The voice of our party would have acted as a wet blanket upon the chauvinistic intoxication of the masses. It would have preserved the intelligent proletariat from delirium, would have it more difficult for imperialism to poison and to stupefy the minds of the people. The crusade against the Social Democracy would have awakened the masses in an incredibly short time.

And as the war went on, as the horror of endless massacre and bloodshed in all countries grew and grew, as its imperialistic hoof became more and more evident, as the exploitation by bloodthirsty speculators became more and more shameless, every live, honest, progressive and humane element in the masses would have rallied to the standard of the Social Democracy. The German Social Democracy would have stood in the midst of this mad whirlpool of collapse and decay, like a rock in a stormy sea, would have been the lighthouse of the whole International, guiding and leading the labor movements of every country of the earth. The unparalleled moral prestige that lay in the hands of the German Socialists would have reacted upon the Socialists of all nations in a very short time. Peace sentiments would have spread like wildfire and the popular demand for peace in all countries would have hastened the end of the slaughter, would have decreased the number of its victims.

The German proletariat would have remained the lighthouse keeper of Socialism and of human emancipation.

Truly this was a task not unworthy of the disciples of Marx, Engels and Lassalle.

## CHAPTER VIII

In spite of military dictatorship and press censorship, in spite of the downfall of the Social Democracy, in spite of fratricidal war, the class struggle arises from civil peace with elemental force. From the blood and smoke of the battlefields the solidarity of international labor arises. Not in weak attempts to artificially galvanize the old International, not in pledges rendered now and here, now there, to stand together after the war is over. No, here, in the war, out of the war, arises, with a new might and intensity, the recognition that the proletarians of all lands have one and the same interest. The world war, itself, utterly disproves the falsehoods it has created.

Victory or defeat? It is the slogan of all-powerful militarism in every belligerent nation, and like an echo, the Social Democratic leaders have adopted it. Victory or defeat has become the highest motive of the workers of Germany, of France, of England and of others, just as for the ruling classes of these nations. When the cannons thunder, all proletarian interests subside before the desire for victory of their own, i.e., for the defeat of the other countries. And yet, what can victory bring to the proletariat?

According to the official version of the leaders of the Social Democracy, that was so readily adopted without criticism, victory of the German forces would mean unhampered, boundless industrial growth for Germany; defeat, however, industrial ruin. On the whole, this conception coincides with that generally accepted during the war of 1870. But the period of capitalist growth that followed the war of 1870 was not caused by the war, but resulted rather from the political union of the various German states, even though this union took the form of the crippled figure that Bismarck established as the German Empire.

Here the industrial impetus came from this union, in spite of the war and the manifold reactionary hindrances that followed in its wake. What the victorious war itself accomplished was to firmly establish the military monarchy and Prussian junkerdom in Germany; the defeat of France led to the liquidation of its empire and the establishment of a republic. But today the situation is different in all of the nations in question. Today war does not function as a dynamic force to provide for rising young capitalism the indispensable political conditions for its "national" development. Modern war appears in this role only in Serbia, and there only as an isolated fragment. Reduced to its objective historic significance, the present world war as a whole is a competitive struggle of a fully developed capitalism for world supremacy, for the exploitation of the last remnant of non-capitalistic world zones. This fact gives to the war and its political after effects an entirely new character. The high stage of world-industrial development in capitalist production finds expression in the extraordinary technical development and destructiveness of the instruments of war, as in their practically uniform degree of perfection in all belligerent countries. The international organization of war industries is reflected in the military instability, that persistently brings back the scales, through all partial decisions and variations, to their true balance, and pushes a general decision further and further into the future. The indecision of military results, moreover, has the effect that a constant stream of new reserves, from the belligerent nations as well as from nations hitherto neutral, are sent to the front. Everywhere war finds material enough for imperialist desires and conflicts; creates new material to feed the conflagration that spreads out like a prairie fire. But the greater the masses, and the greater the number of nations that are dragged into this world war, the longer will it rage. All of these things together prove, even before any military decision of victory or defeat can be established, what the result of the war will be: the economic ruin of all participating nations, and, in a steadily growing measure, of the formally neutral nations, a phenomenon entirely distinct from the earlier wars of modern times. Every month of war affirms and augments this effect, and thus takes away the expected fruits of military victory for a decade to come. This, in the last analysis, neither victory nor defeat can alter; on the contrary, it makes a purely military decision altogether doubtful, and increases the likelihood that the war will finally end through a general and extreme exhaustion. But even a victorious Germany under such circumstances, even if its imperialist war agitators should succeed in carrying on the mass murder to the absolute destruction of their opponents, even if their most daring dreams should be fulfilled—would win but a Pyrrhic victory. A number of annexed territories, impoverished and depopulated, and a grinning ruin under its own roof, would be its trophies. Nothing can hide this, once the painted stage properties of financial war-bond transactions, and the Potemkin villages of an "unalterable prosperity" kept up by war orders, are pushed aside. The most superficial observer cannot but see that even the most victorious nation cannot count on war indemnities that will stand in any relation to the wounds that the war has inflicted. Perhaps they may see in the still greater economic ruin of the defeated opponents, England and France, the very countries with which Germany was most closely united by industrial relations, upon whose recuperation its own prosperity so much depends, a substitute and an augmentation for their victory. Such are the circumstances under which the German people, even after a victorious war, would be required to pay, in cold cash, the war bonds that were "voted" on credit by the patriotic parliament, i.e., to take upon their shoulders an immeasurable burden of taxation, and a strengthened military dictatorship as the only permanent tangible fruit of victory.

Should we now seek to imagine the worst possible effects of a defeat, we shall find that they resemble, line for line, with the exception of imperialistic annexations, the same picture that presented itself as the irrefutable consequence of victory: the effects of war today are so far reaching, so deeply rooted, that its military outcome can alter but little in its final consequences.

But let us assume, for the moment, that the victorious nation should find itself in the position to avoid the great catastrophe for its own people, should be able to throw the whole burden of the war upon the shoulders of its defeated opponent, should be able to choke off the industrial development of the latter by all sorts of hindrances. Can the German labor movement hope for successful development, so long as the activity of the French, English, Belgian and Italian laborers is hampered by industrial retrogression? Before 1870 the labor movements of the various nations grew independently of each other. The action of the labor movement of a single city often controlled the destinies of the whole labor movement. On the streets of Paris the battles of the working class were fought out and decided. The modern labor movement, its laborious daily struggle in the industries of the world, its mass organization, are based upon the cooperation of the workers in all capitalistically producing countries. If the truism that the cause of labor can thrive only upon a virile, pulsating industrial life applies, then it is true not only for Germany, but for France, England, Belgium, Russia, and Italy as well. And if the labor movement in all of the capitalist states of Europe becomes stagnant, if industrial conditions there result in low wages, weakened labor unions, and a diminished power of resistance on the part of labor, labor unionism in Germany cannot possibly flourish. From this point of view the loss sustained by the working class in its industrial struggle is in the last analysis identical, whether German capital be strengthened at the expense of the French or English capital at the expense of the German.

But let us investigate the political effects of the war. Here differentiation should be less difficult than upon the economic side, for the sympathies and the partisanship of the proletariat have always tended toward the side that defended progress against reaction. Which side, in the present war, represents progress, which side reaction? It is clear that this question cannot be decided according to the outward insignias that mark the political character of the belligerent nations as "democracy" and absolutism. They must be judged solely according to the tendencies of their respective world policies.

Before we can determine what a German victory can win for the German proletariat we must consider its effect upon the general status of political conditions all over Europe. A decisive victory for Germany would mean, in the first place, the annexation of Belgium, as well as of a possible number of territories in the East and West and a part of the French colonies; the sustaining of the Hapsburg monarchy and its aggrandizement by a number of new territories; finally the establishment of a fictitious "integrity" of Turkey, under a German protectorate, i.e., the conversion of Asia Minor and Mesopotamia, in one form or another, into German provinces. In the end this would result in the actual military and economic hegemony of Germany in Europe. Not because they are in accord with the desires of imperialist agitators are these consequences of an absolute German military victory to be expected, but because they are the inevitable outgrowth of the world-political position that Germany has adopted, of conflicting interests with England, France and Russia, in which Germany has been involved, and which have grown, during the course of the war, far beyond their original dimensions. It is sufficient to recall these facts to realize that they could under no circumstances establish a permanent world-political equilibrium. Though this war may mean ruin for all of its participants, and worse for its defeated, the preparations for a new world war, under England's leadership, would begin on the day after peace is declared, to shake off the yoke of Prussian-German militarism that would rest upon Europe and Asia. A German victory would be the prelude to an early second world war, and therefore, for this reason, but the signal for new feverish armaments, for the unleashing of the blackest reaction in every country, but particularly in Germany. On the other hand a victory of England or France would mean, in all likelihood, for Germany, the loss of a part of her colonies, as well as of Alsace-Lorraine, and certainly the bankruptcy of the world-political position of German militarism. But this would mean the disintegration of Austria-Hungary and the total liquidation of Turkey. Reactionary as both of these states are, and much as their disintegration would be in line with the demands of progressive development, in the present world-political milieu the disintegration of the Hapsburg monarchy and the liquidation of Turkey would mean the bartering of their peoples to the highest bidder—Russia, England, France, or Italy. This enormous redivision of the world and shifting of the balance of power in the Balkan states and along the Mediterranean would be followed inevitably by another in Asia: the liquidation of Persia and a redivision of China. This would bring the Anglo-Russian as well as the Anglo-Japanese conflict into the foreground of international politics, and may mean, in direct connection with the liquidation of the present war, a new world war, perhaps for Constantinople; would certainly bring it about, inescapably, in the immediate future. So a victory on this side, too, would lead to new, feverish armaments in all nations—defeated Germany, of course, at the head—and would introduce an era of undivided rule for militarism and reaction all over Europe, with a new war as its final goal.

So the proletariat, should it attempt to cast its influence into the balance on one side or the other, for progress or democracy, viewing the world policies in their widest application, would place itself between Scylla and Charybdis. Under the circumstances the question of victory or defeat becomes, for the European working class, in its political, exactly as in its economic aspects, a choice between two beatings. It is, therefore, nothing short of a dangerous madness for the French Socialists to believe that they can deal a death blow to militarism and imperialism, and clear the road for peaceful democracy, by overthrowing Germany. Imperialism, and its servant militarism, will reappear after every victory and after every defeat in this war. There can be but one exception: if the international proletariat, through its intervention, should overthrow all previous calculations.

The important lesson to be derived by the proletariat from this war is the one unchanging fact, that it can and must not become the uncritical echo of the "victory and defeat" slogan, neither in Germany nor in France, neither in England nor in Austria. For it is a slogan that has reality only from the point of view of imperialism, and is identical, in the eyes of every large power, with the question: gain or loss of world-political power, of annexations, of colonies, of military supremacy.

For the European proletariat as a class, victory or defeat of either of the two war groups would be equally disastrous. For war as such, whatever its military outcome may be, is the greatest conceivable defeat of the cause of the European proletariat. The overthrow of war, and the speedy forcing of peace, by the international revolutionary action of the proletariat, alone can bring to it the only possible victory. And this victory, alone, can truly rescue Belgium, can bring democracy to Europe.

For the class conscious proletariat to identify its cause with either military camp is an untenable position. Does that mean that the proletarian policies of the present day demand a return to the "status quo," that we have no plan of action beyond the fond hope that everything may remain as it was before the war? The existing conditions have never been our ideal, they have never been the expression of the self-determination of the people. And more, the former conditions cannot be reinstated, even if the old national boundaries should remain unchanged. For even before its formal ending this war has brought about enormous changes, in mutual recognition of one another's strength, in alliances and in conflict. It has sharply revised the relations of countries to one another, of classes within society, has destroyed so many old illusions and portents, has created so many new forces and new problems, that a return to the old Europe that existed before August 4, 1914, is as impossible as the return to prerevolutionary conditions, even after an unsuccessful revolution. The proletariat knows no going back and can only strive forward and onward, for a goal that lies beyond even the most newly created conditions. In this sense, alone, is it possible for the proletariat to oppose, with its policy, both camps in the imperialist world war.

But this policy cannot concern itself with recipes for capitalist diplomacy worked out individually by the Social Democratic parties, or even together in international conferences, to determine how capitalism shall declare peace in order to assure future peaceful and democratic development. All demands for complete or gradual disarmament, for the abolition of secret diplomacy, for the dissolution of the great powers into smaller national entities, and all other similar propositions, are absolutely Utopian so long as capitalist class rule remains in power. For capitalism, in its present imperialist course, to dispense with present-day militarism, with secret diplomacy, with the centralization of many national states, is so impossible that these postulates might, much more consistently, be united into the simple demand, "abolition of capitalist class society." The proletarian movement cannot reconquer the place it deserves by means of Utopian advice and projects for weakening, taming or quelling imperialism within capitalism by means of partial reforms. The real problem that the world war has placed before the socialist parties, upon whose solution the future of the working class movement depends, *is the readiness of the proletarian masses to act in the fight against imperialism.* The international proletariat suffers, not from a dearth of postulates, programs, and slogans, but from a lack of deeds, of effective resistance, of the power to attack imperialism at the decisive moment, just in times of war. It has been unable to put its old slogan, war against war, into actual practice. Here is the Gordian knot of the proletarian movement and of its future.

Imperialism, with all its brutal policy of force, with the incessant chain of social catastrophe that it itself provokes, is, to be sure, a historic necessity for the ruling classes of the present world. Yet nothing could be more detrimental than that the proletariat should derive, from the present war, the slightest hope or illusion of the possibility of an idyllic and peaceful development of capitalism. There is but one conclusion that the proletariat can draw from the historic necessity of imperialism. To capitulate before imperialism will mean to live forever in its shadow, off the crumbs that fall from the table of its victories.

Historic development moves in contradictions, and for every necessity puts its opposite into the world as well. The capitalist state of society is doubtless a historic necessity, but so also is the revolt of the working class against it. Capital is a historic necessity, but in the same measure is its grave digger, the socialist proletariat. The world rule of imperialism is a historic necessity, but likewise its overthrow by the proletarian international. Side by side the two historic necessities exist in constant conflict with each other. And ours is the necessity of socialism. Our necessity receives its justification with the moment when the capitalist class ceases to be the bearer of historic progress, when it becomes a hindrance, a danger, to the future development of society. The present world war has revealed that capitalism has reached this stage.

Capitalist desire for imperialist expansion, as the expression of its highest maturity in the last period of its life, has the economic tendency to change the whole world into capitalistically producing nations, to sweep away all superannuated, precapitalistic methods of production and society, to subjugate all the riches of the earth and all means of production to capital, to turn the laboring masses of the peoples of all zones into wage slaves. In Africa and in Asia, from the most northern regions to the southernmost point of South America and in the South Seas, the remnants of old communistic social groups, of feudal society, of patriarchal systems, and of ancient handicraft production are destroyed and stamped out by capitalism. Whole peoples are destroyed, ancient civilizations are levelled to the ground, and in their place profiteering in its most modern forms is being established. This brutal triumphant procession of capitalism through the world, accompanied by all the means of force, of robbery, and of infamy, has one bright phase: It has created the premises for its own final overthrow, it has established the capitalist world rule upon which, alone, the socialist world revolution can follow. This is the only cultural and progressive aspect of the great so-called works of culture that were brought to the primitive countries. To capitalist economists and politicians, railroads, matches, sewerage systems and warehouses are progress and culture. Of themselves such works, grafted upon primitive conditions, are neither culture nor progress, for they are too dearly paid for with the sudden economic and cultural ruin of the peoples who must drink down the bitter cup of misery and horror of two social orders, of traditional agricultural landlordism, of super-modern, super-refined capitalist exploitation, at one and the same time. Only as the material conditions for the destruction of capitalism and the abolition of class society, can the effects of the capitalist triumphal march through the world bear the stamp of progress in an historical sense. In this sense imperialism, too, is working in our interest.

The present world war is a turning point in the course of imperialism. For the first time the destructive beasts that have been loosed by capitalist Europe over all other parts of the world have sprung with one awful leap, into the midst of the European nations. A cry of horror went up through the world when Belgium, that priceless little jewel of European culture, when the venerable monuments of art in northern France, fell into fragments before the onslaughts of a blind and destructive force. The "civilized world" that has stood calmly by when this same imperialism doomed tens of thousands of Hereros to destruction; when the desert of Kalahari shuddered with the insane cry of the thirsty and the rattling breath of the dying; when in Putumayo, within ten years forty thousand human beings were tortured to death by a band of European industrial robber-barons, and the remnants of a whole people were beaten into cripples; when in China an ancient civilization was delivered into the hands of destruction and anarchy, with fire and slaughter, by the European soldiery; when Persia gasped in the noose of the foreign rule of force that closed inexorably about her throat; when in Tripoli the Arabs were mowed down, with fire and swords, under the yoke of capital while their civilization and their homes were razed to the ground. This civilized world has just begun to know that the fangs of the imperialist beast are deadly, that its breath is frightfulness, that its tearing claws have sunk deeper into the breasts of its own mother, European culture. And this belated recognition is coming into the world of Europe in the distorted form of bourgeois hypocrisy, that leads each nation to recognize infamy only when it appears in the uniform of the other. They speak of German barbarism, as if every people that goes out for organized murder did not change into a horde of barbarians! They speak of Cossack horrors, as if war itself were not the greatest of all horrors, as if the praise of human slaughter in a Socialist periodical were not mental Cossackdom in its very essence.

But the horrors of imperialist bestiality in Europe have had another effect, that has brought to the "civilized world" no horror stricken eyes, no agonized heart. It is the mass destruction of the European proletariat. Never has a war killed off whole nations; never, within the past century, has it swept over all of the great and established lands of civilized Europe. Millions of human lives were destroyed in the Vosges, in the Ardennes, in Belgium, in Poland, in the Carpathians and on the Save; millions have been hopelessly crippled. But nine-tenths of these millions come from the ranks of the working class of the cities and the farms. It is our strength, our hope that was mowed down there, day after day, before the scythe of death. They were the best, the most intelligent, the most thoroughly schooled forces of international socialism, the bearers of the holiest traditions, of the highest heroism, the modern labor movement, the vanguard of the whole world proletariat, the workers of England, France, Belgium, Germany and Russia who are being gagged and butchered in masses. Only from Europe, only from the oldest capitalist nations, when the hour is ripe, can the signal come for the social revolution that will free the nations. Only the English, the French, the Belgian, the German, the Russian, the Italian workers together, can lead the army of the exploited and oppressed. And when the time comes they alone can call capitalism to account for centuries of crime committed against primitive peoples; they alone can avenge its work of destruction over a whole world. But for the advance and victory of socialism we need a strong, educated, ready proletariat, masses whose strength lies in knowledge as well as in numbers. And these very masses are being decimated all over the world. The flower of our youthful strength, hundreds of thousands whose socialist education in England, in France, in Belgium, in Germany and in Russia was the product of decades of education and propaganda, other hundreds of thousands who were ready to receive the lessons of socialism, have fallen, and are rotting upon the battlefields. The fruit of the sacrifices and toil of generations is destroyed in a few short weeks, the choicest troops of the international proletariat are torn out by the life roots.

The bloodletting of the June battle laid low the French labor movement for a decade and a half. The bloodletting of the Commune massacre again threw it back for more than a decade. What is happening now is a massacre such as the world has never seen before, that is reducing the laboring population in all of the leading nations to the aged, the women and the maimed; a bloodletting that threatens to bleed white the European labor movement.

Another such war, and the hope of socialism will be buried under the ruins of imperialistic barbarism. That is more than the ruthless destruction of Liège and of the Rheims Cathedral.[29] That is a blow, not against capitalist civilization of the past, but against socialist civilization of the future, a deadly blow against the force that carries the future of mankind in its womb, that alone can rescue the precious treasures of the past over into a better state of society. Here capitalism reveals its death's head, here it betrays that it has sacrificed its historic right of existence, that its rule is no longer compatible with the progress of humanity.

But here is proof also that the war is not only a grandiose murder, but the suicide of the European working class. The soldiers of socialism, the workers of England, of France, of Germany, of Italy, of Belgium are murdering each other at the bidding of capitalism, are thrusting cold, murderous irons into each other's breasts, are tottering over their graves, grappling in each other's death-bringing arms.

"Deutschland, Deutschland über alles,"[30] "long live democracy," "long live the Tsar and slavery," "ten thousand tent cloths, guaranteed according to specifications," "hundred thousand pounds of bacon," "coffee substitute, immediate delivery". . . dividends are rising—proletarians falling, and with each one there sinks a fighter of the future, a soldier of the revolution, a savior of humanity from the yoke of capitalism, into the grave.

This madness will not stop, and this bloody nightmare of hell will not cease until the workers of Germany, of France, of Russia and of England will wake up out of their drunken sleep; will clasp each other's hands in brotherhood and will drown the bestial chorus of war agitators and the hoarse cry of capitalist hyenas with the mighty cry of labor, "Proletarians of all countries, unite!"

# 14 — Speeches and Letters on War and Revolution, 1918–19

EDITORS' NOTE: Only two months separated Luxemburg's release from jail in November 1918 and her murder by the counter-revolutionary *Freikorps* on January 15, 1919, upon the defeat of the armed uprising by the Spartacus League. These two months represent some of the most important and creative moments of Luxemburg's life, as she threw herself into the political maelstrom of the German Revolution of 1918 and its aftermath. Workers and Soldiers Councils sprang up around the country, many of which sought to advance the revolution beyond the confines of the reformist Social Democrats, who were now part of the government. The following five writings display the range of Luxemburg's efforts to prepare the ground for social revolution in this period. The first, "The Beginning," was published in *Die Rote Fahne* on November 18, 1918, shortly after Luxemburg was released from jail. The translation is by William D. Graf. The second, "The Socialization of Society," contains one of Luxemburg's fullest discussions of the nature of post-capitalist society. It originally appeared in *Die Junge Garde* of December 1918. The translation is by Dave Hollis. The third, "What Does the Spartacus League Want?" was first published in *Die Rote Fahne*, December 14, 1918. The translation is by Martin Nicolaus. The fourth, "Our Program and the Political Situation," is a speech Luxemburg gave to the founding conference of the German Communist Party on December 31, 1918, of which she and Karl Liebknecht were the major leaders. The translation of the following excerpts of the speech is by Dick Howard. The fifth and last, "Order Reigns in Berlin," was written after the failure of the uprising of the Spartacus League, as Luxemburg was forced into hiding. It is the last words that we have from her pen; she and Liebknecht were murdered by members of the Freikorps, a proto-fascist organization, on the following day. "Order Reigns in Berlin" was originally published in *Die Rote Fahne*, January 14, 1919. The translation is by Peggy Fallen Wright.

## 14A. THE BEGINNING

The revolution has begun. What is called for now is not jubilation at what has been accomplished, not triumph over the beaten foe, but the strictest self-criticism and iron concentration of energy in order to continue the work we have begun. For our accomplishments are small and the foe has not been beaten.

What has been achieved? The monarchy has been swept away, supreme governing power has been transferred into the hands of the workers' and soldiers' representatives.[1] But the monarchy was never the real enemy; it was only a facade, the frontispiece of imperialism. It was not the Hohenzollerns who unleashed the world war, set the four corners of the globe afire, and brought Germany to the brink of the abyss. The monarchy, like every bourgeois government, was the executive of the ruling classes. The imperialist bourgeoisie, the rule of the capitalist class—this is the criminal who must be held accountable for the genocide.

The abolition of the rule of capitalism, the realization of the social order of socialism—this and nothing less is the historical theme of the present revolution. This is a huge work which cannot be completed in the twinkling of an eye by a few decrees from above; it can be born only of the conscious action of the mass of workers in the cities and in the country, and brought successfully through the maze of difficulties only by the highest intellectual maturity and unflagging idealism of the masses of the people.

The path of the revolution follows clearly from its ends, its method follows from its task. All power in the hands of the working masses, in the hands of the workers' and soldiers' councils, protection of the work of revolution against its lurking enemies—this is the guiding principle of all measures to be taken by the revolutionary government.

Every step, every act by the government must, like a compass, point in this direction:

- Reelection and improvement of the local workers' and soldiers' councils so that the first chaotic and impulsive gestures of their formation are replaced by a conscious process of understanding the goals, tasks and methods of the revolution;
- Regularly scheduled meetings of these representatives of the masses and the transfer of real political power from the small committee of the Executive Council into the broader basis of the workers' and soldiers' councils;
- Immediate convocation of the national council of workers and soldiers in order to establish the proletariat of all Germany as a class, as a compact political power,

and to make them the bulwark and impetus of the revolution;

- Immediate organization not of the "farmers," but of the agrarian proletariat and smallholders who, as a class, have until now been outside the revolution;
- Formation of a proletarian Red Guard for the permanent protection of the revolution, and training of a workers' militia in order to prepare the whole proletariat to be on guard at all times;
- Suppression of the old organs of administration, justice, and the army of the absolutist militarist police state;
- Immediate confiscation of the dynastic property and possessions and of landed property as initial temporary measures to guarantee the people's food supply, since hunger is the most dangerous ally of the counterrevolution;
- Immediate convocation of the World Labor Congress in Germany in order to emphasize clearly and distinctly the socialist and international character of the revolution, for only in the International, in the world revolution of the proletariat, is the future of the German revolution anchored.

We have mentioned only the first necessary steps. What is the present revolutionary government doing?

It is leaving the administrative organs of the state intact from top to bottom, in the hands of yesterday's pillars of Hohenzollern absolutism and tomorrow's tools of the counterrevolution;

It is convening the constituent National Assembly, thus creating a bourgeois counterweight to the workers' and soldiers' representatives, and, by doing this, is diverting the revolution on to the track of a bourgeois revolution and spiriting away the socialist goals of the revolution;

It is doing nothing to demolish the continuing power of the capitalist class rule;

It is doing everything to placate the bourgeoisie, to proclaim the sacrosanctity of private property, to safeguard the inviolability of the distribution of capital;

It is allowing the active counterrevolution, which is dogging its every step, to go its own way without appealing to the masses, without loudly warning the people against it.

Law! Order! Order! Law! This is the cry resounding from all sides, in all proclamations of the government; this is the joyous echo from all the bourgeois camps. A strident outcry against the bogey of "anarchy" and "putschism"—the well-known infernal music of a bourgeoisie concerned for its fireproof safes, its property and its profits—is the loudest note of the day, and the revolutionary workers' and soldiers' government is placidly tolerating this general march to mount an offensive against socialism, indeed it is participating in it in word and deed.

The result of the first week of the revolution is as follows: in the state of the Hohenzollerns, not much has basically changed; the workers' and soldiers' government is acting as the deputy of the imperialist government that has gone bankrupt. All its acts and omissions are governed by fear of the working masses. Even before the revolution has acquired verve and momentum, its only vital force, namely its socialist and proletarian character, will have been spirited away.

Everything is in order. The reactionary state of the civilized world will not become a revolutionary people's state within twenty-four hours. Soldiers who yesterday, as gendarmes of the reaction, were murdering the revolutionary proletariat in Finland, Russia and the Ukraine, and workers who calmly allowed this to happen, have not become in twenty-four hours supporters of socialism or clearly aware of their goals.

The picture of the German revolution corresponds to the inner ripeness of the German situation. The government of the German revolution at its present stage is in the hands of Scheidemann and Ebert.[2] And the independents[3] who believe they can make socialism together with Scheidemann and Ebert, and who in *Die Freiheit* solemnly swear that one can form a "purely socialist government" with them, thus qualify themselves as the appropriate partners in the firm at this initial provisional stage.

But revolutions do not stand still. Their vital law is to advance rapidly, to outgrow themselves. It is already being driven forward by its inner contradictions from this initial stage. The situation can be comprehended as a beginning, as a condition untenable over the long haul. If the counterrevolution is not to gain the upper hand all along the line, the masses must be on their guard.

A beginning has been made. What happens next is not in the hands of the dwarfs who would hold up the course of the revolution, who would put a spoke in the wheel of world history. It is the realization of the ultimate goal of socialism which is on today's agenda of world history. The German revolution has now hit upon the path illuminated by this star. Step by step, through storm and stress, through battle and torment and misery and victory, it will reach its goal.

It must!

## 14B. THE SOCIALIZATION OF SOCIETY

The proletarian revolution that has now begun can have no other goal and no other result than the realization of socialism. The working class must above all else strive to get the entire political power of the state into its own hands. Political power, however, is for us socialists only a means. The end for which we must use this power is the fundamental transformation of the entire economic relations.

Currently all wealth—the largest and best estates as well as the mines, works and the factories—belongs to a few Junkers and private capitalists. The great mass of the workers only get from these Junkers[4] and capitalists a meager wage to live on for hard work. The enrichment of a small number of idlers is the aim of today's economy.

This state of affairs should be remedied. All social wealth, the land with all its natural resources hidden in its bowels and on the surface, and all factories and works must be taken out of the hands of the exploiters and taken into common property of the people. The first duty of a real workers' government is to declare by means of a series of decrees the most important means of production to be national property and place them under the control of society. Only then, however, does the real and most difficult task begin: the reconstruction of the economy on a completely new basis.

At the moment production in every enterprise is conducted by individual capitalists on their own initiative. What—and in which way—is to be produced, where, when and how the produced goods are to be sold is determined by the industrialist. The workers do not see to all this, they are just living machines who have to carry out their work.

In a socialist economy this must be completely different! The private employer will disappear. Then no longer is production aimed at the enrichment of one individual, but at delivering to the public at large the means of satisfying all its needs. Accordingly the factories, works and the agricultural enterprises must be reorganized according to a new way of looking at things:

Firstly: if production is to have the aim of securing for everyone a dignified life, plentiful food and providing other cultural means of existence, then the productivity of labor must be a great deal higher than it is now. The land must yield a far greater crop, the most advanced technology must be used in the factories, only the most productive coal and ore mines must be exploited, etc.

It follows from this that socialization will above all extend to the large enterprises in industry and agriculture. We do not need and do not want to dispossess the small farmer and craftsman eking out a living with a small plot of land or workshop. In time they will all come to us voluntarily and will recognize the merits of socialism as against private property.

Secondly: in order that everyone in society can enjoy prosperity, everybody must work. Only somebody who performs some useful work for the public at large, whether by hand or brain, can be entitled to receive from society the means for satisfying his needs. A life of leisure like most of the rich exploiters currently lead will come to an end. A general requirement to work for all who are able to do so, from which small children, the aged and sick are exempted, is a matter of course in a socialist economy. The public at large must provide forthwith for those unable to work—not like now with paltry alms but with generous provision, socialized child-raising, enjoyable care for the elderly, public health care for the sick, etc.

Thirdly, in accordance with same outlook, i.e. for the general well-being, one must sensibly manage and be economic with both the means of production and labor. The squandering that currently takes place wherever one goes must stop. Naturally, the entire war and munitions industries must be abolished since a socialist society does not need murder weapons and, instead, the valuable materials and human labor used in them must be employed for useful products. Luxury industries which make all kinds of frippery for the idle rich must also be abolished, along with personal servants. All the human labor tied up here will be found a more worthy and useful occupation.

If we establish in this way a nation of workers, where everybody works for everyone, for the public good and benefit, then work itself must be organized quite differently. Nowadays work in industry, in agriculture and in the office is mostly a torment and a burden for the proletarians. One only goes to work because one has to, because one would not otherwise get the means to live. In a socialist society, where everyone works together for their own well-being, the health of the workforce and its enthusiasm for work must be given the greatest consideration at work. Short working hours that do not exceed the normal capability, healthy workrooms, all methods of recuperation and a variety of work must be introduced in order that everyone enjoys doing their part. All these great reforms, however, call for a corresponding human material. Currently the capitalist, his works foreman or supervisor stands behind the worker with his whip. Hunger drives the proletarian to work in the factory or in the office, for the Junker or the big farmer. The employers take care that time is not frittered away nor material wasted, and that both good and efficient work is delivered.

In a socialist society the industrialist with his whip ceases to exist. The workers are free and equal human beings who work for their own well-being and benefit. That means by themselves, working on their own initiative, not wasting public wealth, and delivering the most reliable and meticulous work. Every socialist concern needs of course its technical managers who know exactly what they are doing and give the directives so that everything runs smoothly and the best division of labor and the highest efficiency is achieved. Now it is a matter of willingly following these orders in full, of maintaining discipline and order, of not causing difficulties or confusion.

In a word: the worker in a socialist economy must show that he can work hard and properly, keep discipline and give his best without the whip of hunger and without the capitalist and his slave-driver behind him. This calls for inner self-discipline, intellectual maturity, moral ardor, a sense of dignity and responsibility, a complete inner rebirth of the proletarian.

One cannot realize socialism with lazy, frivolous, egoistic, thoughtless and indifferent human beings. A socialist society needs human beings who, whatever their place, are full of passion and enthusiasm for the general well-being, full of self-sacrifice and sympathy for their fellow human beings, full of courage and tenacity in order to dare to attempt the most difficult.

We do not need, however, to wait perhaps a century or a decade until such a species of human beings develop. Right now, in the struggle, in the revolution, the mass of the proletarians learn the necessary idealism and soon acquire the intellectual maturity. We also need courage and endurance, inner clarity and self-sacrifice, to at all be able to lead the revolution to victory. In enlisting capable fighters for the current revolution, we are also creating the future socialist workers which a new order requires as its fundament. The working class youth is particularly well-qualified for these great tasks. As the future generation they will indeed, quite certainly, already constitute the real foundation of the socialist economy. It is already now its job to demonstrate that it is equal to the great task of being the bearer of the humanity's future. An entire old world still needs overthrowing and an entirely new one needs constructing. But we will do it young friends, won't we? We will do it! Just as it says in the song:

> We surely lack nothing, my wife, my child,
> Except all that which prospers through us,
> To be as free as the birds:
> Only the time!

## 14C. WHAT DOES THE SPARTACUS LEAGUE WANT?

### I

On November 9, workers and soldiers smashed the old German regime. The Prussian saber's mania of world rule had bled to death on the battlefields of France. The gang of criminals who sparked a worldwide conflagration and drove Germany into an ocean of blood had come to the end of its rope. The people—betrayed for four years, having forgotten culture, honesty, and humanity in the service of the Moloch, available for every obscene deed— awoke from its four-year-long paralysis, only to face the abyss.

On November 9, the German proletariat rose up to throw off the shameful yoke. The Hohenzollerns were driven out; workers' and soldiers' councils were elected.

But the Hohenzollerns were no more than the front men of the imperialist bourgeoisie and of the Junkers. The class rule of the bourgeoisie is the real criminal responsible for the World War, in Germany as in France, in Russia as in England, in Europe as in America. The capitalists of all nations are the real instigators of the mass murder. International capital is the insatiable god Baal, into whose bloody maw millions upon millions of steaming human sacrifices are thrown.

The World War confronts society with the choice: either continuation of capitalism, new wars, and imminent decline into chaos and anarchy, or abolition of capitalist exploitation.

With the conclusion of world war, the class rule of the bourgeoisie has forfeited its right to existence. It is no longer capable of leading society out of the terrible economic collapse which the imperialist orgy has left in its wake.

Means of production have been destroyed on a monstrous scale. Millions of able workers, the finest and strongest sons of the working class, slaughtered. Awaiting the survivors' return stands the leering misery of unemployment. Famine and disease threaten to sap the strength of the people at its roots. The financial bankruptcy of the state, due to the monstrous burdens of the war debt, is inevitable.

Out of all this bloody confusion, this yawning abyss, there is no help, no escape, no rescue other than socialism. Only the revolution of the world proletariat can bring order into this chaos, can bring work and bread for all, can end the reciprocal slaughter of the peoples, can restore peace, freedom, true culture to this martyred humanity. Down with the wage system! That is the slogan of the hour! Instead of wage labor and class rule there must be collective labor.

The means of production must cease to be the monopoly of a single class; they must become the common property of all. No more exploiters and exploited! Planned production and distribution of the product in the common interest. Abolition not only of the contemporary mode of production, mere exploitation and robbery, but equally of contemporary commerce, mere fraud.

In place of the employers and their wage slaves, free working comrades! Labor as nobody's torture, because everybody's duty! A human and honorable life for all who do their social duty. Hunger no longer the curse of labor, but the scourge of idleness!

Only in such a society are national hatred and servitude uprooted. Only when such a society has become reality will the earth no more be stained by murder. Only then can it be said: This war was the last.

In this hour, socialism is the only salvation for humanity. The words of the *Communist Manifesto* flare like a fiery *menetekel*[5] above the crumbling bastions of capitalist society: Socialism or barbarism![6]

## II

The establishment of the socialist order of society is the mightiest task which has ever fallen to a class and to a revolution in the history of the world. This task requires a complete transformation of the state and a complete overthrow of the economic and social foundations of society.

This transformation and this overthrow cannot be decreed by any bureau, committee, or parliament. It can be begun and carried out only by the masses of people themselves.

In all previous revolutions a small minority of the people led the revolutionary struggle, gave it aim and direction, and used the mass only as an instrument to carry its interests, the interests of the minority, through to victory. The socialist revolution is the first which is in the interests of the great majority and can be brought to victory only by the great majority of the working people themselves.

The mass of the proletariat must do more than stake out clearly the aims and direction of the revolution. It must also personally, by its own activity, bring socialism step by step into life.

The essence of socialist society consists in the fact that the great laboring mass ceases to be a dominated mass, but rather, makes the entire political and economic life its own life and gives that life a conscious, free, and autonomous direction.

From the uppermost summit of the state down to the tiniest parish, the proletarian mass must therefore replace the inherited organs of bourgeois class rule—the assemblies, parliaments, and city councils—with its own class organs—with workers' and soldiers' councils. It must occupy all the posts, supervise all functions, measure all official needs by the standard of its own class interests and the tasks of socialism. Only through constant, vital, reciprocal contact between the masses of the people and their organs, the workers' and soldiers' councils, can the activity of the people fill the state with a socialist spirit.

The economic overturn, likewise, can be accomplished only if the process is carried out by proletarian mass action. The naked decrees of socialization by the highest revolutionary authorities are by themselves empty phrases. Only the working class, through its own activity, can make the word flesh. The workers can achieve control over production, and ultimately real power, by means of tenacious struggle with capital, hand-to-hand, in every shop, with direct mass pressure, with strikes and with the creation of its own permanent representative organs.

From dead machines assigned their place in production by capital, the proletarian masses must learn to transform themselves into the free and independent directors of this process. They have to acquire the feeling of responsibility proper to active members of the collectivity which alone possesses ownership of all social wealth. They have to develop industriousness without the capitalist whip, the highest productivity without slave-drivers, discipline without the yoke, order without authority. The highest idealism in the interest of the collectivity, the strictest self-discipline, the truest public spirit of the masses are the moral foundations of socialist society, just as stupidity, egotism, and corruption are the moral foundations of capitalist society.

All these socialist civic virtues, together with the knowledge and skills necessary to direct socialist enterprises, can be won by the mass of workers only through their own activity, their own experience.

The socialization of society can be achieved only through tenacious, tireless struggle by the working mass along its entire front, on all points where labor and capital, people and bourgeois class rule, can see the whites of one another's eyes. The emancipation of the working class must be the work of the working class itself.

## III

During the bourgeois revolutions, bloodshed, terror, and political murder were an indispensable weapon in the hand of the rising classes.

The proletarian revolution requires no terror for its aims; it hates and despises killing. It does not need these weapons because it does not combat individuals but institutions, because it does not enter the arena with naive illusions whose disappointment it would seek to revenge. It is not the desperate attempt of a minority to mold the world forcibly according to its ideal, but the action of the great massive millions of the people, destined to fulfill a historic mission and to transform historical necessity into reality.

But the proletarian revolution is at the same time the death knell for all servitude and oppression. That is why all capitalists, Junkers, petty bourgeois, officers, all opportunists and parasites of exploitation and class rule rise up to a man to wage mortal combat against the proletarian revolution.

It is sheer insanity to believe that capitalists would good-humoredly obey the socialist verdict of a parliament or of a national assembly, that they would calmly renounce property, profit, the right to exploit. All ruling classes fought to the end, with tenacious energy, to preserve their privileges. The Roman patricians and the medieval feudal barons alike, the English cavaliers and the American slavedealers, the Walachian boyars[7] and the Lyonnais silk manufacturers—they all shed streams of blood, they all marched over corpses, murder, and arson, instigated civil war and treason, in order to defend their privileges and their power.

The imperialist capitalist class, as last offspring of the caste of exploiters, outdoes all its predecessors in brutality, in open cynicism and treachery. It defends its holiest of holies, its profit and its privilege of exploitation, with tooth and nail, with the methods of cold evil which it demonstrated to the world in the entire history of colonial politics and in the recent World War. It will mobilize heaven and hell against the proletariat. It will mobilize the peasants against the cities, the backward strata of the working class against the socialist vanguard; it will use officers to instigate atrocities; it will try to paralyze every socialist measure with a thousand methods of passive resistance; it will force a score of Vendées on the revolution;[8] it will invite the foreign enemy, the murderous weapons of Clemenceau, Lloyd George, and Wilson[9] into the country to rescue it—will turn the country into a smoking heap of rubble rather than voluntarily give up wage slavery.

All this resistance must be broken step by step, with an iron fist and ruthless energy. The violence of the bourgeois counterrevolution must be confronted with the revolutionary violence of the proletariat. Against the attacks, insinuations, and rumors of the bourgeoisie must stand the inflexible clarity of purpose, vigilance, and ever ready activity of the proletarian mass. Against the threatened dangers of the counterrevolution, the arming of the people and disarming of the ruling classes. Against the parliamentary obstructionist maneuvers of the bourgeoisie, the active organization of the mass of workers and soldiers. Against the omnipresence, the thousand means of power of bourgeois society, the concentrated, compact, and fully developed power of the working class. Only a solid front of the entire German proletariat, the south German together with the north German, the urban and the rural, the workers with the soldiers, the living, spirited identification of the German Revolution with the International, the extension of the German Revolution into a world revolution of the proletariat can create the granite foundations on which the edifice of the future can be constructed.

The fight for socialism is the mightiest civil war in world history, and the proletarian revolution must procure the necessary tools for this civil war; it must learn to use them—to struggle and to win.

Such arming of the solid mass of laboring people with all political power for the tasks of the revolution—that is the dictatorship of the proletariat and therefore true democracy. Not where the wage slave sits next to the capitalist, the rural proletarian next to the Junker in fraudulent equality to engage in parliamentary debate over questions of life or death, but where the million-headed proletarian mass seizes the entire power of the state in its calloused fist, like the god Thor his hammer, using it to smash the head of the ruling classes—that alone is democracy, that alone is not a betrayal of the people.

In order to enable the proletariat to fulfill these tasks, the Spartacus League demands:

### I  *As immediate measures to protect the Revolution*:

1. Disarmament of the entire police force and of all officers and nonproletarian soldiers; disarmament of all members of the ruling classes.
2. Confiscation of all weapons and munitions stocks as well as armaments factories by workers' and soldiers' councils.
3. Arming of the entire adult male proletarian population as a workers' militia. Creation of a Red Guard of proletarians as an active part of the militia for the constant protection of the Revolution against counterrevolutionary attacks and subversions.

4. Abolition of the command authority of officers and non-commissioned officers. Replacement of the military cadaver-discipline by voluntary discipline of the soldiers. Election of all officers by their units, with right of immediate recall at any time. Abolition of the system of military justice.
5. Expulsion of officers and capitulationists from all soldiers' councils.
6. Replacement of all political organs and authorities of the former regime by delegates of the workers' and soldiers' councils.
7. Establishment of a revolutionary tribunal to try the chief criminals responsible for starting and prolonging the war, the Hohenzollerrns,[10] Ludendorff, Hindenburg, Tirpitz,[11] and their accomplices, together with all the conspirators of counterrevolution.
8. Immediate confiscation of all foodstuffs to secure the feeding of the people.

## II *In the political and social realm:*

1. Abolition of all principalities; establishment of a united German Socialist Republic.
2. Elimination of all parliaments and municipal councils, and takeover of their functions by workers' and soldiers' councils, and of the latter's committees and organs.
3. Election of workers' councils in all Germany by the entire adult working population of both sexes, in the city and the countryside, by enterprises, as well as of soldiers' councils by the troops (officers and capitulationists excluded). The right of workers and soldiers to recall their representatives at any time.
4. Election of delegates of the workers' and soldiers' councils in the entire country to the central council of the workers' and soldiers' councils, which is to elect the executive council as the highest organ of the legislative and executive power.
5. Meetings of the central council provisionally at least every three months—with new elections of delegates each time—in order to maintain constant control over the activity of the executive council, and to create an active identification between the masses of workers' and soldiers' councils in the nation and the highest governmental organ. Right of immediate recall by the local workers' and soldiers' councils and replacement of their representatives in the central council, should these not act in the interests of their constituents. Right of the executive council to appoint and dismiss the people's commissioners as well as the central national authorites and officials.

6. Abolition of all differences of rank, all orders and titles. Complete legal and social equality of the sexes.
7. Radical social legislation. Shortening of the labor day to control unemployment and in consideration of the physical exhaustion of the working class by world war. Maximum working day of six hours.
8. Immediate basic transformation of the food, housing, health and educational systems in the spirit and meaning of the proletarian revolution.

### III  *Immediate economic demands:*

1. Confiscation of all dynastic wealth and income for the collectivity.
2. Repudiation of the state and other public debt together with all war loans, with the exception of sums of certain level to be determined by the central council of the workers' and soldiers' councils.
3. Expropriation of the lands and fields of all large and medium agricultural enterprises; formation of socialist agricultural collectives under unified central direction in the entire nation. Small peasant holdings remain in the possession of their occupants until the latters' voluntary association with the socialist collectives.
4. Expropriation by the council Republic of all banks, mines, smelters, together with all large enterprises of industry and commerce.
5. Confiscation of all wealth above a level to be determined by the central council.
6. Takeover of the entire public transportation system by the councils' Republic.
7. Election of enterprise councils in all enterprises, which, in coordination with the workers' councils, have the task of ordering the internal affairs of the enterprises, regulating working conditions, controlling production and finally taking over direction of the enterprise.
8. Establishment of a central strike commission which, in constant collaboration with the enterprise councils, will furnish the strike movement now beginning throughout the nation with a unified leadership, socialist direction and the strongest support by the political power of the workers' and soldiers' councils.

### IV  *International tasks:*

Immediate establishment of ties with the fraternal parties in other countries, in order to put the socialist revolution on an international footing and to shape and secure the peace by means of international brotherhood and the revolutionary uprising of the world proletariat.

### v  *That is what the Spartacus League wants!*

And because that is what it wants, because it is the voice of warning, of urgency, because it is the socialist conscience of the Revolution, it is hated, persecuted, and defamed by all the open and secret enemies of the Revolution and the proletariat.

Crucify it! shout the capitalists, trembling for their cashboxes.

Crucify it! shout the petty bourgeois, the officers, the anti-Semites, the press lackeys of the bourgeoisie, trembling for their fleshpots under the class rule of the bourgeoisie.

Crucify it! shout the Scheidemanns, who, like Judas Iscariot, have sold the workers to the bourgeoisie and tremble for their pieces of silver.

Crucify it! repeat like an echo the deceived, betrayed, abused strata of the working class and the soldiers who do not know that, by raging against the Spartacus League, they rage against their own flesh and blood.

In their hatred and defamation of the Spartacus League, all the counter-revolutionaries, all enemies of the people, all the antisocialist, ambiguous, obscure, and unclear elements are united. That is proof that the heart of the Revolution beats within the Spartacus League, that the future belongs to it.

The Spartacus League is not a party that wants to rise to power over the mass of workers or through them.

The Spartacus League is only the most conscious, purposeful part of the proletariat, which points the entire broad mass of the working class toward its historical tasks at every step, which represents in each particular stage of the Revolution the ultimate socialist goal, and in all national questions the interests of the proletarian world revolution.

The Spartacus League refuses to participate in governmental power with the lackeys of the bourgeoisie, with the Scheidemann-Eberts, because it sees in such collaboration a betrayal of the fundamentals of socialism, a strengthening of the counterrevolution, and a weakening of the Revolution.

The Spartacus League will also refuse to enter the government just because Scheidemann–Ebert are going bankrupt and the independents, by collaborating with them, are in a dead-end street.[3]

The Spartacus League will never take over governmental power except in response to the clear, unambiguous will of the great majority of the proletarian mass of all of Germany, never except by the proletariat's conscious affirmation of the views, aims, and methods of struggle of the Spartacus League.

The proletarian revolution can reach full clarity and maturity only by stages, step by step, on the Golgotha-path of its own bitter experiences in struggle, through defeats and victories.

The victory of the Spartacus League comes not at the beginning, but at the end of the Revolution: it is identical with the victory of the great million-strong masses of the socialist proletariat.

Proletarian, arise! To the struggle! There is a world to win and a world to defeat. In this final class struggle in world history for the highest aims of humanity, our slogan toward the enemy is: Thumbs on the eyeballs and knee in the chest![12]

## 14D. OUR PROGRAM AND THE POLITICAL SITUATION

Comrades! Our task today is to discuss and adopt a program. In undertaking this task we are not motivated solely by the formal consideration that yesterday we founded a new independent party and that a new party must formulate an official program. Great historical movements have been the determining causes of today's deliberations. The time has come when the entire Social Democratic socialist program of the proletariat has to be placed on a new foundation. Comrades! In so doing, we connect ourselves to the threads which Marx and Engels spun precisely seventy years ago in the *Communist Manifesto*. As you know, the *Communist Manifesto* dealt with socialism, with the realization of the ultimate goals of socialism as the immediate task of the proletarian revolution. This was the conception advocated by Marx and Engels in the Revolution of 1848; and it was what they conceived as the basis for international proletarian action as well. In common with all the leading spirits in the proletarian movement, both Marx and Engels then believed that the immediate task was the introduction of socialism. All that was necessary, they thought, was to bring about a political revolution, to seize the political power of the state in order to make socialism immediately enter the realm of flesh and blood. Subsequently, as you are aware, Marx and Engels undertook a thoroughgoing revision of this standpoint. In their joint Preface to the republication of the *Communist Manifesto* in 1872, they say:

> No special stress is to be laid on the revolutionary measures proposed at the end of Section II. That passage would, in many respects, be differently worded today.

In view of the gigantic strides of modern industry during the last twenty-five years and of the accompanying progress of the organization of the party of the working class; in view of the practical experience gained, first in the February revolution, and then, still more, in the Paris Commune, where the proletariat for the first time held political power for two months, this program has in some aspects been antiquated. One thing especially was proved by the Commune, namely, that the "working class cannot simply lay hold of the ready-made state machinery and wield it for its own purposes.[13]

What is the actual wording of the passage which is said to be dated? It reads as follows:

The proletariat will use its political supremacy to gradually wrest all capital from the bourgeoisie; to centralize all instruments of production in the hands of the state, i.e., of the proletariat organized as the ruling class; and to increase the total of productive forces as rapidly as possible.

Of course, in the beginning this can only be effected by means of despotic interference into property rights and into the conditions of bourgeois production; by measures, therefore, which appear economically insufficient and untenable, but which, in the course of the movement, go beyond themselves, necessitate further inroads into the old social order, and are unavoidable as a means of revolutionizing the whole mode of production.

The measures will, of course, be different in different countries.

Nevertheless, in the most advanced countries, the following will be generally applicable:

1   Abolition of landed property and application of all land rents to public purposes.
2   Heavy progressive taxes.
3   Abolition of the right of inheritance.
4   Confiscation of the property of all emigrants and rebels.
5   Centralization of credit in the hands of the state by means of a national bank with state capital and an exclusive monopoly.
6   Centralization of the means of communication and transport in the hands of the state.
7   Increase in the number of factories and instruments of production owned by the state; the bringing into cultivation of waste lands, and the improvement of the soil generally, in accordance with a social plan.

8   Equal obligation upon all to labor. Establishment of industrial armies, especially for agriculture.

9   Unification of agricultural and manufacturing industries; gradual abolition of the distinction between town and country.

10  Free education for all children in public schools. Abolition of children's factory labor in its present form. Unification of education with industrial production, etc.[14]

As you see, with a few variations, these are the tasks that confront us today: the introduction, the realization of socialism. Between the time when the above program was formulated and the present moment, there have intervened seventy years of capitalist development, and the dialectical movement of history has brought us back to the conception which Marx and Engels had abandoned in 1872 as erroneous. At that time, there were good reasons for believing that their earlier views had been wrong. The further development of capital has, however, led to the fact that what was incorrect in 1872 has become truth today, so that our immediate task today is to fulfill what Marx and Engels thought they would have to accomplish in 1848. But between that point in the development, that beginning, and our own views and our immediate task, there lies the whole development not only of capitalism but also of the socialist labor movement, above all in Germany as the leading land of the modern proletariat. This development has taken a peculiar form.

When, after the disillusionments of the Revolution of 1848, Marx and Engels had given up the idea that the proletariat could immediately realize socialism, there came into existence in all countries Social Democratic socialist parties inspired with very different conceptions. The immediate task of these parties was declared to be detail work, the petty daily struggle in the political and economic realms, in order, by degrees, to form the armies of the proletariat which would be ready to realize socialism when capitalist development had matured. The socialist program was thereby established upon an utterly different foundation, and in Germany the change took a very typical form. Until the collapse of August 4, 1914, German Social Democracy took its stand upon the Erfurt Program, by which the so-called immediate minimal aims were placed in the forefront, while socialism was no more than a distant guiding star, the ultimate goal. Far more important, however, than what is written in a program is the way in which that program is interpreted in action. From this point of view, great importance must be attached to one of the historical documents of our labor movement, to the Preface written by

Friedrich Engels to the 1895 republication of Marx's *Class Struggles* in France. It is not on mere historical grounds that I now reopen this question. The matter is one of extreme immediacy. It has become our historical duty today to replace our program upon the foundation laid by Marx and Engels in 1848. In view of the changes brought about by historical development, it is our duty to undertake a deliberate revision of the views that guided German Social Democracy until the collapse of August 4. This revision must be officially undertaken today.

Comrades! How did Engels envisage the question in that famous Preface to Marx's *Class Struggles* in France, written in 1895, [twelve years] after the death of Marx? First of all, looking back upon the year 1848, he showed that the belief that the socialist revolution was imminent had become obsolete. He continued as follows:

> History has shown that we, and those who thought like us, were all mistaken. It has shown that the state of economic development on the continent was then far from being ripe for the abolition of capitalist production. It has proved this by the economic revolution which since 1848 has taken place all over the continent. Large-scale industry has been established in France, Austria-Hungary, Poland, and, recently, in Russia. Germany has become a first-rank industrial country. All these changes have taken place upon a capitalist foundation, a foundation which therefore in the year 1848 was still capable of an enormous extension.[15]

After summing up the changes which had occurred in the intervening period, Engels turns to the immediate tasks of the party in Germany:

> As Marx predicted, the war of 1870–1871 and the defeat of the Commune provisionally shifted the center of gravity of the European labor movement from France to Germany. Naturally, many years had to elapse before France could recover from the bloodletting of May 1871.[16] In Germany, on the other hand, in the hothouse atmosphere produced by the influx of the French billions, industry was developing by leaps and bounds. Even more rapid and more enduring was the growth of Social Democracy. Thanks to the agreement in virtue of which the German workers have been able to avail themselves of the universal suffrage introduced in 1866, the astounding growth of the party has been demonstrated to all the world by the testimony of figures whose signficance no one can deny.[17]

Thereupon followed the famous enumeration showing the growth of the party vote in election after election until the figures swelled to millions. From this progress, Engels drew the following conclusion:

> The successful employment of the parliamentary vote, however, entailed an entirely new mode of struggle by the proletariat, and this new method has undergone rapid development. It has been discovered that the political institutions in which the domination of the bourgeoisie is organized offer a fulcrum by means of which the proletariat can combat these very political institutions. The Social Democrats have participated in the elections to the various Diets, to municipal councils, and to industrial courts. Wherever the proletariat could secure an effective voice, the occupation of these electoral strongholds by the bourgeoisie has been contested. Consequently, the bourgeoisie and the government have become much more alarmed at the legal than at the illegal activities of the labor party, dreading the results of elections far more than they dread the results of rebellion.[18]

Engels appends a detailed critique of the illusion that under modern capitalist conditions the proletariat could possibly expect to gain anything by street fighting, by revolution. It seems to me, however, that today, inasmuch as we are in the midst of a revolution, a revolution characterized by street fighting and all that it entails, it is time to put into question the conception which guided the official policy of German Social Democracy down to our own day, the views which share responsibility for our experience of August 4, 1914.

By this, I do not mean to imply that, on account of these declarations, Engels must share personal responsibility for the whole course of the development in Germany. I merely say that this is a classical documentation of the opinions prevailing in German Social Democracy—opinions which proved fatal to it. Here, comrades, Engels demonstrates, using all his knowledge as an expert in military science, that it is a pure illusion to believe that the working people could, in the existing state of military technique and of industry, and in view of the characteristics of the great cities of today, bring about and win a revolution by street fighting. Two important conclusions were drawn from this reasoning. In the first place, the parliamentary struggle was opposed to direct revolutionary action by the proletariat, and was frankly considered as the only means of carrying on the class struggle. The logical conclusion of this critique was the doctrine of "parliamentarism-only." Secondly, the whole military machine, precisely the most powerful organization in the class state, the entire mass of proletarians in military uniform, was declared, in a remarkable way, on a priori grounds, to be immune and absolutely inaccessible to socialist influence. When the Preface declares that, owing to the modern development of gigantic armies, it is insane to suppose that proletarians could stand up against soldiers armed with machine guns and equipped with all the latest technical devices, the assertion is obviously based upon the assumption that anyone who is a soldier is thereby a priori, once and for all, a support of the ruling class.

It would be absolutely incomprehensible, in the light of contemporary experience, that a man who stood at the head of our movement could have committed such an error if we did not know the actual circumstances in which this historical document was composed. To the honor of our two great masters, and especially to the credit of Engels, who died twelve years later than Marx, and was always a faithful champion of his great collaborator's theories, the well-known fact that the Preface was written by Engels under the direct pressure of the parliamentary delegation must be stressed.[19] During the early 1890s after the [anti]socialist law had been repealed, there was in Germany a strong left-radical current within the German labor movement which wanted to save the Party from a total absorption in the parliamentary struggle. In order to defeat the radical elements theoretically, and to neutralize them in practice; in order to keep their views from the attention of the masses through the authority of our great masters, Bebel and comrades (and this was typical of our situation at the time: the parliamentary delegation decided theoretically and tactically the destiny and the tasks of the party) pressed Engels, who lived abroad and had to rely on their assurances, to write that Preface, arguing that it was absolutely essential to save the German labor movement from anarchist deviations. From that time on, the tactics expounded by Engels dominated German Social Democracy in everything that it did and in everything that it left undone, down to the appropriate end, August 4, 1914. The Preface was the proclamation of the parliamentarism only tactic. Engels died the same year, and had therefore no chance to see the practical results of this application of his theory.

I am certain that those who know the works of Marx and Engels, those who are familiar with the living, genuine revolutionary spirit that inspired all their teachings and their writings, will be convinced that Engels would have been the first to protest against the debauch of parliamentarism-only, against the corruption and degradation of the labor movement which was characteristic of Germany before August 4 (1914). August 4 did not come like thunder out of a clear sky; what happened on August 4 was the logical outcome of all that we had been doing day after day for many years. I am certain that

Engels—and Marx, had he been alive—would have been the first to have protested with the utmost energy, and would have used all his forces to keep the vehicle from rolling into the swamp. But Engels died in the same year that he wrote the Preface. After we lost him in 1895, the theoretical leadership unfortunately passed into the hands of Kautsky. The result of this was that at every annual Party congress the energetic protests of the left wing against the policy of parliamentarism-only, its tenacious struggle against the sterility of such a policy whose dangerous results must be clear to everyone, were stigmatized as anarchism, anarcho-socialism, or at least anti-Marxism. What passed officially for Marxism became a cloak for all the hesitations, for all the turnings-away from the actual revolutionary class struggle, for every halfway measure which condemned German Social Democracy, the labor movement in general, and also the trade unions, to vegetate within the framework and on the terrain of capitalist society without any serious attempt to shake or throw that society out of gear.

But today we have reached the point, comrades, when we can say that we have rejoined Marx, that we are advancing under his flag. If today we declare in our program that the immediate task of the proletariat is none other than—in a word—to make socialism a truth and a fact, and to destroy capitalism root and branch, in saying this we take our stand upon the ground occupied by Marx and Engels in 1848, and from which in principle they never swerved. What true Marxism is has now become plain; and what *ersatz* Marxism, which has so long been the official Marxism of Social Democracy, has been is also clear. You see what Marxism of that sort leads to—to the Marxism of those who are the henchmen of Ebert, David, and company. These are the representatives of the doctrine which was trumpeted for decades as true, undefiled Marxism. No, Marxism could not lead in this direction, could not lead to counterrevolutionary activities side by side with men such as Scheidemann. True Marxism fights also against those who seek to falsify it. Burrowing like a mole beneath the foundations of capitalist society, it has worked so well that the better part of the German proletariat is marching today under our banner, the stormy banner of revolution. Even in the opposite camp, even where the counterrevolution still seems to rule, we have adherents and future comrades-in-arms.

Comrades! As I have already noted, the course of the historical dialectic has led us back to the point at which Marx and Engels stood in 1848 when they first unfurled the banner of international socialism. We stand where they stood, but with the advantage that seventy additional years of capitalist development lie behind us. Seventy years ago, to those who reviewed the errors and illusions of 1848, it seemed as if the proletariat still had an infinitely long distance to travel before it could hope to realize socialism. Naturally no serious thinker has ever been inclined to fix a definite date for the collapse of capitalism; but the day of that collapse seemed to lie in the distant future. Such a belief too can be read in every line of the Preface which Engels wrote in 1895. We are now in a position to draw up the account. In comparison with the class struggles of the past, was it not a very short time? The progress of large-scale capitalist development during seventy years has brought us so far that today we can seriously set about destroying capitalism once and for all. No, still more; today we are not only in a position to perform this task, its performance is not only a duty toward the proletariat, but its solution offers the only means of saving human society from destruction.

Comrades! What has the war left of bourgeois society beyond a gigantic heap of ruins? Formally, of course, all the means of production and most of the instruments of power are still in the hands of the ruling classes. We are under no illusions on this score. But what our rulers will be able to achieve with these powers over and above frantic attempts to reestablish their system of exploitation through blood and slaughter will be nothing more than anarchy. Today matters have reached a point at which mankind is faced with the dilemma: either collapse into anarchy, or salvation through socialism. The results of the World War make it impossible for the capitalist classes to find any way out of their difficulties while still maintaining their class rule and capitalism. We are living today, in the strictest sense of the term, the absolute truth of the statement formulated for the first time by Marx and Engels as the scientific basis of socialism in the great charter of our movement, in the Communist Manifesto: Socialism will become an historical necessity. Socialism has become necessary not merely because the proletariat is no longer willing to live under the conditions imposed by the capitalist class but, rather, because if the proletariat fails to fulfill its class duties, if it fails to realize socialism, we shall crash down together to a common doom.

Here, comrades, you have the general foundation of the program we are officially adopting today, whose outline you have all read in the pamphlet *What Does the Spartacus League Want.*[20] Our program is deliberately opposed to the standpoint of the Erfurt Program; it is deliberately opposed to the separation of the immediate, so-called minimal demands formulated for the political and economic struggle from the socialist goal regarded as a maximal program. In this deliberate opposition [to the Erfurt Program] we liquidate the results of seventy years' evolution and above all, the immediate results of the World War, in that we say: For us there is no minimal and no maximal program; socialism is one and the same thing; this is the minimum we have to realize today.

I do not propose to discuss the details of our program. That would take too long, and you will form your own opinions on matters of detail. I consider my task to be merely to sketch and formulate the broad principles which distinguish our program from what has hitherto been the so-called official program of German Social Democracy. I regard it, however, as more important and more pressing that we should come to an understanding in our estimate of the concrete circumstances, of the tactics we have to adopt, and of the practical measures which must be undertaken in view of the political situation, of the course of the revolution until now, and of the probable further lines of its development. We have to judge the political situation according to the outlook I have just tried to characterize—from the standpoint of the realization of socialism as the immediate task which guides every measure and every position that we take.

Comrades! Our Party Congress, the Congress of what I may proudly call the only revolutionary socialist party of the German proletariat, happens to coincide with a turning point in the development of the German revolution. "Happens to coincide," I say; but in truth the coincidence is not an accident. We may assert that after the events of the last few days, the curtain has gone down upon the first act of the German revolution. We are now in the opening of the second act, a further stage in the development, and it is our common duty to submit to self-criticism. We shall be guided more wisely in the future, and we shall gain additional impetus for further advance, if we examine critically all that we have done and created, and all that we have left undone. Let us, then, carefully examine the events of the now-ended first act in the revolution.

The movement began on November 9. The Revolution of November 9 was characterized by inadequacy and weakness. This is not surprising. The revolution followed four years of war, four years during which, schooled by Social Democracy and the trade unions, the German proletariat had behaved with intolerable ignominy and had repudiated its socialist obligations to an extent unparalleled in any other land. We Marxists and socialists, whose guiding principle is a recognition of historical development, could hardly expect that in the Germany which had known the terrible spectacle of August 4, and which during more than four years had reaped the harvest sown on that day, there should suddenly occur on November 9, 1918, a glorious revolution inspired with definite class consciousness and directed toward a conscious aim. What we experienced on November 9 was more the collapse of the existent imperialism than the victory of a new principle.

The moment had come for the collapse of imperialism, a colossus with feet of clay, crumbling from within. The sequel of this collapse was a more or less chaotic movement, one practically devoid of a conscious plan. The only source of union, the persistent and saving principle, was the motto: "Form Workers' and Soldiers' Councils." That was the key notion in this revolution which, in spite of the inadequacy and weakness of the opening phases, immediately gave it the stamp of a proletarian socialist revolution. We should not forget this when we are confronted by those who shower calumnies on the Russian Bolsheviks, and we must answer: "Where did you learn the ABCs of your present revolution? Was it not from the Russians that you learned to demand workers' and soldiers' councils?"[21] Those pygmies who today, as heads of what they falsely term a German socialist government, make it one of their chief tasks to join with the British imperialists in a murderous attack upon the Bolsheviks, also formally base their power on the workers' and soldiers' councils, thereby admitting that the Russian Revolution created the first mottoes for the world revolution. On the basis of the existing situation, we can predict with certainty that in whatever country, after Germany, the proletarian revolution may next break out, the first step will be the formation of workers' and soldiers' councils.

Precisely here lies the bond that unites our movement internationally. This is the slogan which completely distinguishes our revolution from all earlier bourgeois revolutions. And it is very characteristic of the dialectical contradictions in which the revolution, like all others, moves that on November 9, the first cry of the revolution, as instinctive as the cry of a new-born child, found the watchword which will lead us to social-ism: workers' and soldiers' councils. This was the call which rallied everyone-and that the revolution instructively found the word, even though on November 9 it was so inadequate, so feeble, so devoid of initiative, so lacking in clearness as to its own aims, that on the second day of the revolution nearly half of the instruments of power which had been seized on November 9 had slipped from the grasp of the revolution. We see in this, on the one hand, that our revolution is subject to the all-powerful law of historical necessity which guarantees that, despite all difficulties and complications, and notwithstanding all our own errors, we shall nevertheless advance step by step toward our goal. On the other hand, comparing this splendid battle cry with the insufficiency of the practical re-sults which have been achieved through it, we have to admit that these were no more than the first childish and faltering footsteps of the revolution which has many arduous tasks to perform and a long road to travel before fully realizing the promise of the first watchwords.

Comrades! This first act, between November 9 and the present, has been filled with illusions on all sides. The first illusion of the workers and soldiers who made the revolution was: the illusion of unity under the banner of so-called socialism. What could be more characteristic of the internal weakness of the Revolution of November 9 than the fact that at the head of the movement appeared persons who a few hours before the revolution broke out had regarded it as their chief duty to agitate against it—to attempt to make revolution impossible: the Eberts, Scheidemanns, and Haases.[22] The motto of the Revolution of November 9 was the idea of the unity of the various socialist trends in the general exultation—an illusion which was to be bloodily avenged. The events of the last few days have brought a bitter awakening from our dreams. But the self-deception was universal, affecting the Ebert and Scheidemann groups and the bourgeoisie no less than ourselves. Another illusion was that of the bourgeoisie at the end of this stage, believing that by means of the Ebert-Haase combination, by means of the so-called socialist government, they would really be able to bridle the proletarian masses and to strangle the socialist revolution. Yet another illusion was that of the Ebert-Scheidemann government, that with the aid of the soldiers returned from the front, they would be able to hold down the working masses in their socialist class struggle.

Such were the multifarious illusions which explain recent events. One and all, they have now been dissipated into nothingness. It has been shown that the union between Haase and Ebert-Scheidemann under the banner of "socialism" serves merely as a fig leaf for the veiling of a counterrevolutionary policy. We ourselves have been cured of our self-deceptions, as happens in all revolutions. There is a definite revolutionary method by which the people can be cured of illusion, but unfortunately, the cure must be paid for with the blood of the people. In Germany, events have followed a course characteristic of earlier revolutions. The blood of the victims on the Chausseestrasse on December 6,[23] the blood of the sailors on December 24,[24] brought the truth home to the broad masses of the people. They came to realize that what has been pasted together and called a socialist government is nothing but a government representing the bourgeois counterrevolution, and that whoever continues to tolerate such a state of affairs is working against the proletariat and against socialism.

Comrades! It was characteristic of the first period of the revolution, which I have described, until December 24 we might say, that the revolution remained exclusively political. We must be fully conscious of this. This explains the uncertain character, the inadequacy, the halfheartedness, the aimlessness of this revolution. It was the first stage of a revolutionary overthrow whose main tasks lie in the economic field: to make a fundamental conversion of economic conditions. Its steps were as naive and unconscious as those of a child groping its way without knowing where it is going; for at this stage, I repeat, the revolution had a purely political character. Only in the last two or three weeks have strikes broken out quite spontaneously. Let us be clear: it is the very essence of this revolution that strikes will become more and more extensive, that they must become more and more the central focus, the key aspect of the revolution. It then becomes an economic revolution, and at the same time a socialist revolution. The struggle for socialism has to be fought out by the masses, by the masses alone, breast to breast against capitalism, in every factory, by every proletarian against his employer. Only then will it be a socialist revolution.

Certainly, the thoughtless had a different picture of the course of events. They imagined it would be only necessary to overthrow the old government, to set up a socialist government at the head of affairs, and then to inaugurate socialism by decree. Once again, that was an illusion. Socialism will not and cannot be created by decrees; nor can it be established by any government, however socialistic. Socialism must be created by the masses, by every proletarian. Where the chains of capitalism are forged, there they must be broken. Only that is socialism, and only thus can socialism be created.

What is the external form of struggle for socialism? It is the strike. And that is why the economic phase of development has to come to the front in the second act of the revolution. I would like to stress here that this is something on which we may pride ourselves, and no one will dispute that we of the Spartacus League, of the Communist Party of Germany, are the only ones in all Germany who are on the side of the striking and fighting workers. You have read and witnessed again and again the attitude of the Independent Socialists [USPD] toward strikes. There was no difference between the outlook of *Vorwärts* and that of *Freiheit*.[25] Both journals sang the same tune: Be diligent; socialism means much work. Such was their position while capitalism was still in control! Socialism cannot be established in that way, but only by an energetic struggle against capitalism. Yet we see the claims of capitalism defended, not only by the most outrageous intriguers, but also by the Independent Socialists and their organ, *Freiheit*. Our Communist Party stands alone in supporting the workers. This suffices to show that, today, all those who have not taken their stand with. us upon the platform of revolutionary communism fight persistently and violently against the strikes.

The conclusion to be drawn is not only that during the second act of the revolution strikes will become increasingly frequent but, further, that strikes will become the central feature and the decisive factor of the revolution, thrusting purely political questions into the background. You understand that the inevitable consequence of this will be that the economic struggle will be enormously intensified. The revolution will thus strengthening of the economic struggle which will sooner or later cause the government of Ebert and Scheidemann to take its place among the shades.

It is equally difficult to say what will happen to the National Assembly during the second act of the revolution. It is possible that if the Assembly comes into existence, it may prove a new school of education for the working class. But, on the other hand, it seems just as likely that the National Assembly will never come into existence. One cannot make predictions. Let me say parenthetically, to help you understand the grounds on which we were defending our position yesterday, that our only objection was to limiting our tactics to a single alternative.[26] I will not now reopen the whole discussion, but will merely say a word or two lest any of you should falsely imagine that I am blowing hot and cold with the same breath. Our position today is precisely that of yesterday. We do not want to base our tactics in relation to the National Assembly upon what is a possibility but not a certainty. We refuse to stake everything upon the belief that the National Assembly will never come into existence. We want to be prepared for all possibilities, including the possibility of using the National Assembly for revolutionary purposes should it ever come into being. Whether it comes into being or not is a matter of indifference, for whatever happens, the success of the revolution is assured. . . .

Comrades! To resume the thread of my discourse, it is clear that all these machinations, the formation of Iron Divisions and, above all, the above-mentioned agreement with British imperialism, signify nothing but the ultimate reserves with which to throttle the German socialist movement. But the cardinal question, the question of the prospects of peace, is intimately associated with this affair. What can such negotiations lead to but a fresh outbreak of the war? While these scoundrels are playing a comedy in Germany, trying to make us believe that they are working overtime in order to make peace, and declaring that we are the disturbers of the peace who are making the Entente uneasy and retarding the peace settlement, they are themselves preparing a rekindling of the war, a war in the East on which a war on German soil will follow. Once again we have a situation which cannot fail to bring on a period of fresh conflict. We will have to defend not only socialism and the interests of revolution but also the interests of world peace. This is precisely a justification of the tactics which we Spartacists have consistently and at every opportunity pursued throughout the four years of the war. Peace signifies the world revolution of the proletariat! There is no other way of really establishing and safeguarding peace than by the victory of the socialist proletariat!

Comrades! What general tactical considerations must we deduce from this in order to deal with the situation with which we will be confronted in the immediate future? Your first conclusion will doubtless be a hope that the fall of the Ebert-Scheidemann government is at hand, and that it will be replaced by a declared socialist-proletarian-revolutionary government. For my part, I would ask you to direct your attention not to the leadership, not above, but to the base. We must not nourish and repeat the illusion of the first phase of the revolution, that of November 9, thinking that it is sufficient to overthrow the capitalist government and to set up another in its place in order to bring about a socialist revolution. There is only one way of achieving the victory of the proletarian revolution. We must begin by undermining step by step the Ebert-Scheidemann government through a social, revolutionary mass struggle of the proletariat. Moreover, let me remind you of some of the inadequacies of the German revolution which have not been overcome with the close of the first act of the revolution and which show clearly that we are far from having reached a point when the overthrow of the government can ensure the victory of socialism. I have tried to show you that the Revolution of November 9 was, above all, a political revolution, whereas it is necessary that it become in addition and mainly an economic revolution. But further, the revolutionary movement was confined to the cities, and up to the present the rural districts remain practically untouched. It would be a folly to realize socialism while leaving the agricultural system unchanged. From the standpoint of socialist economics in general, manufacturing industry cannot be remodeled unless it is amalgamated with a socialist reorganization of agriculture. The most important idea of the socialist economic order is the abolition of the opposition and the division between city and country. This division, this conflict, this contradiction, is a purely capitalist phenomenon which must be eliminated as soon as we place ourselves upon the socialist standpoint. If socialist reconstruction is to be undertaken in real earnest, we must direct attention just as much to the open country as to the industrial centers. Here, unfortunately, we are not even at the beginning of the beginning. This is essential, not merely because we cannot bring about socialism without socializing agriculture, but also because while we may think that we have reckoned with the last reserves of the counterrevolution against us and our efforts, there remains another important reserve which has not yet been taken into account: the peasantry. Precisely because the peasants are still untouched by socialism they constitute an additional reserve for the counter-revolutionary bourgeoisie. The first thing our enemies will do when the flames of the socialist strikes begin to scorch their heels will be to mobilize the peasants, the fanatical devotees of private property. There is only one way of making headway against this threatening counterrevolutionary power. We must carry the class struggle into the country districts; we must mobilize the landless proletariat and the poorer peasants against the richer peasants.

From this consideration follows what we have to do to insure the presup-positions of the success of the revolution. I would summarize our next tasks as follows: First and foremost, we have to extend in all directions the system of workers' and soldiers' councils, especially those of the workers. What we undertook on November 9 are only weak beginnings, and not even that. Dur-ing the first phase of the revolution we actually lost extensive forces that were acquired at the very outset. You are aware that the counterrevolution has been engaged in the systematic destruction of the system of workers' and sol-diers' councils. In Hesse, the councils have been definitely abolished by the counterrevolutionary government; elsewhere, power has been wrenched from their hands. Therefore, we have not merely to develop the system of workers' and soldiers' councils, but we have to induce the agricultural labor-ers and the poorer peasants to adopt this council system. We have to seize power, and the problem of the seizure of power poses the question: what does each workers' and soldiers' council in all Germany do, what can it do, and what must it do? The power is there! We must undermine the bourgeois state by putting an end everywhere to the cleavage in public powers, to the cleavage between legislative and executive powers. These powers must be united in the hands of the workers' and soldiers' councils.

Comrades, that is an extensive field to till. We must prepare from the base up; we must give the workers' and soldiers' councils so much strength that the overthrow of the Ebert-Scheidemann or any similar government will merely be the final act in the drama. Thus, the conquest of power will not be effected with one blow. It will be a progression; we shall progressively occupy all the positions of the capitalist state and defend them tooth and nail. In my view and in that of my most intimate associates in the Party, the economic struggle, likewise, will be carried on by the workers' councils. The direction of the economic struggle and the continued expansion of the area of this struggle must be in the hands of the workers' councils. The councils must have all power in the state.

We must direct our activities in the immediate future to these ends, and it is obvious that, if we pursue this line and pursue these tasks, there cannot fail to be an enormous intensification of the struggle in the near future. It is a question of fighting step by step, hand-to-hand, in every province, in every city, in every village, in every municipality in order to take and transfer all the powers of the state bit by bit from the bourgeoisie to the workers' and soldiers' councils. But before these steps can be taken, the members of our own Party and the proletarians in general must be educated. Even where workers' and soldiers' councils already exist, there is still a lack of consciousness of the purposes for which they exist.[27] We must make the masses understand that the workers' and soldiers' council is in all senses the lever of the machinery of state, that it must take over all power and must unify the power in one stream—the socialist revolution. The masses of workers who are already organized in workers' and soldiers' councils are still miles away from having adopted such an outlook, and only isolated proletarian minorities are clearly conscious of their tasks. But this is not a lack, but rather the normal state of affairs. The masses must learn how to use power by using power. There is no other way to teach them. Fortunately, we have gone beyond the days when it was proposed to "educate" the proletariat socialistically. Marxists of Kautsky's school still believe in the existence of those vanished days. To educate the proletarian masses socialistically meant to deliver lectures to them, to circulate leaflets and pamphlets among them. No, the school of the socialist proletariat doesn't need all this. The workers will learn in the school of action.

Our motto is: In the beginning was the act. And the act must be that the workers' and soldiers' councils realize their mission and learn to become the sole public power of the whole nation. Only in this way can we mine the ground so that it will be ready for the revolution which will crown our work. This, comrades, is the reason, this is the clear calculation and clear consciousness which led some of us, and me in particular, to say yesterday, "Don't think that the struggle will continue to be so easy." Some comrades have interpreted me as saying that they wanted to boycott the National Assembly and simply to fold their arms. It is impossible, in the time that remains, to discuss this matter fully, but let me say that I never dreamed of anything of the kind. My meaning was that history is not going to make our revolution an easy matter like the bourgeois revolutions in which it sufficed to overthrow that official power at the center and to replace a dozen or so persons in authority. We have to work from beneath, and this corresponds to the mass character of our revolution which aims at the foundation and base of the social constitution; it corresponds to the character of the present proletarian revolution that the conquest of political power must come not from above but from below. The 9th of November was an attempt, a weak, half-hearted, half-conscious, and chaotic attempt to overthrow the existing public power and to put an end to class rule. What now must be done is that with full consciousness all the forces of the proletariat should be concentrated in an attack on the very foundations of capitalist society. There, at the base, where the individual employer confronts his wage slaves; at the base, where all the executive organs of political class rule confront the object of this rule, the masses; there, step by step, we must seize the means of power from the rulers and take them into our own hands. In the form that I depict it, the process may seem rather more tedious than one had imagined it at first. It is healthy, I think, that we should be perfectly clear as to all the difficulties and complications of this revolution. For I hope that, as in my own case, so in yours also, the description of the difficulties of the accumulating tasks will paralyze neither your zeal nor your energy. On the contrary, the greater the task, the more will we gather all of our forces. And we must not forget that the revolution is able to do its work with extraordinary speed. I make no attempt to prophesy how much time will be needed for this process. Who among us cares about the time; who worries, so, long only as our lives suffice to bring it to pass. It is only important that we know clearly and precisely what is to be done; and I hope that my feeble powers have shown you to some extent the broad outlines of that which is to be done.

### 14E. ORDER REIGNS IN BERLIN

"Order reigns in Warsaw," Minister Sebastiani informed the Paris Chamber of Deputies in 1831, when, after fearfully storming the suburb Praga, Paskiewitsch's rabble troops had marched into the Polish capital and begun their hangman's work on the rebels.[28]

"Order reigns in Berlin" is the triumphant announcement of the bourgeois press, of Ebert and Noske, and of the officers of the "victorious troops," who are being cheered by the petty-bourgeois mob in the streets, waving their handkerchiefs and shouting hurrahs. The glory and the honor of the German Army has been saved in the eyes of history. Those who were miserably routed in Flanders and the Argonne have restored their reputation by this shining victory—over the three hundred "Spartacists" in the *Vorwärts*.[29] The days of the first glorious penetration of German troops into Belgium, the days of General von Emmich, the conqueror of Liège, pale before the deeds of this Reinhardt and Company in the streets of Berlin.[30] The massacred mediators, who wanted to negotiate the surrender of the *Vorwärts* and were beaten beyond recognition by rifle butts, so that their bodies could not even be identified; captives who were put up against the wall and murdered in a way that spattered their skulls and brains all over: in the face of such glorious acts, who is still thinking of the ignominious defeats suffered at the hand of the French, the English, or the Americans? "Spartacus" is the name of the enemy; and Berlin, the place where our officers know how to win. Noske, the "worker,"[31] is the name of the general who knows how to organize victories where Ludendorff failed.

Who does not recall here the drunken ecstasy of that pack of "law-and-order" hounds in Paris, the bacchanal of the bourgeoisie on the bodies of the Communards—the very same bourgeoisie who had only just capitulated pitifully to the Prussians and surrendered the nation's capital to the foreign enemy, only to take to their heels themselves like the ultimate coward! But against the badly armed and starving Parisian proletarians, against their defenseless wives and children—how the manly courage of the little sons of the bourgeoisie, of the "golden youth," and of the officers flamed up again! How the courage of these sons of Mars who had broken down before the foreign enemy spent itself in bestial cruelties against the defenseless, against prisoners, and the fallen!

"Order reigns in Warsaw!"—"Order reigns in Paris!"—"Order reigns in Berlin!" And so run the reports of the guardians of "order" every half-century, from one center of the world-historical struggle to another. And the rejoicing "victors" do not notice that an "order" which must be periodically maintained by bloody butchery is steadily approaching its historical destiny, its doom.

What was this recent "Spartacus Week" in Berlin? What has it brought? What does it teach us? Still in the midst of the struggle and the victory cries of the counterrevolution, the revolutionary proletarians have to give an account of what has happened; they must measure the events and their results on the great scale of history. The revolution has no time to lose, it storms onward—past still open graves, past "victories" and "defeats"—toward its great goals. To follow lucidly its principles and its paths is the first task of the fighters for international socialism.

Was an ultimate victory of the revolutionary proletariat to be expected in this conflict, or the overthrow of the Ebert-Scheidemann [government] and establishment of a socialist dictatorship? Definitely not, if all the decisive factors in this issue are taken into careful consideration. The sore spot in the revolutionary cause at this moment—the political immaturity of the masses of soldiers who, even now, are still letting themselves be misused by their officers for hostile, counterrevolutionary purposes—is alone already proof that a lasting victory of the revolution was not possible in this encounter. On the other hand, this immaturity of the military is itself but a symptom of the general immaturity of the German revolution.

The open country, from which a large percentage of the common soldiers come, is still hardly touched by the revolution, the same as always. So far, Berlin is as good as isolated from the rest of the country. Of course, there are revolutionary centers in the provinces—in the Rhineland, on the northern seaboard, in Brunswick, Saxony, and Württemberg—that are heart and soul on the side of the Berlin proletariat. Still what is lacking first of all is the immediate coordination of the march forward, the direct community of action, which would make the thrust and the willingness to fight of the Berlin working class incomparably more effective. Furthermore—and this is but the deeper cause of that political immaturity of the revolution—the economic struggles, the actual volcanic fountain which is continually feeding the revolutionary class struggle, are only in their infancy.

From all this it follows that at this moment a conclusive and lasting victory could not be expected. Was the struggle of the last week therefore a "mistake"? Yes, if it were in fact a matter of a deliberate "attack" or a so-called "putsch"! But what was the starting point for the last week of fighting? The same as in all previous cases, the same as on December 6 and December 24: a brutal provocation by the government! Just as before, in the case of the blood bath involving defenseless demonstrators on the Chausseestrasse, or in the butchery of the sailors, likewise this time the cause of all subsequent events was the assault on the Berlin police headquarters. The revolution does not operate voluntaristically, in an open field, according to a cunning plan laid out by "strategists." Its opponents too have initiative; in fact, as a rule, they exercise it much more than the revolution itself.

Faced with the shameless provocation of the Ebert–Scheidemanns, the revolutionary working class was forced to take up arms. Yes, it was a matter of honor for the revolution to repel the attack immediately and with all due energy, lest the counterrevolution be encouraged to advance further, and lest the revolutionary ranks of the proletariat and the moral credit of the German revolution in the International be shaken.

Immediate resistance came forth spontaneously from the masses of Berlin with such an obvious energy that from the very beginning the moral victory was on the side of the "street."

Now it is an internal law of life of the revolution never to stand still in inaction, in passivity, once a step has been taken. The best parry is a forceful blow. Now more than ever this elementary rule of all struggles governs each step of the revolution. It goes without saying, and it testifies to the sound instinct and fresh internal strength of the Berlin proletariat, that it was not appeased by the reinstatement of Eichhorn, that it spontaneously proceeded to occupy other outposts of the counterrevolution's power: the bourgeois press, the semi-official news agencies, the *Vorwärts*. All these measures resulted from the people's instinctive recognition that, for its part, the counterrevolution would not rest with the defeat it had suffered, but rather would be bent on a general test of strength.

Here, too, we stand before one of the great historical laws of revolution against which are dashed to pieces all the sophistries and the pseudo-science of those little "revolutionaries" of the USPD brand who, in every fight, look only for pretexts for retreating. As soon as the fundamental problem of the revolution has been clearly posed—and in this revolution it is to overthrow the Ebert-Scheidemann regime, the first obstacle to the triumph of socialism—then this problem will recur repeatedly as a pressing need of the moment, and each individual episode of the struggle will broach the problem in its entirety with the fatality of a natural law, however unprepared the revolution may be for its solution, however unripe the situation may still be. "Down with Ebert and Scheidemann!"—this slogan is inevitably heard in every revolutionary crisis as the single formula summing up all partial conflicts, thereby automatically, by its own internal, objective logic, propelling each episode of the struggle to the extreme, whether one wants it or not.

From this contradiction between the increasing gravity of the task and the lack of the preconditions for its solution it follows, in an initial phase of the revolutionary development, that the individual fights of the revolution formally end with a defeat. But revolution is the only form of "war"—this, too, is its particular life principle—in which the final victory can be prepared only by a series of "defeats"!

What does the whole history of modern revolutions and of socialism show us? The first flare-up of the class struggle in Europe—the revolt of the silk weavers of Lyons in 1831—ended with a severe defeat. The Chartist movement in England—with a defeat. The rebellion of the Parisian proletariat in the June days of 1848 ended with a crushing defeat. The Paris Commune ended with a dreadful defeat. The whole path of socialism, as far as revolutionary struggles are concerned, is paved with sheer defeats.

And yet, this same history leads step by step, irresistibly, to the ultimate victory! Where would we be today without those "defeats" from which we have drawn historical experience, knowledge, power, idealism! Today, where we stand directly before the final battle of the proletarian class struggle, we are standing on precisely those defeats, not a one of which we could do without, and each of which is a part of our strength and clarity of purpose.

In this respect, revolutionary struggles are the direct opposite of parliamentary struggles. In the course of four decades we have had nothing but parliamentary "victories" in Germany, we have advanced directly from victory to victory. And with the great test of history on August 4, 1914, the result was: a devastating political and moral defeat, an unprecedented debacle, an unparalleled bankruptcy. Revolutions have brought us nothing but defeat till now, but these unavoidable defeats are only heaping guarantee upon guarantee of the coming final triumph.

On one condition, of course! The question arises, under which circumstances each respective defeat was suffered: whether it resulted from the forward-storming energy of the masses being dashed against the barrier of the lack of maturity of the historical presuppositions, or, on the other hand, whether it resulted from the revolutionary action itself being paralyzed by incompleteness, vacillation, and inner frailties.

Classic examples for both cases are, on the one hand, the French February Revolution, and the German March Revolution on the other. The courageous action of the Parisian proletariat in 1848 has become the living source of class energy for the entire international proletariat. The deplorable facts of the German March Revolution [1848] have clung to the whole development of modern Germany like a ball and chain. In the particular history of official German Social Democracy, they have produced after-effects well into the most recent incidents of the German revolution—and into the dramatic crisis we just experienced.

How does the defeat in this so-called Spartacus Week appear in light of the above historical question? Was it a defeat due to raging revolutionary energy and a situation that was insufficiently ripe, or rather due to frailties and halfway undertakings?

Both! The divided character of this crisis, the contradiction between the vigorous, resolute, aggressive showing of the people of Berlin and the indecision, timidity, and inadequacy of the Berlin leadership is the particular characteristic of this latest episode.

The leadership failed. But the leadership can and must be created anew by the masses and out of the masses. The masses are the crucial factor; they are the rock on which the ultimate victory of the revolution will be built. The masses were up to the task. They fashioned this "defeat" into a part of those historical defeats which constitute the pride and power of international socialism. And that is why this "defeat" is the seed of the future triumph.

"Order reigns in Berlin!" You stupid lackeys! Your "order" is built on sand. The revolution will "raise itself up again clashing," and to your horror it will proclaim to the sound of trumpets: *I was*, *I am*, *I shall be*.[32]

# PART FIVE

# "Like a Clap of Thunder"

In my soul a totally new, original form is ripening that ignores all rules
and conventions. It breaks them by the power of ideas
and strong conviction. I want to affect people like a clap of thunder,
to inflame their minds not by speechifying but with the breadth
of my vision, the strength of my conviction,
and the power of my expression.

—ROSA LUXEMBURG to Leo Jogiches, April 19, 1899

# 15 — Selected Correspondence, 1899-1917

EDITORS' NOTE: Rosa Luxemburg was an energetic correspondent throughout her life. The major historical questions that provide the focus of her public writings and speeches remain in sight. But in her letters she also reveals another side of herself, showing how public events impacted on her as a human being and and the peculiar combination of warmth and principle she brought to her personal relationships. Several of the letters excerpted here were written while she was in prison. The letters to Leo Jogiches are translated by Elzbieta Ettinger, and the other letters by Stephen Eric Bronner.

## TO LEO JOGICHES

Berlin, January 9, 1899

*Dearest Dziodzio.*

. . . Now help me—and fast—to solve the following little problem. With the development of capitalism, contradictions develop and there with both the economic system of capitalism, and the capitalist state, become untenable. The latter—that is to say, capitalist politics—leads likewise to a collapse. An illustration from praxis: in international politics. Five or six years ago, Constantinople played a central role around which the entire international struggle turned. But, since here the conquest of a purely strategic point was directly involved, over the last ten years a policy of stabilizing the integrity of Turkey has emerged in view of maintaining the balance of power. Thus, the Constantinople issue has arrived at dead center, the development of international relations has gotten stuck there.

Around 1895, a basic change occurred: the Japanese war[1] opened the Chinese doors and European politics, driven by capitalist and state interests, intruded into Asia. Constantinople moved into the background. Here the conflict between states, and with it the development of politics, had an extended field before it: the conquest and partition of all Asia became the goal which European politics pursued. An extremely quick dismemberment of China followed. At present, Persia and Afghanistan too have been attacked by Russia and England. From that, the European antagonisms in Africa have received new impulses; there, too, the struggle is breaking out with new force (Fashoda, Delagoa, Madagascar).[2]

It's clear that the dismemberment of Asia and Africa is the final limit beyond which European politics no longer has room to unfold. There follows then another such squeeze as has just occurred in the Eastern question, and the European powers will have no choice other than throwing themselves on one another, until the *period of the final crisis sets in within politics* . . . etc. etc.

Well, you understand the wonderful prospects which this affords. Consider this and, if you have something to add, write me immediately—*and I do mean immediately*. At first this occurred to me as a theme for a beautiful lead article entitled "Shifts in World Politics" but then, instead, I decided to incorporate it organically into my paper on Ede [Bernstein] in order not simply to speak in abstractions, but rather to point to concrete facts.[3]

So much for the time being, my dearest. I am working very hard on Ede; you are mistaken in regard to "English Eyeglasses"—the way I am working it through, it is a very basic part of the argument. For I am slowly coming to the conclusion that in England, where the very first unfolding of capitalism took place, the ossification of capitalism will also first set in, and that this process of ossification has already begun. I have plenty of proof. This shows the conclusions which Ede draws from England in a very peculiar light: turned upside down.

I have been depressed since yesterday and that's why I can't write more. I send you a kiss from my heart, my dearest. Write, don't wait for me. When I am feeling just a bit better, I will write you again.

*Your R*

Berlin, April 19, 1899

*Dyodyo!* Finally I've got a free minute—I sent out the proofs and am exhausted—too tired to sleep. I have to write you now. For a long time I've wanted, actually needed, to tell you something, but there hasn't been a second!!

Do you know what I've been feeling very strongly? Something is moving inside me and wants to come out. It's something intellectual, something I must write. Don't worry, it's not poetry again, or fiction. No, my treasure, it's in my brain that I feel something. I feel I haven't used a tenth or a hundredth part of my powers. I'm not happy with what I've been writing and absolutely and clearly know I can do much better work. In other words, as Heinrich4 says, I need to "say something important."

It's the *form* of my writing that no longer satisfies me. In my "soul" a totally new, original form is ripening that ignores all rules and conventions. It breaks them by the power of ideas and strong conviction. I want to affect people like a clap of thunder, to inflame their minds not by speechifying but with the breadth of my vision, the strength of my conviction, and the power of my expression.

How? What? Where? I still don't know.

*Laugh to your heart's content*, I don't care. I'm convinced that something is stirring inside me, something is being born. You're probably saying, "A great mountain goes into labor and a silly mouse is born." Never mind. We'll see.

I've been thinking again tonight about *your* situation, how and what to do? I'd give anything in the world, half of my life, to have it all settled. Oh, Dyodyo!

Write to me *every day*. I made a decision: to write to you daily, time permitting, even if it's only a line or two. It's dreadful that neither of us has had word of the other for *several* days.

My darling Dyodyuchny, I imagined you today awakened by a special delivery letter, crawling out of bed, cautiously sticking out your sleepy, blond disheveled head through the crack in the door, a silly look on your sweet face, and I was sorry I wasn't standing at the door so I could plant a kiss on that silly nose—so hard it hurts.

*Rózia*

Leipzig got 600 copies of "Social Reform or Revolution" already. Three thousand will sell quickly, and I'll request royalties for the second edition.

I wrote back to Warski5 a long time ago and to the "Warsaw Library" as well.

Berlin, May 1, 1899

*Dziodzio!*

Thanks for yesterday's special-delivery letter. It pleased me greatly, since I sat all alone in the empty house all day—waiting for your [brother] Jozio. Anyway, I had no place to go; it was raining, and I wasn't feeling well at all. Unexpectedly, the mailman rang and brought me the news from you for which I have been waiting the last few days. . . .

You ask whether the speeches for the Party Convention[6] have been assigned. I believe I already told you that Bebel will discuss Bernstein—it's not yet known who will speak about militarism. The other items have nothing to do with us.

Your advice "to attempt to give a speech at any cost" is truly childish. It amazes me that you still keep serving up such inappropriate counsel, and that in such an important matter. Do you seriously believe that there is even the remotest chance for someone to be entrusted with a speech who has only been in the movement for a year, whose presence has only been established through a few articles—even if they are excellent? Someone who does not belong to the clan, who avails herself of no one's protection except for her own elbows? Someone who is not only greatly feared by her enemies (Auer & Co.) but also, in their heart of hearts, by her allies—Bebel, K[arl] K[autsky], Singer etc.? Someone who gives them the feeling that it might be best to put her off for as long as possible, because she might quickly surpass them? Don't you understand any of this? To get the chance to speak without their consent—there is no way to do this for it is clearly they who are pulling the strings behind the scenes.

But I contemplate all this with the deepest calm; I knew in advance that everything would develop as it has, and I know also that in a year or two no intrigue, no fear or envy, will prevent me from achieving one of the premier places in the party. Certainly the situation at the present moment—Bernstein—is an exception. Still, you seem to think, once again, that the navel of the world is right here and that, if action is not taken now—everything is lost. That is nonsense. The party only now (over the last two years) has been entering the whirlpool of ever more difficult tasks, ever more dangerous situations. There will be thousands upon thousands of occasions to show, in daily combat, its strength and indispensability.

At that, I do not have the slightest intention of limiting myself to criticism. On the contrary, I have the intention and desire of actively pushing, not individuals, but the movement as a whole, to reexamine the whole of our positive work, to point to new forms of agitation and praxis—if they can be found, and I don't doubt they can—to fight tedium and sloth, etc. In a word, I wish to be a continual spur for the movement—what Parvus[7] was at the beginning and unfortunately carried on well for only a few months. At any rate, I have the same unshakable belief that Parvus had, that one can do a great deal within the movement, do it daily and for many years to come.

All of our present time is extraordinarily critical. But the fact that there is no one who can take the party by the collar is shown in the problem of the Landtag elections,[8] in which, unfortunately, I got involved too late. But, year by year, there will be hundreds of issues like this one. If you only take the issues of tariffs, foreign affairs, and craft unions—already you have three untapped opportunities. And then there is the oral and written agitation which, petrified in old forms, affects practically no one any longer and which must be directed into new channels; new life must be injected into press, meetings and brochures.

I write you all this in haste and not in any special order, to show you that I am not without a plan and not without ideas while looking at what is happening all over and, second, to remind you that the world does not stop with Bernstein and Hannover. I do not agree with the view that it is foolish to be an idealist in the German movement. To begin with, there are idealists here too—above all, a huge number of the most simple agitators from the working masses and, further—more, even in the leadership, e.g., Bebel. Secondly, the whole matter doesn't concern me because the ultimate principle to which I subscribed during all of my Polish-German revolutionary praxis is to always remain true to oneself without regard for the surroundings and the others. I am and will remain an idealist in the German as well as the Polish movement.

Naturally, that does not mean that I will play the role of an obedient donkey who works for others. Very definitely, I want to strive, and I will strive, for the most influential place in the movement, and that does not in the least contradict my idealism since I will not employ methods other than the use of my own "talent"—insofar as I possess it. . . .

Already I must close for today. I kiss you tenderly.

*Your Rosa*


Berlin-Friedenau, February 11, 1902

*Dear Dziodzio!*

. . . Naturally, as usual, I had a few funny episodes on my trip. After the meeting in Reichenbach—in every city, after the meeting, I must sit with the comrades in a more private setting until 2 A.M. which, by the way, I don't regret in the least!—one of the local big shots said, after he had looked me over for quite some time: "Well, you couldn't be more than twenty-seven years old. And I thought you were around forty-two." But why? —I asked in amazement. "Well, there was that picture in the *Süddeutscher Postillon.*"

You can imagine how I laughed. It turned out that, in their naiveté, they had taken the picture for my actual portrait and that each had solemnly kept a copy.

After the meeting in Meerane (Saxony), on the other hand, I was formally interpellated on the woman's question and on marriage. A splendid young weaver, Hoffman, is zealously studying this question. He has read Bebel, Lili Braun and *Gleichheit* and is carrying on a bitter argument with the older village comrades, who keep maintaining that "a woman's place is in the home," and that we must seek the abolition of factory work for women. When I agreed with Hoffman, what a triumph! "There, you see," he cried, "the voice of authority has spoken for me!"

Answering one of the older men who called it a disgrace that pregnant women should have to scurry around in the factory in the midst of young men, Hoffman cried out: "Those are mistaken moralistic notions! Can you imagine if our Luxemburg were pregnant today while giving her lecture? Then I would like her even better!"

At this unexpected declaration, I almost exploded with laughter. But they took it all so seriously that I had to bite my lips.

Anyway, I must make an effort to be pregnant the next time I go to Reichenbach. Do you hear? After the farewells (at two o'clock in the morning), this young fellow held me a moment longer so that I might answer an important question: Should he get married, even though present-day marriage is a perverse arrangement? Luckily I answered that he should get married, which pleased him greatly, since, as the whispers and laughter of the others, and later his own confession brought out, he was just getting ready to be married—and it's high time too, since his fiancée is exactly in that condition which he likes so very much....

I embrace you.

*Your R*

March 20, 1907

*To Clara Zetkin*

The appeal of the Party Executive has had the same effect on me as it had upon you—that says it all. Since my return from Russia, I have felt rather isolated here. I feel the pettiness and indecisiveness which reigns in our party more brutally and more painfully than ever before. But I do not get as angry as you about it, because it has already become clear to me—shockingly clear—that neither people nor things can be changed until the whole situation has been completely changed. And even then—after cold reflection—I have come to the conclusion that we must count upon the inevitable *resistance* of those people, should we wish to inspire the masses.

The situation is simple: August [Bebel] and still more all the others have given themselves over to parliamentarism without reservation. Whenever events take a turn which goes beyond the limits of parliamentarism, they are lost. No, they are worse than lost, for they seek to lead it all back into parliamentary channels. This is why they furiously attack as an "enemy of the people" any movement or individual who wishes to go further. The masses, and still more the great mass of comrades, in the bottom of their hearts have had enough of this parliamentarism. I have the feeling that a breath of fresh air in our tactics would be greeted with cries of joy. But, still they submit to the heel of the old authorities and, what's more, to the upper strata of opportunist editors, deputies and trade union leaders.

Our task actually consists simply in protesting against the stagnation brought on by these authorities as vigorously as possible. In such actions, according to circumstances, we will find ourselves opposing the opportunists as well as the Party Executive and August. As long as it was a question of defending themselves against Bernstein and friends, August & Co. accepted our help and assistance with pleasure—because they were shaking in their shoes. But, when it comes to any *offensive* action against opportunists, then the veterans stand with Ede [Bernstein], Vollmar and David,[9] against us. This is how I see the situation. And now to what is essential: keep your chin up and stay calm. The tasks are many and I calculate that it should take many years to complete them.

*Rosa*

Wronke, December 28, 1916

*To Emanuel and Mathilde Wurm*

*Dearest Tilde,*

I want to answer your Christmas letter immediately, as long as I am in the state of rage which it has evoked in me. Yes, your letter made me seethe with rage because, despite its brevity, it shows me in every line how *very* much you are again under the influence of your milieu. This whining tone, this "alas" and "alack" about the "disappointments" which you have experienced—disappointments which you blame on others, instead of just looking into the mirror to see the whole of humanity's wretchedness in its most striking likeness! And when you say "we" that now means your boggy, froggish friends, whereas earlier, when you and I were together, it meant *my* company. Just you wait, I will treat "you" in the plural.

In your melancholy view, I have been complaining that you people are not marching up to the cannon's mouth. "Not marching" is a good one! You people do not march; you do not even walk; you creep. It is not simply a difference of degree, but rather of kind. On the whole, *you* people are a different zoological species than I, and your grousing, peevish, cowardly and half-hearted nature has never been as alien, as hateful to me, as it is now. You think that audacity would surely please you, but because of it one can be thrown into the cooler and one is then "of little use!" Ach! —you miserable little mercenaries. *You* would be ready enough to put a little bit of "heroism" up for sale—but only "for cash," even if only for three mouldy copper pennies. After all, one must immediately see its "use" on the sales counter.

For you people, the simple words of honest and upright men have not been spoken: "Here I stand, I can't do otherwise; God help me!"[10] Luckily, world history, up until this point, has not been made by people like yourselves. Otherwise, we wouldn't have had a Reformation, and we probably would still be living in the *ancien régime.*

As for me, although I have never been soft, lately I have grown hard as polished steel, and I will no longer make the smallest concession either in political or personal intercourse. When I think of your heroes, a creepy feeling comes over me: the adorable Haase; Dittmann with the lovely beard and those lovely Reichstag speeches; the uncertain pastor Kautsky whom your Emmo naturally follows through thick and thin; the magnificent Arthur [Stadthagen][11]—Ah, there's no end to it!

I swear to you: I would rather do time for years on end—and I do not mean to say here, where after all compared to those previous places, I am in heaven, but rather in the joint on Alexanderplatz[12] where, morning and night without light, I was squeezed between the C (but without the W) and the iron cot in an 11 cubic meter cell and where I recited my Mörike[13]—than (excuse the expression) "struggle" along with your heroes, or, generally speaking, have anything to do with them! Even Count Westarp[14] would be better—and not because in the Reichstag he spoke of my "almond-shaped velvet eyes," but because he is a *man*!

Let me tell you, as soon as I can stick my nose outside again, I will chase and hunt your company of frogs with trumpet calls, cracks of the whip and bloodhounds—I was going to say like Penthesilea,[15] but by God, not one of you is an Achilles!

Do you have enough now for a New Year's greeting? Then see that you remain a *Mensch!* Being a *Mensch is* the main thing! And that means to be firm, lucid and cheerful. Yes, cheerful despite everything and anything—since whining is the business of the weak. Being a *Mensch* means happily throwing one's life "on fate's great scale" if necessary, but, at the same time, enjoying every bright day and every beautiful cloud. Oh, I can't write you a prescription for being a *Mensch.* I only know how one *is a Mensch,* and you used to know it too when we went walking for a few hours in the Südende fields with the sunset's red light falling on the wheat.

The world is so beautiful even with all its horrors, and it would be even more beautiful if there were no weaklings or cowards. Come, you still get a kiss, because you are a sincere little dear. Happy New Year!

   *R*


                                        Wronke i.P. Fortress, February 16, 1917

*To Emanuel and Mathilde Wurm*

(Send your *sealed* letters here directly, and without marking them "prisoner-of-war" letters.)


*Dearest Tilde,*

Received letter, card and biscuits—many thanks. Don't worry, despite the boldness of your parry, even to the point where you declare war, I will remain as fond of you as always. I had to smile: you want to "fight" me. Young lady, I sit tall in the saddle. No one has yet laid me low, and I would be curious to know the one who can do it. But I had to smile for yet another reason: because you do not even want to "fight" me, and also you are more dependent upon me politically than you would wish to believe. I will always remain your compass, because your straightforward nature tells you that I have the most infallible judgment—because with me all the annoying side issues are forgotten: anxiousness, routine, parliamentary cretinism, which cloud the judgment of others. Your whole argument against my watchword—"Here I stand, I can't do otherwise!" —amounts to the following: Good, so be it, but the masses are too cowardly and weak for such heroism. *Ergo,* one must fit tactics to their weakness and to the axiom: "Walk softly, and you'll walk safely."

What a narrow historical view, my little lamb! There is nothing more mutable than human psychology. The psyche of the masses like the eternal sea always carries all the latent possibilities: the deathly calm and the roaring storm, the lowest cowardice and the wildest heroism. The mass is always that which it *must* be according to the circumstances of the time, and the mass is always at the point of becoming something entirely different than what it appears to be. A fine captain he would be who would chart his course only from the momentary appearance of the water's surface and who would not know how to predict a coming storm from the signs in the sky or from the depths! My little girl, the "disappointment over the masses" is always the most shameful testimony for a political leader. A leader in the grand style does not adapt his tactics to the momentary mood of the masses, but rather to the iron laws of development; he holds fast to his tactics in spite of all "disappointments" and, for the rest, calmly allows history to bring its work to maturity. With that, let us "close the debate. I will gladly remain your friend. Whether, as you wish, I am to remain your teacher, that depends on *you*.

You remind me of an evening six years ago, when we went to Schlachtensee together to wait for the comet. Strange—I can't recall it at all. But you awaken another memory in me. At the time, on an October evening, I was sitting with Hans Kautsky (the painter) at the Havel river, opposite the Peacock Island, and we were also awaiting the comet. There was a deep twilight, yet a dark purple streak was still gleaming on the horizon, which was reflected in the Havel, and which transformed the water's surface into a huge rose petal. A white squall passed over it, and created dark scales on the water, which was sprinkled with a swarm of black dots. These were wild ducks, which had stopped in their flight for a rest on the Havel, and their muted cries—in which so much longing and breadth resounded—were transmitted over to us.

There was a wonderful ambience and we sat quietly, as if bewitched. I looked at the Havel, and Hans accidentally looked at me. Suddenly he rose in terror, and grabbed my hand: "What's the matter with you?" he shouted. You see, a meteor had descended behind his back and had bathed me in a phosphorescent green light; I must have appeared as pale as a corpse. And since I had jumped violently seeing this strange spectacle which was invisible to him, Hans probably could not help thinking that I was dying. (Later he made a beautiful, large painting of that evening at the Havel.)

That you now have neither time nor interest for anything except the "single issue," namely the quandary of the party, is calamitous. For such one-sidedness also clouds one's political judgment; and above all, one must live as a full person at all times.

But look, Lady, since you so rarely get to open a book, at least read only *good* books and not kitsch like the "Spinoza-novel" which you sent to me. What do you want with this particular suffering of the Jews? The poor victims on the rubber plantations in Putumayo, the Negroes in Africa with whose bodies the Europeans play a game of catch, are just as near to me. Do you remember the words written on the work of the Great General Staff about Trotha's campaign in the Kalahari desert? "And the death-rattles, the mad cries of those dying of thirst, faded away into the sublime silence of eternity."

Oh, this "sublime silence of eternity" in which so many screams have faded away unheard. It rings within me so strongly that I have no special corner of my heart reserved for the ghetto: I am at home wherever in the world there are clouds, birds and human tears. . . .

*Your R*

Wronke, May 2, 1917

*To Sonja Liebknecht*

One morning last April, you may remember, I urgently called the two of you on the telephone at ten o'clock to go hear the nightingale who was giving a full concert in the botanical gardens. Once there, we sat quietly on the rocks, by a little trickling pool of water hidden in the dense shrubbery. After the nightingale had finished, however, we suddenly heard a monotonous plaintive call which sounded something like: Gligligligliglick! I said that it sounded like some type of marsh or aquatic bird and Karl[16] agreed, but we were absolutely unable to find out what it was.

Just imagine that a few days ago, early in the morning I suddenly heard the same sound here, nearby. My heart pounded with impatience finally to learn what it could be. I had no peace until I found out today: it is not an aquatic bird, but rather a wryneck, a kind of grey woodpecker. It is only a little bigger than a sparrow, and it takes its name from the fact that, when in danger, it attempts to frighten its enemies through comical gestures and contortions of its head. It lives only on ants, which it collects on its sticky tongue like the anteater. That's why the Spaniards call it *Hormiguero*—the ant-bird.

By the way, Mörike wrote a very pretty comical poem about the bird; Hugo Wolf[17] set it to music. For me, it's as if I had received a present, since I learned the nature of this bird with the wailing voice. Perhaps you could also write Karl about it, it would please him.

What am I reading? For the most part, natural science: geography of plants and animals. Only yesterday I read why the warblers are disappearing from Germany. Increasingly systematic forestry, gardening and agriculture are, step by step, destroying all natural nesting and breeding places: hollow trees, fallow land, thickets of shrubs, withered leaves on the garden grounds. It pained me *so* when I read that. Not because of the song they sing for people, but rather it was the picture of the silent, irresistible extinction of these defenseless little creatures which hurt me to the point where I had to cry. It reminded me of a Russian book which I read while still in Zurich, a book by Professor Sieber[18] about the ravage of the redskins in North America. In exactly the same way, step by step, they have been pushed from their land by civilized men and abandoned to perish silently and cruelly.

I suppose I must be out of sorts to feel everything so intensely. You know, sometimes, it seems to me that I am not really a human being at all, but rather a bird or beast in human form. Inwardly, I feel so much more at home in a plot of garden like the one here, and still more in the meadows when the grass is humming with bees, than at one of our party congresses. Surely I can tell you this, since you will not immediately suspect me of betraying socialism! You know that, in spite of it all, I really hope to die at my post, in a street fight or in prison.

But, my innermost self belongs more to my titmice than to the "comrades." And not because I find a restful refuge in nature like so many morally bankrupt politicians. On the contrary, in nature too, with every step, I find so much that is cruel that I suffer very much. For example, imagine that I cannot get the following little experience out of my mind. Last spring, I was coming home from a walk in the fields, along my silent, empty street, when I noticed a little dark spot on the pavement. I bent down and saw a silent tragedy: a big dung beetle lay on its back, helplessly defending itself with its legs, while a large group of tiny ants swarmed around on top of it and ate it alive! It made my flesh crawl! I took out my handkerchief and began to chase away the brutal little beasts. But, they were so insolent and stubborn that I had to fight a long struggle against them. When I finally freed the poor victim, and placed it faraway on the grass, I saw that two of its legs had already been eaten away. . . . I walked away with the agonizing feeling that in the long run I had done it a very dubious favor.

Now, in the evenings, the twilights are long. How I used to love this hour! In Südende there were many blackbirds, here I neither see nor hear any. I fed a pair all through the winter, and now they have vanished. In Südende, around this time of evening, I used to saunter around the streets; it's so lovely when, still in the last violet light of day, suddenly the rosy gaslights on the street lamps flicker on and still look so strange in the twilight as if they felt a bit ashamed of themselves. Through the streets, the vague figure of some tardy woman scurries by, a porter or a servant girl running to the baker's or grocer's in order to buy something. The shoemaker's children, with whom I have made friends, would still play in the dark street until, from the corner, they would be vigorously called to come home. At this hour, some blackbird would remain who couldn't settle down and who suddenly, like a naughty child, would screech in his sleep and then noisily fly from one tree to another. And I would stand there, in the middle of the street, counting the first stars, not wanting to go home and get out of the mild air and the twilight, in which the day and the night would so softly nestle against one another.

Sonjuscha, I will write you again soon. Be calm and cheerful. Everything will be all right—for Karl too. So long, until the next letter.

I embrace you.

*Your Rosa*

Mid-December 1917

*To Sophie Liebknecht*

Karl has been in Luckau prison for a year now. I have been thinking of that so often this month and of how it is just a year since you came to see me at Wronke, and gave me that lovely Christmas tree. This time I arranged to get one here, but they have brought me such a shabby little tree, with some of its branches broken off—there's no comparison between it and yours. I'm sure I don't know how I shall manage to fix the eight candles that I have got for it. This is my third Christmas under lock and key, but you needn't take it to heart. I am as tranquil and cheerful as ever. Last night I lay awake for a long time. I have to go to bed at ten, but can never get to sleep before one in the morning, so I lie in the dark, pon-dering many things. Last night my thoughts ran this wise: "How strange it is that I am always in a sort of joyful intoxica-tion, though without sufficient cause. Here I am lying in a dark cell upon a mattress hard as stone; the building has its usual churchyard quiet, so that one might as well be already entombed; through the window there falls across the bed a glint of light from the lamp which burns all night in front of the prison. At intervals I can hear faintly in the distance the noise of a passing train or close at hand the dry cough of the prison guard as in his heavy boots, he takes a few slow strides to stretch his limbs. The grind of the gravel beneath his feet has so hopeless a sound that all the weariness and futility of existence seems to be radiated thereby into the damp and gloomy night. I lie here alone and in silence, enveloped in the manifold black wrappings of darkness, tedium, unfreedom, and winter—and yet my heart beats with an immeasurable and incomprehensible inner joy, just as if I were moving in the brilliant sunshine across a flowery mead. And in the darkness I smile at life, as if I were the possessor of a charm which would enable me to transform all that is evil and tragical into serenity and happiness." But when I search my mind for the cause of this joy, I find there is no cause, and can only laugh at myself. I believe that the key to the riddle is simply life itself. This deep darkness of night is soft and beautiful as velvet, if only one looks at it in the right way. The grind of the damp gravel beneath the slow and heavy tread of the prison guard is likewise a lovely little song of life—for one who has ears to hear. At such moments I think of you, and would that I could hand over this magic key to you also. Then, at all times and in all places, you would be able to see the beauty and the joy of life; then you also could live in the sweet intoxication, and make your way across a flowery mead. Do not think that I am offering you imaginary joys, or that I am preaching asceticism. I want you to taste all the real pleasures of the senses. My one desire is to give you in addition my inexhaustible sense of inward bliss. Could I do so, I should be at ease about you, knowing that in your passage through life you were clad in a star-bespangled cloak which would protect you from everything petty, trivial, or harassing.

I am interested to hear of the lovely bunch of berries, black ones and reddish-violet ones you picked in Steglitz Park. The blackberries may have been elder—of course you know the elder berries which hang in thick and heavy clusters among fan-shaped leaves. More probably, however, they were privet, slender and graceful, upright spikes of berries, amid narrow, elongated green leaves. The reddish-violet berries, almost hidden by small leaves, must have been those of the dwarf medlar; their proper color is red, but at this late season, when they are overripe and beginning to rot, they often assume a violet tinge. The leaves are like those of the myrtle, small, pointed, dark green in color, with a leathery upper surface, but rough beneath.

Sonyusha, do you know Platen's *Verhängnisvolle Gabel?*[19] Could you send it to me, or bring it when you come? Karl told me he had read it at home. George's poems[20] are beautiful. Now I know where you got the verse, "And amid the rustling of ruddy corn," which you were fond of quoting when we were walking in the country. I wish you would copy out for me "The Modern Amades" when you have time. I am so fond of the poem (a knowledge of which I owe to Hugo Wolf's setting) but I have not got it here. Are you still reading the *Lessing Legende*? I have been rereading Lange's *His-*

*tory of Materialism²¹*, which I always find stimulating and invigorating. I do so hope you will read it some day.

Sonichka, dear, I had such a pang recently. In the courtyard where I walk, army lorries often arrive, laden with haversacks or old tunics and shirts from the front; sometimes they are stained with blood. They are sent to the women's cells to be mended, and then go back for use in the army. The other day one of these lorries was drawn by a team of buffaloes instead of horses. I had never seen the creatures close at hand before. They are much more powerfully built than our oxen, with flattened heads, and horns strongly recurved, so that their skulls are shaped something like a sheep's skull. They are black, and have huge, soft eyes. The buffaloes are war trophies from Rumania. The soldier-drivers said that it was very difficult to catch these animals, which had always run wild, and still more difficult to break them in to harness. They had been unmercifully flogged—on the principle of "vae victis." There are about a hundred head in Breslau alone. They have been accustomed to the luxuriant Rumanian pastures and have here to put up with lean and scanty fodder. Unsparingly exploited, yoked to heavy loads, they are soon worked to death. The other day a lorry came laden with sacks, so overladen indeed that the buffaloes were unable to drag it across the threshold of the gate. The soldier-driver, a brute of a fellow, belabored the poor beasts so savagely with the butt end of his whip that the wardress at the gate, indignant at the sight, asked him if he had no compassion for animals. "No more than anyone has compassion for us men," he answered with an evil smile, and redoubled his blows. At length the buffaloes succeeded in drawing the load over the obstacle, but one of them was bleeding. You know their hide is proverbial for its thickness and toughness, but it had been torn. While the lorry was being unloaded, the beasts, which were utterly exhausted, stood perfectly still. The one that was bleeding had an expression on its black face and in its soft black eyes like that of a weeping child—one that has been severely thrashed and does not know why, nor how to escape from the torment of ill-treatment. I stood in front of the team; the beast looked at me; the tears welled from my own eyes. The suffering of a dearly loved brother could hardly have moved me more profoundly than I was moved by my impotence in face of this mute agony. Far distant, lost forever, were the green, lush meadows of Rumania. How different there the light of the sun, the breath of the wind; how different there the song of the birds and the melodious call of the herdsman. Instead, the hideous being at one with you in my pain, my weakness, and my street, the fetid stable, the rank hay mingled with moldy straw, the strange and terrible men—blow upon blow, and blood running from gaping wounds. Poor wretch, I am as powerless, as dumb, as yourself; I am longing.

Meanwhile the women prisoners were jostling one another as they busily unloaded the dray and carried the heavy sacks into the building. The driver, hands in pockets, was striding up and down the courtyard, smiling to himself as he whistled a popular air. I had a vision of all the splendor of war! . . .

Write soon, darling Sonichka.

*Your Rosa*

Never mind, my Sonyusha; you must be calm and happy all the same. Such is life, and we have to take it as it is, valiantly, heads erect, smiling ever— despite all.

# Notes

### INTRODUCTION

1 See Tych's introduction to Luxemburg, *Briefe an Leon Jogiches* (Frankfurt: Europäische Verlaganstalt, 1971).

2 Cited in Paul Frölich, *Rosa Luxemburg: Her Life and Work* (New York: Monthly Review Press, 1972), p. 14.

3 Letter to Mathilde Jacob of April 9, 1915, in *The Letters of Rosa Luxemburg*, ed. Stephen Eric Bronner (Boulder: Westview Press, 1978), p. 163.

4 The phrase was used by Richard Fischer, a managing editor of *Vorwärts*, the main publication of the German Social Democratic Party. See *Protokoll über die Verhandlungen des Parteitages der Sozialdemokratischen Partei Deutschlands, September 22–28, 1901* (Berlin: SPD, 1901), p. 191.

5 "Perspectives and Projects," in *Die Internationale*, no. 1, April 1915. That these words were directed against Kautsky, who had *defended* Luxemburg's earlier critique of Bernstein (though somewhat belatedly), suggests that his overall position was not as totally opposed to Bernstein's as appeared to many at the time.

6 See the excerpts from *Reform or Revolution*, p. 137, below.

7 This passage from *Reform or Revolution*, not included in this *Reader*, can be found in Luxemburg, *Selected Political Writings*, ed. Dick Howard (New York: Monthly Review Press, 1971), p. 81.

8 J.P. Nettl, *Rosa Luxemburg* (London: Oxford University Press, 1966), p. 246.

9 "Rede auf Parteitag der Sozialdemokratischen Partei Deutschlands von 17 bis 23 September 1905 in Jena," in Luxemburg, *Gesammelte Werke*, Band 1/2 (Berlin: Dietz Verlag, 1974), p. 601.

10 See the excerpts from *The Mass Strike, the Party, and the Trade Unions*, p.198, below.

11 Letter to Emanuel and Mathilde Wurm of July 18, 1906, in Bronner, *Letters*, p. 119.

12 See "Die badische Budgetabstimmung," *Bremer Bürgerzeitung*, August 10, 1910, in Luxemburg, *Gesammelte Werke*, Band 2, pp. 427–28.

13 Letter to Clara Zetkin of March 20, 1907. See p. 385, below.

14 Letter to Konstantin Zetkin of March 20, 1907, in Luxemburg, *Gesammelte Briefe*, Band 2 (Berlin: Dietz Verlag, 1982), p. 282.

15 Letter of June 27, 1908 to Konstantin Zetkin in *Gesammelte Briefe*, Band 2, pp. 556-58.

16 For excerpts, see this volume, chapter 8.

17 Cited in Raya Dunayevskaya, *Rosa Luxemburg, Women's Liberation, and Marx's Philosophy of Revolution* (Urbana and Chicago: University of Illinois Press, 1991), p. 27.

18 Leon Trotsky's response was no better. In 1911, he wrote to Kautsky that Luxemburg's sharp critique was due

to "impatience" stemming from her Russian character, also assuring him that none of the Russians, not even the Bolsheviks, supported her. (Cited by Nettl, *Rosa Luxemburg*, p. 433.) Years later, in a defense of Luxemburg against slanders from Stalin, Trotsky acknowledged that Luxemburg had been ahead of Lenin and himself in recognizing Kautsky's opportunism: "Lenin . . . did not support Luxemburg up to 1914. . . . In Lenin's eyes, Bebel and Kautsky stood immeasurably higher as revolutionists than in the eyes of Rosa Luxemburg, who observed them at closer range, in action, and who was much more directly subjected to the atmosphere of German politics." See Trotsky's "Hands off Rosa Luxemburg" (1932), in *Rosa Luxemburg Speaks*, ed. Mary-Alice Waters (New York: Pathfinder, 1970), p. 443.

19   Letter of January 9, 1899. See pp. 380–81, below.

20   Letter of February 16, 1917. For the full text, see p. 390, below.

21   Frölich, *Rosa Luxemburg*, p. 148.

22   See "What Is Economics?" in *Rosa Luxemburg Speaks*, pp. 219–49.

23   Michael Löwy, "Le communisme primitif dans les écrits économiques de Rosa Luxemburg," in *Rosa Luxemburg aujourd'hui*, edited by Claudie Weill and Gilbert Badia (Vincennes: Presses Universitaires de Vincennes, 1986), p. 68. Besides Löwy's, the few other discussions of the *Introduction to Political Economy*—in Frölich's biography, in Ernest Mandel's lengthy preface to the French edition (*Introduction à l'économie politique,* Paris: Éditions Anthropos, 1970), and in the East German introduction to its republication in

Luxemburg's *Gesammelte Werke*, Vol. 5 (Berlin: Dietz Verlag, 1975)—give short shrift to Luxemburg's lengthy treatment of these precapitalist social formations.

24   See "The Dissolution of Primitive Communism," p. 110, below.

25   See the multilingual *Ethnological Notebooks of Karl Marx*, ed. Lawrence Krader (Assen: Van Gorcum, 1972; all-English edition by David Norman Smith, forthcoming from Yale University Press) and *Karl Marx über Formen vorkapitalischer Produktion,* ed. Hans-Peter Harstick (Frankfurt: Campus Verlag, 1977), for two of Marx's most important writings from his last decade on technologically underdeveloped societies. Although Engels made use of some of some passages from *The Ethnological Notebooks* for his *Origin of the Family, Private Property, and the State* (1884), there were considerable differences between his approach and Marx's. An even larger group of these notebooks from Marx's last years will appear in Vol. IV/27 of the ongoing *Marx-Engels Gesamtausgabe*. For an overview of this volume, see Kevin B. Anderson, "Marx's Late Writings on Non-Western and Pre-Capitalist Societies and Gender," *Rethinking Marxism.* 14:4 (2003), pp. 84–96.

26   Narihiko Ito, "Erstveröffentlichung von Rosa Luxemburgs Schrift 'Sklaverei'," in *Jahrbuch für Historische Kommunismus-Forschung,* 2002, p. 175. Ito's substantial introduction also contains a list of over fifty previously unknown Luxemburg texts that were recently unearthed in the former Communist Party archives in Moscow.

27  The English editions of Luxemburg's *Accumulation of Capital*, including the latest one (London: Routledge, 2003), have not included the subtitle.

28  See excerpts from *The Accumulation of Capital*, p. 50–51, below.

29  See excerpts from *The Accumulation of Capital*, p. 55–56, below.

30  The best-known early critique was Nicolai Bukharin's *Imperialism and the Accumulation of Capital* (New York: Monthly Review Press, 1972), first published in Russian in 1924. For some fairly recent critiques, see Dunayevskaya, *Rosa Luxemburg*, and Paul Mattick, Sr., "Rosa Luxemburg in Retrospect," *Root and Branch*, No. 6, 1978. For a recent elaboration of Luxemburg's theory of accumulation and a response to her critics, from Bukharin and Henryk Grossmann to Mattick, Dunayevskaya, and Paul Sweezy, see Paul Zarembka, "Rosa Luxemburg's *Accumulation of Capital*: Critics Try to Bury the Message," *Current Perspectives in Social Theory*, Vol. 21 (2002), pp. 3–45

31  On this point, Luxemburg's earliest critic was Lenin. See especially his 1916 article, "The Junius Pamphlet," where he wrote that Luxemburg "applies Marxist dialectics only half way" by failing to differentiate between progressive and reactionary forms of nationalism. Lenin, *Collected Works*, Vol. 22 (Moscow: Progress Publishers, 1964), p. 316.

32  Luxemburg, *The Accumulation of Capital—An Anti-Critique* (New York: Monthly Review Press, 1972), p. 148.

33  Paul Le Blanc, "Introduction" to *Rosa Luxemburg: Reflections and Writings*, ed. Le Blanc (Amherst, N.Y.: Humanity Books, 1999), p. 10.

34  Andrea Nye, "Luxemburg and Socialist Feminism" in Le Blanc, *Rosa Luxemburg*, p. 105.

35  Frigga Haug, "Rosa Luxemburg and Women's Politics" (orig. 1988), in Haug, *Beyond Female Masochism: Memory-Work and Politics* (London: Verso, 1992), p. 221.

36  In her *Rosa Luxemburg: A Life* (Boston: Beacon Press, 1986), Elzbieta Ettinger characterizes their relationship rather differently, but without providing any evidence to support her claim: "That Luxemburg did not share Zetkin's views on or commitment to women's causes did not affect their friendship" (p. 102).

37  Luxemburg, "A Tactical Question," this volume. See p. 236, below.

38  Luxemburg, "The Proletarian Woman," this volume. See p. 244–45, below.

39  Richard Abraham, *Rosa Luxemburg: A Life for the International* (Oxford: Berg, 1989), p. 67. Inexplicably, Abraham writes at a later point, however, "For Luxemburg, national independence was a bourgeois fetish on a par with the 'women's rights' she scorned with special vehemence" (p. 97). Such a comparison between Luxemburg's attitude toward the national question and women's rights is unjustified; while she vehemently opposed national self-determination in all forms, she supported the struggle for women's rights.

40  Letter of June 27, 1908, to Konstantin Zetkin in *Gesammelte Briefe*, Band 2, pp. 356–58.

41  Dunayevskaya, *Rosa Luxemburg*, pp. 91–93.

42  Adrienne Rich, "Raya Dunayevskaya's Marx" in Rich, *Arts of the Possible: Essays and Conversations* (New York: W. W. Norton, 2001), pp. 95–96.

43 See especially Luxemburg, *The Russian Revolution and Leninism or Marxism?* ed. Bertram Wolfe (Ann Arbor: University of Michigan Press, 1961). The title "Leninism or Marxism?" was supplied by Wolfe.

44 See the excerpts from *Reform or Revolution*, p. 130, below

45 Annelies Laschitza, *Im Lebensrausch, trotz alledem. Rosa Luxemburg, Eine Biographie* (Berlin: Aufbau-Verlag, 1996), p. 404.

46 Ever since 1922, when Lenin and Trotsky attacked its publication by Luxemburg's friend Paul Levi, who had been expelled from the Communist Party, there has been much speculation over whether Luxemburg actually intended to publish this essay containing so many strong critiques of the new Bolshevik regime. This question was settled over a decade ago, however, when some previously unknown Luxemburg letters surfaced that made clear her intention to publish this essay. See Feliks Tych, "Drei unbekannte Briefe Rosa Luxemburgs über die Oktoberrevolution," *IWK Internationale wissenschaftliche Korrespondenz zür Geschichte der deutsche Arbeiterbewegung* 27: 3 (1991), pp. 357–66.

47 In keeping with Trotsky's unquestioned importance at the time, before this was covered over by decades of Stalinist falsification, Luxemburg again and again refers to the policies of "Lenin and Trotsky."

48 The view of Luxemburg's critique of Lenin as reflecting a failure on her part to seize the historical initiative has been put forth by Slavoj Zizek in "George Lukács as the Philosopher of Lenin," in *A Defense of History and Class Consciousness: Tailism and the Dialectic*, by Georg Lukács (London: Verso, 2000). For a critique of Zizek's contention, see Peter Hudis, "Lukács's *History and Class Consciousness* Reconsidered," *News & Letters* (June 2001), pp. 5, 10.

49 See the excerpts from *The Russian Revolution*, pp. 306–8, below.

50 Letter to Luise Kautsky of January 26, 1917, in Luxemburg, *Letters to Karl and Luise Kautsky from 1896 to 1918*, ed. Luise Kautsky (New York: Robert M. McBride & Co., 1925), pp. 187–94.

51 This letter of August 11, 1908, is published in Henrietta Roland-Holst, *Rosa Luxemburg* (Zürich: Jean Christophe Verlag, 1977), p. 221.

52 Cited in Frölich, *Rosa Luxemburg*, p. 259. However, Nettl writes in his *Rosa Luxemburg* that this phrase "cannot be attributed to him with certainty" (p. 737).

53 See "Ein Pyrrhussieg," *Die Rote Fahne*, Dec. 21, 1918, in *Gesammelte Werke*, Band 4, p. 471.

54 See "Our Program and the Political Situation," p. XXX, below.

55 Lelio Basso's contention that Luxemburg found it hard to effect a complete break with the SPD because "Marx and Engels had considered it their party" is hardly sustainable in light of Marx's 1875 sharp critique of the unity congress that gave shape to German Social Democracy. See Basso's *Rosa Luxemburg: A Reappraisal* (London: Cox & Wyman, 1970), p. 127. For discussions on the concept of organization found in Marx's *Critique of the Gotha Program,* see Dunayevskaya, *Rosa Luxemburg*, pp. 153–57 and István Mézsáros, *Beyond Capital: Toward a Theory of Transition* (London: Merlin Press, 1995), pp. 694–703 .

56  For an important reevaluation of
    Luxemburg's role in the events of
    January 1919, see Ottokar Luban,
    "Demokratische Sozialistin oder
    'blutige Rosa'?" *IWK* 35:2 (1999),
    pp. 176–97. See also William A. Pelz,
    *The Spartakusbund and the
    German Working-Class Movement,
    1914–1919* (Lewiston, N.Y.:
    Edwin Mellen Press, 1987).


CHAPTER 1

1   For Marx's diagrams on expanded
    reproduction, see *Capital,* Vol. II
    (London: Vintage, 1978), chapter 21,
    section 3, "Schematic Presentation
    of Accumulation," pp. 581–597.
2   Marx, *Capital,* Vol. I (New York:
    Vintage, 1976), pp. 726–27.
3   Mikhail Ivanovich Tugan-Baranovski
    (1865–1919) was a Ukrainian-born
    economist who argued that over-
    investment was the cause of recessions.
    In his *Theoretical Groundwork of
    Marxism* (1905) he attacked Marx's
    theory of capitalist crisis, arguing that
    it was possible for capitalist economies
    to maintain a long-term state of steady
    equilibrium and balanced growth.
    Luxemburg critiqued his views in
    chapter 23 of *The Accumulation of
    Capital.*
4   *Capital,* Vol. I, p. 636.
5   *Capital,* Vol. II, p. 408.
6   *Capital,* Vol. II, p. 422.
7   *Capital,* Vol. II, p. 497.
8   *Capital,* Vol. III (New York: Vintage,
    1981), pp. 614–15.
9   *Theories of Surplus Value,* in *Marx-
    Engels Collected Works* (hereafter
    MECW), Vol. 32 (New York:
    International Publishers, 1989), p. 124.
10  See *Capital,* Vol. II, pp. 589–95.

11  "It is never the original thinkers
    who draw the absurd conclusions.
    They leave that to the Says and
    MacCullochs" (*Capital,* Vol. II,
    p. 466)—and we might add—to the
    Tugan-Baranovskis. (RL)
12  To illustrate the problem of expanded
    reproduction, in Vol. II of *Capital*
    Marx divided social production into
    two departments: Department I is
    production of means of production,
    while Department II is production
    of means of consumption.
13  The figures result from the difference
    between the amounts of constant
    capital in Department I under condi-
    tions of technical progress, and under
    Marx's stable conditions. (RL)
14  Jean Charles Leonard Sismondi
    (1773–1842) was an early critic of
    industrialism. His *New Principles of
    Political Economy* (1819) argued for
    state regulation of economic competi-
    tion in order to create a balance
    between production and consumption.
15  *Theories of Surplus Value,* MECW 32,
    p. 116.
16  *Capital,* Vol. III, pp. 351–53.
17  David Ricardo (1772–1823), the noted
    English political economist who
    developed the implications of the
    labor theory of value. He authored
    *Principles of Political Economy and
    Taxation* (1817).
18  Adam Smith (1723–1790) developed
    the labor theory of value in his *Wealth
    of Nations* (1776). Marx subjected his
    work to a detailed critique in Vol. II
    of *Capital.*
19  *Theories of Surplus Value,* MECW 32,
    p. 154.
20  *Capital,* Vol. III, p. 420.
21  "If capital and the productivity of labor
    advance and the standard of capitalist

production in general is on a higher level of development, then there is a correspondingly greater mass of commodities passing through the market from production to individual and industrial consumption, greater certainty that each particular capital will find the conditions for its reproduction available in the market" (*Theories of Surplus Value*, MECW 32, pp. 115-16). (RL)

22  *Theories of Surplus Value*, MECW 32, pp. 115-16. Marx's italics. (RL)

23  Thomas Robert Malthus (1766-1834), whom Marx frequently attacked, was an economist who argued that human population growth will outstrip the supply of food. Vasily Pavlovich Vorontsov (1847-1918) was a Russian liberal Populist who argued that capitalism could not be implanted in Russia. Peter Struve (1870-1944) was a founding member of the Russian Social Democratic Labor Party who edited the journal *Osvoboshdenye* (Liberation). A "legal Marxist," he moved to the right after the 1905 Revolution and joined the liberal Constitutional Democratic Party (Cadets).

24  Nicolayon, the pen-name of Nikolai Frantsevich Danielson (1844-1918), was a leading Russian Populist who corresponded with Marx for many years and participated in the translation of Vol. I of *Capital* into Russian in 1872. He argued that Russia could reach socialism without going through capitalist industrialization.

25  Karl Johann Rodbertus (1805-1875) was a German economist who developed a labor theory of value and defended a version of statist socialism. His theory of underconsumption was very influential among the German

Social Democrats. Julius Hermann von Kirchmann (1802-99) was a German economist and philosopher who argued that economic crises result from a lack of markets. Luxemburg discusses his view in detail in chapter 15 of *The Accumulation of Capital*.

26  Luxemburg is here referring to Marx's detailed effort in Part 3 of Vol. II of *Capital* to expose what he considered Adam Smith's "incredible aberration," that of "spiriting away" the constant portion of capital in *The Wealth of Nations*.

27  The following figures plainly show the importance of the cotton industry for English exports: In 1893, cotton exports to the amount of £ 64,000,000 made up 23 percent, and iron and other metal exports not quite 17 percent, of the total export of manufactured goods, amounting to £ 277,000,000 in all.

In 1898, cotton exports to the amount of £ 65,000,000 made up 28 percent, and metal exports 22 per cent, of the total export of manufactured goods, amounting to £ 233,400,000 in all.

In comparison, the figures for the German Empire show the following result: in 1898, cotton exports to the amount of £ 11,595,000 made up 5.75 percent of the total exports, amounting to £ 200,500,000. 5,250,000,000 yards of cotton bales were exported in 1898, 2,250,000,000 of them to India (E. Jaffé: *Die englische Baumwollindustrie und die Organization des Exporthandels*. Schmoller's Jahrbücher, vol. XXIV, p. 1033). In 1908, British exports of cotton yarn alone amounted to £ 13,100,000 (*Statist. Jahrb. für das deutsche Reich*, 1910).

28  One-fifth of German aniline dyes,
and one-half of her indigo, goes to
countries such as China, Japan, British
India, Egypt, Asiatic Turkey, Brazil,
and Mexico. (RL)

29  *Capital*, Vol. I, pp. 751–52.

30  The English Blue Book on the
practices of the Peruvian Amazon
Company Ltd., in Putumayo, has
recently revealed that in the free
republic of Peru and without the
political form of colonial supremacy,
international capital can, to all intents
and purposes, enslave the natives, so
that it may appropriate the means of
production of the primitive countries
by exploitation on the greatest scale.
Since 1900, this company, financed by
English and foreign capitalists, has
thrown upon the London market
approximately four thousand tons
of Putumayo rubber. During this time,
thirty thousand natives were killed
and most of the ten thousand survivors
were crippled by beatings. (RL)

31  *Capital*, Vol. I, pp. 727. Similarly in
another passage: "One part of the
surplus value, of the surplus means of
subsistence produced, must then be
converted into variable capital for the
purpose of purchasing new labor.
This can only be done if the number
of workers grows or if their working
time is prolonged.... This, however,
cannot be considered a ready measure
for accumulation. The working
population can increase if formerly
unproductive workers are transformed
into productive ones, or if parts of the
population who previously performed
no work, such as women, children
and paupers, are drawn into the
process of production. Here, however,
we shall ignore this aspect. Lastly, the

working population can increase
through an absolute increase in population. If accumulation is to proceed
steadily and continuously, it must be
grounded in an absolute growth of the
population, though this may decline in
comparison with the capital employed.
An expanding population appears
as the basis of accumulation conceived
as a steady process. An indispensable
condition for this is an average wage
which is adequate not only to the
reproduction of the working population but permits its continual increase"
(*Theories of Surplus Value*, MECW 32,
pp. 109–10. (RL)

32  *Capital*, Vol. I, pp. 781–794.

33  A table published in the United States
shortly before the War of Secession
contained the following data about the
value of the annual production of the
Slave States and the number of slaves
employed—for the greatest part
on cotton plantations:

| Year | Cotton (Dollars): | Slaves |
|---|---|---|
| 1800 | 5,200,000 | 893,041 |
| 1810 | 15,000,000 | 1,191,364 |
| 1820 | 26,300,000 | 1,543,688 |
| 1830 | 34,100,000 | 2,009,053 |
| 1840 | 74,600,000 | 2,487,255 |
| 1850 | 101,800,000 | 3,197,509 |
| 1851 | 137,300,000 | 3,200,000 |

Simons, "Class Struggles in American
History." Supplement to *Neue Zeit*
(*Klassenkämpfe in der Geschichte
Amerikas. Ergänzungsheft der "Neue
Zeit"*), Nr. 7, p. 39.

34  Bryce, a former English Minister,
describes a model pattern of such
hybrid forms in the South African
diamond mines: "the most striking
sight at Kimberley, and one unique in

the world, is furnished by the two so-called 'compounds' in which the natives who work in the mines are housed and confined. They are huge inclosures, unroofed, but covered with a wire netting to prevent anything from being thrown out of them over the walls, and with a subterranean entrance to the adjoining mine. The mine is worked on the system of three eight-hour shifts, so that the workman is never more than eight hours together underground. Round the interior of the wall are built sheds or huts in which the natives live and sleep when not working. A hospital is also provided within the inclosure, as well as a school where the workpeople can spend their leisure in learning to read and write. No spirits are sold. . . . Every entrance is strictly guarded, and no visitors, white or native, are permitted, all supplies being obtained from the store within, kept by the company. The De Beers mine compound contained at the time of my visit 2,600 natives, belonging to a great variety of tribes, so that here one could see specimens of the different native types from Natal and Pondoland, in the south, to the shores of Lake Tanganyika in the far north. They come from every quarter, attracted by the high wages, usually eighteen to thirty shillings a week, and remain for three months or more, and occasionally even for longer periods. . . . In the vast oblong compound one sees Zulus from Natal, Fingos, Pondos, Tembus, Basutos, Bechuanas, Gungunhana's subjects from the Portuguese territories, some few Matabili and Makalaka; and plenty of Zambesi boys from the tribes on both sides of that great river, a living ethnological collection such as can be examined nowhere else in South Africa. Even Bushmen, or at least natives with some bushman blood in them, are not wanting. They live peaceably together, and amuse themselves in their several ways during their leisure hours. Besides games of chance, we saw a game resembling 'fox and geese' played with pebbles on a board; and music was being discoursed on two rude native instruments, the so-called 'Kaffir piano' made of pieces of iron of unequal length fastened side by side in a frame, and a still ruder contrivance of hard bits of wood, also of unequal size, which when struck by a stick emit different notes, the first beginning of a tune. A very few were reading or writing letters, the rest busy with their cooking or talking to one another. Some tribes are incessant talkers, and in this strange mixing-pot of black men one may hear a dozen languages spoken as one passes from group to group" (James Bryce, *Impressions of South Africa*, London, 1897, pp. 242 ff.).

After several months of work, the negro as a rule leaves the mine with the wages he has saved up. He returns to his tribe, buying a wife with his money, and lives again his traditional life. Cf. also in the same book the most lively description of the methods used in South Africa to solve the "labor-problem." Here we are told the negroes are compelled to work in the mines and plantations of Kimberley, Witwatersrand, Natal, Matabeleland, by stripping them of all land and cattle, i.e. depriving them of their means of existence, by making them into proletarians and also demoralizing them with alcohol. (Later, when they are already within the "enclosure" of capital, spirits, to which they have just been accustomed, are strictly prohibited—the object of exploitation must be kept fit for use.) Finally, they are simply pressed into the wage system of capital by force, by imprisonment, and flogging. (RL)

35 Jean-Baptiste Say (1767–82) was a French economist who propounded "Say's law"—the thesis that every act of production creates the purchasing power to buy the product.

36 The relations between Germany and England provide a typical example. (RL)

37 The Nogaian Tatars were allies of Tamerlane (Timur), who conquered northern India in 1398.

38 James Mill (1773–1836), British economist and philosopher whose work Marx closely studied and critiqued. His *History of British India* was very influential among commentators of the time.

39 Mill, in his history of British India, substantiates the thesis that under primitive conditions the land belongs always and everywhere to the sovereign, on evidence collected at random and quite indiscriminately from the most varied sources (Mungo Park, Herodotus, Volney, Acosta, Garcilasso de la Vega, Abbé Grosier, Barrow, Diodorus, Strabo and others). Applying this thesis to India, he goes on to say: "From these facts only one conclusion can be drawn, that the property of the soil resided in the sovereign; for if it did not reside in him, it will be impossible to show to whom it belonged" (James Mill, *History of British India* (4th edition, 1840), vol. I, p. 311). Mill's editor, H. H. Wilson who, as Professor of Sanskrit at Oxford University, was thoroughly versed in the legal relations of Ancient India, gives an interesting

commentary to this classical deduction. Already in his preface he characterizes the author as a partisan who has juggled with the whole history of British India in order to justify the theories of Mr. Bentham and who, with this end, has used the most dubious means for his portrait of the Hindus which in no way resembles the original and almost outrages humanity. He appends the following footnote to our quotation: "The greater part of the text and of the notes here is wholly irrelevant. The illustrations drawn from the Mahometan practice, supposing them to be correct, have nothing to do with the laws and rights of the Hindus. They are not, however, even accurate and Mr. Mill's guides have misled him." Wilson then contests outright the theory of the sovereign's right of ownership in land, especially with reference to India. (Ibid., p. 305, footnote.) Henry Maine, too, is of the opinion that the British attempted to derive their claim to Indian land from the Mahometans in the first place, and he recognizes this claim to be completely unjustified. "The assumption which the English first made was one which they inherited from their Mahometan predecessor. It was that all the soil belonged in absolute property to the sovereign,—and that all private property in land existed by his sufferance. The Mahometan theory and the corresponding Mahometan practice had put out of sight the ancient view of the sovereign's rights which, though it assigned to him a far larger share of the produce of the land than any Western ruler has ever claimed, yet in nowise denied the existence of private property in land" (*Village Communities in the East and West* (5th edition, vol. 2, 1890, p. 104). Maxim Kovalevski, on the other hand, has proved thoroughly that this alleged "Mahometan theory and practice" is an exclusively British legend. (Cf. his excellent study, written in Russian, *On the Causes, the Development and the Consequences of the Disintegration of Communal Ownership of Land* (Moscow, 1879), part I.) Incidentally, British experts and their French colleagues at the time of writing maintain an analogous legend about China, for example, asserting that all the land there had been the Emperor's property. (Cf. the refutation of this legend by Dr. O. Franke, *Die Rechtsverhältnisse am Grundeigentum in China*, 1903.) (RL)

40 "The partitions of inheritances and execution for debt levied on land are destroying the communities—this is the formula heard nowadays everywhere in India" (Henry Maine, *Village Communities in the East and West*, p. 113). (RL)

41 This view of British colonial policy, expounded e.g. by Lord Roberts of Kandahar (for many years a representative of British power in India) is typical. He can give no other explanation for the Sepoy Mutiny than mere "misunderstandings" of the paternal intentions of the British rulers. "The alleged unfairness of what was known in India as the land settlement, under which system the right and title of each landholder to his property was examined, and the amount of revenue to be paid by him to the paramount Power, as owner of the soil, was regulated . . . as peace and order were established, the system of land revenue, which had been enforced

in an extremely oppressive and corrupt manner under successive Native Rulers and dynasties, had to be investigated and revised. With this object in view, surveys were made, and inquiries instituted into the rights of ownership and occupancy, the result being that in many cases it was found that families of position and influence had either appropriated the property of their humbler neighbors, or evaded an assessment proportionate to the value of their estates. Although these inquiries were carried out with the best intentions, they were extremely distasteful to the higher classes, while they failed to conciliate the masses. The ruling families deeply resented our endeavors to introduce an equitable determination of rights and assessment of land revenue. . . . On the other hand, although the agricultural population greatly benefited by our rule, they could not realise the benevolent intentions of a Government which tried to elevate their position and improve their prospects" (*Forty One Years in India*, London, 1901, p. 233). (RL)

42 Tamerlane or Timur (1336–1405), the Turkmen Mongol conqueror who created an empire ranging from India to the Mediterranean, invaded northern India in 1398. He captured Delhi and massacred its inhabitants.

43 In his *Maxims on Government* (translated from the Persian into English in 1783), Timur says: "And I commanded that they should build places of worship, and monasteries in every city; and that they should erect structures for the reception of travellers on the high roads, and that they should make bridges across the rivers.

"And I commanded that the ruined bridges should be repaired; and that bridges should be constructed over the rivulets, and over the rivers; and that on the roads, at the distance of one stage from each other, Kauruwansarai should be erected; and that guards and watchmen should be stationed on the road, and that in every Kauruwansarai people should be appointed to reside . . .

"And I ordained, whoever undertook the cultivation of waste lands, or built an aqueduct, or made a canal, or planted a grove, or restored to culture a deserted district, that in the first year nothing should be taken from him, and that in the second year, whatever the subject voluntarily offered should be received, and that in the third year, duties should be collected according to the regulation" (James Mill, *History of British India*, vol. II, pp. 493, 498). (RL)

44 Count Warren, *De L'État moral de la population indigène.* Quoted by Kovalevski, *On the Causes, the Development and the Consequences of the Disintegration of Communal Ownership of Land*, p. 164. (RL)

45 *Historical and Descriptive Account of British India* from the most remote period to the conclusion of the Afghan war by Hugh Murray, James Wilson, Greville, Professor Jameson, William Wallace and Captain Dalrymple (Edinburgh, 4th edition, 1843), vol. II, p. 427. Quoted by Kovalevski, *On the Causes, the Development and the Consequences of the Disintegration of Communal Ownership of Land*. (RL)

46 Victor v. Leyden, *Agrarverfassung und Grundsteuer in Britisch-Ostindien. Jahrb. F. Ges., Verw. u. Volksw.*, vol. XXXVI, no. 4, p. 1855. (RL)

47 The *zadruga* consisted of a family group of 100 or more individuals who worked the land communally under the direction of family elders.

48 "When dying, the father of the family nearly always advises his children to live in unity, according to the example of their elders. This is his last exhortation, his dearest wish" (A. Hanotaux et A. Letournaux, *La Kabylie et les Coûtumes Kabyles*, vol. II, 1873, "Droit Civil", pp. 468–73). The authors, by the way, appraised this impressive description of communism in the clan with this peculiar sentence: "Within the industrious fold of the family association, all are united in a common purpose, all work for the general interest—but no one gives up his freedom or renounces his hereditary rights. In no other nation does the organization approach so closely to equality, being yet so far removed from communism." (RL)

49 The 1830 revolution in France.

50 Louis Philippe (1773–1850), French monarch brought to power by the July Revolution of 1830 and overthrown by the 1848 Revolution.

## CHAPTER 2

1 The "mark" was an ancient Germanic communal form of village organization that survived in modified form into the modern period. Luxemburg uses the term more universally, applying to what she saw as similar forms in various societies around the world.

2 See Georg Ludwig von Maurer, *Geschichte der Markenverfassung in Deutschland* (Erlangen, 1856), p. 119.

3 The artisan in the Greek community of the Homeric period had exactly the

same position: "All these people (metalworkers, carpenters, musicians, doctors) are *demiurgoi* (from demos = people); that is, they work for the members of the community, not for themselves; they are personally free, but they are not considered full members; they are beneath the actual members of the community, the small peasant. They are often transients; they move from place to place or, if they have a name, they are summoned from afar." (Eduard Meyer, *Die wirtschaftliche Entwicklung des Altertums* [Jena 1895], p. 17)—RL.

4  The Inca Empire was in fact formed several centuries later.

5  Luxemburg actually writes "Vechua" rather than "Keshua," the standard German for "Quechua," apparently transliterating directly from one of her principal sources, the Russian anthropologist Maxim Kovalevsky's book, *Obscinnoe Zemlevladenie. Priciny, khod i posledstvija ego razlozenija* [Communal Land ownership: The Causes, Processes, and Consequences of Its Disintegration] (Moscow, 1879). Marx knew Kovalevsky and made notes on his book shortly after it appeared. It is likely that Luxemburg was aware of this. A translation of most of Marx's notes can be found in the appendix to Lawrence Krader, *The Asiatic Mode of Production* (Assen: Van Gorcum, 1975); the full version appeared in Hans-Peter Harstick, ed., *Karl Marx über Formen vorkapitalistischer Produktion* (Frankfurt: Campus Verlag, 1977).

6  Max Weber, "Agrargeschichte. I. Agrarverhältnisse im Altertum." In *Hand-

wörterbuch der Staatswissenschaften*, 2nd ed., vol. 1 (Jena, 1898), p. 69—RL.

7  Theopompus of Chios, a fourth century B.C.E. Greek historian.

8  Ettore Ciccotti, *Der Untergang der Sklaverei im Altertum* (Berlin, 1910), p. 37-38—RL.

9  [Bartolemé de Las Casas,] *Brevissima Relación de la destruycion de las Indias* (Sevilla, 1552), cited in Kovalevsky, p. 47—RL.

10  Heinrich Handelmann, *Geschichte der Insel Hayti* (Kiel, 1856), p. 6—RL.

11  Luxemburg actually refers to the island of "Kumagna" and the port of "Kumani," transliterating both names directly from Kovalevsky (p. 51), who cites Girolamo Benzoni's *Storia del mundo nuovo* (Venice, 1565). Consulting Benzoni directly, we have identified "Kumani" as the port city of Cumana in present-day Venezuela, but were unable to identify "Kumagna."

12  Girolamo Benzoni, *Storia del mundo nuovo* (Venezia 1565), as cited in Kovalevsky, pp. 51-52—RL.

13  [Pierre-François-David de] Charleroix, *Histoire de l'Isle Espagnole ou de St. Dominique* (Paris, 1730), Part I, p. 228, as cited in Kovalevsky, p. 50—RL.

14  [José de] Acosta, *Historia natural y moral de las Indias* (Barcelona, 1591), as cited in Kovalevsky, p. 52—RL.

15  In the manuscript, Luxemburg used the Hebrew name for Ham, "Cham."

16  Ujiji, on Lake Tanganyika, was a center of the East African slave trade.

17  *The Life and African Explorations of Dr. David Livingstone* (New York: Cooper Square Press, 2002, orig. 1874), pp. 328-29.

[…o de] Zurita, p. 57-59, as cited
Kovalevsky, p. 62—RL.
At this point, Luxemburg wrote in
the margin: "Relations here similar to
India, Algeria, (Russia), Java, etc."

20 Zurita, p. 329, as cited in Kovalevsky,
pp. 62-63—RL.

21 Zurita, p. 295, as cited in Kovalevsky,
p. 65—RL.

22 Cited in Kovalevsky, p. 66.

23 Zurita, p. 87, cited in Kovalevsky,
p. 69—RL.

24 Zurita, p. 341, cited in Kovalevsky,
p. 60—RL.

25 *Memorial que presenta a su Magestad
el licenciado Juan Ortiz de Cervantes,
Abogado y Procurador general del
Reyno del Peru y encomenderos, sobre
pedir remedio del danno y diminución
des los indios*, 1619, cited in Kovalevsky,
p. 61—RL.

26 Friedrich Wilhelm Herschel
(1738-1822), German-born British
astronomer, who discovered the
planet Uranus and hypothesized that
nebulae are composed of stars.

27 At this point, Luxemburg writes
in the margin: "1. Canal building
(division of labor). Despite this, mark
community. 2. Several types
(Kovalevsky) of society. 3. All this
remains despite the Muslim conquest
and feudalization. 4. English!"

28 Timur's forces massacred tens of
thousands at Delhi in 1398.

29 The *zadruga* consisted of a family group
of a hundred or more working the land
under the direction of family elders.

30 At this point, Luxemburg writes
in the margin: "James Mill!!"

31 Marx, *Capital*, Vol. I. (London:
Penguin, 1976), pp. 477-79.

32 The terms in parenthesis are drawn
from Kovalevsky, pp. 84-85, who
leaves them in the Western alphabet.
He sources an 1845 British report on
the Northwest Frontier Provinces,
a Pashto-speaking area of present-day
Pakistan and Afghanistan. In Pashto,
"*wund*" also refers to the periphery
of a village. "*Lulmee*" refers to land
that lacks natural or artificial irrigation
and thus depends for its fertility
upon rainfall.

33 The discussion of Algeria is missing
in the manuscript and may have been
used in *Accumulation of Capital*.

34 Boris Nikolaievich Chicherin (1828-
1904), liberal historian and philosopher
who advocated emancipation of the
serfs and who also wrote on Hegel.

35 See the new edition of the *Handwörterbuch* on Plekhanov and Russian
Social Democracy. However, Engels
in "Afterword [1894] to 'On Social
Relations in Russia'," [MECW 27,
pp. 432-33]. Eduard Meyer—RL.

36 See V. G. Trirogov, *Obschina i podat*
(St. Petersburg, 1882), p. 49—RL.

37 The first "revision" enacted by a ukase
by Peter in 1719, was organized like
a kind of penal expedition on foreign
soil. The military was commissioned
to handcuff defaulting governors and
place them under arrest in their own
offices, and leave them there "until
they improve." The clerics, who were
assigned the task of implementing
the peasant list and who allowed the
concealment of "souls" to go on, were
relieved of their positions and "after
being subjected to a relentless beating
upon the body, had to submit to penal
servitude, even if they were advanced

in age." People who were suspected of hiding "souls" were placed on tenterhooks. The later "revisions" continued to be just as bloody, though they were carried out with decreasing stringency—RL.

38  A reference to the horrific 1865–66 famine in British-ruled India.

39  See C. Lehmann and Parvus, *Das hungernde Russland. Reiseeindrücke, Beobachtungen und Untersuchungen* (Stuttgart, 1900)—RL.

40  Sergei Witte (1849–1915), high official who sought to carry out Western-style modernization while maintaining absolutism.

41  In fact, Mwata Kembe was the leader of the eighteenth century Lunda Empire, located in what is today the border region of Zambia and Congo. This state supplied slaves to the Portuguese for the international slave trade.

42  A Bantu-speaking people of present-day Malawi.

43  Here Luxemburg's sources included: *Stanleys und Camerons Reisen durch Afrika* (Leipzig, 1879), pp. 74–80; Richard Oberländer, *Livingstones Nachfolger. Afrika von Osten nach Westen quer durchwandert von Stanley und Cameron. Nach den Tagebüchern, Berichten und Aufzeichnungen der Reisenden* (Leipzig 1879).

44  Henry Sumner Maine, important nineteenth-century British colonial official and ethnologist, whose writings Marx excerpted and critiqued in his *Ethnological Notebooks of 1880–82*, edited by Krader (Assen: Van Gorcum, 1972; English version edited by David Norman Smith, forthcoming from Yale University Press).

## CHAPTER 3

1  Solon, an Athenian statesman, carried out social and economic reforms that diluted the power of the aristocracy.

2  Likely Karl J. Ploetz, a writer on world history.

3  Karl Johann Rodbertus, a German economist and conservative socialist, elaborated a labor theory of value. Luxemburg is probably referring to his *Zur Frage des Sachwerths des Geldes in Altertum* (1870).

4  Karl Bücher, author of books on the Roman economy and society. Marx made notes of his 1874 book on slave revolts, which will appear for the first time in Vol. IV/27 of the *Marx-Engels Gesamtausgabe*.

5  In the original, the word *comrade* is crossed out.

6  Social historian of the ancient world Karl Julius Beloch.

## CHAPTER 4

1  A reference to the outbreak of the 1848 revolutions in Europe.

2  In 1898 France and England almost went to war over a conflict in Fashoda, Sudan.

3  A reference to the Spanish-American War of 1898, in which the U.S. took possession of the Philippines and Cuba. This occurred not six but *four* years previously.

4  "The ramparts of Praga" refers to a massacre by the Russian army against a Polish uprising in Praga, a suburb of Warsaw, in 1831.

5  A reference to the brutal suppression of the Paris Commune of 1871, in which thousands of revolutionaries

were slaughtered by French
government forces.

CHAPTER 5

1  For the English translation, see
*Evolutionary Socialism*, translated
by Edith C. Harvey (New York:
Schocken, 1961).

2  Ferdinand Lassalle (1825–64) founded
the General Association of German
Workers in 1863, the first mass party
of the German proletariat. Though
Lassalle sought to enlist Marx's
support, Marx always kept some
distance between them. For example,
Marx sharply opposed his efforts
to advance socialism by making
alliances with the landed aristocracy.

3  That is, cartels and trusts.

4  *Neue Zeit*, 1897–98, No. 18, S. 555. (RL)

5  *Neue Zeit*, 1897–98, No. 18, S. 554. (RL)

6  Isaac Péreire (1806–80) was a French
financier who founded the Crédit
Mobilier. He was originally a follower
of Saint-Simon. Marx first studied his
work in 1845 and often commented on it.

7  Added to second edition: "In a note
to the third volume of *Capital*, Engels
wrote in 1894: 'Since the above was
written (1865), competition on the
world market has been considerably
intensified by the rapid development
of industry in all civilized countries,
especially in America and Germany.
The fact that the rapidly and enormously expanding modern productive forces
grow beyond the control of the laws of
the capitalist mode of exchange within
which they are supposed to move
impresses itself nowadays more and
more even on the minds of the

capitalists. This is shown especially
by two symptoms. First, by the new and
general mania for protective tariffs
which differs from the old protectionism especially by the fact that now the
articles which are capable of being
exported are the best protected. In the
second place, it is shown by the cartels
(trusts) of manufacturers in whole large
spheres of production for the regulation
of production, and thus of prices and
profits. It goes without saying that these
experiments are practicable only so long
as the economic weather is relatively
favorable. The first storm must upset
them, and prove that although production assuredly needs regulation, it is
certainly not the capitalist class which is
fitted for the task. Meanwhile, the trusts
have no other mission but to see to it
that the little fish are swallowed by the
big fish still more rapidly than before'."
(RL) (See *Capital*, Vol. III, p. 215.)

8  *Capital*, Vol. III, p. 368.

9  Konrad Schmidt (1865–1932) was a
leading Social-Democrat and
economist who corresponded with
Engels. He was a founder of one
of the main revisionist journals in
Germany, *Sozialistische Monatschaft*.

10  Wolfgang Heine (1861–1944) was a
major supporter of Bernstein who
at the time proposed a "policy
of compensation" in which the SPD
would agree to higher defense
spending in exchange for obtaining a
more democratic suffrage system. After
1910 he moved closer to Luxemburg's
position on military questions.

11  Gustav von Scholler (1838–1917) was an
influential economist and statist socialist
who founded the Association for Social

Reform in 1872 to encourage a nexus between industry, the corporate state, and labor. He was derided by liberals and leftists as one of the *Kathedersozialisten*, or "Socialists of the Chair."

12  In the second edition, Luxemburg added the following footnote: "In 1872, Professors Wagner, Schmoller, Brentano, and others held a Congress at Eisenach at which they proclaimed noisily and with much publicity that their goal was the introduction of social reforms for the protection of the working class. These gentlemen, whom the liberal, Oppenheimer, calls *'Kathedersozialisten'* [Socialists of the Chair, or Academic Socialists] formed a *Verein für Sozialreform* [Association for Social Reform]. Only a few years later, when the fight against Social Democracy grew sharper, as representatives in the Reichstag these pygmies of *'Kathedersozialismus'* voted for the extension of the Antisocialist Law. Beyond this, all of the activity of the Association consists in its yearly general assemblies at which a few professorial reports on different themes are read. Further, the Association has published over one hundred thick volumes on economic questions. Not a thing has been done for social reform by the professors—who, in addition, support protective tariffs, militarism, etc. Finally, the Association has given up social reforms and occupies itself with the problem of crises, cartels, and the like."

13  This part answers Bernstein's book *Die Voraussetzungen des Sozialismus und die Aufgaben der Sozialdemokratie* (Stuttgart: Verlag von J.H.W. Dietz Nachf, 1899), in which Bernstein responded to Luxemburg's critique of his position. Page references in parentheses in the text are to the English translation by Edith C. Harvey.

14  Richard van de Borght, *Handwörterbuch der Staatswissenschaften*, I. (RL)

15  *Nota bene*! In the great diffusion of small shares, Bernstein obviously finds a proof that social wealth is beginning to pour shares on all little men. Indeed, who but petty bourgeois and even workers could buy shares for the bagatelle of one pound sterling or 20 marks? Unfortunately his supposition rests on a simple miscalculation. We are operating here with the nominal value of shares instead of their market value, something entirely different. For example, on the mining market, South African Rand mine shares are on sale. These shares, like most mining values, are quoted at one pound sterling or 20 paper marks. But already in 1899, they sold at 43 pounds sterling, that is to say, not at 20 but at 860 marks. And it is generally so in all cases. So that these shares are perfectly bourgeois, and not at all petty-bourgeois or proletarian "bonds on social wealth," for they are bought at their nominal value only by a small minority of shareholders. (RL)

16  Wilhelm Weitling (1808–71) was a self-educated worker who wrote a number of important works on socialism in the 1830s and 1840s. Marx at first spoke highly of him, though he soon became critical of Weitling's voluntarist approach. After 1848 Weitling emigrated to the United States, where he became a supporter of the Democratic Party.

17  The following footnote appears only
in the first edition: "It is true that
Bernstein answered our first series of
articles in the *Leipziger Volkszeitung*
[i.e., Part I of this essay] in a seemingly
broad manner, but in a way which
merely betrayed his embarrassment.
For example, he makes it easy for
himself to answer our critique of his
skepticism concerning crises by
arguing that we have made the whole
Marxist theory of crises into music
of the future. But this is an extremely
free interpretation of our words, for
we merely explained the regular
*mechanical periodicity* of the crises—
more precisely, the ten-year cycle of
crises—as a schema which corresponds only to the fully developed
world market. As for the *content* of the
Marxist theory of crises, we explained
it as the only scientific formulation of
the mechanism, as well as of the inner
economic causes of *all* previous crises.

"Bernstein's answers to other
points of our critique are still more
astounding. To the argument, for example, that already, by their very nature, the
cartels could offer no defense against the
capitalist anarchy because-as the sugar
industry shows—they create an exacerbated competition on the world market,
Bernstein answers that this may very
well be true, but the exacerbated sugar
competition in England created a large
fabrication of marmalade and preserves
(p. 89). An answer which makes us
think of the conversation exercises in
Ollendorf's *Teach Yourself Language*
book: 'The sleeve is short *but* the shoe
is tight. The father is tall *but* the
mother has gone to bed'."

"In the same logical context, Bernstein
answers our proof that *credit* too cannot
be a means of adaptation' against
capitalist anarchy because, on the
contrary, it increases this anarchy.
Credit, he believes, alongside its
disruptive character also has a positive
'Production-creative' character which
Marx himself is said to have recognized. This argument about credit is
not at all new to anyone who, basing
himself on Marxist theory, sees in the
capitalist society all the positive points
of departure for the future socialist
transformation of society. The question
at issue was whether this positive character of credit which points it beyond
capitalism can come to fruition in the
capitalist society as well, whether it can
master capitalist anarchy, as Bernstein
thinks, or whether it itself does not
rather degenerate into contradictions
and only increase once more the anarchy, as we showed. Bernstein's repeated
reference to the 'production creative
capacity of credit,' which in fact forms
the point of departure for the whole
debate, is in this light merely a
'theoretical flight into the beyond'—
of the domain of the discussion."

18  Eugen Böhm-Bawerk (1851–1914)
founded the Austrian marginal utility
school of economics. William Stanley
Jevons (1835–82) was a major English
theorist of marginal utility. Karl
Menger (1840–1921) was a member
of the Austrian psychological school
which led to the development
of marginalist economics.

19  Paragraph 14 of the Austrian Constitution gave the Hapsburg monarchy the
right to suspend constitutional liberties.

20 A reference to the period prior to the revolution of March 1848 that obtained some important liberal reforms.

21 Marinism is the naval equivalent of militarism. Beginning in 1890 Germany sought to become a major naval power, leading to serious tensions with England.

22 Kiao-Cheou (Tsingtao) was an area of China occupied by Germany from 1898 to 1919.

23 In the second edition, the bracketed portion is replaced by: "In Germany, the era of great armaments begun in 1893, and the policy of world politics inaugurated with Kiao-Cheou, were paid for immediately with the following sacrificial victim: the decomposition of liberalism, the change of the Center Party (which passed from opposition to government). The recent Reichstag elections of 1907, fought under the sign of colonial policy, are at the same time the historical burial of German liberalism." (In the 1907 Reichstag elections the SPD's share of seats fell to forty-three, compared with eighty-one in the 1903 elections—its most severe electoral setback to date. In response, SPD leaders increasingly moved away from taking radical and anti-imperialist positions in order to garner additional votes.—Eds.)

24 Karl Kautsky (1854–1938), the leading theoretician of the Second International and one of the most important figures in German Social Democracy. He founded *Neue Zeit* as the SPD's main theoretical journal in 1883, co-authored the Erfurt Program (1891) which served as the progammatic basis of the Second International, and authored numerous works on Marxist theory and history. Though at first he demurred from entering the debate over revisionism, he supported Luxemburg's position. Luxemburg broke with him in 1910. For the circumstances of their break, see chapter 8, below.

25 A reference to Marx's critique of Proudhon; Marx had written, "Proudhon wants to be a synthesis— he is a composite error." See *The Poverty of Philosophy*, MECW, p. 178.

26 For Luxemburg's estimate of Engels' Introduction to Marx's *Class Struggles in France* in subsequent years, see "Our Program and the Political Situation" (1918), below.

27 A reference to a phrase used in a debate with Luxemburg by Georg Vollmar (1850–1922), a reformist leader of the SPD from Bavaria, who said the effects of the Paris Commune of 1871 were so disastrous that the workers would have been better off going to sleep than initiating the revolution.

28 Followers of August Blanqui (1805–81), French socialist who held that a small grouping of resolute revolutionists could seize power on behalf of the proletariat. Blanqui participated in the 1830 Revolution and organized an unsuccessful insurrection in 1839. He was involved in numerous conspiratorial coups and spent a total of 35 years in prison.

29 The *Vossiche Zeitung* was a liberal journal that advocated peaceful reform and state socialism. The *Frankfurter Zeitung* was a liberal journal edited by Friedrich Naumann (1860–1919), founder of the National Socialist Association. The *Frankfurter Zeitung*

later seems to have coined the phrase "bloody Rosa."

30 In 1884 and 1885 Bismarck proposed that the government award subsidies to steamship companies that linked Germany to its colonies. The Social Democratic representatives to the Reichstag were divided on the issue.

31 "Vollmar's state socialism" refers to Vollmar's belief that state intervention from above was needed to gradually introduce socialism. "The vote on the Bavarian budget" refers to the practice of Bavarian socialists (led by Vollmar) to vote for the budget proposed by the government of Bavaria—an act widely opposed at the time by other sections of the SPD. The "agrarian socialism of South Germany" refers to Vollmar's opposition to the dominant SPD position that the development of agribusiness would inevitably transform the peasantry into a rural proletariat and that this would be a historically "progressive" development. Max Schippel (1859–1928) was a right-wing SPD leader who opposed the creation of a people's militia and supported the existing military system. He also defended German expansion.

32 "Movement of the independents" was a group associated with the *Junge*, who were anarchists expelled from the SPD in 1894. Though she often critiqued anarchists, Luxemburg opposed their expulsion from the Party. She wrote in 1906: "Anarchism in our ranks is nothing but a left reaction against the excessive demands of the right. Since we have never kicked out anyone on the far right, we do not now have the right to evict the far left" (quoted in J. P. Nettl, *Rosa Luxemburg* [London: Oxford University Press, 1969], p. 248.

33 In one of Aesop's fables, this is addressed to a braggart who claimed to have made a great leap in Rhodes. It more generally means "now show us what you can do." In *The Eighteenth Brumaire of Louis Bonaparte* (1852), Marx uses this expression to illustrate what he termed the way in which, unlike "bourgeois revolutions," which "storm swiftly from success to success. . . proletarian revolutions. . . criticize themselves constantly . . . recoil again and again from the indefinite prodigiousness of their own aims, until a situation has been created which makes all turning back impossible, and the conditions themselves cry out: *Hic Rhodus, hic salta!"* [MECW 11, pp. 106–7]. Earlier, Hegel referred to this expression in the Preface to his *Philosophy of Right* (1820).

## CHAPTER 6

1 Kurt Eisner (1867–1919) was a journalist and editor of *Vorwärts*, the leading Social Democratic newspaper in Germany, from 1898 to 1905. Initially a revisionist, he often clashed with Luxemburg. He opposed World War I on pacifist grounds and moved toward the left, later helping to found the United Social-Democratic Party (USPD), in which Kautsky also participated. In November 1918 he was a leader of the revolution in Bavaria. He was murdered in February 1919 by a reactionary.

2 *Kladderadatsch* means a great noise, muddle, or confusion.

3   The Cologne Trade Union Congress of
    1905 opposed the concept of a mass
    strike. The trade union leaders passed a
    resolution (by 200 to 17) which effective-
    ly prohibited even any discussion of it.

4   Robert von Puttkammer (1828–1900)
    was a conservative Minister of the
    Interior who enforced Bismarck's anti-
    socialist law and forcibly suppressed
    strikes in the 1870s and 1880s.

5   See "Eine Probe aufs Exempel,"
    *Sachsiche Arbeiterzeitung* (Dresden),
    52, March 3, 1905.

6   The Russian Duma or parliament
    was first established under the impact
    of the 1905 Revolution.

7   The September 1905 Jena Congress of
    the SPD approved a vague resolution
    submitted by Bebel which approved of
    the mass strike, but the resolution lim-
    ited it to a purely defensive weapon in
    the event of possible government
    attempts to restrict suffrage or trade
    union rights. Though Luxemburg did
    not think the resolution went far
    enough, she still thought it was a victo-
    ry that the SPD had approved it.

8   The Russo-Japanese war of 1904–05.

9   Sergey Vasilyevich Zubatov (1864–1917)
    was a Tsarist colonel who established a
    system of surveillance to monitor
    revolutionary organizations as head of
    the *Okhrana* or secret police. Originally
    a revolutionist, he became a police
    agent in the 1880s. Starting in 1901 he
    organized the Moscow Society for
    Mutual Aid to Workingmen in an effort
    to prevent workers from joining Social
    Democratic unions. He committed sui-
    cide after the February 1917 revolution.

10  That is, of passing ardor.

11  The *Zemstvos* were a system of rural

assemblies in Tsarist Russia, formed in
1864 and given limited powers to deal
with economic and cultural issues.
They tended to be dominated by the
landed gentry. Zemstvo-Liberalism
refers to efforts to reform the Tsarist
system through constitutional means,
based on the *Zemstvo* system.

12  On October 30, 1905, the Tsar was
    forced to agree to a more representative
    constitutional parliamentary system.

13  In the first two weeks of June 1906 alone
    the following wage struggles were con-
    ducted: by the printers in Petersburg,
    Moscow, Odessa, Minsk, Vilna, Aratov,
    Mogilev, and Tambov, for an eight-hour
    day and Sunday holiday; a general strike
    of seamen in Odessa, Nicholaiev,
    Kertch, in the Crimea, in the Caucasus,
    in the Volga Fleet, in Warsaw and Plock
    for the recognition of the trade union
    and the release of the arrested workers
    delegates; by the dockers in Saratov,
    Nicholaiev, Tsaritzin, Archangel,
    Nizhni-Novgorod, and Rubinsk. The
    bakers struck in Kiev, Archangel, Bia-
    lystok, Vilna, Odessa, Kharkov, Brest-
    Litovsk, Radom, and Tiflis; the
    agricultural workers in the districts of
    Verchne-Dneprovski, Vorosovsk, and
    Simferopol; in the governments, of
    Podolsk, Tula and Kurak, in the districts
    of Koslov and Lijpovet, in Finland, in
    the government of Kiev and in the dis-
    trict of Elizavetgrad. In this period
    almost all branches of industry in sever-
    al towns struck work simultaneously, as
    at Saratov, Archangel, Kertch, and Kre-
    mentchug. In Bachmut there was a
    strike of colliers of the whole district.
    In other towns the wages movement in
    the same two weeks seized all ranches of

industry, one after the other, as in Kiev, Petersburg, Warsaw, Moscow, and in the district of Ivanovo-Voznosensk. Object of the strikers everywhere: shortening of the working day, Sunday holiday, and wage increases. Most of the strikes ran a victorious course. It is emphasized in the local reports that some strata of the workers were affected who took part for the first time in a wage movement. (RL)

14 The Bulygin Duma was Russia's first parliament, announced on August 10, 1905. It was intended as a consultative body only. It never convened, since by October 1905 the Tsar was forced to agree to a more representative Duma (the Witte Duma) which granted a restricted franchise to workers.

15 Martin Kasprzak (1860–1905) was a leader of the Proletariat Party, an early socialist group in Poland. He knew Luxemburg as a youth and helped smuggle her out of Poland in 1889. He later worked closely with her in Germany. Active in Poland during the 1905 Revolution, he was imprisoned and then hanged by the government.

16 The Social Democratic movement in Hamburg was known as one of the most radical in all of Germany. On January 17, 1906, workers there called a "trial mass strike." The Hamburg Left later played an important role in the 1918 German Revolution.

17 The mass strike of January 22, 1905 marked the beginning of the 1905 Revolution. A mass demonstration in front of the Tsar's palace in St. Petersburg, led by an orthodox priest, Father Georgi Gapon, was fired upon by government troops. It was known thereafter as "Bloody Sunday."

## CHAPTER 7

1 The Jena Congress of the SPD took place from September 17 to 23, 1905, and passed a resolution presented by Luxemburg entitled, "On the Political Mass Strike and the Social-Democracy."

2 The manifesto issued by Tsar Nicholas II in October 1905, providing for a limited constitutional monarchy.

3 "The December crisis in Moscow" refers to the arrest of the members of the St. Petersburg Soviet in December 1905. This was followed by a massive workers' insurrection in Moscow, which was bloodily suppressed.

4 A daily newspaper edited by Marx from June 1848 until May 19, 1849, hereafter abbreviated as *NRZ*.

5 Ludolf Camphausen (1803–90) headed the liberal ministry appointed by King Frederick William IV of Prussia after the revolutionary upsurge of March 1848. He resigned in June 1848. David Justus Hansemann (1790–1864) was a cabinet minister in Camphausen's government.

6 The liberal-dominated Frankfurt National Assembly was convened on May 18, 1848. Its aim was to help unify Germany and draw up a national constitution. However, it failed to make headway in these areas and ended by supporting monarchist forces.

## CHAPTER 8

1 Unless otherwise indicated, all quotes from Kautsky are from his article "A New Strategy," *Neue Zeit*, no. 28, 2, June 10–24, 1910, pp. 332–41, 364–74, 412–21.

2 "What Next," *Arbeiter-Zeitung* (Dortmund), March 14–15, 1910. An English translation, entitled "The Next

Step," can be found in *Rosa Luxemburg: Selected Political Writings*, ed. Robert Looker (New York: Grove Press, 1974), pp. 148–59.

3   See Marx's *Critique of the Gotha Program*, MECW 24, pp. 81–99.

4   The Erfurt Program, adopted in 1891 after being drafted by Kautsky and Bernstein, was the guiding programmatic doctrine of German Social Democracy and the Second International. For Engels's criticism of the program, see "A Critique of the Draft Social Democratic Program of 1891," MECW 27, pp. 225–32.

5   August Bebel (1840–1913) founded the Eisenach group in 1869, which claimed adherence to Marx's views. He became one of the most influential leaders of the SPD and the Second International. A longtime deputy in the Reichstag, he was known for his fiery oratory. He was also the author of *Woman and Socialism*. He often clashed with Luxemburg, at times making sexist comments about her in private correspondence with other male leaders.

6   Wilhelm Liebknecht (1826–1900), associate of Marx during his London exile, joined forces with Bebel to form the Eisenach group. He was a leading member of the SPD from its founding to his death. He was a friend and associate of Luxemburg, though they often differed on political issues.

7   *Neue Zeit*, 20, 1, pp. 11–12. (RL) See Engels's "A Critique of the Draft Social Democratic Program," MECW 27, pp. 225, 227, 228, 229.

8   Hermann Tessendorf was Berlin police prosecutor from 1873 to 1879.

9   The "Exceptional Powers Law"

(*Ausnahme Gesetz*), also known as the "Anti-Socialist Law," was in effect in Germany from 1878 to 1890. It placed severe restrictions on freedom of speech, press, and association.

10   *Neue Zeit*, 9, 1, p. 573. (RL) See Marx's *Critique of the Gotha Program*, MECW 24, pp. 95–96.

11   A reference to a bill passed in the Prussian lower house on June 1910 which greatly increased the monies paid to the Prussian court.

12   A government-sponsored bill that was defeated in the Reichstag in 1899 that proposed abolishing the right to organize and strike.

13   "Comrade Frohme" refers to Karl Frohme, a reformist Social Democrat and Reichstag deputy. His most famous work was *Die Entwicklung der Eigentums-Verhältnisse* (Bockenheim, 1884).

14   The English edition of the *The Social Revolution*, translated by A. M. and Maywood Simons (Chicago: Charles Kerr & Co., 1902), is based on the first German edition of 1902. Since the first edition was written before the 1905 Revolution, it did not contain the passage quoted by Luxemburg. In the third German edition of 1911 (*Die Soziale Revolution* [Berlin: Verlag Buchhandlung Vorwärts]) Kautsky removed the sentence commending Luxemburg's position.

15   Albert Graf von Waldersee (1832–1904) was the German army chief of staff who suppressed the anti-imperialist uprising of I Ho Ch'uan (the Boxer Uprising) in China in 1899.

16   The Hereros and Nama (a Khoikhoi people) are ethnic groups indigenous to Namibia. "Hottentot" was a deroga-

tory Afrikaner name for all Khoikhoi. The Hereros and Nama were almost wiped out by German imperialism in the early nineteenth century, when troops led by General Lothar von Trotha (1848–1920) massacred tens of thousands of them when they resisted German occupation and colonization. The extermination drive against the Herero and Namib peoples established the paradigm for Hitler's later drive to exterminate the Jews.

17  "The State of the Reich," *Neue Zeit*, 25, 1, December 1906, p. 427. (RL)

18  During the Reichstag elections of 1907 Chancellor Bernhard von Bülow campaigned on an imperialist platform and attacked the Social Democrats as traitors. The SPD lost thirty-eight seats in the Reichstag election.

19  Correspondence Bulletin of the General Commission of German Unions, 1909, no. 7, Statistical Supplement. (RL)

20  The Crimmitschau strike, involving thousands of textile workers, took place in August 1903. The intervention of reformist union leaders forced an end to the strike in January 1904, leaving the workers with virtually no gains.

21  *Neue Zeit*, 23, 1, pp. 780, 781. (RL)

22  A reference to Luxemburg's essay "Attrition or Collision?" *Neue Zeit*, 28, 2, 1909/10, pp. 257–66, 291–305.

23  Karl Kautsky, "What Now?" *Neue Zeit*, 28, 2, April 15, 1910, p 80.

24  "Revolutionaries Everywhere," *Neue Zeit*, 22, 1, p. 736. My emphasis. (RL)

25  See Luxemburg's *Mass Strike, Party and Trade Unions* in this volume.

26  "Driving Forces and Perspectives of the Russian Revolution," *Neue Zeit*, 25, 1, p. 333. (RL)

27  *The Social Revolution*, 2nd ed., p. 60. (RL)

28  Karl Kautsky, "The Lessons of the Miners' Strikes," *Neue Zeit*, 23, 1, p. 781.

29  Oda Olberg, "The Italian General Strike," *Neue Zeit*, 23, 1, p. 19.

## CHAPTER 9

1  At their March 30–31, 1902, Party Conference, held during Easter weekend, the Belgian Workers' Party had called for one man, one vote, but had put aside their long standing demand for women's suffrage.

2  In this weighed voting system, the votes of those with more education or property could be counted twice, or even three times.

3  In Euripides's *The Trojan Women*, Hecuba, wife of King Priam of Troy, is parceled out to the victorious Greeks as spoils of war. While there are several versions of the Hecuba story, this is probably the one to which Luxemburg was referring here.

4  August Dewinne, a reformist Social Democrat.

5  n 1899, Alexandre-Étienne Millerand, a French reformist leader, became the first Social Democrat to accept a post in a "bourgeois" government.

6  Eduard Anseele, an important reformist Social Democrat.

7  Title supplied by the editors. The conference took place in Stuttgart.

8  The International Socialist Congress was held in Amsterdam in 1904.

9  The Conference voted to found an International Women's Secretariat to gather information on working women's struggles. Zetkin became its

leader and her newspaper, *Gleichheit* (Equality), its official organ.

10  This is a quote from the refrain of a well-known German song, by Viktor Scheffel (1826–1886), "Behüt Dich Gott," from his opera *Der Trompeter von Säckingen.*

11  Emma Ihrer (1857–1911) was an important leader of the German women's movement. In 1885 she founded the Berliner Arbeiterinnenverein, which promoted the interests of women workers. In 1891 she edited a women's paper that later became *Gleichheit*, the chief publication of the socialist women's movement, to which Luxemburg contributed.

12  Clara Zetkin (1857–1933) was a leading activist and theorist in the German women's movement who edited *Gleichheit*, the SPD's women's paper. She was a close friend and supporter of Luxemburg and corresponded regularly with her. She consistently took leftist positions in the disputes in the SPD, earning her the enmity of many of its leaders. She was a founding member of the Spartacus League and the German Communist Party.

13  The "women's section" was instituted in 1902 by the Prussian Minister von Hammerstein. It stipulated that a special section of a room be reserved for women at political meetings.

14  François Fourier (1772–1837), a utopian socialist who encouraged the development of agricultural communities based on mutual cooperation. His advocacy of the liberation of women and unfettered sexuality were far in advance of his time.

15  Luxemburg could not have known, since it was not published until after her death, that Marx projected a similar idea in his *Economic and Philosophical Manuscripts of 1844*: "The direct, natural, and necessary relation of person to person is the relation of man to woman. . . . From this relationship one can therefore judge humanity's whole level of development." See MECW 3, pp. 295–96.

16  March 8, International Women's Day, began the German Social Democratic Party's "Red Week" for the year 1914. This was a period of demonstrations, meetings, and recruitment.

17  A reference to the genocidal "Herero War" in Namibia in 1904.

18  A reference to the outright enslavement of the rubber workers of Putumayo, Colombia, and elsewhere in the Amazon Basin in the early years of the twentieth century.

CHAPTER 10

1  See Manifesto of the Communist Party, MECW 6, p. 492.

2  A reference to the second congress of the RSDLP, held in August 1903, where the split between the Mensheviks and Bolsheviks first took place.

3  Lenin's book was published in May 1904. See Lenin's *Collected Works*, Vol. 7 (Moscow: Progress Publishers, 1964), pp. 203–524.

4  A reference to the way in which the Austrian Social Democrats provided for a federal party structure that allowed for autonomy for its national sections, as a response to the multinational character of the Austro-Hungarian Empire.

5  In *One Step Forward, Two Steps Back*

Lenin wrote: "These 'dreadful words'—Jacobinism and the rest—are expressive of *opportunism* and nothing else. A Jacobin who wholly identifies himself with the *organization* of the proletariat . . . is a *revolutionary Social Democrat*. A Girondist . . . who is afraid of the dictatorship of the proletariat, and who yearns for the absolute value of democratic demands, is an *opportunist*." See Lenin, CW 7, p. 383. During the French Revolution, 1789–94, the Jacobin faction won out over the more moderate Girondin one.

6   This famous quote is from Goethe's *Faust*.

7   Parvus, pseudonym of Alexander Helphand (1867–1924), was a Russian revolutionary active in the left wing of the SPD after 1891. One of the first to issue an attack on Bernstein's revisionism, he often worked closely with Luxemburg prior to World War I. She broke off relations with him after 1914, when he supported Germany's side in World War I and obtained large sums from the government to help foment revolution in Russia.

8   A synonym for an authoritarian state.

9   Lenin, CW 7, pp. 273–74.

10  Lenin, CW 7, pp. 396.

11  The revisionists in the SPD often argued for local autonomy of SPD electoral districts against the "excessive centralism" of the SPD, as a way to promote reformist policies.

12  French for "beware of all politicians," a syndicalist slogan.

13  *Rabochaya Mysl* (Workers Thought) was the organ of the St. Petersburg Committee of the RSDLP from 1897 to 1902.

14  A reference to the critical philosophy of

Immanuel Kant (1724–1804). This is one of the relatively few times that Luxemburg refers to a classical philosopher in her writings. A number of reformist leaders of the SPD were Kantians.

15  "Going to the people" was a slogan of the Russian populist intelligentsia in the 1870s and 1880s.

16  For Lassalle's General German Workers' Union, see note 2 of chapter 5, above.

17  A reference to Jean Jaurès (1854–1914), a reformist French socialist leader who founded the newspaper *L'Humanité* in 1904 and helped lead the defense of Captain Eduard Dreyfus. Luxemburg debated with him many times, though she held him in high regard. He was assassinated on the eve of World War I because of his opposition to war.

18  Narodnaya Volya (People's Will), founded in August 1879, was a Russian populist organization that practiced revolutionary terrorism. On March 1, 1881, members of the group assassinated Tsar Alexander II. Soon afterward, the Russian government eliminated the group through fierce repression.

CHAPTER 11

1   Title provided by the editors of this volume. The original manuscript is untitled. There is a note at the beginning in Leo Jogiches's handwriting, "Received by Adolf [Jogiches] October 11." Other handwritten additions or deletions by Jogiches are indicated in the footnotes.

2   The meeting of the Central Committee of the Russian Social Democratic Party (RSDRP) abroad took place at the initiative of the Bolsheviks, and was endorsed by Luxemburg's Social

Democratic Party of the Kingdom of Poland and Lithuania (SDKPiL). Participating for the SDKPiL were Feliks Dzerzhinsky and Jogiches, and for the Bolsheviks, Lenin, Alexei Rykov, and Grigory Zinoviev. Also present were the Menshevik Boris Goldman-Gorev, Mark Liber of the Bund, and M.V. Ozolin-Martyn of the Latvian Social Democrats. The main focus of the meeting was calling a Party Conference of the RSDRP. To this end, a Technical Commission and a Foreign Commission were formed to deal with the party press, the illegal transport of literature to Russia, etc. (In this context, "foreign" refers to those Social Democrats residing outside the Russian Empire, who in fact constituted the real leadership of the Party.)

3   At this meeting, the SDKPiL was represented by Jogiches and Adolf Warski. Under the influence of the SDKPiL and the representatives of the "conciliatory" Bolshevik group, they had agreed, against the wishes of Lenin and his group, on the dissolution of the Party factions and an end to factional organs. The Party funds (the so-called Schmitt Legacy), which had been up to that point in the hands of the Bolsheviks, were placed in escrow with three representatives of the German Social Democracy: Karl Kautsky, Franz Mehring, and Clara Zetkin, who were to function as trustees.

4   At this point, Jogiches added: "It proved their unanimous, unfaltering will."

5   At this point, Jogiches added: "less about two separately organized, factional camps within the Party itself."

6   The "Liquidators" were part of the Menshevik wing of the RSDRP, whereas "Ostzovism" resided in its (non-Leninist) Bolshevik wing. The Third Imperial Duma lasted from November 1907 to June 1912.

7   The most recent Party Congress of the unified RSDRP had taken place in May 1907 in London, with Luxemburg in attendance (see chapter 7 of this volume for her speech). Subsequent Party Congresses of the RSDRP took place with a divided party.

8   *Golos Sotsial-Demokrata*, newspaper of the Menshevik Liquidators, appeared from February 1908 to December 1911, initially in Geneva, then in Paris. The central organ of the RSDRP, *Sotsial Demokrata*, was published from 1908 to 1913 in Paris and was, after November 1911, the *de facto* paper of the Bolsheviks. Rosa Luxemburg is referring to the Mensheviks Feodor Dan and Julius Martov, when she speaks of the boycott of the latter newspaper by the Mensheviks. Under pressure from Lenin, both permanently left the editorial staff in June 1911. In November 1911, the representative of the SDKPiL also resigned.

9   Luxemburg's party, the Social Democratic Party of the Kingdom of Poland and Lithuania.

10  At this point, Jogiches wrote "above!" in the margin.

11  This wing of the Mensheviks did not share the views of the Liquidators and wanted to maintain a unified RSDRP.

12  *Vperyod* [Forward], a publication of the Left Bolsheviks during 1910 and 1911, had Maxim Gorki, A.V. Lunacharsky, and Alexander Bogdanov among its contributors.

13  *Pravda* proclaimed itself a "non-factional" newspaper of the RSDRP.

14  This brochure, issued in May 1911 in Russian and German, contained sharp attacks on Lenin and the Bolsheviks.

15  At this point, Jogiches inserts the word "naturally."

16  That is, since the accession of the SDKPiL to the unified Russian Social Democracy at the Fourth Party Conference in April 1906 in Stockholm.

17  Last clause of this sentence crossed out by Jogiches.

18  Tsar Nicholas II's prime minister, A. Stolypin (1906–11) bloodily suppressed the Revolution of 1905–1907 and dissolved the pro-revolutionary Second Duma in June 1907. He enacted a new voting law, which secured a parliamentary majority for the representatives of the wealthiest classes. He also attempted to modernize agriculture along capitalist lines. In September 1911, he was assassinated by a Social Revolutionary.

19  The Congress never materialized, and the then merely advisory Duma was finished by the Russian general strike of October 1905. After the defeat of the Revolution, the Mensheviks seized again upon the idea of a "broad Workers' Congress" aimed at gaining a legal existence for Social Democracy within the Stolypin system. Lenin as well as Luxemburg strongly opposed this, and obtained a resolution to that effect at the 1907 London Congress of the RSDRP.

20  A reference to her own article, "Organizational Questions of the Russian Social Democracy" (1904), chapter 10 of this volume.

21  These took place in September and October 1912.

22  At this point, Jogiches wrote "Trotsky" in the margin.

## CHAPTER 12

1  Pavel Borisovich Axelrod (1850–1929) was early leader of the RSDLP and a prominent Menshevik, who after 1903 edited *Golos Sotsial-Demokrata*. Feodor Ilich Dan (1871–1947) was a leading Menshevik who opposed World War I on pacifist grounds. Like Axelrod, he also opposed the Bolshevik Revolution of 1917.

2  Friedrich Stampfer (1874–1857) journalist and SPD leader who rook a centrist position during World War I.

3  Alexei Maximovitch Kaledin (1861–1918) was a field commander in the Russian Army during World War I. After the Russian Revolution of 1917, he organized an army of Don Cossacks and sought to overthrow the Soviet regime. He committed suicide shortly after the Bolshevik forces routed his army in January 1918.

4  A reference to Kautsky's apologia for the events of August 4, 1914; he argued that since the Second International was "an instrument designed for peace," it was "not suited for times of war."

5  The populist Social Revolutionary Party was formed in Russia in 1901 to represent the interests of the poorer peasants. In October 1917 the SRs split, with its left wing forming a coalition government with the Bolsheviks. The left-SRs quit the government in March 1918, over the signing of the Brest-Litovsk Peace Treaty with Germany.

6  John Lilburne (1614–1657) was a leader
   of the Levellers, a radical democratic
   party during the English Civil War that
   advocated the transfer of sovereignty to
   the House of Commons and that the
   government be run on a decentralized,
   communal basis. Their name was given
   by their enemies to suggest they wanted to "level men's estates."

7  The Diggers were a group of agrarian
   communists during the English Civil
   War, led by Gerrard Winstanley and
   William Everard.

8  Iraklii Georgievich Tseretelli (1882–
   1959) was a leading Menshevik from
   Georgia who was Minister of the Interior in Kerensky's government in 1917.

9  Jean-Paul Marat (1743–1793) was a
   French revolutionary journalist and
   politician who was a leader of the
   Jacobin faction during the French Revolution. He was assassinated by Char-
   lotte Corday, a royalist sympathizer.

10 Pavel Nikolaievich Miliukov
   (1859–1943) was a leader of the Constitutional Democratic Party (Cadets)
   who served as Foreign Minister in the
   provisional government from March to
   July 1917. Alexander Kerensky
   (1881–1970), a former Social-Revolu-
   tionary who supported World War I,
   served as Prime Minister of the provisional government that was overthrown
   by the Bolsheviks in October 1917.

11 Brest-Litovsk was the town where the
   Soviet government negotiated a peace
   treaty with Germany in May 1918.

12 The Constituent Assembly was dissolved by the Bolsheviks at its first session in January 1918.

13 Mykola Liubyinski (1891–1936), a
   Ukrainian Social Democrat who

opposed the Bolsheviks, was Ukrainian Foreign Minister in early 1918 and
represented Ukraine in the peace negotiations at Brest-Litovsk. Rafael Erich
was a Finnish nationalist and member
of the Finnish government in 1918 who
pushed for an alliance with German
imperialism. General Karl Manner-
heim (1867–1951) led anti-Bolshevik
forces in the Finnish civil war of 1918
and later became president of Finland.

14 The *Wasserkante* is a region in
   Germany where the dialect called
   *Plattdeutsch* is spoken.

15 An apparent reference to the
   Bolsheviks' July 1918 execution of
   some of those charged with the
   assassination of German Ambassador
   Count Wilhelm von Mirbach by
   members of the Socialist Revolutionary Party, who opposed the signing
   of the treaty of Brest-Litovsk.

16 See Trotsky's *Von der Oktober-Revolu-
   tion bis zum Bresterfriedensvertrag*
   (Belp-Bern: Promachus Verlag, 1918),
   p. 90.

17 Nicolai Avksentiev (1878–1943), a
   founder of the Socialist Revolutionary
   Party, took part in Kerensky's government in 1917 and was a delegate to the
   Constituent Assembly. During the
   Russian Civil War he took part in the
   Provisional Siberian Government,
   which was supported by Allied troops
   invading Russia.

18 Luxemburg is in error here, since the
   elections to the Constituent Assembly
   took place *after*, not *before*, the Bolshevik seizure of power, although they had
   been planned beforehand.

19 "Little Scheidemen," a play on the name
   of the leader of the German government.

20 This paragraph was a note found on an unnumbered sheet of the manuscript. It was placed here by the editors of the original German edition of *The Russian Revolution*.

21 Heinrich Cunow (1862–1936), a German social democrat and ethnographer, opposed revisionism before World War I but after 1914 supported the war and was a close associate of Scheidemann. Paul Lensch (b. 1873) was part of the SPD's left wing before 1914, but he became a pro-war chauvinist at the start of the war.

## CHAPTER 13

1 A reference to the German military's plan to capture Paris within six weeks upon the outbreak of war between France and Germany. Drawn up by Army Chief of Staff Count Alfred von Schlieffen (1833–1913) in 1899, the Schlieffen plan stalled after a few days in 1914 in the face of Belgian and French resistance.

2 A reference to unfounded rumors that circulated in the first days of the war to justify Germany's declaration of war. One of them was that French airmen had bombed the German city of Nuremberg.

3 In the southern Russian city of Kishinev (now part of Moldova) in April 1903, a vicious pogrom was carried out during Passover against Jews, with the encouragement of Tsarist officials. Over forty-five Jews were killed.

4 This refers to the fact that almost all royal families in Europe were related by blood and marriage. For example, both King George V of England and Kaiser Wilhelm of Germany were grandchildren of Queen Victoria and hence cousins.

5 On August 4, 1914, the SPD Deputies in the Reichstag voted war credits to the German government. Though 14 of the 119 SPD Deputies did not favor voting for war credits, none at the time broke party discipline by making their views public to Luxemburg, August 4, 1914 signaled the collapse of the German Social Democracy and the Second International.

6 *Via Dolorossa* means "Path of Sorrow," Jesus's road to Calvary.

7 The Franco-German War of 1870, in which Germany defeated France.

8 See Engels' "Introduction to *The Class Struggles in France*" [1895], MECW 27, p. 521. For Luxemburg's later reevaluation of Engels' Introduction, see "Our Program and the Political Situation," in chapter 14 of this volume.

9 The *Wiener Arbeiter Zeitung* was the major newspaper of the Austrian Social Democracy.

10 The International Socialist Bureau was the Executive Committee of the Second International, headquartered in Brussels.

11 See Marx's *Civil War in France*, MECW 10, p. 117.

12 "Twilight of the Gods." Wagner used the phrase as the title for the concluding opera of his *Ring* cycle.

13 In July 1911 the German government sent the warship *Panther* to waters off Agadir, Morocco, in a bid to challenge French imperialism in the region. The SPD failed to take an unequivocal stand against this move because it feared jeopardizing its chances in upcoming

parliamentary elections. Luxemburg sharply attacked the SPD leadership for "playing it cool" on the Morocco affair, viewing it as a failure to take a firm stand against German imperialism.

14  "Go for broke."

15  The Peace Conference at Basel, Switzerland, was held on November 24–25, 1912. The last pre-war general meeting of the Second International, it was called in response to the outbreak of the First Balkan War in 1912. The conference pledged that socialists would oppose all "imperialist wars."

16  Victor Adler (1852–1918) was founder and leader of Austrian Social Democracy. He was a close friend of Bebel and an opponent of Luxemburg. At an ISB meeting on July 19, 1914, on the eve of World War I, Adler stated that if war should break out, the Second International would have to choose between the destruction of organized socialism or capitulating to "the patriotism of the crowds." When war broke out he chose the latter course, later becoming Minister of Foreign Affairs in the liberal government that followed the collapse of the Hapsburg monarchy.

17  Pieter Jelles Troelstra (1860–1930) was a Dutch socialist who opposed the left-wing elements in the Second International.

18  By tradition, the Ruetli pledge was made in 1291, when a secret meeting of Swiss patriots in the Ruetli forest pledged to oust the Austrians from Switzerland.

19  Eduard David (1863–1930), reformist SPD leader who worked closely with Vollmar. He was a fervent supporter of German expansionism in World War I.

20  "Die Weltgeschichte ist das Weltgericht" means "World History is the Last Judgment." Often quoted by Marxists, the phrase is from para. 340 of *Hegel's Philosophy of Right*.

21  Luxemburg probably has in mind a passage in the *Communist Manifesto* where Marx and Engels speak of class struggles resulting in "either a revolutionary constitution of society at large . . . or the common ruin of the contending classes." See MECW 6, p. 482.

22  Golgotha was the site of Jesus's crucifixion.

23  "June Combatants" refers to the workers who rose up on June 23, 1848, in Paris against the new liberal republic, in quest of a social republic that would address issues such as unemployment.

24  In his *Eighteenth Brumaire of Louis Bonaparte*, Marx refers to the "party of order" as the representatives of the big bourgeoisie, who in 1849 outmaneuvered the more liberal wing of bourgeois democracy, helping to pave the way for the Bonapartist coup of 1851.

25  Marie Joseph Thiers (1797–1877) organized the suppression of the Paris Commune. Claude Favre (1809–1880), a minister in Thiers' government who negotiated the surrender of the French Army to Bismarck, also helped crush the Paris Commune.

26  See *Civil War in France*, MECW 22, p. 353–54.

27  The March Revolution was the German revolution of 1848, sparked by an attack by troops on demonstrators in Berlin. The mass revolt that followed led to the formation of the National Assembly at Frankfurt.

28  Ignaz Auer (1846–1907) led the SPD

along with Bebel and Liebknecht and served as party secretary for many years, often siding with reformist currents against Luxemburg. At the height of the revisionism controversy he famously wrote Bernstein, "one doesn't *say* such things, one simply *does* them."

29  In August 1914 the fortress of Liège in Belgium was destroyed by a German siege. In September 1914 the Cathedral of Rheims, where every French King from Clovis to Louis XVI had been crowned, was heavily shelled.

30  "Deutschland über alles" means " Germany above everything." The phrase is from a song by Heinrich Hoffman von Fallersleben (1798–1876).

## CHAPTER 14

A)  *The Beginning*

1   With the collapse of the Western front and the emergence of outright revolution, as workers' and soldiers' councils spring up around Germany, Kaiser Wilhelm II abdicated and fled to the Netherlands in early November 1918.

2   Friedrich Ebert (1871–1925) became chairman of the SPD after Bebel's death in 1913. He was part of the SPD majority during the war and vigorously opposed social revolution. He helped form a provisional government on November 9, 1918, after the abdication of the Kaiser. He was a leading figure in the government that crushed the Spartacus uprising of January 1919 and which had a hand in Luxemburg's death. He was President of the Weimar Republic from 1919 to 1925. Philipp Scheidemann (1865–1939) was a right-wing Social Democrat who became

part of the provisional government in November 1918. He worked closely with Ebert in crushing the Spartacus uprising. He resigned from the government in 1919 because of his opposition to the Treaty of Versailles.

3   "The independents" refers to the Independent Social-Democratic Party (USPD), founded at Gotha in March 1917 by longtime SPD leaders, including Kautsky and Bernstein, who opposed the SPD leadership's uncritical support of World War I. Adopting a centrist position, the USPD joined the Ebert–Scheidemann government in November 1918 but left it on December 29, 1918. The party split in 1922, with some of its leaders (like Kautsky and Bernstein) returning to the SPD. Most of its members joined the German Communist Party, however.

B)  *The Socialization of Society*

4   The Junker aristocracy claimed descent from the Teutonic Knights who settled in the eastern part of Germany in the thirteenth century. They were large landowners who kept the area under feudal control. They were also staunch militarists.

C)  *What Does the Spartacus League Want?*

5   A *mene-tekel* is a Hebrew sign of impending doom.

6   Marx's exact phrase is "either a revolutionary reconstitution of society at large. . . . or the common ruin of the contending classes." See *The Communist Manifesto*, MECW 6, p. 482.

7   Wallachian boyars were the landowning class in what is now Romania.

8   The Vendée region, near Lyon, was the
    site of counterrevolutionary insurrec-
    tions and Jacobin terror in 1793–94.

9   Georges Clemenceau (1841–1929), a
    socialist in his youth, moved to the right,
    was Prime Minister of France in 1906–
    09 and 1917–19, and was also a convener
    of the conference that drew up the
    Treaty of Versailles. The British Liberal
    politician David Lloyd George (1863–
    1945) was War Minister during World
    War I and Prime Minister from 1918 to
    1921. Woodrow Wilson (1856–1924) was
    U.S. President from 1912 to 1920.

10  The Hohenzollerns were the ruling
    family in the Prussian monarchy that
    took over the whole of Germany in 1871.

11  General Paul von Hindenburg
    (1847–1934) fought in the Franco-Pruss-
    ian war of 1870–71 and was Field Mar-
    shal of German forces on the eastern
    front in World War I. He replaced Ebert
    as President of the Weimar Republic in
    1925 and appointed Adolf Hitler as
    Chancellor of Germany in 1933. General
    Erich Ludendorff (1865–1937) was
    Hindenburg's Chief of Staff during
    World War I. After the war, he flirted
    with National Socialism and was
    involved in the Kapp putsch of 1920 and
    Hitler's Münich "beer hall putsch" in
    1923. Alfred von Tirpitz (1849–1930)
    was Grand Admiral of the German
    Navy in World War I. He was an advo-
    cate of unrestricted submarine warfare.

12  This was a well-known slogan of
    Ferdinand Lassalle's.

D)  *Our Program and the Political Situation*

13  "Preface to the 1872 German Edition of
    the *Manifesto of the Communist Party*,"
    MECW 23, pp. 174–75.

14  *The Communist Manifesto*, MECW 6,
    pp. 504–5.

15  See Engels's 1895 "Introduction to *Class
    Struggles in France*," MECW 27, p. 512.

16  That is, the crushing of the Paris
    Commune.

17  "Introduction to *The Class Struggles
    in France*," MECW 27, pp. 514–15.

18  "Introduction to *The Class Struggles
    in France*," MECW 27, p. 516.

19  Luxemburg could not have known at
    the time that the "error" committed by
    Engels in his "Introduction to *The
    Class Struggles in France*" was actually
    the fault of the leaders of the German
    Social-Democratic Party. The Party
    leaders, fearful that any revolutionary
    language might give the government an
    excuse to pass a new anti-socialist law,
    eliminated all the passages in Engels's
    Introduction that they considered too
    radical. In one of the deleted passages,
    Engels argued that street battles still
    retained their relevance for social revo-
    lution. Engels protested privately
    against these deletions by the SPD
    leaders, but he died before any changes
    could be made in the text. The original
    manuscript, with the deletions by the
    Party leaders, was rediscovered only
    after Luxemburg's death.

20  See the previous section of this chapter.

21  The Ebert-Scheidemann government
    made a major effort to gain the support
    of the workers' and soldiers' councils.
    In Berlin, they were largely successful in
    this, as seen in the refusal of the
    provisional executive of the workers'
    and soldiers' councils there to support
    the January 1919 uprising against the
    Ebert-Scheidemann government. On
    the other hand, Luxemburg's Spartacus

League had a considerable influence in workers' councils in several other cities, especially Brunswick and Stuttgart.

22  Hugo Haase (1863–1919) became leader of the SPD's Reichstag delegation after Bebel's death. In 1914 he opposed the voting of war credits, but chose not to break party discipline by making his views public. He instead delivered the speech to the Reichstag declaring that the SPD would not "abandon the government in its moment of need." He helped found the USPD in 1916 and was Minister of Foreign Affairs in Ebert's government until resigning on December 19, 1918. He was assassinated by a monarchist.

23  The Chausseestrasse massacre of December 6, 1918, was an armed assault by forces controlled by the Ebert-Scheidemann government against the Spartacus League, in which several of the latter were killed. The government justified its action on the grounds that the Spartacus League and some of the workers' and soldiers' councils were attempting a putsch, but other evidence suggests that the government provoked the incident in order to crack down on the Left.

24  On December 24, 1918, a division of revolutionary-minded sailors in Berlin refused to obey government orders and arrested Otto Wels, the SPD military chief of Berlin. The Ebert-Scheidemann government sent troops against the sailors, killing a dozen of them.

25  At the time, *Vorwärts* was the SPD's paper and *Freiheit* was the USPD's paper.

26  "Our position" refers to that of the Central Committee of the Spartacus League. At Luxemburg's urging it proposed that the soon-to-be-formed Communist Party take part in the elections for a National Assembly, but this was voted down by 62–23 at the Party's founding conference. Jogiches was prepared to leave the Party over the vote (he was also a member of the central committee) but Luxemburg convinced him not to do so.

27  A reference to the tendency of the Berlin workers' and soldiers' councils to support many of the policies of the Ebert-Scheidemann government. Luxemburg and Liebknecht wanted to join the provisional executive committee of the Berlin councils, but the request was denied on the grounds that they were neither workers nor soldiers.

E) *Order Reigns in Berlin*

28  A reference to the crushing of the Polish insurrection of 1830–31 by the Russian General Ivan Fyodorovich Paskiewitsch (1782–1856). His troops massacred thousands of freedom fighters upon entering Warsaw in 1831. In 1849 Paskiewitsch, also the Commander in Chief of the Russian Army, crushed the Hungarian Revolution, thus bringing to an end the revolutions begun across Europe in 1848.

29  On January 13, 1919, the Ebert-Scheidemann government sent troops against supporters of the Spartacus League who had occupied the headquarters of *Vorwärts*. The troops' victory over the revolutionaries marked the beginning of the end of the Spartacus uprising.

30  German General von Emmich (d. 1915) was Commanding General of the 10th Army Corps, which carried out the

bloody siege of Liège, Belgium, in August 1914.

31  Gustav Noske (1868–1946), a former furniture worker, was a right wing SPD member who was a specialist on military affairs before World War I. He became Defense Minister of the Ebert-Scheidemann government in 1918 and was responsible for the bloody suppression of the Spartacus uprising and also allowed the murder of Luxemburg and Liebknecht.

32  "Raise itself up again clashing" is a line from the poem *Abschiedswort* (A Word of Farewell) by Friedrich Freiligrath, a close friend of Marx. Marx published it in the final issue of the *Neue Rheinische Zeitung* after the defeat of the 1848 revolution; the entire issue was printed in red ink. "I was, I am, I shall be" is a line from Freiligrath's poem *Die Revolution*, written in 1851.

## CHAPTER 15

1  A reference to the Sino-Japanese War of 1895, in which Japan defeated China.

2  The Fashoda incident refers to the conflict that arose between England and France over control of the Sudanese outpost of Fashoda in 1898, which almost led to war between the two countries. Delagoa Bay is in Mozambique, then a Portuguese colony. In 1898 the British sought to secure control of Delagoa as part of their struggle against the South African Boers. In the same year the French declared a protectorate over the island of Madagascar.

3  A reference to Luxemburg's plan to incorporate these ideas into her *Reform or Revolution*.

4  Wladyslaw Heinrich (1869–1957) knew Luxemburg from her days at the University of Zurich and was a member in the 1890s of the Social Democracy of the Kingdom of Poland (SDKP), the forerunner of the SDKPiL. He later became a prominent Polish philosopher.

5  "Warski" was his pseudonym of Adloph Warzawski (1868–1937), co-founder of the SDKP and a longtime leader of the SDKPiL. He befriended Luxemburg while they were students and later became editor of *Sprawa* Robotnicz, and worked closely with for the next two decades. After 1918 he became a major figure in the Russian Communist Party under Lenin. He was murdered by Stalin during his purge of the Polish Communist Party in 1937.

6  A reference to the upcoming SPD Convention in Hannover.

7  Parvus was the pseudonym of Alexander Helphand (1867–1924), a Russian revolutionary who met Luxemburg when she was a student in Zurich and later became active as a leftist in the SPD. He was was one of the first to attack Bernstein's revisionism (while editor of the *Sachische Arbeiterzeiting*) but he stopped being involved in the debate after a few months. He returned to Russia in 1905 and became president of the St. Petersburg Soviet after the arrest of Leon Trotsky. After moving to Turkey in 1910, he made a fortune as a businessman. He supported Germany in World War I and during the war worked as a paid agent of the German Foreign Ministry.

8  This refer to elections to provincial parliaments in 1898 and 1899, which

the revisionist wing of the SPD tended to dominate.

9   Eduard David (1863-1930) was a revisionist who worked closely with. He supported World War I and served as Minister Without Portfolio in an SPD government in 1919-20.

10  These words, uttered by Martin Luther before Emperor Charles V, are credited with ushering in the Protestant Reformation.

11  Hugo Haase (1863-1919) was an SPD Reichstag deputy from 1897-1918 and leader of the SPD Reichstag delegation in 1914. He opposed the voting of war credits in 1914, but he declined to break party discipline over it and gave the speech annnouncing the vote. He helped found the USPD in 1917 and became Foreign Minister in Ebert's government until resigning on December 19, 1918. In 1919 he was assassinated by a monarchist. Wilhelm Dittman (1874-1954) was a SPD member who became leader of the USPD. He rejoined the SPD in 1920. Arthur Stadthagen ( 1857-1917) was an SPD Reichstag delegate from 1890-1917 and member of the editorial board of *Vorwärts*. A lawyer, he several times worked to get Luxemburg out of jail. They broke off relations after 1914 over his support for the World War I.

12  Alexanderplatz was the notorious prison in Berlin were Luxemburg was incarcerated for six weeks in 1916. It later became a headquarters for Hitler's Gestapo. Luxemburg later called her incarceration there the most difficult period of her life.

13  Eduard Friedrich Morike (1804-75), a German poet.

14  Count Kuno von Westarp (1864-1945) was leader of the conservatives in the Reichstag.

15  In Heinrich von Kleist's (1771-1811) drama *Penthesilea*, the Queen of the Amazons kills and then eats her lover, Achilles.

16  Karl Liebknecht (1871-1919) was a son of Wilhelm Liebknecht and a prominent anti-militarist and youth activist prior to World War I. Though he knew Luxemburg before 1914, they began to work closely together only after the outbreak of the World War I, when he was one of the few members of the SPD Reichstag delegation to oppose the voting of war credits. He worked closely with Luxemburg in helping to found the Spartacus League and was a pivotal figure in the opposition to World War I. After being released from jail in 1918 he helped galvanize left-wing opposition to Ebert and Scheidemann's government and helped found the German Communist Party. He was murdered along with Luxemburg in January 1919.

17  Hugo Wolf (1860-1903), a classical musician, was a follower of Wagner. One of his major works was *Penthesilea*.

18  Nikolai Sieber (1844-1888), Russian economist and historian who was one of the first to comment on Marx's *Capital* in Russia.

19  August von Platen (1796-1835), German poet and playwright.

20  Stefan George (1869-1933), influential German poet who opposed mass culture and consumerism.

21  Friedrich Lange (1828-1875), a neo-Kantian German philosopher and economist.

# Acknowledgments

In preparing this volume, we have received assistance from a number of scholars in Asia, Europe, and the United States.

Several people offered valuable comments on drafts of the Introduction: Janet Afary, Olga Domanski, Narihiko Ito, Paul Le Blanc, Albert Resis, and especially Ottokar Luban.

Concerning the newly translated material, we would like to thank our primary translator, Ashley Passmore. We are also grateful to Feliks Tych, both for his previous scholarly publications on Luxemburg's "Credo" and for providing us with a copy of the handwritten Polish original of this article. Urszula Wislanka checked our translation from the German with the Polish original. Narihiko Ito generously made available his transcription and scholarly analysis of Luxemburg's "Slavery." Earlier, he informed us about recently unearthed Luxemburg texts. We would also like to thank the following people for background information for the notes and for other forms of help: Olga Avedeyeva, A. Z. Hilali, Waheed Khan, and Albert Resis. In addition, we acknowledge financial support from the Monthly Review Foundation for the new translations.

At Purdue University, we thank the staff of the Department of Political Science, especially Michelle Conwell, for photocopying and wordprocessing help; we are also grateful to the Inter-Library Loan staff at Purdue's Humanities, Social Sciences, and Education Library for help with source materials.

Finally, we would like to thank our editor, Andrew Nash, for his good judgment and patience in helping to see this project through to completion.

The editor and publishers gratefully acknowledge the following sources:

"The Historical Conditions of Accumulation," from *The Accumulation of Capital* (New York: Monthly Review Press, 1951).

*Social Reform or Revolution*, "What Does the Spartacus League Want?," "Our Program and the Political Situation," and "Order Reigns in Berlin" from *Selected Political Writings of Rosa Luxemburg*, ed. Dick Howard (New York: Monthly Review Press, 1971).

*The Mass Strike, the Political Party, and the Trade Unions*
(Detroit: Marxist Educational Society, 1925).

"Address to the Fifth Congress of the Russian Social-Democratic Labor Party,"
from Raya Dunayevskaya, *Rosa Luxemburg, Women's Liberation, and Marx's
Philosophy of Revolution* (Urbana-Champaign, Ill.: University of Illinois Press, 1991).

*Theory and Practice* (Detroit: News and Letters, 1980).

"Organizational Questions of Russian Social Democracy,"
from Neil Harding, ed., *Marxism in Russia: Key Documents, 1879–1906*
(Cambridge: Cambridge University Press, 1983).

*The Russian Revolution*, ed. Bertram D. Wolfe
(Ann Arbor: University of Michigan Press, 1961).

*The Junius Pamphlet: The Crisis in German Social Democracy*
(New York: Socialist Publication Society, 1918).

"The Beginning," from Robert Looker, ed., *Rosa Luxemburg:
Selected Political Writings* (New York: Grove Press, 1974).

"The Socialization of Society," Luxemburg Internet Archive, www.marxists.org

Letters to Leo Jogiches, from Elzbieta Ettinger, ed., *Comrade and Lover:
Rosa Luxemburg's Letters to Leo Jogiches* (Cambridge, Mass.: MIT Press, 1979).

Letters to Clara Zetkin, Emanuel and Mathilde Wurm, and Sonja Liebknecht,
from Stephen Eric Bronner, ed., *The Letters of Rosa Luxemburg*
(Boulder, Colo.: Westview Press, 1978).

Letter to Sophie Liebknecht, from Paul Le Blanc, ed., *Rosa Luxemburg:
Reflections and Writings* (Amherst, N.Y.: Humanity Books, 1999).

# Index

Abraham, Richard, 22

absolutism, 152, 153, 181, 345; in Russia, 178–179, 201, 285; struggle against, 182, 205, 207, 226. *See also* monarchy; Tsarism

*Accumulation of Capital, The* (Luxemburg), 18–20

accumulation theory. *See* Marx's diagram of accumulation

Acosta, José de, 85, 407n14

Adler, Victor, 318, 425n16

Africa, 106–110, 124; despotism in, 107–109, 110; diamond mines in, 402–404n; Herero people of, 15, 22, 244, 339, 418n16

African slaves, 59, 85–86, 88

agriculture, 54; socialization of, 370–371. *See also* primitive communism

Alexander II, Tsar of Russia, 96, 421n18

Alexander III, Tsar of Russia, 99

Alexander of Macedon, 92

Algeria, French rule of, 20, 64, 68–70, 95

American Indians, extermination of, 83. *See also* Inca Empire; Putumayo

American War of Secession (Civil War), 55, 56, 402n33

Americas, Spanish colonialism in, 83–89

anarchism, 168–169, 182, 363, 414n32

anarchy, 9, 166, 344, 364; capitalist, 10, 133, 149, 412n17

Anseele, Eduard, 236, 419n6

*Anti-Dühring* (Engels), 111

Anti-Socialist Law (Germany, 1878), 213, 214, 249, 330, 411n12, 417n9

Arab family associations, 68–69, 70

aristocracy, 66, 81–82, 100, 101, 104–105; African tribal, 108, 109; ancient Greek, 115–117. *See also* Junkers; ruling class

Aristotle, 120, 122

arms competition, 326

Auer, Ignaz, 330, 426n28

Austria, 152, 201, 251; strikes in, 197, 228–229

Austria-Hungary, 335

Avksentiev, Nicolai, 300, 424n17

Axelrod, Pavel Borisovich, 282, 286, 422n1

Bahamas, 83

balance of power, 335, 380

Baltic countries, 295, 296, 326

Bebel, August, 11, 209, 317, 383, 384, 415n7; Liebknecht and, 330, 331; parliamentarism and, 362, 386; sexism of, 14, 417n5

Belgium, 339, 374; mass strikes in, 228; suffrage in, 152, 233–236

Beloch, Karl Julius, 119

Bennett, Gordon, 86

Benzoni, Girolamo, 83, 84, 407nn11–12

Berlin, counterrevolution in, 373–376, 378

Berlin Armory, storming of the, 205

Bernstein, Eduard, 9, 14, 119, 168, 383, 384; as opportunist, 386; revisionism of, 11, 420n7. *See also* Social Democracy, Bernstein on

Bismarck, Otto von, 249, 323, 324, 332, 414n30; armament policy of, 326

Blanqui, August, 413–414n

Blanquism, 149, 156, 158, 159, 251–253

Bohemia, strikes in, 230

Haase, Hugo, 367, 428n22, 430n11

Haiti, 83

Hamburg, strike in, 193, 197, 201–202, 416n16

Handelmann, Heinrich, 83

Hannover, 384

Hansemann, David Justus, 205, 417n5

Hapsburg monarchy, 335

Haug, Frigga, 21

Heine, Wolfgang, 163, 410n10

helots, 80, 82, 113–114. *See also* Greece, slavery in

Herero people, 15, 22, 244, 339, 418n16

Herschel, Friedrich Wilhelm, 89, 301, 408n26

Hindenburg, Paul von, 354, 427n11

*Historia natural y moral de las Indias* (Acosta), 85

historical crisis, leadership in, 329

historical process, 264–265

*History of British India* (Mill), 404nn38–39, 406n34

Hohenzollern, 161, 214, 343, 345, 349, 354

Humbert (Deputy), 70

idealists, 199, 384

Ihrer, Emma, 237, 419n11

imperialism, 14–15, 18, 19–20, 30; capitalist class and, 352; collapse of, 366; German, 281, 282, 295, 297, 298, 309; militarism and, 336, 337; national self-determination and, 324–326, 327; proletariat subservient to, 315, 337–338; World War I and, 321, 339, 340. *See also* British imperialism; colonial exploitation

*Imperialism and Socialism* (leaflet), 317

Inca Empire, 75–79, 80–81, 92, 112, 114

Independent Social-Democratic Party (USPD), 426n3

Independent Socialist Party (USPD), 368, 376

India, 60; under British rule, 20, 64, 65–68, 95, 325, 326, 404–406n;

village community, 65–68, 89–95

Indians, American, 83–89. *See also* Inca Empire

industry, socialist economy and, 346–348

inequality/equality, 78, 109

inheritance, 72. *See also* property rights

intelligentsia, 303; opportunism and, 257–262

International, 284, 319, 331, 345. *See also* Second International

International Peace Conference (1912), 318

international socialism, 340; Russian Revolution and, 283–284, 309

International Socialist Bureau (Brussels), 236–237

international trade, 56. *See also* global capitalism

*Introduction to Political Economy* (Luxemburg), 15–16

invasion, fear of, 322–324

irrigation systems, 66–67, 91, 104

Iskra, 250

Islam, in Algeria, 69, 70

Islamic rule, 109–110

Ito, Narihiko, 17, 397n26

Jacobins, 251, 253, 288, 290, 307, 322, 420n5, 423n9. *See also* French Revolution

Japan. *See* Russo-Japanese War (1904-1905)

Jaurés, Jean, 11, 263, 319, 326, 420n17

Jena resolution (1905), 172, 201, 223–224, 415n7, 416n1

Jevons, William Stanley, 150, 413n18

Jews, 11, 15, 424n3

Jogiches, Leo (Tyshka), 8–9, 22, 27, 275, 279

*Junius Pamphlet* (Luxemburg), 26, 311–341; on class struggle and fear of invasion, 322–324; on Engels, 320–321, 428n19; on imperialism, 337–338, 339; on labor movement, 314–315, 316, 317, 334; on leadership, 317, 320–321, 329; Marx's prophecy, 316–317; pre-World

INDEX 447

354, 366, 371–372; Ebert-Schiedemann government and, 371, 428n21, 429n27
working class, 49, 131, 154, 340; consumption of, 37; counterrevolution and, 375; demonstrations by, 28; growth in, 402n31; labor-power of, 34–35; propagation of, 57–58; socialist economy and, 142, 347–348. *See also* labor; proletariat
"Working Women in the Class Struggle" (Ihrer), 237–238
world economy, 137, 138, 153. *See also* global capitalism
World Labor Congress, 345
world politics, 153–154, 155
World War I, 339–341, 349, 365; German

militarism and, 324, 325, 335; Marx's prophecy of, 316–317; national self-determination and, 298; opposition to, 26–27; peace, 285–286, 287, 369–370; as reversion to barbarism, 321; Russian Revolution (1917) and, 281

Yakut people, 105

zadruga (family group), 68, 406n47, 408n29
*Zemstvos* (rural assemblies), 183, 415n11
Zetkin, Clara, 9, 14, 21, 22, 237, 419n12
Zubatov, Sergey Vasilyevich, 176–177, 179, 415n9
Zurita, Alonso de, 86–89